Kizzi Magazine Presents...The Greek Philosophers. Vol 2. 2021.

This book is presented solely for educational and entertainment purposes. The author and publisher are not offering it as legal, accounting, or other professional services advice.

While best efforts have been used in preparing this book, the author and publisher make no representations or warranties of any kind and assume no liabilities of any kind with respect to the accuracy or completeness of the contents and specifically disclaim any implied warranties of merchantability or fitness of use for a particular purpose.

Neither the author nor the publisher shall be held liable or responsible to any person or entity with respect to any loss or incidental or consequential damages caused, or alleged to have been caused, directly or indirectly, by the information

Visit Kizzi Magazine at www.kizzi.biz

Also by Mithra and Athena Publishing

Escape Your 9-5 And Do Something Amazing

Customer Service

SocMed: Social Media For Business

How To Start A Business With Little Or No Cash

Facebook For Business

Social Media Marketing: Write Up your Tweet

Getting Your Business LinkedIn

It's That Easy! Online Marketing 3.0

Business, Business, Business!

Mind Your Own Business

Insiders Know-how: Running A PR Agency

Energy Efficiency

Social PR

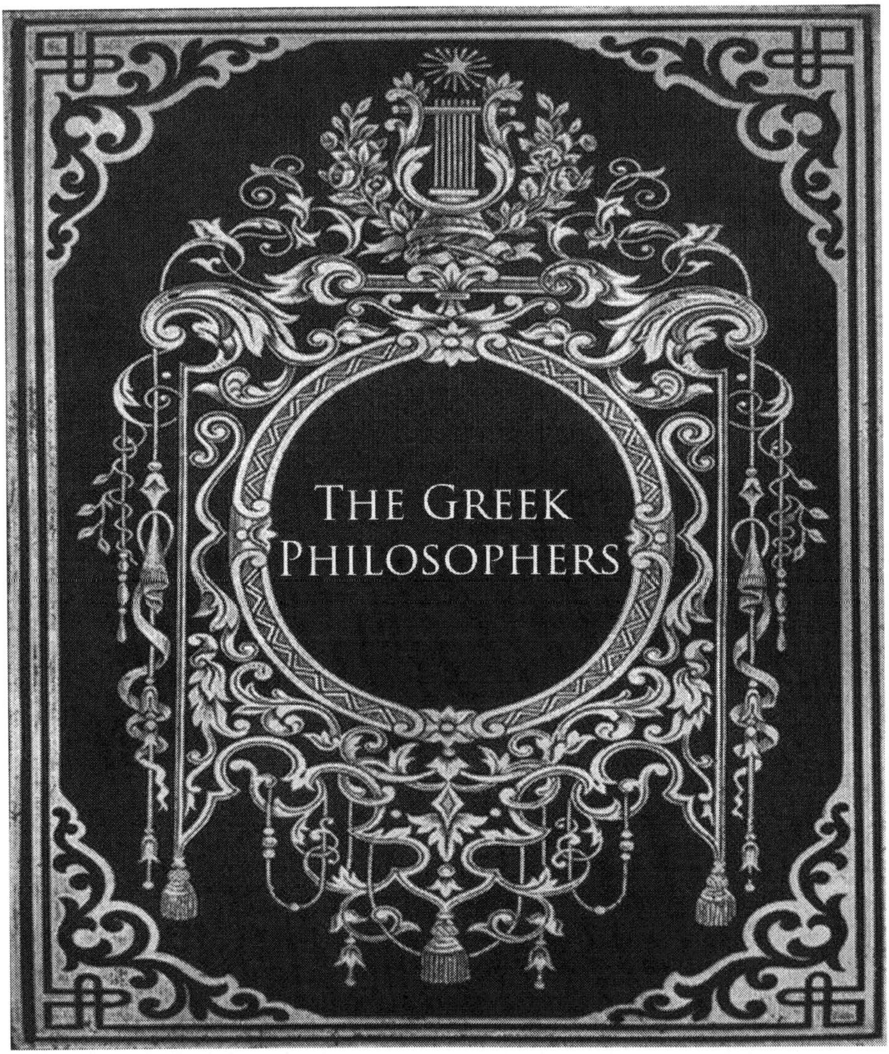
THE GREEK
PHILOSOPHERS

THE GREEK PHILOSOPHERS

BY ALFRED WILLIAM BENN. IN TWO VOLUMES.

VOL. 2.

Table of contents

Welcome to The Greek Philosophers

"I know that I know nothing"

Socrates (c. 470–399 BCE) quoted in Plato's Apology from The Last Days of Socrates.

As a young student I read this remarkable proposition for the first time and, in that instant, I was hooked on philosophy. This quote is perhaps the most philosophical quote of them all. Reflective knowledge is so important, Socrates claims, that to discover you don't actually know anything is a positive thing. After that moment, I hurried to the library (we had them in those days) and picked up a copy of Bertram Russell's 'The History of Western Philosophy' and my life changed forever. By turning my young mind to the consideration of the most basic questions concerning reality, human existence, and God, I opened up myself to a world of possibilities for understanding the world and our place in it. Exercising my sponge-like young mind in the disciplines of critical and logical thought, I helped gain the ability to imagine, debate, and clarify the nature of the good life.

Even at that tender age of 14 I was fascinated by the idea that the soul – that immaterial essence and totality of who I am at a core level – played such a critical role to my development as a human being. In the words of Socrates:

"I try to persuade you, whether younger or older, to give less priority, and devote less zeal, to the care of your bodies or of your money than to the care of your soul and trying to make it as good as it can be."

The inescapable fact is that philosophy is essential to life. Not only for our development as human beings, but also for life in general, philosophy matters. Philosophy can reveal to our minds the nature of justification: that is, by what measure is something justified? Philosophy can aid in our understanding the problems of good and evil. Philosophy likewise requires, and thus reveals to us, meta-thinking: to think about first principles. And least of all, philosophy has, of all the disciplines, the greatest potential to make us open-minded. When we turn our minds to the consideration of the most basic questions concerning reality, human existence, and God, we open ourselves to a world of possibilities for understanding the world and our place in it. By exercising our mind in the disciplines of critical and logical thought, we gain the ability to imagine, debate, and clarify the nature of the good life.

For readers not familiar with philosophy and its proponents, there can be no better introduction to the subject than The Greek Philosophers by Alfred William Benn. Presented in two volumes, The Greek Philosophers has been selected by scholars as being culturally important, and is part of the knowledge base of civilization as we know it. Spanning the works of Plato, Socrates and Aristotle through to Epicurus and Lucretius and eventually arriving at the spiritualism of Plotinus, The Greek Philosophers is perhaps one of the most significant and influential books on Greek philosophy ever written. It is our pleasure to bring you this marvel.

Kizzi, Creator of Kizzi Magazine and Business Game Changer Magazine

CHAPTER I.
THE STOICS.

I.

The systems of Plato and Aristotle were splendid digressions from the main line of ancient speculation rather than stages in its regular development. The philosophers who came after them went back to an earlier tradition, and the influence of the two greatest Hellenic masters, when it was felt at all, was felt almost entirely as a disturbing or deflecting force. The extraordinary reach of their principles could not, in truth, be appreciated until the organised experience of mankind had accumulated to an extent requiring the application of new rules for its comprehension and utilisation; and to make such an accumulation possible, nothing less was needed than the combined efforts of the whole western world. Such religious, educational, social, and political reforms as those contemplated in Plato's Republic, though originally designed for a single city-community, could not be realised, even approximately, within a narrower field than that offered by the mediaeval church and the feudal state. The ideal theory first gained practical significance in connexion with the metaphysics of Christian theology. The place given by Plato to mathematics has only been fully justified by the development of modern science. So also, Aristotle's criticism became of practical importance only when the dreams against which it was directed had embodied themselves in a fabric of oppressive superstition. Only the vast extension of reasoned knowledge has enabled us to disentangle the vitally important elements of Aristotle's logic from the mass of useless refinements in which they are imbedded; his fourfold division of causes could not be estimated rightly even by Bacon, Descartes, or Spinoza; while his arrangement of the sciences, his remarks on classification, and his contributions to comparative biology bring us up to the very verge of theories whose first promulgation is still fresh in the memories of men.

Plato and Aristotle

Again, the spiritualism taught by Plato and Aristotle alike—by the disciple, indeed, with even more distinctness than by the master—was so entirely inconsistent with the common belief of antiquity as to remain a dead letter for nearly six centuries—that is, until the time of Plotinus. The difference between body and mind was recognised by every school, but only as the difference between solid and gaseous matter is recognised by us; while the antithesis between conscious and unconscious existence, with all its momentous consequences, was recognised by none. The old hypothesis had to be thoroughly thought out before its insufficiency could be completely and irrevocably confessed.

Nor was this the only reason why the spiritualists lost touch of their age. If in some respects they were far in advance of early Greek thought, in other respects they were far behind it. Their systems were pervaded by an unphilosophical dualism which tended to undo much that had been achieved by their less prejudiced predecessors. For this we have partly to blame their environment. The opposition of God and the world, heaven and earth, mind and matter, necessity in Nature and free-will in man, was a concession—though of course an unconscious concession—to the stupid bigotry of Athens. Yet at the same time they had failed to solve those psychological problems which had most interest for an Athenian public. Instead of following up the attempt made by the Sophists and Socrates to place morality on a scientific foundation, they busied themselves with the construction of a new machinery for diminishing the efficacy of temptation or for strengthening the efficacy of law. To the question, What is the highest good? Plato gave an answer which nobody could understand, and Aristotle an answer which was almost absolutely useless to anybody but himself. The other great problem, What is the ultimate foundation of knowledge? was left in an equally unsatisfactory state. Plato never answered it at all; Aristotle merely pointed out the negative conditions which must be fulfilled by its solution.

It is not, then, surprising that the Academic and Peripatetic schools utterly failed to carry on the great movement inaugurated by their respective founders. The successors of Plato first lost themselves in a labyrinth of Pythagorean mysticism, and then sank into the position of mere moral instructors. The history of that remarkable revolution by which the Academy regained a foremost place in Greek thought, will form the subject of a future chapter: here we may anticipate so far as to observe that it was effected by taking up and presenting in its original purity a tradition of older date than Platonism, though presented under a new aspect and mixed with other elements by Plato. The heirs of Aristotle, after staggering on a few paces under the immense burden of his encyclopaedic bequest, came to a dead halt, and contented themselves with keeping the treasure safe until the time should arrive for its appropriation and reinvestment by a stronger speculative race.

No sooner did the two imperial systems lose their ascendency than the germs which they had temporarily overshadowed sprang up into vigorous vitality, and for more than five centuries dominated the whole course not only of Greek but of European thought. Of these by far the most important was the naturalistic idea, the belief that physical science might be substituted for religious superstitions and local conventions as an impregnable basis of conduct. In a former chapter[1] we endeavoured to show that, while there are traces of this idea in the philosophy of Heracleitus, and while its roots stretch far back into the literature and popular faith of Greece, it was formulated for the first time by the two great Sophists, Prodicus and Hippias, who, in the momentous division between Nature and Law, placed themselves—Hippias more particularly—on the side of Nature. Two causes led to the temporary discredit of their teaching. One was the perversion by which natural right became the watchword of those who, like Plato's Callicles, held that nothing should stand between the strong man and the gratification of his desire for pleasure or for power. The other was the keen criticism of the Humanists, the friends of social convention, who held with Protagoras that Nature was unknowable, or with Gorgias that she did not exist, or with Socrates that her laws were the secret of the gods. It was in particular the overwhelming personal influence of Socrates which triumphed. He drew away from the Sophists their strongest disciple, Antisthenes, and convinced him that philosophy was valuable only in so far as it became a life-renovating power, and that, viewed in this light, it had no relation to anything outside ourselves. But just as Socrates had discarded the physical speculations of former teachers, so also did Antisthenes discard the dialectic which Socrates had substituted for them, even to the extent of denying that definition was possible.[2] Yet he seems to have kept a firm hold on the two great ideas that were the net result of all previous philosophy, the idea of a cosmos, the common citizenship of which made all men potentially equal,[3] and the idea of reason as the essential prerogative of man.[4]

Antisthenes pushed to its extreme consequences a movement begun by the naturalistic Sophists. His doctrine was what would now be called anarchic collectivism. The State, marriage, private property, and the then accepted forms of religion, were to be abolished, and all mankind were to herd promiscuously together.[5] Either he or his followers, alone among the ancients, declared that slavery was wrong; and, like Socrates, he held that the virtue of men and women was the same.[6] But what he meant by this broad human virtue, which according to him was identical with happiness, is not clear. We only know that he dissociated it in the strongest manner from pleasure. 'I had rather be mad than delighted,' is one of his characteristic sayings.[7] It would appear, however, that what he really objected to was self-indulgence—the pursuit of sensual gratification for its own sake—and that he was ready to welcome the enjoyments naturally accompanying the healthy discharge of vital function.[8]

Antisthenes and his school, of which Diogenes is the most popular and characteristic type, were afterwards known as Cynics; but the name is never mentioned by Plato and Aristotle, nor do they allude to the scurrility and systematic indecency afterwards associated with it. The anecdotes relating to this unsavoury subject should be received with extreme suspicion. There has always been a tendency to believe that philosophers carry out in practice what are vulgarly believed to be the logical consequences of their theories. Thus it is related of Pyrrho the Sceptic that when out walking he never turned aside to avoid any obstacle or danger, and was only saved from destruction by the vigilance of his friends.[9] This is of course a silly fable; and we have Aristotle's word for it that the Sceptics took as good care of their lives as other people.[10] In like manner we may conjecture that the Cynics, advocating as they did a return to Nature and defiance of prejudice, were falsely credited with what was falsely supposed to be the practical exemplification of their precepts. It is at any rate remarkable that Epictêtus, a man not disposed to undervalue the obligations of decorum, constantly refers to Diogenes as a kind of philosophical saint, and that he describes the ideal Cynic in words which would apply without alteration to the character of a Christian apostle.[11]

Cynicism, if we understand it rightly, was only the mutilated form of an older philosophy having for its object to set morality free from convention, and to found it anew on a scientific knowledge of natural law. The need of such a system was not felt so long as Plato and Aristotle were unfolding their wonderful schemes for a reorganisation of action and belief. With the temporary collapse of those schemes it came once more to the front. The result was a new school which so thoroughly satisfied the demands of the age, that for five centuries the noblest spirits of Greece and Rome, with few exceptions, adhered to its doctrines; that in dying it bequeathed some of their most vital elements to the metaphysics and the theology by which it was succeeded; that with their decay it reappeared as an important factor in modern thought; and that its name has become imperishably associated in our own language with the proud endurance of suffering, the self-sufficingness of conscious rectitude, and the renunciation of all sympathy, except what may be derived from contemplation of the immortal dead, whose heroism is recorded in history, or of the eternal cosmic forces performing their glorious offices with unimpassioned energy and imperturbable repose.

II.

One day, some few years after the death of Aristotle, a short, lean, swarthy young man, of weak build, with clumsily shaped limbs, and head inclined to one side, was standing in an Athenian bookshop, intently studying a roll of manuscript. His name was Zeno, and he was a native of Citium, a Greek colony in Cyprus, where the Hellenic element had become adulterated with a considerable Phoenician infusion. According to some accounts, Zeno had come to the great centre of intellectual activity to study, according to others for the sale of Tyrian purple. At any rate the volume which he held in his hand decided his vocation. It was the second book of Xenophon's Memoirs of Socrates. Zeno eagerly asked where such men as he whose sayings stood recorded there were to be found. At that moment the Cynic Crates happened to pass by. 'There is one of them,' said the bookseller, 'follow him.'[12]

Zeno

The history of this Crates was distinguished by the one solitary romance of Greek philosophy. A young lady of noble family, named Hipparchia, fell desperately in love with him, refused several most eligible suitors, and threatened to kill herself unless she was given to him in marriage. Her parents in despair sent for Crates. Marriage, for a philosopher, was against the principles of his sect, and he at first joined them in endeavouring to dissuade her. Finding his remonstrances unavailing, he at last flung at her feet the staff and wallet which constituted his whole worldly possessions, exclaiming, 'Here is the bridegroom, and that is the dower. Think of this matter well, for you cannot be my partner unless you follow the same calling with me.' Hipparchia consented, and thenceforth, heedless of taunts, conformed her life in every respect to the Cynic pattern.[13]

Zeno had more delicacy or less fortitude than Hipparchia; and the very meagre intellectual fare provided by Crates must have left his inquisitive mind unsatisfied. Accordingly we find him leaving this rather disappointing substitute for Socrates, to study philosophy under Stilpo the Megarian dialectician and Polemo the head of the Academy;[14] while we know that he must have gone back to Heracleitus for the physical basis from which contemporary speculation had by this time cut itself completely free. At length, about the beginning of the third century B.C., Zeno, after having been a learner for twenty years, opened a school on his own account. As if to mark the practical bearing of his doctrine he chose one of the most frequented resorts in the city for its promulgation. There was at Athens a portico called the Poecile Stoa, adorned with frescoes by Polygnôtus, the greatest painter of the Cimonian period. It was among the monuments of that wonderful city, at once what the Loggia dei Lanzi is to Florence, and what Raphael's Stanze are to Rome; while, like the Place de la Concorde in Paris, it was darkened by the terrible associations of a revolutionary epoch. A century before Zeno's time fourteen hundred Athenian citizens had been slaughtered under its colonnades by order of the Thirty. 'I will purify the Stoa,' said the Cypriote stranger;[15] and the feelings still associated with the word Stoicism prove how nobly his promise was fulfilled.

How much of the complete system known in later times under this name was due to Zeno himself, we do not know; for nothing but a few fragments of his and of his immediate successors' writings is left. The idea of combining Antisthenes with Heracleitus, and both with Socrates, probably belongs to the founder of the school. His successor, Cleanthes, a man of character rather than of intellect, was content to hand on what the master had taught. Then came another Cypriote, Chrysippus, of whom we are told that without him the Stoa would not have existed;[16] so thoroughly did he work out the system in all its details, and so strongly did he fortify its positions against hostile criticism by a framework of elaborate dialectic. 'Give me the propositions, and I will find the proofs!' he used to say to Cleanthes.[17] After him, nothing of importance was added to the doctrines of the school;

although the spirit by which they were animated seems to have undergone profound modifications in the lapse of ages.

In reality, Stoicism was not, like the older Greek philosophies, a creation of individual genius. It bears the character of a compilation both on its first exposition and on its final completion. Polemo, who had been a fine gentleman before he became a philosopher, taunted Zeno with filching his opinions from every quarter, like the cunning little Phoenician trader that he was.[18] And it was said that the seven hundred treatises of Chrysippus would be reduced to a blank if everything that he had borrowed from others were to be erased. He seems, indeed, to have been the father of review-writers, and to have used the reviewer's right of transcription with more than modern license. Nearly a whole tragedy of Euripides reappeared in one of his 'articles,' and a wit on being asked what he was reading, replied, 'the Medea of Chrysippus.'[19]

In this respect Stoicism betrays its descent from the encyclopaedic lectures of the earlier Sophists, particularly Hippias. While professedly subordinating every other study to the art of virtuous living, its expositors seem to have either put a very wide interpretation on virtue, or else to have raised its foundation to a most unnecessary height. They protested against Aristotle's glorification of knowledge as the supreme end, and declared its exclusive pursuit to be merely a more refined form of self-indulgence;[20] but, being Greeks, they shared the speculative passion with him, and seized on any pretext that enabled them to gratify it. And this inquisitiveness was apparently much stronger in Asiatic Hellas, whence the Stoics were almost entirely recruited, than in the old country, where centuries of intellectual activity had issued in a scepticism from which their fresher minds revolted.[21] It is mentioned by Zeller as a proof of exhaustion and comparative indifference to such enquiries, that the Stoics should have fallen back on the

Heracleitean philosophy for their physics.[22] But all the ideas respecting the constitution of Nature that were then possible had already been put forward. The Greek capacity for discovery was perhaps greater in the third century than at any former time; but from the very progress of science it was necessarily confined to specialists, such as Aristarchus of Samos or Archimedes. And if the Stoics made no original contributions to physical science, they at least accepted what seemed at that time to be its established results; here, as in other respects, offering a marked contrast to the Epicurean school. If a Cleanthes assailed the heliocentric hypothesis of Aristarchus on religious grounds, he was treading in the footsteps of Aristotle. It is far more important that he or his successors should have taught the true theory of the earth's shape, of the moon's phases, of eclipses, and of the relative size and distance of the heavenly bodies.[23] On this last subject, indeed, one of the later Stoics, Posidonius, arrived at or accepted conclusions which, although falling far short of the reality, approximated to it in a very remarkable manner, when we consider what imperfect means of measurement the Greek astronomers had at their disposition.[24]

In returning to one of the older cosmologies, the Stoics placed themselves in opposition to the system of Aristotle as a whole, although on questions of detail they frequently adopted his conclusions. The object of Heracleitus, as against the Pythagoreans, had been to dissolve away every antithesis in a pervading unity of contradictories; and, as against the Eleatics, to substitute an eternal series of transformations for the changeless unity of absolute existence. The Stoics now applied the same method on a scale proportionate to the subsequent development of thought. Aristotle had carefully distinguished God from the world, even to the extent of isolating him from all share in its creation and interest in its affairs. The Stoics declared that God and the world were one. So far, it is allowable to call them pantheists. Yet their pantheism was very different from what we are accustomed to denote by that name; from the system of Spinoza, for example. Their strong faith in final causes and in Providence—a faith in which they closely followed Socrates—would be hardly consistent with anything but the ascription of a distinct and individual consciousness to the Supreme Being, which is just what modern pantheists refuse to admit. Their God was sometimes described as the soul of the world, the fiery element surrounding and penetrating every other kind of matter. What remained was the body of God; but it was a body which he had originally created out of his own substance, and would, in the fulness of time, absorb into that substance again.[25] Thus they kept the future conflagration foretold by Heracleitus, but gave it a more religious colouring. The process of creation was then to begin over again, and all things were to run the same course as before down to the minutest particulars, human history repeating itself, and the same persons returning to live the same lives once more.[26] Such a belief evidently involved the most rigid fatalism: and here again their doctrine offers a pointed contrast to that of Aristotle. The Stagirite, differing, as it would seem, in this respect from all the older physicists, maintained that there was an element of chance and spontaneity in the sublunary sphere; and without going very deeply into the mechanism of motives or the theory of moral responsibility, he had claimed a similar indeterminateness for the human will. Stoicism would hear of neither; with it, as with modern science, the chain of causation is unbroken from first to last, and extends to all phenomena alike. The old theological notion of an omnipotent divine will, or of a destiny superior even to that will, was at once confirmed and continued by the new theory of natural law; just as the predestination of the Reformers reappeared in the metaphysical rationalism of Spinoza.[27]

This dogma of universal determinism was combined in the Stoical system with an equally outspoken materialism. The capacity for either acting or being acted on was, according to Plato, the one convincing evidence of real existence; and he had endeavoured to prove that there is such a thing as mind apart from matter by its possession of this characteristic mark.[28] The Stoics simply reversed his argument. Whatever acts or is acted on, they said, must be corporeal; therefore the soul is a kind of body.[29] Here they only followed the common opinion of all philosophers who believed in an external world, except Plato and Aristotle, while to a certain extent anticipating the scientific automatism first taught in modern times by Spinoza, and simultaneously revived by various thinkers in our own day. To a certain extent only; for they did not recognise the independent reality of a consciousness in which the mechanical processes are either reflected, or represented under a different aspect. And they further gave their theory a somewhat grotesque expression by interpreting those qualities and attributes of things, which other materialists have been content to consider as belonging to matter, as themselves actual bodies. For instance, the virtues and vices were, according to them, so many gaseous currents by which the soul is penetrated and shaped—a materialistic rendering of Plato's theory that qualities are distinct and independent substances.[30]

We must mention as an additional point of contrast between the Stoics and the subsequent schools which they most resembled, that while these look on the soul as inseparable from the body, and sharing its fortunes from first to last, although perfectly distinct from it in idea, they emphasised the antithesis between the two just as strongly as Plato, giving the soul an absolutely infinite power of self-assertion during our mortal life, and allowing it a continued, though not an immortal, existence after death.[31]

What has been said of the human soul applies equally to God, who is the soul of the world. He also is conceived under the form of a material but very subtle and all-penetrating element to which our souls are much more closely akin than to the coarse clay with which they are temporarily associated. And it was natural that the heavenly bodies, in whose composition the ethereal element seemed so visibly to predominate, should pass with the Stoics, as with Plato and Aristotle, for conscious beings inferior only in sacredness and majesty to the Supreme Ruler of all.[32] Thus, the philosophy which we are studying helps to prove the strength and endurance of the religious reaction to which Socrates first gave an argumentative expression, and by which he was ultimately hurried to his doom. We may even trace its increasing ascendency through the successive stages of the Naturalistic school. Prodicus simply identified the gods of polytheism with unconscious physical forces;[33] Antisthenes, while discarding local worship, believed, like Rousseau, in the existence of a single deity;[34] Zeno, or his successors, revived the whole pantheon, but associated it with a pure morality, and explained away its more offensive features by an elaborate system of allegorical interpretation.[35]

It was not, however, by its legendary beliefs that the living power of ancient religion was displayed, but by the study and practice of divination. This was to the Greeks and Romans what priestly direction is to a Catholic, or the interpretation of Scripture texts to a Protestant believer. And the Stoics, in their anxiety to uphold religion as a bulwark of morality, went entirely along with the popular superstition; while at the same time they endeavoured to reconcile it with the universality of natural law by the same clumsily rationalistic methods that have found favour with some modern scientific defenders of the miraculous. The signs by which we are enabled to predict an event entered, they said, equally with the event itself, into the order of Nature, being either connected with it by direct causation, as is the configuration of the heavenly bodies at a man's birth with his after fortunes, or determined from the beginning of the world to precede it according to an invariable rule, as with the indications derived from inspecting the entrails of sacrificial victims. And when sceptics asked of what use was the premonitory sign when everything was predestined, they replied that our behaviour in view of the warning was predestined as well.[36]

To us the religion of the Stoics is interesting chiefly as a part of the machinery by which they attempted to make good the connexion between natural and moral law, assumed rather than proved by their Sophistic and Cynic precursors. But before proceeding to this branch of the subject we must glance at their mode of conceiving another side of the fundamental relationship between man and the universe. This is logic in its widest sense, so understood as to include the theory of the process by which we get our knowledge and of the ultimate evidence on which it rests, no less than the theory of formal ratiocination.

III.

In their theory of cognition the Stoics chiefly followed Aristotle; only with them the doctrine of empiricism is enunciated so distinctly as to be placed beyond the reach of misinterpretation. The mind is at first a tabula rasa, and all our ideas are derived exclusively from the senses.[37] But while knowledge as a whole rests on sense, the validity of each particular sense-perception must be determined by an appeal to reason, in other words, to the totality of our acquired experience.[38] So also the first principles of reasoning are not to be postulated, with Aristotle, as immediately and unconditionally certain; they are to be assumed as hypothetically true and gradually tested by the consequences deducible from them.[39] Both principles well illustrate the synthetic method of the Stoics—their habit of bringing into close connexion whatever Aristotle had studiously held apart. And we must maintain, in opposition to the German critics, that their method marks a real advance on his. It ought at any rate to find more favour with the experiential school of modern science, with those who hold that the highest mathematical and physical laws are proved, not by the impossibility of conceiving their contradictories, but by their close agreement with all the facts accessible to our observation.

It was a consequence of the principle just stated that in formal logic the Stoics should give precedence to the hypothetical over the categorical syllogism.[40] From one point of view their preference for this mode of stating an argument was an advance on the method of Aristotle, whose reasonings, if explicitly set out, would have assumed the form of disjunctive syllogisms. From another point of view it was a return to the older dialectics of Socrates and Plato, who always looked on their major premises as possessing only a conditional validity—conditional, that is to say, on the consent of their interlocutor. We have further to note that both the disjunctive and the hypothetical syllogism were first recognised as such by the Stoics; a discovery connected with the feature which most profoundly distinguishes their logic from Aristotle's logic. We showed, in dealing with the latter, that it is based on an analysis of the concept, and that all its imperfections are due to that single circumstance. It was the Stoics who first brought judgment, so fatally neglected by the author of the Analytics, into proper prominence. Having once grasped propositions as the beginning and end of reasoning, they naturally and under the guidance of common language, passed from simple to complex assertions, and immediately detected the arguments to which these latter serve as a foundation. And if we proceed to ask why they were more interested in judgment than in conception, we shall probably find the explanation to be that their philosophy had its root in the ethical and practical interests which involve a continual process of injunction and belief, that is to say, a continual association of such disparate notions as an impression and an action; while the Aristotelian philosophy, being ultimately derived from early Greek thought, had for its leading principle the circumscription of external objects and their representation under the form of a classified series. Thus the naturalistic system, starting with the application of scientific ideas to human life, ultimately carried back into science the vital idea of Law; that is, of fixed relations subsisting between disparate phenomena. And this in turn led to the reinterpretation of knowledge as the subsumption of less general under more general relations.

Under the guidance of a somewhat similar principle the Stoic logicians attempted a reform of Aristotle's categories. These they reduced to four: Substance, Quality, Disposition, and Relation (τὸ ὑποκείμενον, τὸ ποιὸν, τὸ πῶς ἔχον, and τὸ πρός τι πῶς ἔχον[41]); and the change was an improvement in so far as it introduced a certain method and subordination where none existed before; for each category implies, and is contained in, its predecessor; whereas the only order traceable in Aristotle's categories refers to the comparative frequency of the questions to which they correspond.

With the idea of subsumption and subordination to law, we pass at once to the Stoic ethics. For Zeno, the end of life was self-consistency; for Cleanthes, consistency with Nature; for Chrysippus, both the one and the other.[42] The still surviving individualism of the Cynics is represented in the first of these principles; the religious inspiration of the Stoa in the second; and the comprehensiveness of its great systematising intellect in the last. On the other hand, there is a vagueness about the idea of self-consistency which seems to date from a time when Stoicism was less a new and exclusive school than an endeavour to appropriate whatever was best in the older schools. For to be consistent is the common ideal of all philosophy, and is just what distinguishes it from the uncalculating impulsiveness of ordinary life, the chance inspirations of ordinary thought. But the Peripatetic who chose knowledge as his highest good differed widely from the Hedonist who made pleasure or painlessness his end; and even if they agreed in thinking that the highest pleasure is yielded by knowledge, the Stoic himself would assert that the object of their common pursuit was with both alike essentially unmoral. He would, no doubt, maintain that the self-consistency of any theory but his own was a delusion, and that all false moralities would, if consistently acted out, inevitably land their professors in a contradiction.[43] Yet the absence of contradiction, although a valuable verification, is too negative a mark to serve for the sole test of rightness; and thus we are led on to the more specific standard of conformability to Nature, whether our own or that of the universe as a whole. Here again a difficulty presents itself. The idea of Nature had taken such a powerful hold on the Greek mind that it was employed by every school in turn—except perhaps by the extreme sceptics, still faithful to the traditions of Protagoras and Gorgias—and was confidently appealed to in support of the most divergent ethical systems. We find it occupying a prominent place both in Plato's *Laws* and in Aristotle's *Politics*; while the maxim, Follow Nature, was borrowed by Zeno himself from Polemo, the head of the Academy, or perhaps from Polemo's predecessor, Xenocrates. And Epicurus, the great opponent of Stoicism, maintained, not without plausibility, that every animal is led by Nature to pursue its own pleasure in preference to any other end.[44] Thus, when Cleanthes declared that pleasure was unnatural,[45] he and the Epicureans could not have been talking about the same thing. They must have meant something different by pleasure or by nature or by both.

The last alternative seems the most probable. Nature with the Stoics was a fixed objective order whereby all things work together as co-operant parts of a single system. Each has a certain office to perform, and the perfect performance of it is the creature's virtue, or reason, or highest good: these three expressions being always used as strictly synonymous terms. Here we have the teleology, the dialectics, and the utilitarianism of Socrates, so worked out and assimilated that they differ only as various aspects of a single truth. The three lines of Socratic teaching had also been drawn to a single point by Plato; but his idealism had necessitated the creation of a new world for their development and concentration. The idea of Nature as it had grown up under the hands of Heracleitus, the Sophists, and Antisthenes, supplied Zeno with a ready-made mould into which his reforming aspirations could be run. The true Republic was not a pattern laid up in heaven, nor was it restricted to the narrow dimensions of a single Hellenic state. It was the whole real universe, in every part of which except in the works of wicked men a divine law was recognised and obeyed.[46] Nay, according to Cleanthes, God's law is obeyed even by the wicked, and the essence of morality consists only in its voluntary fulfilment. As others very vividly put it, we are like a dog tied under a cart; if we do not choose to run we shall be dragged along.[47]

It will now be better understood whence arose the hostility of the Stoics to pleasure, and how they could speak of it in what seems such a paradoxical style. It was subjective feeling as opposed to objective law; it was relative, particular, and individual, as opposed to their formal standard of right; and it was continually drawing men away from their true nature by acting as a temptation to vice. Thus, probably for the last reason, Cleanthes could speak of pleasure as contrary to Nature; while less rigorous authorities regarded it as absolutely indifferent, being a consequence of natural actions, not an essential element in their performance. And when their opponents pointed to the universal desire for pleasure as a proof that it was the natural end of animated beings, the Stoics answered that what Nature had in view was not pleasure at all, but the preservation of life itself.[48]

Such an interpretation of instinct introduces us to a new principle—self-interest; and this was, in fact, recognised on all hands as the foundation of right conduct; it was about the question, What is our interest? that the ancient moralists were disagreed. The Cynics apparently held that, for every being, simple existence is the only good, and therefore with them virtue meant limiting oneself to the bare necessaries of life; while by following Nature they meant reducing existence to its lowest terms, and assimilating our actions, so far as possible, to those of the lower animals, plants, or even stones, all of which require no more than to maintain the integrity of their proper nature.

Where the Cynics left off the Stoics began. Recognising simple self-preservation as the earliest interest and duty of man, they held that his ultimate and highest good was complete self-realisation, the development of that rational, social, and beneficent nature which distinguishes him from the lower animals.[49] Here their teleological religion came in as a valuable sanction for their ethics. Epictêtus, probably following older authorities, argues that self-love has purposely been made identical with sociability. 'The nature of an animal is to do all things for its own sake. Accordingly God has so ordered the nature of the rational animal that it cannot obtain any particular good without at the same time contributing to the common good. Because it is self-seeking it is not therefore unsocial.'[50] But if our happiness depends on external goods, then we shall begin to fight with one another for their possession:[51] friends, father, country, the gods themselves, everything will, with good reason, be sacrificed to their attainment. And, regarding this as a self-evident absurdity, Epictêtus concludes that our happiness must consist solely in a righteous will, which we know to have been the doctrine of his whole school.

We have now reached the great point on which the Stoic ethics differed from that of Plato and Aristotle. The two latter, while upholding virtue as the highest good, allowed external advantages like pleasure and exemption from pain to enter into their definition of perfect happiness; nor did they demand the entire suppression of passion, but, on the contrary, assigned it to a certain part in the formation of character. We must add, although it was not a point insisted on by the ancient critics, that they did not bring out the socially beneficent character of virtue with anything like the distinctness of their successors. The Stoics, on the other hand, refused to admit that there was any good but a virtuous will, or that any useful purpose could be served by irrational feeling. If the passions agree with virtue they are superfluous, if they are opposed to it they are mischievous; and once we give them the rein they are more likely to disagree with than to obey it.[52] The severer school had more reason on their side than is commonly admitted. Either there is no such thing as duty at all, or duty must be paramount over every other motive—that is to say, a perfect man will discharge his obligations at the sacrifice of every personal advantage. There is no pleasure that he will not renounce, no pain that he will not endure, rather than leave them unfulfilled. But to assume this supremacy over his will, duty must be incommensurable with any other motive; if it is a good at all, it must be the only good. To identify virtue with happiness seems to us absurd, because we are accustomed to associate it exclusively with those dispositions which are the cause of happiness in others, or altruism; and happiness itself with pleasure or the absence of pain, which are states of feeling necessarily conceived as egoistic. But neither the Stoics nor any other ancient moralists recognised such a distinction. All agreed that public and private interest must somehow be identified; the only question being, should one be merged in the other, and if so, which? or should there be an illogical compromise between the two. The alternative chosen by Zeno was incomparably nobler than the method of Epicurus, while it was more consistent than the methods of Plato and Aristotle. He regarded right conduct exclusively in the light of those universal interests with which alone it is properly concerned; and if he appealed to the motives supplied by personal happiness, this was a confusion of phraseology rather than of thought.

The treatment of the passions by the Stoic school presents greater difficulties, due partly to their own vacillation, partly to the very indefinite nature of the feelings in question. It will be admitted that here also the claims of duty are supreme. To follow the promptings of fear or of anger, of pity or of love, without considering the ulterior consequences of our action, is, of course, wrong. For even if, in any particular instance, no harm comes of the concession, we cannot be sure that such will always be the case; and meanwhile the passion is strengthened by indulgence. And we have also to consider the bad effect produced on the character of those who, finding themselves the object of passion, learn to address themselves to it instead of to reason. Difficulties arise when we begin to consider how far education should aim at the systematic discouragement of strong emotion. Here the Stoics seem to have taken up a position not very consistent either with their appeals to Nature or with their teleological assumptions. Nothing strikes one as more unnatural than the complete absence of human feeling; and a believer in design might plausibly maintain that every emotion conduced to the preservation either of the individual or of the race. We find, however, that the Stoics, here as elsewhere reversing the Aristotelian method, would not admit the existence of a psychological distinction between reason and passion. According to their analysis, the emotions are so many different forms of judgment. Joy and sorrow are false opinions respecting good and evil in the present: desire and fear, false opinions respecting good and evil in the future.[53] But, granting a righteous will to be the only good, and its absence the only evil, there can be no room for any of these feelings in the mind of a truly virtuous man, since his opinions on the subject of good are correct, and its possession depends entirely on himself. Everything else arises from an external necessity, to strive with which would be useless because it is inevitable, foolish because it is beneficent, and impious because it is supremely wise.

It will be seen that the Stoics condemned passion not as the cause of immoral actions but as intrinsically vicious in itself. Hence their censure extended to the rapturous delight and passionate grief which seem entirely out of relation to conduct properly so called. This was equivalent to saying that the will has complete control over emotion; a doctrine which our philosophers did not shrink from maintaining. It might have been supposed that a position which the most extreme supporters of free-will would hardly accept, would find still less favour with an avowedly necessarian school. And to regard the emotions as either themselves beliefs, or as inevitably caused by beliefs, would seem to remove them even farther from the sphere of moral responsibility. The Stoics, however, having arrived at the perfectly true doctrine that judgment is a form of volition, seem to have immediately invested it as such with the old associations of free choice which they were at the same time busily engaged in stripping off from other exercises of the same faculty. They took up the Socratic paradox that virtue is knowledge; but they would not agree with Socrates that it could be instilled by force of argument. To them vice was not so much ignorance as the obstinate refusal to be convinced.[54]

The Stoic arguments are, indeed, when we come to analyse them, appeal to authority rather than to the logical understanding. We are told again and again that the common objects of desire and dread cannot really be good or evil, because they are not altogether under our control.[55] And if we ask why this necessarily excludes them from the class of things to be pursued or avoided, the answer is that man, having been created for perfect happiness, must also have been created with the power to secure it by his own unaided exertions. But, even granting the very doubtful thesis that there is any ascertainable purpose in creation at all, it is hard to see how the Stoics could have answered any one who chose to maintain that man is created for enjoyment; since, judging by experience, he has secured a larger share of it than of virtue, and is just as capable of gaining it by a mere exercise of volition. For the professors of the Porch fully admitted that their ideal sage had never been realised; which, with their opinions about the indivisibility of virtue, was equivalent to saying that there never had been such a thing as a good man at all. Or, putting the same paradox into other words, since the two classes of wise and foolish divide humanity between them, and since the former class has only an ideal existence, they were obliged to admit that mankind are not merely most of them fools, but all fools. And this, as Plutarch has pointed out in his very clever attack on Stoicism, is equivalent to saying that the scheme of creation is a complete failure.[56]

IV.

The inconsistencies of a great philosophical system are best explained by examining its historical antecedents. We have already attempted to disentangle the roots from which Stoicism was nourished, but one of the most important has not yet been taken into account. This was the still continued influence of Parmenides, derived, if not from his original teaching, then from some one or more of the altered shapes through which it had passed. It has been shown how Zeno used the Heracleitean method to break down all the demarcations laboriously built up by Plato and Aristotle. Spirit was identified with matter; ideas with aerial currents; God with the world; rational with sensible evidence; volition with judgment; and emotion with thought. But the idea of a fundamental antithesis, expelled from every other department of enquiry, took hold with all the more energy on what, to Stoicism, was the most vital of all distinctions—that between right and wrong.[57] Once grasp this transformation of a metaphysical into a moral principle, and every paradox of the system will be seen to follow from it with logical necessity. What the supreme Idea had been to Plato and self-thinking thought to Aristotle, that virtue became to the new school, simple, unchangeable, and self-sufficient. It must not only be independent of pleasure and pain, but absolutely incommensurable with them; therefore there can be no happiness except what it gives. As an indivisible unity, it must be possessed entirely or not at all; and being eternal, once possessed it can never be lost. Further, since the same action may be either right or wrong, according to the motive of its performance, virtue is nothing external, but a subjective disposition, a state of the will and the affections; or, if these are to be considered as judgments, a state of the reason. Finally, since the universe is organised reason, virtue must be natural, and especially consonant to the nature of man as a rational animal; while, at the same time, its existence in absolute purity being inconsistent with experience, it must remain an unattainable ideal.

It has been shown in former parts of this work how Greek philosophy, after straining an antithesis to the utmost, was driven by the very law of its being to close or bridge over the chasm by a series of accommodations and transitions. To this rule Stoicism was no exception; and perhaps its extraordinary vitality may have been partly due to the necessity imposed on its professors of continually revising their ethics, with a view to softening down its most repellent features. We proceed to sketch in rapid outline the chief artifices employed for this purpose.

The doctrine, in its very earliest form, had left a large neutral ground between good and evil, comprehending almost all the common objects of desire and avoidance. These the Stoics now proceeded to divide according to a similar principle of arrangement. Whatever, without being morally good in the strictest sense, was either conducive to morality, or conformable to human nature, or both, they called preferable. Under this head came personal advantages, such as mental accomplishments, beauty, health, strength, and life itself; together with external advantages, such as wealth, honour, and high connexions. The opposite to preferable things they called objectionable; and what lay between the two, such as the particular coin selected to make a payment with, absolutely indifferent.[58]

The thorough-going condemnation of passion was explained away to a certain extent by allowing the sage himself to feel a slight touch of the feelings which fail to shake his determination, like a scar remaining after the wound is healed; and by admitting the desirability of sundry emotions, which, though carefully distinguished from the passions, seem to have differed from them in degree rather than in kind.[59]

In like manner, the peremptory alternative between consummate wisdom and utter folly was softened down by admitting the possibility of a gradual progress from one to the other, itself subdivided into a number of more or less advanced grades, recalling Aristotle's idea of motion as a link between Privation and Form.[60]

If there be a class of persons who although not perfectly virtuous are on the road to virtue, it follows that there are moral actions which they are capable of performing. These the Stoics called intermediate or imperfect duties; and, in accordance with their intellectual view of conduct, they defined them as actions for which a probable reason might be given; apparently in contradistinction to those which were deduced from a single principle with the extreme rigour of scientific demonstration. Such intermediate duties would have for their appropriate object the ends which, without being absolutely good, were still relatively worth seeking, or the avoidance of what, without being an absolute evil, was allowed to be relatively objectionable. They stood midway between virtue and vice, just as the progressive characters stood between the wise and the foolish, and preferable objects between what was really good and what was really evil.

The idea of such a provisional code seems to have originated with Zeno;[61] but the form under which we now know it is the result of at least two successive revisions. The first and most important is due to Panaetius, a Stoic philosopher of the second century B.C., on whose views the study of Plato and Aristotle exercised a considerable influence. A work of this teacher on the Duties of Man furnished Cicero with the materials for his celebrated De Officiis, under which form its lessons have passed into the educational literature of modern Europe. The Latin treatise is written in a somewhat frigid and uninteresting style, whether through the fault of Cicero or of his guide we cannot tell. The principles laid down are excellent, but there is no vital bond of union holding them together. We can hardly imagine that the author's son, for whom the work was originally designed, or anyone else since his time, felt himself much benefited by its perusal. Taken, however, as a register of the height reached by ordinary educated sentiment under the influence of speculative ideas, and of the limits imposed by it in turn on their vagaries, after four centuries of continual interaction, the De Officiis presents us with very satisfactory results. The old quadripartite division of the virtues is reproduced; but each is treated in a large and liberal spirit, marking an immense advance on Aristotle's definitions, wherever the two can be compared. Wisdom is identified with the investigation of truth; and there is a caution against believing on insufficient evidence, which advantageously contrasts with what were soon to be the lessons of theology on the same subject. The other great intellectual duty inculcated is to refrain from wasting our energies on difficult and useless enquiries.[62] This injunction has been taken up and very impressively repeated by some philosophers in our own time; but in the mouth of Cicero it probably involved much greater restrictions on the study of science than they would be disposed to admit. And the limits now prescribed to speculation by Positivism will perhaps seem not less injudicious, when viewed in the light of future discoveries, than those fixed by the ancient moralists seem to us who know what would have been lost had they always been treated with respect.

The obligations of justice come next. They are summed up in two precepts that leave nothing to be desired: the first is to do no harm except in self-defence; the second, to bear our share in a perpetual exchange of good offices. And the foundation of justice is rightly placed in the faithful fulfilment of contracts—an idea perhaps suggested by Epicurus.[63] The virtue of fortitude is treated with similar breadth, and so interpreted as to cover the whole field of conduct, being identified not only with fearlessness in the face of danger, but with the energetic performance of every duty. In a word, it is opposed quite as much to slothfulness and irresolution as to physical timidity.[64] Temperance preserves its old meaning of a reasonable restraint exercised over the animal passions and desires; and furthermore, it receives a very rich significance as the quality by which we are enabled to discern and act up to the part assigned to us in life by natural endowment, social position, and individual choice. But this, as one of the most important ideas contributed by Stoicism to subsequent thought, must be reserved for separate discussion in the following section.

In addition to its system of intermediate duties, the Stoic ethics included a code of casuistry which, to judge by some recorded specimens, allowed a very startling latitude both to the ideal sage and to the ordinary citizen. Thus, if Sextus Empiricus is to be believed, the Stoics saw nothing objectionable about the trade of a courtesan.[65] Chrysippus, like Socrates and Plato, denied that there was any harm in falsehoods if they were told with a good intention.

Chrysippus

Diogenes of Seleucia thought it permissible to pass bad money,[66] and to sell defective articles without mentioning their faults;[67] he was, however, contradicted on both points by another Stoic, Antipater. Still more discreditable were the opinions of Hecato, a disciple of Panaetius. He discussed the question whether a good man need or need not feed his slaves in a time of great scarcity, with an evident leaning towards the latter alternative; and also made it a matter of deliberation whether in case part of a ship's cargo had to be thrown overboard, a valuable horse or a worthless slave should be the more readily sacrificed. His answer is not given; but that the point should ever have been mooted does not say much for the rigour of his principles or for the benevolence of his disposition.[68] Most outrageous of all, from the Stoic point of view, is the declaration of Chrysippus that Heracleitus and Pherecydes would have done well to give up their wisdom, had they been able by so doing to get rid of their bodily infirmities at the same time.[69] That overstrained theoretical severity should be accompanied by a corresponding laxity in practice is a phenomenon of frequent occurrence; but that this laxity should be exhibited so undisguisedly in the details of the theory itself, goes beyond anything quoted against the Jesuits by Pascal, and bears witness, after a fashion, to the extraordinary sincerity of Greek thought.[70]

It was not, however, in any of these concessions that the Stoics found from first to last their most efficient solution for the difficulties of practical experience, but in the countenance they extended to an act which, more than any other, might have seemed fatally inconsistent both in spirit and in letter with their whole system, whether we choose to call it a defiance of divine law, a reversal of natural instinct, a selfish abandonment of duty, or a cowardly shrinking from pain. We allude, of course, to their habitual recommendation of suicide. 'If you are not satisfied with life,' they said, 'you have only got to rise and depart; the door is always open.' Various circumstances were specified in which the sage would exercise the privilege of 'taking himself off,' as they euphemistically expressed it. Severe pain, mutilation, incurable disease, advanced old age, the hopelessness of escaping from tyranny, and in general any hindrance to leading a 'natural' life, were held to be a sufficient justification for such a step.[71] The first founders of the school set an example afterwards frequently followed. Zeno is said to have hanged himself for no better reason than that he fell and broke his finger through the weakness of old age; and Cleanthes, having been ordered to abstain temporarily from food, resolved, as he expressed it, not to turn back after going half-way to death.[72] This side of the Stoic doctrine found particular favour in Rome, and the voluntary death of Cato was always spoken of as his chief title to fame. Many noble spirits were sustained in their defiance of the imperial despotism by the thought that there was one last liberty of which not even Caesar could deprive them. Objections were silenced by the argument that, life not being an absolute good, its loss might fairly be preferred to some relatively greater inconvenience.[73] But why the sage should renounce an existence where perfect happiness depends entirely on his own will, neither was, nor could it be, explained.

V.

If now, abandoning all technicalities, we endeavour to estimate the significance and value of the most general ideas contributed by Stoicism to ethical speculation, we shall find that they may be most conveniently considered under the following heads. First of all, the Stoics made morality completely inward. They declared that the intention was equivalent to the deed, and that the wish was equivalent to the intention—a view which has been made familiar to all by the teaching of the Gospel, but the origin of which in Greek philosophy has been strangely ignored even by rationalistic writers.[74] From the inaccessibility of motives and feelings to direct external observation, it follows that each man must be, in the last resort, his own judge. Hence the notion of conscience is equally a Stoic creation. That we have a mystical intuition informing us, prior to experience, of the difference between right and wrong is, indeed, a theory quite alien to their empirical derivation of knowledge. But that the educated wrong-doer carries in his bosom a perpetual witness and avenger of his guilt, they most distinctly asserted.[75] The difference between ancient and modern tragedy is alone sufficient to prove the novelty and power of this idea; for that the Eumenides do not represent even the germ of a conscience is as certain as anything in mythology can be.[76] On the other hand, the fallibility of conscience and the extent to which it may be sophisticated were topics not embraced within the limits of Stoicism, and perhaps never adequately illustrated by any writer, even in modern times, except the great English novelist whose loss we still deplore.

The second Stoic idea to which we would invite attention is that, in the economy of life, every one has a certain function to fulfil, a certain part to play, which is marked out for him by circumstances beyond his control, but in the adequate performance of which his duty and dignity are peculiarly involved. It is true that this idea finds no assignable place in the teaching of the earliest Stoics, or rather in the few fragments of their teaching which alone have been preserved; but it is touched upon by Cicero under the head of Temperance, in the adaptation from Panaetius already referred to; it frequently recurs in the lectures of Epictêtus; and it is enunciated with energetic concision in the solitary meditations of Marcus Aurelius.[77] The belief spoken of is, indeed, closely connected with the Stoic teleology, and only applies to the sphere of free intelligence a principle like that supposed to regulate the activity of inanimate or irrational beings. If every mineral, every plant, and every animal has its special use and office, so also must we, according to the capacity of our individual and determinate existence. By accomplishing the work thus imposed on us, we fulfil the purpose of our vocation, we have done all that the highest morality demands, and may with a clear conscience leave the rest to fate. To put the same idea into somewhat different terms: we are born into certain relationships, domestic, social, and political, by which the lines of our daily duties are prescribed with little latitude for personal choice. What does depend upon ourselves is to make the most of these conditions and to perform the tasks arising out of them in as thorough a manner as possible. 'It was not only out of ivory,' says Seneca, 'that Pheidias could make statues, but out of bronze as well; had you offered him marble or some cheaper material still, he would have carved the best that could be made out of that. So the sage will exhibit his virtue in wealth, if he be permitted; if not, in poverty; if possible, in his own country; if not, in exile; if possible, as a general; if not, as a soldier; if possible, in bodily vigour; if not, in weakness. Whatever fortune be granted him, he will make it the means for some memorable achievement.' Or, to take the more homely comparisons of Epictêtus: 'The weaver does not manufacture his wool, but works up what is given him.' 'Remember that you are to act in whatever drama the manager may choose, a long or short one according to his pleasure. Should he give you the part of a beggar, take care to act that becomingly; and the same should it be a lame man, or a magistrate, or a private citizen. For your business is to act well the character that is given to you, but to choose it is the business of another.'So spoke the humble freedman; but the master of the world had also to recognise what fateful limits were imposed on his beneficent activity. 'Why wait, O man!' exclaims Marcus Aurelius. 'Do what Nature now demands; make haste and look not round to see if any know it; nor hope for Plato's Republic, but be content with the smallest progress, and consider that the result even of this will be no little thing.'[78] Carlyle was not a Stoic; but in this respect his teaching breathes the best spirit of Stoicism; and, to the same extent also, through his whole life he practised what he taught.

The implications of such an ethical standard are, on the whole, conservative; it is assumed that social institutions are, taking them altogether, nearly the best possible at any moment; and that our truest wisdom is to make the most of them, instead of sighing for some other sphere where our grand aspirations or volcanic passions might find a readier outlet for their feverish activity. And if the teaching of the first Stoics did not take the direction here indicated, it was because they, with the communistic theories inherited from their Cynic predecessors, began by condemning all existing social distinctions as irrational. They wished to abolish local religion, property, the family, and the State, as a substitute for which the whole human race was to be united under a single government, without private possessions or slaves, and with a complete community of women and children.[79] It must, however, have gradually dawned on them that such a radical subversion of the present system was hardly compatible with their belief in the providential origin of all things; and that, besides this, the virtues which they made it so much their object to recommend, would be, for the most part, superfluous in a communistic society. At the same time, the old notion of Sôphrosynê as a virtue which consisted in minding one's own business, or, stated more generally, in discerning and doing whatever work one is best fitted for, would continue to influence ethical teaching, with the effect of giving more and more individuality to the definition of duty. And the Stoic idea of a perfect sage, including as it did the possession of every accomplishment and an exclusive fitness for discharging every honourable function, would seem much less chimerical if interpreted to mean that a noble character, while everywhere intrinsically the same, might be realised under as many divergent forms as there are opportunities for continuous usefulness in life.[80]

We can understand, then, why the philosophy which, when first promulgated, had tended to withdraw its adherents from participation in public life, should, when transplanted to Roman soil, have become associated with an energetic interest in politics; why it was so eagerly embraced by those noble statesmen who fought to the death in defence of their ancient liberties; how it could become the cement of a senatorial opposition under the worst Caesars; how it could be the inspiration and support of Rome's Prime Minister during that quinquennium Neronis which was the one bright episode in more than half a century of shame and terror; how, finally, it could mount the throne with Marcus Aurelius, and prove, through his example, that the world's work might be most faithfully performed by one in whose meditations mere worldly interests occupied the smallest space. Nor can we agree with Zeller in thinking that it was the nationality, and not the philosophy, of these disciples which made them such efficient statesmen.[81] On the contrary, it seems to us that the 'Romanism' of these men was inseparable from their philosophy, and that they were all the more Roman because they were Stoics as well.

The third great idea of Stoicism was its doctrine of humanity. Men are all children of one Father, and citizens of one State; the highest moral law is, Follow Nature, and Nature has made them to be social and to love one another; the private interest of each is, or should be, identified with the universal interest; we should live for others that we may live for ourselves; even to our enemies we should show love and not anger; the unnaturalness of passion is proved by nothing more clearly than by its anti-social and destructive tendencies. Here, also, the three great Stoics of the Roman empire—Seneca, Epictêtus, and Marcus Aurelius—rather than the founders of the school, must be our authorities;[82] whether it be because their lessons correspond to a more developed state of thought, or simply because they have been more perfectly preserved. The former explanation is, perhaps, the more generally accepted. There seems, however, good reason for believing that the idea of universal love—the highest of all philosophical ideas next to that of the universe itself—dates further back than is commonly supposed. It can hardly be due to Seneca, who had evidently far more capacity for popularising and applying the thoughts of others than for original speculation, and who on this subject expresses himself with a rhetorical fluency not usually characterising the exposition of new discoveries. The same remark applies to his illustrious successors, who, while agreeing with him in tone, do not seem to have drawn on his writings for their philosophy. It is also clear that the idea in question springs from two essentially Stoic conceptions: the objective conception of a unified world, a cosmos to which all men belong; and the subjective conception of a rational nature common to them all. These, again, are rooted in early Greek thought, and were already emerging into distinctness at the time of Socrates. Accordingly we find that Plato, having to compose a characteristic speech for the Sophist Hippias, makes him say that like-minded men are by nature kinsmen and friends to one another.[83] Nature, however, soon came to be viewed under a different aspect, and it was maintained, just as by some living philosophers, that her true law is the universal oppression of the weak by the strong. Then the idea of mind came in as a salutary corrective. It had supplied a basis for the ethics of Protagoras, and still more for the ethics of Socrates; it was now combined with its old rival by the Stoics, and from their union arose the conception of human nature as something allied with and illustrated by all other forms of animal life, yet capable, if fully developed, of rising infinitely above them. Nevertheless, the individual and the universal element were never quite reconciled in the Stoic ethics. The altruistic quality of justice was clearly perceived; but no attempt was made to show that all virtue is essentially social, and has come to be recognised as obligatory on the individual mainly because it conduces to the safety of the whole community.

The learner was told to conquer his passions for his own sake rather than for the sake of others; and indulgence in violent anger, though more energetically denounced, was, in theory, placed on a par with immoderate delight or uncontrollable distress. So also, vices of impurity were classed with comparatively harmless forms of sensuality, and considered in reference, not to the social degradation of their victims, but to the spiritual defilement of their perpetrators.

Yet, while the Stoics were far from anticipating the methods of modern Utilitarianism, they were, in a certain sense, strict Utilitarians—that is to say, they measured the goodness or badness of actions by their consequences; in other words, by their bearing on the supposed interest of the individual or of the community. They did not, it is true, identify interest with pleasure or the absence of pain; but although, in our time, Hedonism and Utilitarianism are, for convenience, treated as interchangeable terms, they need not necessarily be so. If any one choose to regard bodily strength, health, wealth, beauty, intellect, knowledge, or even simple existence, as the highest good and the end conduciveness to which determines the morality of actions, he is a Utilitarian; and, even if it could be shown that a maximum of happiness would be ensured by the attainment of his end, he would not on that account become a Hedonist. Now it is certain that the early Stoics, at least, regarded the preservation of the human race as an end which rightfully took precedence of every other consideration; and, like Charles Austin, they sometimes pushed their principles to paradoxical or offensive extremes, apparently for no other purpose than that of affronting the common feelings of mankind,[84] without remembering that such feelings were likely to represent embodied experiences of utility. Thus—apart from their communistic theories—they were fond of specifying the circumstances in which incest would become legitimate; and they are said not only to have sanctioned cannibalism in cases of extreme necessity, but even to have recommended its introduction as a substitute for burial or cremation; although this, we may hope, was rather a grim illustration of what they meant by moral indifference than a serious practical suggestion.[85]

Besides the encouragement which it gave to kind offices between friends and neighbours, the Stoic doctrine of humanity and mutual love was honourably exemplified in Seneca's emphatic condemnation of the gladiatorial games and of the horrible abuses connected with domestic slavery in Rome.[86] But we miss a clear perception that such abuses are always and everywhere the consequences of slavery; and the outspoken abolitionism of the naturalists alluded to by Aristotle does not seem to have been imitated by their successors in later ages.[87] The most one can say is that the fiction of original liberty was imported into Roman jurisprudence through the agency of Stoic lawyers, and helped to familiarise men's minds with the idea of universal emancipation before political and economical conditions permitted it to be made a reality.

VI.

It is probable that the philanthropic tendencies of the Stoics were, to a great extent, neutralised by the extreme individualism which formed the reverse side of their philosophical character; and also by what may be called the subjective idealism of their ethics. According to their principles, no one can really do good to any one else, since what does not depend on my will is not a good to me. The altruistic virtues are valuable, not as sources of beneficent action, but as manifestations of benevolent sentiment. Thus, to set on foot comprehensive schemes for the relief of human suffering seemed no part of the Stoic's business. And the abolition of slavery, even had it been practicable, would have seemed rather superfluous to one who held that true freedom is a mental condition within the reach of all who desire it,[88] while the richest and most powerful may be, and for the most part actually are, without it. Moreover, at the time when philosophy gained its greatest ascendency, the one paramount object of practical statesmen must have been to save civilisation from the barbarians, a work to which Marcus Aurelius devoted his life. Hence we learn without surprise that the legislative efforts of the imperial Stoic were directed to the strengthening, rather than to the renovation, of ancient institutions.[89] Certain enactments were, indeed, framed for the protection of those who took part in the public games. It was provided, with a humanity from which even our own age might learn something, that performers on the high rope should be ensured against the consequences of an accidental fall by having the ground beneath them covered with feather beds; and the gladiators were only allowed to fight with blunted weapons.[90] It must, however, be noted that in speaking of the combats with wild beasts which were still allowed to continue under his reign, Marcus Aurelius dwells only on the monotonous character which made them exceedingly wearisome to a cultivated mind; just as a philosophic sportsman may sometimes be heard to observe that shooting one grouse is very like shooting another; while elsewhere he refers with simple contempt to the poor wretches who, when already half-devoured by the wild beasts, begged to be spared for another day's amusement.[91] Whether he knew the whole extent of the judicial atrocities practised on his Christian subjects may well be doubted; but it maybe equally doubted whether, had he known it, he would have interfered to save them. Pain and death were no evils; but it was an evil that the law should be defied.[92]

Those manifestations of sympathy which are often so much more precious than material assistance were also repugnant to Stoic principles. On this subject, Epictêtus expresses himself with singular harshness. 'Do not,' he says, 'let yourself be put out by the sufferings of your friends. If they are unhappy, it is their own fault. God made them for happiness, not for misery. They are grieved at parting from you, are they? Why, then, did they set their affections on things outside themselves? If they suffer for their folly it serves them right.'[93]

On the other hand, if Stoicism did not make men pitiful, it made them infinitely forgiving. Various causes conspired to bring about this result. If all are sinners, and if all sins are equal, no one has a right, under pretence of superior virtue, to cast a stone at his fellows. Such is the point of view insisted on with especial emphasis by Seneca, who, more perhaps than other philosophers, had reason to be conscious how far his practice fell short of his professions.[94] But, speaking generally, pride was the very last fault with which the Stoics could be charged. Both in ancient and modern times, satirists have been prone to assume that every disciple of the Porch, in describing his ideal of a wise man, was actually describing himself. No misconception could be more complete. It is like supposing that, because Christ commanded his followers to be perfect even as their heavenly Father is perfect, every Christian for that reason thinks himself equal to God. The wise man of the Stoics had, by their own acknowledgment, never been realised at all; he had only been approached by three characters, Socrates, Antisthenes, and Diogenes.[95] 'May the sage fall in love?' asked a young man of Panaetius. 'What the sage may do,' replied the master, 'is a question to be considered at some future time. Meanwhile, you and I, who are very far from being sages, had better take care not to let ourselves become the slaves of a degrading passion.'[96]

In the next place, if it is not in the power of others to injure us, we have no right to resent anything that they can do to us. So argues Epictêtus, who began to learn philosophy when still a slave, and was carefully prepared by his instructor, Musonius, to bear without repining whatever outrages his master might choose to inflict on him. Finally, to those who urged that they might justly blame the evil intentions of their assailants, Marcus Aurelius could reply that even this was too presumptuous, that all men did what they thought right, and that the motives of none could be adequately judged except by himself.[97] And all the Stoics found a common ground for patience in their optimistic fatalism, in the doctrine that whatever happens is both necessarily determined, and determined by absolute goodness combined with infallible wisdom.[98]

Doctrines like these, if consistently carried out, would have utterly destroyed so much of morality as depends on the social sanction; while, by inculcating the absolute indifference of external actions, they might ultimately have paralysed the individual conscience itself. But the Stoics were not consistent. Unlike some modern moralists, who are ready to forgive every injury so long as they are not themselves the victims, our philosophers were unsparing in their denunciations of wrong-doing; and it is very largely to their indignant protests that we are indebted for our knowledge of the corruption prevalent in Roman society under the Empire. It may even be contended that, in this respect, our judgment has been unfairly biassed. The picture drawn by the Stoics, or by writers trained under their influence, seems to have been too heavily charged with shadow; and but for the archaeological evidence we should not have known how much genuine human affection lay concealed in those lower social strata whose records can only be studied on their tombs.[99] It was among these classes that Christianity found the readiest acceptance, simply because it gave a supernatural sanction to habits and sentiments already made familiar by the spontaneous tendencies of an unwarlike régime.

VII.

Before parting with Stoicism we have to say a few words on the metaphysical foundation of the whole system—the theory of Nature considered as a moral guide and support. It has been shown that the ultimate object of this, as of many other ethical theories, both ancient and modern, was to reconcile the instincts of individual self-preservation with virtue, which is the instinct of self-preservation in an entire community. The Stoics identified both impulses by declaring that virtue is the sole good of the individual no less than the supreme interest of the whole; thus involving themselves in an insoluble contradiction. For, from their nominalistic point of view, the good of the whole can be nothing but an aggregate of particular goods, or else a means for their attainment; and in either case the happiness of the individual has to be accounted for apart from his duty. And an analysis of the special virtues and vices would equally have forced them back on the assumption, which they persistently repudiated, that individual existence and pleasure are intrinsically good, and their opposites intrinsically evil. To prove their fundamental paradox—the non-existence of individual as distinguished from social interest—the Stoics employed the analogy of an organised body where the good of the parts unquestionably subserves the good of the whole;[100] and the object of their teleology was to show that the universe and, by implication, the human race, were properly to be viewed in that light. The acknowledged adaptation of life to its environment furnished some plausible arguments in support of their thesis; and the deficiencies were made good by a revival of the Heracleitean theory in which the unity of Nature was conceived partly as a necessary interdependence of opposing forces, partly as a perpetual transformation of every substance into every other. Universal history also tended to confirm the same principle in its application to the human race. The Macedonian, and still more the Roman empire, brought the idea of a world-wide community living under the same laws ever nearer to its realisation; the decay of the old religion and the old civic patriotism set free a vast fund of altruism which now took the form of simple philanthropy; while a rank growth of immorality offered ever new opportunities for an indignant protest against senseless luxury and inhuman vice. This last circumstance, however, was not allowed to prejudice the optimism of the system; for the fertile physics of Heracleitus suggested a method by which moral evil could be interpreted as a necessary concomitant of good, a material for the perpetual exercise and illustration of virtuous deeds.[101]

Yet, if the conception of unity was gaining ground, the conceptions of purpose and vitality must have been growing weaker as the triumph of brute force prolonged itself without limit or hope of redress. Hence Stoicism in its later form shows a tendency to dissociate the dynamism of Heracleitus from the teleology of Socrates, and to lean on the former rather than on the latter for support. One symptom of this changed attitude is a blind worship of power for its own sake. We find the renunciation of pleasure and the defiance of pain appreciated more from an aesthetic than from an ethical point of view; they are exalted almost in the spirit of a Red Indian, not as means to higher ends, but as manifestations of unconquerable strength; and sometimes the highest sanction of duty takes the form of a morbid craving for applause, as if the universe were an amphitheatre and life a gladiatorial game.[102]

The noble spirit of Marcus Aurelius was, indeed, proof against such temptations: and he had far more to dread than to hope from the unlightened voice of public opinion; but to him also, 'standing between two eternities,' Nature presented herself chiefly under the aspect of an overwhelming and absorbing Power. Pleasure is not so much dangerous as

Marcus Aurelius

worthless, weak, and evanescent. Selfishness, pride, anger, and discontent will soon be swept into abysmal gulfs of oblivion by the roaring cataract of change. Universal history is one long monotonous procession of phantasms passing over the scene into death and utter night. In one short life we may see all that ever was, or is, or is to be; the same pageant has already been and shall be repeated an infinite number of times. Nothing endures but the process of unending renovation: we must die that the world may be ever young. Death itself only reunites us with the absolute All whence we come, in which we move, and whither we return.[103] But the imperial sage makes no attempt to explain why we should ever have separated ourselves from it in thought; or why one life should be better worth living than another in the universal vanity of things.

The physics of Stoicism was, in truth, the scaffolding rather than the foundation of its ethical superstructure. The real foundation was the necessity of social existence, formulated under the influence of a logical exclusiveness first introduced by Parmenides, and inherited from his teaching by every system of philosophy in turn. Yet there is no doubt that Stoic morality was considerably strengthened and steadied by the support it found in conceptions derived from a different order of speculations; so much so that at last it grew to conscious independence of that support.

Marcus Aurelius, a constant student of Lucretius, seems to have had occasional misgivings with respect to the certainty of his own creed; but they never extended to his practical beliefs. He was determined that, whatever might be the origin of this world, his relation to it should be still the same. 'Though things be purposeless, act not thou without a purpose.' 'If the universe is an ungoverned chaos, be content that in that wild torrent thou hast a governing reason within thyself.'[104]

There seems, then, good reason for believing that the law of duty, after being divorced from mythology, and seriously compromised by its association, even among the Stoics themselves, with our egoistic instincts, gained an entirely new authority when placed, at least in appearance, under the sanction of a power whose commands did not even admit of being disobeyed. And the question spontaneously presents itself whether we, after getting rid of the old errors and confusions, may profitably employ the same method in defence of the same convictions, whether the ancient alliance between fact and right can be reorganised on a basis of scientific proof.

A great reformer of the last generation, finding that the idea of Nature was constantly put forward to thwart his most cherished schemes, prepared a mine for its destruction which was only exploded after his death. Seldom has so powerful a charge of logical dynamite been collected within so small a space as in Mill's famous Essay on Nature. But the immediate effect was less than might have been anticipated, because the attack was supposed to be directed against religion, whereas it was only aimed at an abstract metaphysical dogma, not necessarily connected with any theological beliefs, and held by many who have discarded all such beliefs. A stronger impression was, perhaps, produced by the nearly simultaneous declaration of Sir W. Gull—in reference to the supposed vis medicatrix naturae—that, in cases of disease, 'what Nature wants is to put the man in his coffin.' The new school of political economists have also done much to show that legislative interference with the 'natural laws' of wealth need by no means be so generally mischievous as was once supposed. And the doctrine of Evolution, besides breaking down the old distinctions between Nature and Man, has represented the former as essentially variable, and therefore, to that extent, incapable of affording a fixed standard for moral action. It is, however, from this school that a new attempt to rehabilitate the old physical ethics has lately proceeded. The object of Mr. Herbert Spencer's Data of Ethics is, among other points, to prove that a true morality represents the ultimate stage of evolution, and reproduces in social life that permanent equilibration towards which every form of evolution constantly tends. And Mr. Spencer also shows how evolution is bringing about a state of things in which the self-regarding shall be finally harmonised with the social impulses. Now, it will be readily admitted that morality is a product of evolution in this sense that it is a gradual formation, that it is the product of many converging conditions, and that it progresses according to a certain method. But that the same method is observed through all orders of evolution seems less evident. For instance, in the formation, first of the solar system, and then of the earth's crust, there is a continual loss of force, while in the development of organic life there is as continual a gain; and on arriving at subjective phenomena, we are met by facts which, in the present state of our knowledge, cannot advantageously be expressed in terms of force and matter at all. Even if we do not agree with George Sand in thinking that self-sacrifice is the only virtue, we must admit that the possibility, at least, of its being sometimes demanded is inseparable from the idea of duty. But self-sacrifice cannot be conceived without consciousness; which is equivalent to saying that it involves other than mechanical notions. Thus we are confronted by the standing difficulty of all evolutionary theories, and on a point where that difficulty is peculiarly sensible. Nor is this an objection to be got rid of by the argument that it applies to all philosophical systems alike. To an idealist, the dependence of morality on consciousness is a practical confirmation of his professed principles. Holding that the universal forms of experience are the conditions under which an object is apprehended, rather than modifications imposed by an unknowable object on an unknowable subject, and that these forms are common to all intelligent beings, he holds also that the perception of duty is the widening of our individual selves into that universal self which is the subjective side of all experience.

Again, whatever harmony evolution may introduce into our conceptions, whatever hopes it may encourage with regard to the future of our race, one does not see precisely what sanction it gives to morality at present—that is to say, how it makes self-sacrifice easier than before. Because certain forces have been unconsciously working towards a certain end through ages past, why should I consciously work towards the same end? If the perfection of humanity is predetermined, my conduct cannot prevent its consummation; if it in any way depends on me, the question returns, why should my particular interests be sacrificed to it? The man who does not already love his contemporaries whom he has seen is unlikely to love them the more for the sake of a remote posterity whom he will never see at all. Finally, it must be remembered that evolution is only half the cosmic process; it is partially conditioned at every stage by dissolution, to which in the long run it must entirely give way; and if, as Mr. Spencer observes, evolution is the more interesting of the two,[105] this preference is itself due to the lifeward tendency of our thoughts; in other words, to those moral sentiments which it is sought to base on what, abstractedly considered, has all along been a creation of their own.

The idea of Nature, or of the universe, or of human history as a whole—but for its evil associations with fanaticism and superstition, we should gladly say the belief in God—is one the ethical value of which can be more easily felt than analysed. We do not agree with the most brilliant of the English Positivists in restricting its influence to the aesthetic emotions.[106] The elevating influence of these should be fully recognised; but the place due to more severely intellectual pursuits in moral training is greater far. Whatever studies tend to withdraw us from the petty circle of our personal interests and pleasures, are indirectly favourable to the preponderance of social over selfish impulses; and the service thus rendered is amply repaid, since these very studies necessitate for their continuance a large expenditure of moral energy. It might even be contended that the influence of speculation on practice is determined by the previous influence of practice on speculation. Physical laws act as an armature to the law of duty, extending and perpetuating its grasp on the minds of men; but it was through the magnetism of duty that their confused currents were first drawn into parallelism and harmony with its attraction. We have just seen how, from this point of view, the interpretation of evolution by conscience might be substituted for the interpretation of conscience by evolution. Yet those who base morality on religion, or give faith precedence over works, have discerned with a sure though dim instinct the dependence of noble and far-sighted action on some paramount intellectual initiative and control; in other words, the highest ethical ideals are conditioned by the highest philosophical generalisations. Before the Greeks could think of each man as a citizen of the world, and as bound to all other rational beings by virtue of a common origin and a common abode, it was first necessary that they should think of the world itself as an orderly and comprehensive whole. And what was once a creative, still continues to work as an educating force. Our aspirations towards agreement with ourselves and with humanity as a whole are strengthened by the contemplation of that supreme unity which, even if it be but the glorified reflection of our individual or generic identity, still remains the idea in and through which those lesser unities were first completely realised—the idea which has originated all man's most fruitful faiths, and will at last absorb them all. Meanwhile our highest devotion can hardly find more fitting utterance than in the prayer which once rose to a Stoic's lips:—

But Jove all-bounteous! who, in clouds

enwrapt, the lightning wieldest;

May'st Thou from baneful Ignorance

the race of men deliver!

This, Father! scatter from the soul,

and grant that we the wisdom

May reach, in confidence of which,

Thou justly guidest all things;

That we, by Thee in honour set,

with honour may repay Thee,

Raising to all thy works a hymn

perpetual; as beseemeth

A mortal soul: since neither man

nor god has higher glory

Than rightfully to celebrate

Eternal Law all-ruling.[107]

CHAPTER II.
EPICURUS AND LUCRETIUS.

I.

Among the systems of ancient philosophy, Epicureanism is remarkable for the completeness with which its doctrines were worked out by their first author, and for the fidelity with which they were handed down to the latest generation of his disciples. For a period of more than five hundred years, nothing was added to, and nothing was taken away from, the original teaching of Epicurus. In this, as in other respects, it offers a striking contrast to the system which we last reviewed. In our sketch of the Stoic philosophy, we had to notice the continual process of development through which it passed, from its commencement to its close. There is a marked difference between the earlier and the later heads of the school at Athens—between these, as a class, and the Stoics of the Roman empire—and, finally, even between two Stoics who stood so near to one another as Epictêtus and Marcus Aurelius. This contrast cannot be due to external circumstances, for the two systems were exactly coeval, and were exposed, during their whole lifetime, to the action of precisely the same environment. The cause must be sought for in the character of the philosophies themselves, and of the minds which were naturally most amenable to their respective influence. Stoicism retained enough of the Socratic spirit to foster a love of enquiry for its own sake, and an indisposition to accept any authority without a searching examination of its claims to obedience or respect. The learner was submitted to a thorough training in dialectics; while the ideal of life set before him was not a state of rest, but of intense and unremitting toil. Whatever particular conclusions he might carry away with him from the class-room were insignificant in comparison with the principle that he must be prepared to demonstrate them for himself with that self-assurance happily likened by Zeno to the feeling experienced when the clenched fist is held within the grasp of the other hand.

Epictêtus

Epicurus, on the contrary, did not encourage independent thought among his disciples; nor, with one exception hereafter to be noticed, did his teaching ever attract any very original or powerful intellect. From the first a standard of orthodoxy was erected; and, to facilitate their retention, the leading tenets of the school were drawn up in a series of articles which its adherents were advised to learn by heart. Hence, as Mr. Wallace observes,[108] while the other chief sects among which philosophy was divided—the Academicians, the Peripatetics, and the Stoics—drew their appellation, not from their first founder, but from the locality where his lectures had been

Epicurus

delivered, the Epicureans alone continued to bear the name of a master whom they regarded with religious veneration. Hence, also, we must add with Zeller,[109] and notwithstanding the doubt expressed by Mr. Wallace,[110] on the subject, that our acquaintance with the system so faithfully adhered to may be regarded as exceptionally full and accurate. The excerpts from Epicurus himself, preserved by Diogenes Laertius, the poem of Lucretius, the criticisms of Cicero, Plutarch, and others, and the fragments of Epicurean literature recovered from the Herculanean papyri, agree so well where they cover the same ground, that they may be fairly trusted to supplement each other's deficiencies; and a further confirmation, if any was needed, is obtained by consulting the older sources, whence Epicurus borrowed most of his philosophy.

It may safely be assumed that the prejudices once entertained against Epicureanism are now extinct. Whatever may have been the speculative opinions of its founder, he had as good a right to them as the Apostles had to theirs; nor did he stand further aloof from the popular religion of any age than Aristotle, who has generally been in high favour with theologians. His practical teaching was directed towards the constant inculcation of virtue;

nor was it belied by the conduct either of himself or of his disciples, even judged by the standard of the schools to which they were most opposed. And some of his physical theories, once rejected as self-evidently absurd, are now proved to be in harmony with the sober conclusions of modern science. At any rate, it is not in this quarter, as our readers will doubtless have already perceived, that the old prejudices, if they still exist, are likely to find an echo. Just now, indeed, the danger is not that Epicurus should be depreciated, but that his merits should obtain far more than their proper meed of recognition. It seems to be forgotten that what was best in his physics he borrowed from others, and that what he added was of less than no value; that he was ignorant or careless of demonstrated truths; that his avowed principles of belief were inconsistent with any truth rising above the level of vulgar apprehension; and finally, that in his system scientific interests were utterly subordinated to practical interests.

In the face of such facts, to say, as Mr. Froude does, that Epicureanism was 'the creed of the men of science' in the time of Julius Caesar[111]—an assertion directly contradicted by Lange[112]—is perhaps only of a piece with Mr. Froude's usual inaccuracy when writing about ancient history; but such declarations as that of Mr. Frederic Pollock, that the Epicurean system 'was a genuine attempt at a scientific explanation of the world; and was in its day the solitary protest against the contempt of physics which prevailed in the other post-Aristotelian schools;'[113] of Prof. Trezza, that the Epicurean school 'summed up in itself the most scientific elements of Greek antiquity;'[114] of Dr. Woltjer, that 'with respect to the laws and principles of science, the Epicureans came nearest of all the ancients to the science of our own time;'[115] and finally, of M. Ernest Renan, that Epicureanism was 'the great scientific school of antiquity,'[116] are absolutely amazing. The eminent French critic just quoted has elsewhere observed, with perfect justice, that the scientific spirit is the negation of the supernatural; and perhaps he argues that the negation of the supernatural must, reciprocally, be the scientific spirit. But this is only true when such a negation is arrived at inductively, after a disinterested survey of the facts. Epicurus started with the denial of supernatural interference as a practical postulate, and then hunted about for whatever explanations of natural phenomena would suit his foregone conclusion. Moreover, an enquirer really animated by the scientific spirit studies the facts for their own sake; he studies them as they actually are, not resting content with alternative explanations; and he studies them to the fullest extent of which his powers are capable. Epicurus, on the contrary, declares that physics would not be worth attending to if the mind could be set free from religious terrors in any other manner;[117] he will not let himself be tied down to any one theory if there are others equally inconsistent with divine agency to be had;[118] and when his demands in this respect are satisfied, that is, when the appearances vulgarly ascribed to supernatural causation have been provided with natural causes, he leaves off.

To get rid of superstitious beliefs was, no doubt, a highly meritorious achievement, but it had been far more effectually performed by the great pre-Socratic thinkers, Heracleitus, Empedocles, Anaxagoras, and Democritus. These men or their followers had, besides, got hold of a most important principle—the vital principle of all science—which was the reign of law, the universality and indefeasibility of physical causation. Now, Epicurus expressly refused to accept such a doctrine, declaring that it was even worse than believing in the gods, since they could be propitiated, whereas fate could not.[119] Again, Greek physical philosophy, under the guidance of Plato, had been tending more and more to seek for its foundation in mathematics. Mathematical reasoning was seen to be the type of all demonstration; and the best hopes of progress were staked on the extension of mathematical methods to every field of enquiry in turn. How much might be done by following up this clue was quickly seen not only in the triumphs of geometry, but in the brilliant astronomical discoveries by which the shape of the earth, the phases of the moon, and the cause of eclipses were finally cleared up and placed altogether outside the sphere of conjecture. Nor was a knowledge of these truths confined to specialists: they were familiar alike to the older Academy, to the Peripatetic, and to the Stoic schools; so that, with the exception of those who doubted every proposition, we may assume them to have been then, as now, the common property of all educated men. Epicurus, on the other hand, seems to have known nothing of mathematics, or only enough to dispute their validity, for we are told that his disciple Polyaenus, who had previously been eminent in that department, was persuaded, on joining the school, to reject the whole of geometry as untrue;[120] while, in astronomy, he pronounced the heavenly bodies to be no larger than they appear to our senses, denied the existence of Antipodes, and put the crudest guesses of early philosophy on the same footing with the best-authenticated results of later observation. It is no wonder, then, that during the whole continuance of his school no man of science ever accepted its teaching, with the single exception of Asclepiades, who was perhaps a Democritean rather than a disciple of the Garden, and who, at any rate, as a physiologist, would not be brought into contact with its more flagrant absurdities.

In order to understand how so vigorous an intellect could go so wildly astray, we must glance at his personal history, and at the manner in which his system seems to have been gradually built up.

II.

Epicurus was born 341 B.C., about the same time as Zeno the Stoic. Unlike all the other philosophers of his age, he was of Athenian parentage; that is to say, he belonged to a race of exclusively practical tendencies, and marked by a singular inaptitude or distaste for physical enquiries.

His father, a poor colonist in Samos, was, apparently, not able to give him a very regular education. At eighteen he was sent to Athens, but was shortly afterwards obliged to rejoin his family, who were driven from Samos in 322, along with the other Athenian settlers, by a political revolution, and had taken refuge in Colophon, on the Asiatic coast. In the course of his wanderings, the future philosopher came across some public lecturers, who seem to have instructed him in the physics of Democritus, and perhaps also in the scepticism of Pyrrho; but of such a steady discipline as Plato passed through during his ten years' intercourse with Socrates, Aristotle during his twenty years' studies under Plato, and Zeno during his similarly protracted attendance at the various schools of Athens, there is no trace whatever. Epicurus always described himself as self-taught, meaning that his knowledge had been acquired by reading instead of by listening; and we find in him the advantages as well as the defects common to self-taught men in all ages—considerable freshness and freedom from scholastic prejudices, along with a certain narrowness of sympathies, incompleteness of information, inaptitude for abstract reasoning, and last, but not least, an enormous opinion of his own abilities, joined to an overweening contempt for those with whose opinions he did not agree. After teaching for some time in Mitylênê, Epicurus established himself as the head of a school in Athens, where he bought a house and garden. In the latter he lectured and gathered round him a band of devoted friends, among whom women were included, and who were wont to assemble for purposes of social recreation not less than of philosophic discipline. Just before his death, which occurred in the year 270, he declared in a letter to his friend and destined successor Hermarchus, that the recollection of his philosophical achievements had been such a source of pleasure as to overcome the agonies of disease, and to make the last day the happiest of his life.[121] For the rest, Epicurus secluded himself, on principle, from the world, and few echoes of his teaching seem to have passed beyond the circle of his immediate adherents. Thus, whatever opportunities might otherwise have offered themselves of profiting by adverse criticism were completely lost.[122]

Epicureanism was essentially a practical philosophy. The physical, theological, and logical portions of the system were reasoned out with exclusive reference to its ethical end, and their absolute subordination to it was never allowed to be forgotten. It is therefore with the moral theory of Epicurus that we must begin.

From the time of Socrates on, the majority of Greeks, had they been asked what was the ultimate object of endeavour, or what made life worth living, would have answered, pleasure. But among professional philosophers such a definition of the supreme good met with little favour. Seeing very clearly that the standard of conduct must be social, and convinced that it must at the same time include the highest good of the individual, they found it impossible to believe that the two could be reconciled by encouraging each citizen in the unrestricted pursuit of his own private gratifications. Nor had such an idea as the greatest happiness of the greatest number ever risen above their horizon; although, from the necessities of life itself, they unconsciously assumed it in all their political discussions. The desire for pleasure was, however, too powerful a motive to be safely disregarded. Accordingly we find Socrates frequently appealing to it when no other argument was likely to be equally efficacious, Plato striving to make the private satisfaction of his citizens coincide with the demands of public duty, and Aristotle maintaining that this coincidence must spontaneously result from the consolidation of moral habits; the true test of a virtuous disposition being, in his opinion, the pleasure which accompanies its exercise. One of the companions of Socrates, Aristippus the Cyrenaean, a man who had cut himself loose from every political and domestic obligation, and who was remarkable for the versatility with which he adapted himself to the most varying circumstances, went still further. He boldly declared that pleasure was the sole end worth seeking, and on the strength of this doctrine came forward as the founder of a new philosophical school. According to his system, the summum bonum was not the total amount of enjoyment secured in a lifetime, but the greatest single enjoyment that could be secured at any moment; and this principle was associated with an idealistic theory of perception, apparently suggested by Protagoras, but carrying his views much further. Our knowledge, said Aristippus, is strictly limited to phenomena; we are conscious of nothing beyond our own feelings; and we have no right to assume the existence of any objects by which they are caused. The study of natural science is therefore waste of time; our whole energies should be devoted to the interests of practical life.[123] Thus Greek humanism seemed to have found its appropriate sequel in hedonism, which, as an ethical theory, might quote in its favour both the dictates of immediate feeling and the sanction of public opinion.

The Cyrenaic school ended, curiously enough, in pessimism. The doctrine that pleasure is the only good, and the doctrine that life yields a preponderance of painful over pleasurable feelings, are severally compatible with a preference of existence to non-existence; when united, as they were by Hêgêsias, a Cyrenaic professor, they logically lead to suicide; and we are told that the public authorities of Alexandria were obliged to order the discontinuance of his lectures, so great was their effect in promoting self-destruction.[124]

Meanwhile, hedonism had been temporarily taken up by Plato, and developed into the earliest known form of utilitarianism. In his Protagoras, he endeavours to show that every virtue has for its object either to secure a greater pleasure by the sacrifice of a lesser pleasure, or to avoid a greater pain by the endurance of a lesser pain; nothing being taken into account but the interests of the individual agent concerned. Plato afterwards discarded the theory sketched in the Protagoras for a higher and more generous, if less distinctly formulated morality; but while ceasing to be a hedonist he remained a utilitarian; that is to say, he insisted on judging actions by their tendency to promote the general welfare, not by the sentiments which they excite in the mind of a conventional spectator.

The idea of virtue as a hedonistic calculus, abandoned by its first originator, and apparently neglected by his immediate successors, was taken up by Epicurus; for that the latter borrowed it from Plato seems to be proved by the exact resemblance of their language;[125] and M. Guyau is quite mistaken when he represents his hero as the founder of utilitarian morality.[126] It was not enough, however, to appropriate the cast-off ideas of Plato; it was necessary to meet the arguments by which Plato had been led to think that pleasure was not the supreme good, and to doubt whether it was, as such, a good at all. The most natural course would have been to begin by exhibiting the hedonistic ideal in a more favourable light. Sensual gratifications, from their remarkable intensity, had long been the accepted types of pleasurable feeling, and from their animal character, as well as from other obvious reasons, had frequently been used to excite a prejudice against it. On the other hand, Plato himself, and Aristotle still more, had brought into prominence the superiority, simply as pleasures, of those intellectual activities which they considered to be, even apart from all pleasure, the highest good. But Epicurus refused to avail himself of this opportunity for effecting a compromise with the opposite school, boldly declaring that he for his part could not conceive any pleasures apart from those received through the five senses, among which he, characteristically enough, included aesthetic enjoyments. The obvious significance of his words has been explained away, and they have been asserted to contain only the very harmless proposition that our animal nature is the basis, the condition, of our spiritual nature.[127] But, if this were the true explanation, it would be possible to point out what other pleasures were recognised by Epicurus. These, if they existed at all, must have belonged to the mind as such. Now, we have it on Cicero's authority that, while admitting the existence of mental feelings, both pleasurable and painful, he reduced them to an extension and reflection of bodily feelings, mental happiness properly consisting in the assurance of prolonged and painless sensual gratification. This is something very different from saying that the highest spiritual enjoyments are conditioned by the healthy activity of the bodily organs, or that they cannot be appreciated if the animal appetites are starved. It amounts to saying that there are no specific and positive pleasures apart from the five senses as exercised either in reality or in imagination.[128] And even without the evidence of Cicero, we can see that some such conclusion necessarily followed from the principles elsewhere laid down by Epicurus. To a Greek, the mental pleasures, par excellence, were those derived from friendship and from intellectual activity. But our philosopher, while warmly panegyrising friendship, recommends it not for the direct pleasure which it affords, but for the pain and danger which it prevents;[129] while his restriction of scientific studies to the office of dispelling superstitious fears seems meant for a direct protest against Aristotle's opinion, that the highest pleasure is derived from those studies. Equally significant is his outspoken contempt for literary culture.[130] In this respect, he offers a marked contrast to Aristippus, who, when asked by some one what good his son would get by education, answered, 'This much, at least, that when he is at the play he will not sit like a stone upon a stone,'[131] the customary attitude, it would seem, of an ordinary Athenian auditor.

It appears, then, that the popular identification of an Epicurean with a sensualist has something to say in its favour. Nevertheless, we have no reason to think that Epicurus was anything but perfectly sincere when he repudiated the charge of being a mere sensualist.[132] But the impulse which lifted him above sensualism was not derived from his own original philosophy. It was due to the inspiration of Plato; and nothing testifies more to Plato's moral greatness than that the doctrine most opposed to his own idealism should have been raised from the dust by the example of its flight. We proceed to show how the peculiar form assumed by Epicureanism was determined by the pressure brought to bear on its original germ two generations before.

It had been urged against hedonism that pleasure is a process, a movement; whereas the supreme good must be a completed product—an end in which we can rest. Against sensual enjoyments in particular, it had been urged that they are caused by the satisfaction of appetite, and, as such, must result in a mere negative condition, marking the zero point of pleasurable sentiency. Finally, much stress had been laid on the anti-social and suicidal consequences of that selfish grasping at power to which habits of unlimited self-indulgence must infallibly lead. The form given to hedonism by Epicurus is a reaction against these criticisms, a modification imposed on it for the purpose of evading their force. He seems to admit that bodily satisfaction is rather the removal of a want, and consequently of a pain, than a source of positive pleasure. But the resulting condition of liberation from uneasiness is, according to him, all that we can desire; and by extending the same principle to every other good, he indirectly brings back the mental felicity which at first sight his system threatened either to exclude or to reduce to a mere shadow of sensual enjoyment. For, in calculating the elements of unhappiness, we have to deal, not only with present discomfort, but also, and to a far greater extent, with the apprehension of future evil. We dread the loss of worldly goods, of friends, of reputation, of life itself. We are continually exposed to pain, both from violence and from disease. We are haunted by visions of divine vengeance, both here and hereafter. To get rid of all such terrors, to possess our souls in peace, is the highest good—a permanent, as distinguished from a transient state of consciousness—and the proper business of philosophy is to show us how that consummation may be attained. Thus we are brought back to that blissful self-contemplation of mind which Aristotle had already declared to be the goal of all endeavour and the sole happiness of God.

But Epicurus could only borrow the leading principle of his opponents at the expense of an enormous inconsistency. It was long ago pointed out by the Academicians—and the objection has never been answered—that pleasure and mere painlessness cannot both be the highest good, although the one may be an indispensable condition of the other. To confound the means with the end was, indeed, a common fault of Greek philosophy; and the Stoics also were guilty of it when they defined self-preservation to be the natural object of every creature, and yet attached a higher value to the instruments than to the aims of that activity. In Epicureanism, however, the change of front was more open, and was attempted under the eyes of acute and vigilant enemies. If the total absence of pain involves a pleasurable state of consciousness, we have a right to ask for a definition or description of it, and this, so far as can be made out, our philosopher never pretended to supply. Of course, a modern psychologist can point out that the functions of respiration, circulation, secretion, and absorption are constantly going on, and that, in their normal activity, they give rise to a vast sum of pleasurable consciousness, which far more than makes up in volume for what it wants in acuteness. But, whatever his recent interpreters may say,[133] Epicurus nowhere alludes to this diffused feeling of vitality; had he recognised it, his enumeration of the positive sensations, apart from which the good is inconceivable, would have seemed as incomplete to him as it does to us. If, on the other hand, the complete removal of pain introduces us to a state of consciousness, which, without being positively pleasurable, has a positive value of some kind, we ought to be told wherein it differs from the ideals of the spiritualist school; while, if it has no positive value at all, we ought equally to be told wherein it differs from the unconsciousness of sleep or of death.

III.

We have now to see how, granting Epicurus his conception of painlessness as the supreme good, he proceeds to evolve from it a whole ethical, theological, and physical system. For reasons already mentioned, the ethical development must be studied first. We shall therefore begin with an analysis of the particular virtues. Temperance, as the great self-regarding duty, obviously takes precedence of the others. In dealing with this branch of his subject, there was nothing to prevent Epicurus from profiting by the labours of his predecessors, and more especially of the naturalistic school from Prodicus down. So far as moderation is concerned, there need be little difference between a theory of conduct based exclusively on the interests of the individual, and a theory which regards him chiefly as a portion of some larger whole. Accordingly, we find that our philosopher, in his praises of frugality, closely approximated to the Cynic and Stoic standards—so much so, indeed, that his expressions on the subject are repeatedly quoted by Seneca as the best that could be found. Perhaps the Roman moralist valued them less for their own sake than as being, to some extent, the admissions of an opponent. But, in truth, he was only reclaiming what the principles of his own sect had originally inspired. To be content with the barest necessaries was a part of that Nature-worship against which Greek humanism, with its hedonistic and idealistic offshoots, had begun by vigorously protesting. Hence many passages in Lucretius express exactly the same sentiments as those which are most characteristic of Latin literature at a time when it is completely dominated by Stoic influences.

It is another Cynic trait in Epicurus that he should address himself to a much wider audience than the Sophists, or even than Socrates and his spiritualistic successors. This circumstance suggested a new argument in favour of temperance. His philosophy being intended for the use of all mankind without exception, was bound to show that happiness is within the reach of the poor as well as of the rich; and this could not be did it depend, to any appreciable extent, on indulgences which wealth alone can purchase. And even the rich will not enjoy complete tranquillity unless they are taught that the loss of fortune is not to be feared, since their appetites can be easily satisfied without it. Thus the pains arising from excess, though doubtless not forgotten, seem to have been the least important motive to restraint in his teaching. The precepts of Epicurus are only too faithfully followed in the southern countries for whose benefit they were first framed. It is a matter of common observation, that the extreme frugality of the Italians, by leaving them satisfied with the barest sufficiency, deprives them of a most valuable spur to exertion, and allows a vast fund of possible energy to moulder away in listless apathy, or to consume itself more rapidly in sordid vice. Moreover, as economists have long since pointed out, where the standard of comfort is high, there will be a large available margin to fall back upon in periods of distress; while where it is low, the limit of subsistence will be always dangerously near.

The enemies of hedonism had taken a malicious satisfaction in identifying it with voluptuous indulgence, and had scornfully asked if that could be the supreme good and proper object of virtuous endeavour, the enjoyment of which was habitually associated with secresy and shame. It was, perhaps, to screen his system from such reproaches that Epicurus went a long way towards the extreme limit of asceticism, and hinted at the advisability of complete abstinence from that which, although natural, is not necessary to self-preservation, and involves a serious drain on the vital energies.[134] In this respect, he was not followed by Lucretius, who has no objection to the satisfaction of animal instinct, so long as it is not accompanied by personal passion.[135] Neither the Greek moralist nor the Roman poet could foresee what a great part in the history of civilisation chivalrous devotion to a beloved object was destined to play, although the uses of idealised desire had already revealed themselves to Plato's penetrating gaze.

With regard to those more refined aspects of temperance, in which it appears as a restraint exercised by reason over anger, pity, and grief, Epicurus and his followers refused to go all lengths with the Stoics in their effort to extirpate emotion altogether. But here they seem not to have proceeded on any fixed principle, except that of contradicting the opposite school. That the sage will feel pity, and sometimes shed tears,[136] is a sentiment from which few are now likely to dissent; yet the absolute impassivity at which Stoicism aimed seems still more consistent with a philosophy whose ideal was complete exemption from pain; while in practice it would be rather easier to attain than the power of feeling quite happy on the rack, which the accomplished Epicurean was expected to possess.[137]

Next to Temperance comes Fortitude; and with it the difficulties of reconciling Epicureanism with the ordinary morality are considerably increased. The old conception of this virtue was willingness to face pain and death on behalf of a noble cause,[138] which would be generally understood to mean the salvation of family, friends, and fatherland; and the ultimate sanction of such self-devotion was found in the pressure of public opinion. Idealistic philosophy, taking still higher ground, not only refused to balance the fear of pain and death against the fear of infamy or the hope of applause, but added public opinion to the considerations which a good man in the discharge of his duty would, if necessary, despise. Epicurus also inculcated disregard for reputation, except when it might lead to inconveniences of a tangible description;[139] but he had nothing beyond the calculations of self-interest to put in its place. A modern utilitarian is bound to undergo loss and suffering in his own person for the prevention of greater loss and suffering elsewhere; an egoistic hedonist cannot consistently be brave, except for the sake of his own future security. The method by which Epicurus reconciled interest with courage was to minimise the importance of whatever injuries could be inflicted by external circumstances; just as in his theory of Temperance he had minimised the importance of bodily pleasures. How he disposed of death will best be seen in connexion with his physical philosophy. Pain he encountered by emphasising, or rather immensely exaggerating, the mind's power of annulling external sensation by concentrating its whole attention on remembered or anticipated pleasures, or else on the certainty that present suffering must come to an end, and to a more speedy end in proportion to its greater severity. We are to hold a fire in our hand, partly by thinking of the frosty Caucasus, partly by the comforting reflection that the pain of a burn, being intense, will not be of long duration; while, at worst, like the Stoics, we have the resource of suicide as a last refuge from intolerable suffering.[140]

With the Epicurean theory of Justice, the distortion, already sufficiently obvious, is carried still further; although we must frankly admit that it includes some aperçus strikingly in advance of all that had hitherto been written on the subject. Justice, according to our philosopher, is neither an internal balance of the soul's faculties, nor a rule imposed by the will of the stronger, but a mutual agreement to abstain from aggressions, varying from time to time with the varying interests of society, and always determined by considerations of general utility.[141] This is excellent: we miss, indeed, the Stoic idea of a common humanity, embracing, underlying, and transcending all particular contracts; but we have, in exchange, the idea of a general interest equivalent to the sum of private interests, together with the means necessary for their joint preservation; and we have also the form under which the notion of justice originates, though not the measure of its ultimate expansion, which is regard for the general interest, even when we are not bound by any contract to observe it. But when we go on to ask why contracts should be adhered to, Epicurus has no reason to offer beyond dread of punishment. His words, as translated by Mr. Wallace, are:—'Injustice is not in itself a bad thing, but only in the fear arising from anxiety on the part of the wrong-doer that he will not always escape punishment.'[142] This was evidently meant for a direct contradiction of Plato's assertion, that, apart from its penal consequences, injustice is a disease of the soul, involving more mischief to the perpetrator than to the victim. Mr. Wallace, however, takes a different view of his author's meaning. According to him,

If we interpret this doctrine, after the example of some of the ancients, to mean that any wrong-doing would be innocent and good, supposing it escaped detection, we shall probably be misconstruing Epicurus. What he seems to allude to is rather the case of strictly legal enactments, where, previously to law, the action need not have been particularly moral or immoral; where, in fact, the common agreement has established a rule which is not completely in harmony with the 'justice of nature.' In short, Epicurus is protesting against the conception of injustice, which makes it consist in disobedience to political and social rules, imposed and enforced by public and authoritative sanctions. He is protesting, in other words, against the claims of the State upon the citizens for their complete obedience; against the old ideas of the divine sanctity and majesty of law as law; against theories like that maintained by contemporaries of Socrates, that there could be no such thing as an unjust law.[143]

Epicurus was assuredly not a master of language, but had he meant all that is here put into his mouth, he would hardly have been at a loss for words to say it. Remembering that the Κύριαι δόξαι constituted a sort of creed drawn up by the master himself for his disciples to learn by heart,[144] and that the incriminated passage is one of the articles in that creed, we need only look at the context to make certain that it has been entirely misread by his apologist.[145] In the three preceding articles, we are told that justice is by nature a contract for the prevention of aggressions, that it does not exist among animals which are unable, nor among tribes of men which are either unable or unwilling to enter into such an agreement, and—with reiterated emphasis—that, apart from contracts, it has no original existence (οὐκ ῆν τὶ καθ' ἑαυτὸ δικαιοσύνη). There is nothing at all about a true as distinguished from a false justice; there is no allusion whatever to the theories of any 'contemporaries of Socrates;' the polemic reference, if any, is to Plato, and to Plato alone. Then comes the declaration quoted above, to the effect that injustice is not an evil in itself, but only an evil through the dread of punishment which it produces. Now, by injustice, Epicurus must simply mean the opposite of what he defined justice to be in the preceding paragraph—that is, a breach of the agreement not to hurt one another (μὴ βλάπτειν ἀλλήλους). The authority of the State is evidently conceived, not as superseding, but as enforcing agreements. The succeeding article still further confirms the view rejected by Mr. Wallace. Epicurus tells us that no man who stealthily evades the contract to abstain from mutual aggressions can be sure of escaping detection. This is evidently added to show that, apart from any mystical sanctions, fear of punishment is quite enough to deter a prudent man from committing crimes. And we can see that no other deterrent was recognised by Lucretius, when, in evident reference to his master's words, he mentions the fears of those who offend—not against mere conventional rules, but against human rights in general—as the great safeguard of justice.[146]

We may, indeed, fairly ask what guarantee against wrong-doing of any kind could be supplied by a system which made the supreme good of each individual consist in his immunity from pain and fear, except that very pain or fear which he was above all things to avoid? The wise man might reasonably give his assent to enactments intended for the common good of all men, including himself among the number; but when his concrete interest as a private citizen came into collision with his abstract interests as a social unit, one does not see how the quarrel was to be decided on Epicurean principles, except by striking a balance between the pains respectively resulting from justice and injustice. Here, Epicurus, in his anxiety to show that hedonism, rightly understood, led to the same results as the accepted systems of morality, over-estimated the policy of honesty. There are cases in which the wrong-doer may count on immunity from danger with more confidence than when entering on such ordinary enterprises as a sea-voyage or a commercial speculation; there are even cases where a single crime might free him from what else would be a lifelong dread. And, at worst, he can fall back on the Epicurean arguments proving that neither physical pain nor death is to be feared, while the threats of divine vengeance are a baseless dream.[147]

The radical selfishness of Epicureanism comes out still more distinctly in its attitude towards political activity. Not only does it systematically discourage mere personal ambition—the desire of possessing political power for the furtherance of one's own ends—but it passes a like condemnation on disinterested efforts to improve the condition of the people by legislation; while the general rule laid down for the wise man in his capacity of citizen is passive obedience to the established authorities, to be departed from only when the exigencies of self-defence require it. On this Mr. Wallace observes that 'political life, which in all ages has been impossible for those who had not wealth, and who were unwilling to mix themselves with vile and impure associates, was not to the mind of Epicurus.'[148] No authority is quoted to prove that the abstention recommended by Epicurus was dictated by purist sentiments of any kind; nor can we readily admit that it is impossible to record a vote, to canvass at an election, or even to address a public meeting, without fulfilling one or other of the conditions specified by Mr. Wallace; and we know by the example of Littré that it is possible for a poor man to take a rather prominent part in public life, without the slightest sacrifice of personal dignity.[149] It must also be remembered that Epicurus was not speaking for himself alone; he was giving practical advice to all whom it might concern—advice of which he thought, aeque pauperibus prodest, locupletibus aeque; so that when Mr. Wallace adds that, 'above all, it is not the business of a philosopher to become a political partisan, and spend his life in an atmosphere of avaricious and malignant passions,'[150] we must observe that Epicureanism was not designed to make philosophers, but perfect men. The real question is whether it would serve the public interest were all who endeavour to shape their lives by the precepts of philosophy to withdraw themselves entirely from participation in the affairs of their country. And, having regard to the general character of the system now under consideration, we may not uncharitably surmise that the motive for abstention which it supplied was selfish love of ease far more than unwillingness to be mixed up with the dirty work of politics.

Epicureanism allotted a far larger place to friendship than to all the other social virtues put together; and the disciple was taught to look to it not only for the satisfaction of his altruistic impulses, but for the crowning happiness of his life. The egoistic basis of the system was, indeed, made sufficiently prominent even here; utility and pleasure, which Aristotle had excluded from the notion of true friendship, being declared its proper ends. All the conditions of a disinterested attachment were, however, brought back by a circuitous process. It was argued that the full value of friendship could not be reaped except by those whose affection for each other went to the extent of complete self-devotion; but the Epicureans were less successful in showing how this happy condition could be realised consistently with the study of his own interest by each individual. As a matter of fact, it was realised; and the members of this school became remarkable, above all others, for the tenderness and fidelity of their personal attachments. But we may suspect that formal precepts had little to do with the result. Estrangement from the popular creed, when still uncommon, has always a tendency to draw the dissidents together;[151] and where other ties, whether religious, domestic, or patriotic, are neglected, the ordinary instincts of human nature are likely to show themselves with all the more energy in the only remaining form of union. Moreover, the cheerful, contented, abstemious, unambitious characters who would be the most readily attracted to the Epicurean brotherhood supplied the very materials that most readily unite in placid and enduring attachments. A tolerably strict standard of orthodoxy provided against theoretical dissensions: nor were the new converts likely to possess either daring or originality enough to excite controversies where they did not already exist.

IV.

After eliminating all the sources of misery due to folly and vice, Epicurus had still to deal with what, in his opinion, were the most formidable obstacles to human happiness, dread of the divine anger and dread of death, either in itself, or as the entrance on another life. To meet these, he compiled, for we can hardly say constructed, an elaborate system of physical philosophy, having for its object to show that Nature is entirely governed by mechanical causes, and that the soul perishes with the body. We have already mentioned that for science as such and apart from its ethical applications he neither cared nor pretended to care in the least. It seems, therefore, rather surprising that he could not manage, like the Sceptics before him, to get rid of supernaturalism by a somewhat more expeditious method. The explanation seems to be that to give some account of natural phenomena had become, in his time, a necessity for every one aspiring to found a philosophical system. A brilliant example had been set by Plato and Aristotle, of whom the former, too, had apparently yielded to the popular demand rather than followed the bent of his own genius, in turning aside from ethics to physics; and Zeno had similarly included the whole of knowledge in his teaching. The old Greek curiosity respecting the causes of things was still alive; and a similar curiosity was doubtless awakening among those populations to whom Greek civilisation had been carried by colonisation, commerce, and conquest. Now, those scientific speculations are always the most popular which can be shown to have some bearing on religious belief, either in the way of confirmation or of opposition, according as faith or doubt happens to be most in the ascendent. Fifty years ago, among ourselves, no work on natural philosophy could hope for a large circulation unless it was filled with teleological applications. At present, liberal opinions are gaining ground; and those treatises are most eagerly studied which tend to prove that everything in Nature can be best explained through the agency of mechanical causation. At neither period is it the facts themselves which have excited most attention, but their possible bearing on our own interests. Among the contemporaries of Epicurus, the two currents of thought that in more recent times have enjoyed an alternate triumph, seem to have co-existed as forces of about equal strength. The old superstitions were rejected by all thinking men; and the only question was by what new faith they should be replaced. Poets and philosophers had alike laboured to bring about a religious reformation by exhibiting the popular mythology in its grotesque deformity, and by constructing systems in which pure monotheism was more or less distinctly proclaimed. But it suited the purpose, perhaps it gratified the vanity of Epicurus to talk as if the work of deliverance still remained to be done, as if men were still groaning under the incubus of superstitions which he alone could teach them to shake off. He seems, indeed, to have confounded the old and the new faiths under a common opprobrium, and to have assumed that the popular religion was mainly supported by Stoic arguments, or that the Stoic optimism was not less productive of superstitious terrors than the gloomy polytheism which it was designed to supersede.[152]

Again, while attacking the belief in human immortality, Epicurus seems to direct his blows against the metaphysical reasonings of Plato,[153] as well as against the indistinct forebodings of primitive imagination. The consequences of this two-edged polemic are very remarkable. In reading Lucretius, we are surprised at the total absence of criticisms like those brought to bear on Greek mythology with such formidable effect, first by Plato and, long afterwards, by Lucian. There is a much more modern tone about his invectives, and they seem aimed at an enemy familiar to ourselves. One would suppose that the advent of Catholicism had been revealed in a prophetic vision to the poet, and that this, rather than the religion of his own times, was the object of his wrath and dread; or else that some child of the Renaissance was seeking for a freer utterance of his own revolt against all theology, under the disguise of a dead language and of a warfare with long-discredited gods. For this reason, Christians have always regarded him, with perfect justice, as a dangerous enemy; while rationalists of the fiercer type have accepted his splendid denunciations as the appropriate expression of their own most cherished feelings.

The explanation of this anomaly is, we believe, to be found in the fact that Catholicism did, to a great extent, actually spring from a continuation of those widely different tendencies which Epicurus confounded in a common assault. It had an intellectual basis in the Platonic and Stoic philosophies, and a popular basis in the revival of those manifold superstitions which, underlying the brilliant civilisations of Greece and Rome, were always ready to break out with renewed violence when their restraining pressure was removed. The revival of which we speak was powerfully aided from without. The same movement that was carrying Hellenic culture into Asia was bringing Oriental delusions by a sort of back current into the Western world. Nor was this all. The relaxation of all political bonds, together with the indifference of the educated classes, besides allowing a rank undergrowth of popular beliefs to spring up unchecked, surrendered the regulation of those beliefs into the hands of a profession which it had hitherto been the policy of every ancient republic to keep under rigid restraint—the accredited or informal ministers of religion.[154] Now, the chief characteristic of a priestly order has always and everywhere been insatiable avarice. When forbidden to acquire wealth in their individual capacity, they grasp at it all the more eagerly in their corporate capacity. And, as the Epicureans probably perceived, there is no engine which they can use so effectually for the gratification of this passion as the belief in a future life. What they have to tell about this is often described by themselves and their supporters as a message of joy to the weary and afflicted. But under their treatment it is very far from being a consolatory belief. Dark shades and lurid lights predominate considerably in their pictures of the world beyond the grave; and here, as we shall presently show, they are aided by an irresistible instinct of human nature. On this subject, also, they can speak with unlimited confidence; for, while their other statements about the supernatural are liable to be contradicted by experience, the abode of souls is a bourne from which no traveller returns to disprove the accuracy of their statements.

That such a tendency was at work some time before the age of Epicurus is shown by the following passage from Plato's Republic:—

Mendicant prophets go to rich men's doors and persuade them that they have a power committed to them of making atonement for their sins or those of their fathers by sacrifices or charms.... And they produce a host of books ... according to which they perform their ritual, and persuade not only individuals but whole cities, that expiations and atonements for sin may be made by sacrifices and amusements which fill a vacant hour,[155] and are equally at the service of the living and the dead; the latter sort they call mysteries, and they redeem us from the pains of hell, but if we neglect them no one knows what awaits us.[156]

Let us now pass over fourteen centuries and see to what results the doctrine taught by Plato himself led when it had entered into an alliance with the superstitions which he denounced. Our illustration shall be taken from a sainted hero of the Catholic Church. In a sermon preached before Pope Nicholas II. at Arezzo, the famous Hildebrand, afterwards Gregory VII., relates the following story:—

In one of the provinces of Germany there died, about ten years ago, a certain count, who had been rich and powerful, and, what is astonishing for one of that class, he was, according to the judgment of man, pure in faith and innocent in his life. Some time after his death, a holy man descended in spirit to hell, and beheld the count standing on the topmost rung of a ladder. He tells us that this ladder stood unconsumed amid the crackling flames around; and that it had been placed there to receive the family of the aforesaid count. There was, moreover, the black and frightful abyss out of which rose the fatal ladder. It was so ordered that the last comer took his stand at the top of the ladder, and when the rest of the family arrived he went down one step, and all below him did likewise.

As the last of the same family who died came and took his place, age after age, on this ladder, it followed inevitably that they all successively reached the depth of hell. The holy man who beheld this thing, asked the reason of this terrible damnation, and especially how it was that the seigneur whom he had known and who had lived a life of justice and well-doing should be thus punished. And he heard a voice saying, 'It is because of certain lands belonging to the church of Metz, which were taken from the blessed Stephen by one of this man's ancestors, from whom he was the tenth in descent, and for this cause all these men have sinned by the same avarice and are subjected to the same punishment in eternal fire.'[157]

In view of such facts as these, we cannot blame the Epicureans if they regarded the doctrine of future retribution as anything but a consolatory or ennobling belief, and if they deemed that to extirpate it was to cut out a mischievous delusion by the roots:—

Et merito: nam si certain finem esse viderent

Aerumnarum homines aliqua ratione valerent

Relligionibus, atque minis obsistere vatum:

Nunc ratio nulla 'st restandi, nulla facultas,

Aeternas quoniam poenas in morte timendum.'[158]

And it is no wonder that the words of their great poet should read like a prophetic exposure of the terrors with which the religious revival, based on a coalition of philosophy and superstition, was shortly to overspread the whole horizon of human life.

So strong, however, was the theological reaction against Greek rationalism that Epicurus himself came under its influence. Instead of denying the existence of the gods altogether, or leaving it uncertain like Protagoras, he asserted it in the most emphatic manner. Their interference with Nature was all that he cared to dispute. The egoistic character of his whole system comes out once more in his conception of them as beings too much absorbed in their own placid enjoyments to be troubled with the work of creation and providence. He was, indeed, only repeating aloud what had long been whispered in the free-thinking circles of Athenian society. That the gods were indifferent to human interests was a heresy indignantly denounced by Aeschylus,[159] maintained by Aristodêmus, the friend of Socrates, and singled out as a fit subject for punishment by Plato. Nor was the theology of Aristotle's Metaphysics practically distinguishable from such a doctrine. Although essential to the continued existence of the cosmos, considered as a system of movements, the Prime Mover communicates the required impulse by the mere fact of his existence, and apparently without any consciousness of the effect he is producing. Active beneficence had, in truth, even less to do with the ideal of Aristotle than with the ideal of Epicurus, and each philosopher constructed a god after his own image; the one absorbed in perpetual thought, the other, or more properly the others, in perpetual enjoyment; for the Epicurean deities were necessarily conceived as a plurality, that they might not be without the pleasure of friendly conversation. Nevertheless, the part assigned by Aristotle to his god permitted him to offer a much stronger proof of the divine existence and attributes than was possible to Epicurus, who had nothing better to adduce than the universal belief of mankind,—an argument obviously proving too much, since it told, if anything, more powerfully for the interference than for the bare reality of supernatural agents.

Our philosopher appears to more advantage as a critic than as a religious dogmatist. He meets the Stoic belief in Providence by pointing out the undeniable prevalence of evils which omnipotent benevolence could not be supposed to tolerate; the Stoic optimism, with its doctrine, still a popular one, that all things were created for the good of man, by a reference to the glaring defects which, on that hypothesis, would vitiate the arrangements of Nature; the Stoic appeal to omens and prophecies by showing the purely accidental character of their fulfilment.[160] But he trusts most of all to a radically different explanation of the world, an explanation which everywhere substitutes mechanical causation for design. Only one among the older systems—the atomism of Democritus—had consistently carried out such a conception of Nature, and this, accordingly, Epicurus adopts in its main outlines.

V.

It is generally assumed by the German critics that the atomic theory was peculiarly fitted to serve as a basis for the individualistic ethics of

Epicureanism. To this we can hardly agree. The insignificance and powerlessness of the atoms, except when aggregated together in enormous numbers, would seem to be naturally more favourable to a system where the community went for everything and the individual for nothing; nor does the general acceptance of atomism by modern science seem to be accompanied by any relaxation of the social sentiment in its professors. Had the Stoics followed Democritus and Epicurus Heracleitus—at least a conceivable hypothesis—some equally cogent reason would doubtless have been forthcoming to indicate the appropriateness of their choice.[161] As it is, we have no evidence that Epicurus saw anything more in the atomic theory than a convenient explanation of the world on purely mechanical principles.

The division of matter into minute and indestructible particles served admirably to account for the gradual formation and disappearance of bodies without necessitating the help of a creator. But the infinities assumed as a condition of atomism were of even greater importance. Where time and space are unlimited, the quantity of matter must be equally unlimited, otherwise, being composed of loose particles, it would long since have been dissipated and lost in the surrounding void. Now, given infinite time and space, and infinite atoms capable of combining with one another in various ways, all possible combinations must already have been tried, not once or twice, but infinitely often. Of such combinations, that which best fulfils the conditions of mechanical stability will last the longest, and, without being designed, will present all the characters of design. And this, according to Epicurus, is how the actual frame of things comes to be what it is. Nor was it only the world as a whole that he explained by the theory of a single happy accident occurring after a multitude of fortuitous experiments. The same process repeats itself on a smaller scale in the production of particular compounds. All sorts of living bodies were originally throw up from the earth's bosom, but many of them instantly perished, not being provided with the means of nutrition, propagation, or self-defence. In like manner we are enabled to recall a particular thought at pleasure, because innumerable images are continually passing through the mind, none of which comes into the foreground of consciousness until attention is fixed on it; though how we come to distinguish it from the rest is not explained. So also, only those societies survived and became civilised where contracts were faithfully observed. All kinds of wild beasts have at different times been employed in war, just as horses and elephants are now, but on trial were found unmanageable and given up.[162]

It will be seen that what has been singled out as an anticipation of the Darwinian theory was only one application of a very comprehensive method for eliminating design from the universe. But of what is most original and essential in Darwinism, that is, the modifiability of specific forms by the summing up of spontaneous variations in a given direction, the Epicureans had not the slightest suspicion. And wherever they or their master have, in other respects, made some approach to the truths of modern science, it may fairly be explained on their own principle as a single lucky guess out of many false guesses.

The modern doctrine of evolution, while relying largely on the fertility of multiplied chances, is not obliged to assume such an enormous number of simultaneous coincidences as Epicurus. The ascription of certain definite attractions and repulsions to the ultimate particles of matter would alone restrict their possible modes of aggregation within comparatively narrow limits. Then, again, the world seems to have been built up by successive stages, at each of which some new force or combination of forces came into play, a firm basis having been already secured for whatever variations they were capable of producing. Thus the solar system is a state of equilibrium resulting from the action of two very simple forces, gravitation and heat. On the surface of the earth, cohesion and chemical affinity have been superadded. When a fresh equilibrium had resulted from their joint energy, the more complex conditions of life found free scope for their exercise. The transformations of living species were similarly effected by variation on variation. And, finally, in one species, the satisfaction of its animal wants set free those more refined impulses by which, after many experiments, civilisation has been built up. Obviously the total sum of adaptations necessary to constitute our actual world will have the probabilities of its occurrence enormously increased if we suppose the more general conditions to be established prior to, and in complete independence of, the less general, instead of limiting ourselves, like the ancient atomists, to one vast simultaneous shuffle of all the material and dynamical elements involved.

Returning to Epicurus, we have next to consider how he obtained the various motions required to bring his atoms into those infinite combinations of which our world is only the most recent. The conception of matter naturally endowed with capacities for moving in all directions indifferently was unknown to ancient physics, as was also that of mutual attraction and repulsion. Democritus supposed that the atoms all gravitated downward through infinite space, but with different velocities, so that the lighter were perpetually overtaken and driven upwards by the heavier, the result of these collisions and pressures being a vortex whence the world as we see it has proceeded.[163] While the atomism of Democritus was, as a theory of matter, the greatest contribution ever made to physical science by pure speculation, as a theory of motion it was open to at least three insuperable objections. Passing over the difficulty of a perpetual movement through space in one direction only, there remained the self-contradictory assumption that an infinite number of atoms all moving together in that one direction could find any unoccupied space to fall into.[164] Secondly, astronomical discoveries, establishing as they did the sphericity of the earth, had for ever disproved the crude theory that unsupported bodies fall downward in parallel straight lines. Even granting that the astronomers, in the absence of complete empirical verification, could not prove their whole contention, they could at any rate prove enough of it to destroy the notion of parallel descent; for the varying elevation of the pole-star demonstrated the curvature of the earth's surface so far as it was accessible to observation, thus showing that, within the limits of experience, gravitation acted along convergent lines. Finally, Aristotle had pointed out that the observed differences in the velocity of falling bodies were due to the atmospheric resistance, and that, consequently, they would all move at the same rate in such an absolute vacuum as atomism assumed.[165] Of these objections Epicurus ignored the first two, except, apparently, to the extent of refusing to believe in the antipodes. The third he acknowledged, and set himself to evade it by a hypothesis striking at the root of all scientific reasoning. The atoms, he tells us, suffer a slight deflection from the line of perpendicular descent, sufficient to bring them into collision with one another; and from this collision proceeds the variety of movement necessary to throw them into all sorts of accidental combinations. Our own free will, says Lucretius, furnishes an example of such a deflection whenever we swerve aside from the direction in which an original impulse is carrying us.[166] That the irregularity thus introduced into Nature interfered with the law of universal causation was an additional recommendation of it in the eyes of Epicurus, who, as we have already mentioned, hated the physical necessity of the philosophers even more than he hated the watchful interfering providence of the theologians. But, apparently, neither he nor his disciples saw that in discarding the invariable sequence of phenomena, they annulled, to the same extent, the possibility of human foresight and adaptation of means to ends. There was no reason why the deflection, having once occurred, should not be repeated infinitely often, each time producing effects of incalculable extent. And a further inconsequence of the system is that it afterwards accounts for human choice by a mechanism which has nothing to do with free-will.[167]

The Epicurean cosmology need not delay us long. It is completely independent of the atomic theory, which had only been introduced to explain the indestructibility of matter, and, later on, the mechanism of sensation. In describing how the world was first formed, Epicurus falls back on the old Ionian meteorology. He assumes the existence of matter in different states of diffusion, and segregates fluid from solid, light from heavy, hot from cold, by the familiar device of a rapid vortical movement.[168] For the rest, as we have already noticed, Epicurus gives an impartial welcome to the most conflicting theories of his predecessors, provided only that they dispense with the aid of supernatural intervention; as will be seen by the following summary, which we quote from Zeller:—

Possibly the world may move, and possibly it may be at rest. Possibly it may be round, or else it may be triangular, or have any other shape. Possibly the sun and the stars may be extinguished at setting, and be lighted afresh at their rising: it is, however, equally possible that they may only disappear under the earth and reappear again, or that their rising and setting is due to yet other causes. Possibly the waxing and waning of the moon may be caused by the moon's revolving; or it may be due to the atmospheric change, or to an actual increase or decrease in the moon's size, or to some other cause. Possibly the moon may shine with borrowed light, or it may shine with its own, experience supplying us with instances of bodies which give their own light, and of others which have their light borrowed. From these and such like statements it appears that questions of natural science in themselves have no value for Epicurus. Whilst granting that only one natural explanation of phenomena is generally possible, yet in any particular case it is perfectly indifferent which explanation is adopted.[169]

This was the creed professed by 'the great scientific school of antiquity,' and this was its way of protesting 'against the contempt of physics which prevailed' among the Stoics!

So far as he can be said to have studied science at all, the motive of Epicurus was hatred for religion far more than love for natural law. He seems, indeed, to have preserved that aversion for Nature which is so characteristic of the earlier Greek Humanists. He seems to have imagined that by refusing to tie himself down to any one explanation of external phenomena, he could diminish their hold over the mind of man. For when he departs from his usual attitude of suspense and reserve, it is to declare dogmatically that the heavenly bodies are no larger than they appear to our senses, and perhaps smaller than they sometimes appear.[170] The only arguments adduced on behalf of this outrageous assertion were that if their superficial extension was altered by transmission, their colour would be altered to a still greater degree; and the alleged fact that flames look the same size at all distances.[171] It is evident that neither Epicurus nor Lucretius, who, as usual, transcribes him with perfect good faith, could ever have looked at one lamp-flame through another, or they would have seen that the laws of linear perspective are not suspended in the case of self-luminous bodies—a fact which does not tell much for that accurate observation supposed to have been fostered by their philosophy.[172] The truth is, that Epicurus disliked the oppressive notion of a sun several times larger than the earth, and was determined not to tolerate it, be the consequences to fact and logic what they might.

VI.

The Epicurean philosophy of external Nature was used as an instrument for destroying the uncomfortable belief in Divine Providence. The Epicurean philosophy of mind was used to destroy the still more uncomfortable belief in man's immortality. As opinions then stood, the task was a comparatively easy one. In our discussion of Stoicism, we observed that the spiritualism of Plato and Aristotle was far before their age, and was not accepted or even understood by their countrymen for a long time to come. Moreover, Aristotle did not agree with his master in thinking that the personal eternity of the soul followed from its immateriality. The belief of the Stoics in a prolongation of individual existence until the destruction of all created things by fire, was, even in that very limited form, inconsistent with their avowed materialism, and had absolutely no influence on their practical convictions. Thus Plato's arguments were alone worth considering. For Epicurus, the whole question was virtually settled by the principle, which he held in common with the Stoics, that nothing exists but matter, its attributes, and its relations. He accepted, it is true, the duality of soul and body, agreeing, in this respect also, with the Stoics and the earlier physicists; and the familiar antithesis of flesh and spirit is a survival of his favourite phraseology;[173] but this very term 'flesh' was employed to cover the assumption that the body to which he applied it differed not in substance but in composition from its animating principle. The latter, a rather complex aggregate, consists proximately of four distinct elements, imagined, apparently, for the purpose of explaining its various functions, and, in the last analysis, of very fine and mobile atoms.[174] When so much had been granted, it naturally followed that the soul was only held together by the body, and was immediately dissolved on being separated from it—a conclusion still further strengthened by the manifest dependence of psychic on corporeal activities throughout the period of their joint existence. Thus all terrors arising from the apprehension of future torments were summarily dispelled.

The simple dread of death, considered as a final annihilation of our existence, remained to be dealt with. There was no part of his philosophy on which Epicurus laid so much stress; he regarded it as setting the seal on those convictions, a firm grasp of which was essential to the security of human happiness. Nothing else seemed difficult, if once the worst enemy of our tranquillity had been overcome. His argument is summed up in the concise formula: when we are, death is not; when death is, we are not; therefore death is nothing to us.[175] The pleasures of life will be no loss, for we shall not feel the want of them. The sorrow of our dearest friends will be indifferent to us in the absence of all consciousness whatever. To the consideration that, however calmly we may face our own annihilation, the loss of those whom we love remains as terrible as ever, Lucretius replies that we need not mourn for them, since they do not feel any pain at their own extinction.[176]

There must, one would suppose, be some force in the Epicurean philosophy of death, for it has been endorsed by no less a thinker and observer than Shakspeare. To make the great dramatist responsible for every opinion uttered by one or other of his characters would, of course, be absurd; but when we find personages so different in other respects as Claudio, Hamlet, and Macbeth, agreeing in the sentiment that, apart from the prospect of a future judgment, there is nothing to appal us in the thought of death, we cannot avoid the inference that he is here making them the mouthpiece of his own convictions, even, as in Hamlet's famous soliloquy, at the expense of every dramatic propriety. Nevertheless, the answer of humanity to such sophisms will always be that of Homer's Achilles, 'μὴ δή μοι θάνατόν γε παραύδα'—'Talk me not fair of death!' A very simple process of reasoning will make this clear. The love of life necessarily involves a constant use of precautions against its loss. The certainty of death means the certainty that these precautions shall one day prove unavailing; the consciousness of its near approach means the consciousness that they have actually failed. In both cases the result must be a sense of baffled or arrested effort, more or less feeble when it is imagined, more or less acute when it it is realised. But this diversion of the conscious energies from their accustomed channel, this turning back of the feelings on themselves, constitutes the essence of all emotion; and where the object of the arrested energies was to avert a danger, it constitutes the emotion of fear. Thus, by an inevitable law, the love of life has for its reverse side the dread of death. Now the love of life is guaranteed by the survival of the fittest; it must last as long as the human race, for without it the race could not last at all. If, as Epicurus urged, the supreme desirability of pleasure is proved by its being the universal object of pursuit among all species of animals,[177] the supreme hatefulness of death is proved by an analogous experience; and we may be sure that, even if pessimism became the accepted faith, the darkened prospect would lead to no relaxation of our grasp on life. A similar mode of reasoning applies to the sorrow and anguish, mortis comites et funeris atri, from which the benevolent Roman poet would fain relieve us. For, among a social species, the instinct for preserving others is second only to the instinct of self-preservation, and frequently rises superior to it. Accordingly, the loss of those whom we love causes, and must always cause us, a double distress. There is, first, the simple pain due to the eternal loss of their society, a pain of which Lucretius takes no account. And, secondly, there is the arrest of all helpful activity on their behalf, the continual impulse to do something for them, coupled with the chilling consciousness that it is too late, that nothing more can be done. So strong, indeed, is this latter feeling that it often causes the loss of those whose existence was a burden to themselves and others, to be keenly felt, if only the survivors were accustomed, as a matter of duty, to care for them and to struggle against the disease from which they suffered. Philosophy may help to fill up the blanks thus created, by directing our thoughts to objects of perennial interest, and she may legitimately discourage the affectation or the fostering of affliction; but the blanks themselves she cannot explain away, without forfeiting all claim on our allegiance as the ultimate and incorruptible arbitress of truth.

We are now in a position to understand how far Epicurus was justified in regarding the expectation of immortality as a source of dread rather than of consolation. In this respect also, the survival of the fittest has determined that human nature shall not look forward with satisfaction to the termination of its earthly existence. Were any race of men once persuaded that death is the passage to a happier world, it would speedily be replaced by competitors holding a belief better adapted to the conditions of terrestrial duration. Hence, practically speaking, the effect of religious dogmas has been to make death rather more dreaded than it would have been without their aid; and, as already observed, their natural tendency has been powerfully stimulated by the cupidity of their professional expositors. The hope of heaven, to exist at all, must be checked by a considerably stronger apprehension of hell. There is a saying in America that the immortality of the soul is too good to be true. We suspect that the immortality in which most religious Americans still believe hardly deserves such a compliment; but it accurately expresses the incredulity with which a genuine message of salvation would be received by most men; and this explains why Universalism, with the few who have accepted it, is but the transition stage to a total rejection of any life beyond the grave. No doubt, in the first flush of fanaticism, the assurance of an easy admission to paradise may do much to win acceptance for the religion which offers it; but when such a religion ceases to make new conquests, its followers must either modify their convictions, or die out under the competition of others by whom mortal life is not held so cheap.

We must add, that while Epicurus was right in regarding the beliefs entertained about a future life as a source of painful anxiety, he was only justified in this opinion by the deeper truth, which he ignored, that they are simply the natural dread of death under another form.[178] The most appalling pictures of damnation would, taken by themselves, probably add but little to human misery. The alarming effect even of earthly punishments is found to depend on their certainty much more than on their severity; and the certainty of suffering what nobody has ever experienced must be small indeed. Besides, the class most interested in enlarging on the dark side of immortality are also interested in showing that its dangers may be bought off at a comparatively trifling cost. What Epicurus said about the inexorable fate of the physicists might here be turned against himself. He removed terrors which there was a possibility of exorcising, and substituted a prospect of annihilation whence there was no escape.[179]

It is, after all, very questionable whether human happiness would be increased by suppressing the thought of death as something to be feared. George Eliot, in her Legend of Jubal, certainly expresses the contrary opinion.[180] The finest edge of enjoyment would be taken off if we forgot its essentially transitory character. The free man may, in Spinoza's words, think of nothing less than of death; but he cannot prevent the sunken shadow from throwing all his thoughts of life into higher and more luminous relief. The ideal enjoyment afforded by literature would lose much of its zest were we to discard all sympathy with the fears and sorrows on which our mortal condition has enabled it so largely to draw—the lacrimae rerum, which Lucretius himself has turned to such admirable account. And the whole treasure of happiness due to mutual affection must gain by our remembrance that the time granted for its exercise is always limited, and may at any moment be brought to an end—or rather, such an effect might be looked for were this remembrance more constantly present to our minds.

Lucretius dwells much on the dread of death as a source of vice and crime. He tells us that men plunge into all sorts of mad distractions or unscrupulous schemes of avarice and ambition in their anxiety to escape either from its haunting presence, or from the poverty and disrepute which they have learned to associate with it.[181] Critics are disposed to think that the poet, in his anxiety to make a point, is putting a wrong interpretation on the facts. Yet it should be remembered that Lucretius was a profound observer, and that his teaching, in this respect, may be heard repeated from London pulpits at the present day. The truth seems to be, not that he went too far, but that he did not go far enough. What he decries as a spur to vicious energy is, in reality, a spur to all energy. Every passion, good or bad, is compressed and intensified by the contracting limits of mortality; and the thought of death impels men either to wring the last drop of enjoyment from their lives, or to take refuge from their perishing individualities in the relative endurance of collective enterprises and impersonal aims.

Let none suppose that the foregoing remarks are meant either to express any sympathy with a cowardly shrinking from death, or to intimate that the doctrine of evolution tends to reverse the noblest lessons of ancient wisdom. In holding that death is rightly regarded as an evil, and that it must always continue to be so regarded, we do not imply that it is necessarily the greatest of all evils for any given individual. It is not, as Spinoza has shown, by arguing away our emotions, but by confronting them with still stronger emotions, that they are, if necessary, to be overcome.[182] The social feelings may be trusted to conquer the instinct of self-preservation, and, by a self-acting adjustment, to work with more intensity in proportion to the strength of its resistance. The dearer our lives are to us, the greater will be the glory of renouncing them, that others may be better secured in the enjoyment of theirs. Aristotle is much truer, as well as more human, than Epicurus, when he observes that 'the more completely virtuous and happy a man is, the more will he be grieved to die; for to such a one life is worth most, and he will consciously be renouncing the greatest goods, and that is grievous. Nevertheless, he remains brave, nay, even the braver for that very reason, because he prefers the glory of a warrior to every other good.'[183] Nor need we fear that a race of cowards will be the fittest to survive, when we remember what an advantage that state has in the struggle for existence, the lives of whose citizens are most unrestrictedly held at its disposal. But their devotion would be without merit and without meaning, were not the loss of existence felt to be an evil, and its prolongation cherished as a gain.

VII.

Next to its bearing on the question of immortality, the Epicurean psychology is most interesting as a contribution to the theory of cognition. Epicurus holds that all our knowledge is derived from experience, and all our experience, directly or indirectly, from the presentations of sense. So far he says no more than would be admitted by the Stoics, by Aristotle, and indeed by every Greek philosopher except Plato. There is, therefore, no necessary connexion between his views in this respect and his theory of ethics, since others had combined the same views with a very different standard of action. It is in discussing the vexed question of what constitutes the ultimate criterion of truth that he shows to most disadvantage in comparison with the more intellectual schools. He seems to have considered that sensation supplies not only the matter but the form of knowledge; or rather, he seems to have missed the distinction between matter and form altogether. What the senses tell us, he says, is always true, although we may draw erroneous inferences from their statements.[184] But this only amounts to the identical proposition that we feel what we feel; for it cannot be pretended that the order of our sensations invariably corresponds to the actual order of things in themselves. Even confining ourselves to individual sensations, or single groups of sensations, there are some that do not always correspond to the same objective reality, and others that do not correspond to any reality at all; while, conversely, the same object produces a multitude of different sensations according to the subjective conditions under which it affects us. To escape from this difficulty, Epicurus has recourse to a singularly crude theory of perception, borrowed from Empedocles and the older atomists. What we are conscious of is, in each instance, not the object itself, but an image composed of fine atoms thrown off from the surfaces of bodies and brought into contact with the organs of sense. Our perception corresponds accurately to an external image, but the image itself is often very unlike the object whence it originally proceeded. Sometimes it suffers a considerable change in travelling through the atmosphere. For instance, when a square tower, seen at a great distance, produces the impression of roundness, this is because the sharp angles of its image have been rubbed off on the way to our eyes. Sometimes the image continues to wander about after its original has ceased to exist, and that is why the dead seem to revisit us in our dreams. And sometimes the images of different objects coalesce as they are floating about, thus producing the appearance of impossible monsters, such as centaurs and chimaeras.[185]

It was with the help of this theory that Epicurus explained and defended the current belief in the existence of gods. The divine inhabitants of the intermundia, or empty spaces separating world from world, are, like all other beings, composed of atoms, and are continually throwing off fine images, some of which make their way unaltered to our earth and reveal themselves to the senses, particularly during sleep, when we are most alive to the subtlest impressions on our perceptive organs. With the usual irrationality of a theologian, Epicurus remained blind to the fact that gods who were constantly throwing off even the very thinnest films could not possibly survive through all eternity. Neither did he explain how images larger than the pupil of the eye could pass through its aperture while preserving their original proportions unaltered.

We have seen how Epicurus erected the senses into ultimate arbiters of truth. By so doing, however, he only pushed the old difficulty a step further back. Granting that our perceptions faithfully correspond to certain external images, how can we be sure that these images are themselves copies of a solid and permanent reality? And how are we to determine the validity of general notions representing not some single object but entire classes of objects? The second question may be most conveniently answered first. Epicurus holds that perception is only a finer sort of sensation. General notions are material images of a very delicate texture formed, apparently, on the principle of composition-photographs by the coalescence of many individual images thrown off from objects possessing a greater or less degree of resemblance to one another.[186] Thought is produced by the contact of such images with the soul, itself, it will be remembered, a material substance.

The rules for distinguishing between truth and falsehood are given in the famous Epicurean Canon. On receiving an image into the mind, we associate it with similar images formerly impressed on us by some real object. If the association or anticipation (πρόληψις) is confirmed or not contradicted by subsequent experience, it is true; false, if contradicted or not confirmed.[187] The stress laid on absence of contradictory evidence illustrates the great part played by such notions as possibility, negation, and freedom in the Epicurean system. In ethics this class of conceptions is represented by painlessness, conceived first as the condition, and finally as the essence of happiness; in physics by the infinite void, the inane profundum of which Lucretius speaks with almost religious unction; and in logic by the absence of contradiction considered as a proof of reality. Here, perhaps, we may detect the Parmenidean absolute under a new form; only, by a curious reversal, what Parmenides himself strove altogether to expel from thought has become its supreme object and content.[188]

The Epicurean philosophy of life and mind is completed by a sketch of human progress from its earliest beginnings to the complete establishment of civilisation. Here our principal authority is Lucretius; and no part of his great poem has attracted so much attention and admiration in recent times as that in which he so vividly places before us the condition of primitive men with all its miseries, and the slow steps whereby family life, civil society, religion, industry, and science arose out of the original chaos and war of all against each. But it seems likely that here, as elsewhere, Lucretius did no more than copy and colour the outlines already traced by his master's hand.[189] How far Epicurus himself is to be credited with this brilliant forecast of modern researches into the history of civilisation, is a more difficult question. When we consider that the most important parts of his philosophy were compiled from older systems, and that the additions made by himself do not indicate any great capacity for original research, we are forced to conclude that, here also, he is indebted to some authority whose name has not been preserved. The development of civilisation out of barbarism seems, indeed, to have been a standing doctrine of Greek Humanism, just as the opposite doctrine of degeneracy was characteristic of the naturalistic school. It is implied in the discourse of Protagoras reported by Plato, and also, although less fully, in the introduction to the History of Thucydides. Plato and Aristotle trace back the intellectual and social progress of mankind to very rude beginnings; while both writers assume that it was effected without any supernatural aid—a point marked to the exclusive credit of Epicurus by M. Guyau.[190] The old notion of a golden age, accepted as it was by so powerful a school as Stoicism, must have been the chief obstacle to a belief in progress; but the Prometheus of Aeschylus, with its vivid picture of the miseries suffered by primitive men through their ignorance of the useful arts, shows that a truer conception had already gained ground quite independently of philosophic theories. That the primitive state was one of lawless violence was declared by another dramatic poet, Critias, who has also much to say about the civilising function of religion;[191] and shortly before the time of Epicurus the same view was put forward by Euphorion, in a passage of which, as it will probably be new to many of our readers, we subjoin a translation:—

There was a time when mortals lived like brutes

In caves and unsunned hollows of the earth,

For neither house nor city flanked with towers

Had then been reared: no ploughshare cut the clod

To make it yield a bounteous harvest, nor

Were the vines ranked and trimmed with pruning-knives,

But fruitless births the sterile earth did bear.

Men on each other fed with mutual slaughter,

For Law was feeble, Violence enthroned,

And to the strong the weaker fell a prey.
But soon as Time that bears and nurtures all
Wrought out another change in human life,—
Whether some rapt Promethean utterance,
Or strong Necessity, or Nature's teaching
Through long experience, their deliverance brought,—
Holy Dêmêter's fruit it gave them; the sweet spring
Of Bacchus they discovered, and the earth,
Unsown before, was ploughed with oxen; cities then
They girt with towers and sheltering houses raised,
And turned their savage life to civil ways;
And after that Law bade entomb the dead
And measure out to each his share of dust,
Nor leave unburied and exposed to sight
Ghastly reminders of their former feasts.[192]

The merit of having worked up these loose materials into a connected sketch was, no doubt, considerable; but, according to Zeller, there is reason for attributing it to Theophrastus or even to Democritus rather than to Epicurus.[193] On the other hand, the purely mechanical manner in which Lucretius supposes every invention to have been suggested by some accidental occurrence or natural phenomenon, is quite in the style of Epicurus, and reminds us of the method by which he is known to have explained every operation of the human mind.[194]

VIII.

We have already repeatedly alluded to the only man of genius whom Epicureanism ever counted among its disciples. It is time that we should determine with more precision the actual relation in which he stood to the master whom, with a touching survival of religious sentiment, he revered as a saviour and a god.

Lucretius has been called Rome's only great speculative genius. This is, of course, absurd. A talent for lucid exposition does not constitute speculative genius, especially when it is unaccompanied by any ability to criticise the opinions expounded. The author of the De Rerum Naturâ probably had a lawyer's education. He certainly exhibits great forensic skill in speaking from his brief. But Cicero and Seneca showed the same skill on a much more extensive scale; and the former in particular was immensely superior to Lucretius in knowledge and argumentative power. Besides, the poet, who was certainly not disposed to hide his light under a bushel, and who exalts his own artistic excellences in no measured terms, never professes to be anything but a humble interpreter of truths first revealed to his Greek instructor's vivid intellect. It has, indeed, been claimed for Lucretius that he teaches a higher wisdom than his acknowledged guide.[195] This assertion is, however, not borne out by a careful comparison between the two.[196] In both there is the same theory of the universe, of man, and of the relations connecting them with one another. The idea of Nature in Lucretius shows no advance over the same idea in Epicurus. To each it expresses, not, as with the Stoics, a unifying power, a design by which all things work together for the best, but simply the conditions of a permanent mechanical aggregation. When Lucretius speaks of foedera Naturai, he means, not what we understand by laws of nature, that is, uniformities of causation underlying all phenomenal differences, to understand which is an exaltation of human dignity through the added power of prevision and control which it bestows, but rather the limiting possibilities of existence, the barriers against which human hopes and aspirations dash themselves in vain—an objective logic which guards us against fallacies instead of enabling us to arrive at positive conclusions. We have here the pervadingly negative character of Epicureanism, though probably presented with something of Roman solemnity and sternness. The idea of individuality, with which Lucretius has also been credited, occupies but a small place in his exposition, and seems to have interested him only as a particular aspect of the atomic theory. The ultimate particles of matter must be divided into unlike groups of units, for otherwise we could not explain the unlikenesses exhibited by sensible objects. This is neither the original Greek idea, that every man has his own life to lead, irrespective of public opinion or arbitrary convention; nor is it the modern delight in Nature's inexhaustible variety as opposed to the poverty of human invention, or to the restrictions of fashionable taste. Nor can we admit that Lucretius developed Epicurean philosophy in the direction of increased attention to the external world. The poet was, no doubt, a consummate observer, and he used his observations with wonderful felicity for the elucidation and enforcement of his philosophical reasoning; but in this respect he has been equalled or surpassed by other poets who either knew nothing of systematic philosophy, or, like Dante, were educated in a system as unlike as possible to that of Epicurus. There is, therefore, every reason for assuming that he saw and described phenomena not by virtue of his scientific training, but by virtue of his artistic endowment. And the same may be said of the other points in which he is credited with improvements on his master's doctrine. There is, no doubt, a strong consciousness of unity, of individuality, and of law running through his poem. But it is under the form of intuitions or contemplations, not under the form of speculative ideas that they are to be found. And, as will be presently shown, it is not as attributes of Nature but as attributes of life that they present themselves to his imagination.

In ethics, the dependence of Lucretius on his master is not less close than in physics. There is the same inconsistent presentation of pleasure conceived under its intensest aspect, and then of mere relief from pain, as the highest good;[197] the same dissuasion from sensuality, not as in itself degrading, but as involving disagreeable consequences;[198] the same inculcation of frugal and simple living as a source of happiness; the same association of justice with the dread of detection and punishment;[199] the same preference—particularly surprising in a Roman—of quiet obedience to political power;[200] finally, the same rejection, for the same reason, of divine providence and of human immortality, along with the same attempt to prove that death is a matter of indifference to us, enforced with greater passion and wealth of illustration, but with no real addition to the philosophy of the subject.[201]

Nevertheless, after all has been said, we are conscious of a great change in passing from the Greek moralist to the Roman poet. We seem to be breathing a new atmosphere, to find the old ideas informed with an unwonted life, to feel ourselves in the presence of one who has a power of stamping his convictions on us not ordinarily possessed by the mere imitative disciple. The explanation of this difference, we think, lies in the fact that Lucretius has so manipulated the Epicurean doctrines as to convert them from a system into a picture; and that he has saturated this picture with an emotional tone entirely wanting to the spirit of Epicureanism as it was originally designed. It is with the latter element that we may most conveniently begin.

Attention has already been called to the fact that Epicurus, although himself indifferent to physical science, was obliged, by the demands of the age, to give it a place, and a very large place, in his philosophy. Now it was to this very side of Epicureanism that the fresh intellect of Rome most eagerly attached itself. It is a great mistake to suppose that the Romans, or rather the ancient Italians, were indifferent to speculations about the nature of things. No one has given more eloquent expression to the enthusiasm excited by such enquiries than Virgil. Seneca devoted a volume to physical questions, and regretted that worldly distractions should prevent them from being studied with the assiduity they deserved. The elder Pliny lost his life in observing the eruption of Vesuvius. It was probably the imperial despotism, with its repeated persecutions of the 'Mathematicians,' which alone prevented Italy from entering on the great scientific career for which she was predestined in after ages. At any rate, a spirit of active curiosity was displaying itself during the last days of the republic, and we are told that nearly all the Roman Epicureans applied themselves particularly to the physical side of their master's doctrine.[202] Most of all was Lucretius distinguished by a veritable passion for science, which haunted him even in his dreams.[203] Hence, while Epicurus regarded the knowledge of Nature simply as a means for overthrowing religion, with his disciple the speculative interest seems to precede every other consideration, and religion is only introduced afterwards as an obstacle to be removed from the enquirer's path. How far his natural genius might have carried the poet in this direction, had he fallen into better hands, we cannot tell. As it was, the gift of what seemed a complete and infallible interpretation of physical phenomena relieved him from the necessity of independent investigation, and induced him to accept the most preposterous conclusions as demonstrated truths. But we can see how he is drawn by an elective affinity to that early Greek thought whence Epicurus derived whatever was of any real value in his philosophy.

It has been doubted, we think with insufficient reason, that Lucretius was acquainted at first hand with Empedocles.[204] But, by whatever channel it reached him, the enthusiasm of Empedocles and the Eleates lives in his verse no less truly than the inspiration of Aeolian music in the song of his younger contemporary, Catullus. The atomic theory, with its wonderful revelations of invisible activity and unbroken continuity underlying the abrupt revolutions of phenomenal existence, had been the direct product of those earliest struggles towards a deeper vision into the mysteries of cosmic life; and so Lucretius was enabled through his grasp of the theory itself to recover the very spirit and passion from which it sprang.[205]

But the enthusiasm for science, however noble in itself, would not alone have sufficed to mould the Epicurean philosophy into a true work of art. The De Rerum Naturâ is the greatest of all didactic poems, because it is something more than didactic. Far more truly than any of its Latin successors, it may claim comparison with the epic and dramatic masterpieces of Greece and Christian Europe; and that too not by virtue of any detached passages, however splendid, but by virtue of its composition as a whole. The explanation of this extraordinary success is to be sought in the circumstance that the central interest whence Lucretius works out in all directions is vital rather than merely scientific. The true heroine of his epic is not Nature but universal life—human life in the first instance, then the life of all the lower animals, and even of plants as well. Not only does he bring before us every stage of man's existence from its first to its last hour with a comprehensiveness, a fidelity, and a daring unparalleled in literature; but he exhibits with equal power of portrayal the towered elephants carrying confusion into the ranks of war, or girdling their own native India with a rampart of ivory tusks; the horse with an eagerness for the race that outruns even the impulse of his own swift limbs, or fiercely neighing with distended nostrils on the battlefield; the dog snuffing an imaginary scent, or barking at strange faces in his dreams; the cow sorrowing after her lost heifer; the placid and laborious ox; the flock of pasturing sheep seen far off, like a white spot on some green hill; the tremulous kids and sportive lambs; the new-fledged birds filling all the grove with their fresh songs; the dove with her neck-feathers shifting from ruby-red to sky-blue and emerald-green; the rookery clamouring for wind or rain; the sea birds screaming over the salt waves in search of prey; the snake sloughing its skin; the scaly fishes cleaving their way through the yielding stream; the bee winging its flight from flower to flower; the gnat whose light touch on our faces passes unperceived; the grass refreshed with dew; the trees bursting into sudden life from the young earth, or growing, flourishing, and covering themselves with fruit, dependent, like animals, on heat and moisture for their increase, and glad like them:—all these helping to illustrate with unequalled variety, movement, and picturesqueness the central idea which Lucretius carries always in his mind.

The keynote of the whole poem is struck in its opening lines. When Venus is addressed as Nature's sole guide and ruler, this, from the poet's own point of view, is not true of Nature as a whole, but it is eminently true of life, whether we identify Venus with the passion through which living things are continually regenerated, or with the pleasure which is their perpetual motive and their only good. And it is equally appropriate, equally characteristic of a consummate artist, that the interest of the work should culminate in a description of this same passion, no longer as the source of life, but as its last outcome and full flower, yet also, when pushed to excess, the illusion by which it is most utterly disappointed and undone; and that the whole should conclude with a description of death, not as exemplified in any individual tragedy, but in such havoc as was wrought by the famous plague at Athens on man and beast alike. Again, it is by the orderly sequence of vital phenomena that Lucretius proves his first great principle, the everlasting duration and changelessness of matter. If something can come out of nothing, he asks us, why is the production of all living things attached to certain conditions of place and season and parentage, according to their several kinds? Or if a decrease in the total sum of existence be possible, whence comes the inexhaustible supply of materials needed for the continual regeneration, growth, and nourishment of animal life? It is because our senses cannot detect the particles of matter by whose withdrawal visible objects gradually waste away that the existence of extremely minute atoms is assumed; and, so far, there is also a reference to inorganic bodies; but the porosity of matter is proved by the interstitial absorption of food and the searching penetration of cold; while the necessity of a vacuum is established by the ability of fish to move through the opposing stream. The generic differences supposed to exist among the atoms are inferred from the distinctions separating not only one animal species from another, but each individual from all others of the same species. The deflection of the atoms from the line of perpendicular descent is established by the existence of human free-will. So also, the analysis which distinguishes three determinate elements in the composition of the soul finds its justification in the diverse characters of animals—the fierceness of the lion, the placidity of the ox, and the timorousness of the deer—qualities arising from the preponderance of a fiery, an aërial, and a windy ingredient in the animating principle of each respectively. Finally, by another organic illustration, the atoms in general are spoken of as semina rerum—seeds of things.

At the same time Lucretius is resolved that no false analogy shall obscure the distinction between life and the conditions of life. It is for attempting, as he supposes, to efface this distinction that he so sharply criticises the earlier Greek thinkers. He scoffs at Heracleitus for imagining that all forms of existence can be deduced from the single element of fire. The idea of evolution and transformation seems, under some of its aspects, utterly alien to our poet. His intimacy with the world of living forms had accustomed him to view Nature as a vast assemblage of fixed types which might be broken up and reconstructed, but which by no possibility could pass into one another. Yet this rigid retention of characteristic differences in form permits a certain play and variety of movement, an individual spontaneity for which no law can be prescribed. The foedera Naturai, as Prof. Sellar aptly observes, are opposed to the foedera fati.[206] And this is just what might be expected from a philosophy based on the contemplation of life. For, while there is no capriciousness at all about the structure of animals, there is apparently a great deal of capriciousness about their actions. On the other hand, the Stoics, who derived their physics in great part from Heracleitus, came nearer than Lucretius to the standpoint of modern science. With them, as with the most advanced thinkers now, it is the foedera Naturai—the uniformities of co-existence—which are liable to exception and modification, while the foedera fati—the laws of causation—are necessary and absolute.

In like manner, Lucretius rejects the theory that living bodies are made up of the four elements, much as he admires its author, Empedocles. It seemed to him a blind confusion of the inorganic with the organic, the complex harmonies of life needing a much more subtle explanation than was afforded by such a crude intermixture of warring principles. If the theory of Anaxagoras fares no better in his hands, it is for the converse reason. He looks on it as an attempt to carry back purely vital phenomena into the inorganic world, to read into the ultimate molecules of matter what no analysis can make them yield—that is, something with properties like those of the tissues out of which animal bodies are composed.

Thus, while the atomic theory enables Lucretius to account for the dependent and perishable nature of life, the same theory enables him to bring out by contrast its positive and distinguishing characteristics. The bulk, the flexibility, the complexity, and the sensibility of animal bodies are opposed to the extreme minuteness, the absolute hardness, the simplicity, and the unconsciousness of the primordial substances which build them up.

On passing from the ultimate elements of matter to those immense aggregates which surpass man in size and complexity as much as the atoms fall below him, but on whose energies his dependence is no less helpless and complete—the infinite worlds typified for us by this one system wherein we dwell, with its solid earthly nucleus surrounded by rolling orbs of light—Lucretius still carries with him the analogies of life; but in proportion to the magnitude and remoteness of the objects examined, his grasp seems to grow less firm and his touch less sure. In marked contrast to Plato, Aristotle, and the Stoics, he argues passionately against the ascription of a beneficent purpose to the constitution of the world; but his reasonings are based solely on its imperfect adaptation to the necessities of human existence. With equal vigour he maintains, apparently against Aristotle, that the present system has had a beginning; against both Aristotle and Plato that, in common with all systems, it will have an end—a perfectly true conclusion, but evidently based on nothing stronger than the analogies of vital phenomena. And everywhere the subjective standpoint, making man the universal measure, is equally marked. Because our knowledge of history does not go far back, we cannot be far removed from its absolute beginning; and the history of the human race must measure the duration of the visible world. The earth is conceived as a mother bringing forth every species of living creature from her teeming bosom; and not only that, but a nursing mother feeding her young offspring with abundant streams of milk—an unexpected adaptation from the myth of a golden age. If we no longer witness such wonderful displays of fertility, the same elastic method is invoked to explain their cessation. The world, like other animals, is growing old and effete. The exhaustion of Italian agriculture is adduced as a sign of the world's decrepitude with no less confidence than the freshness of Italian poetry as a sign of its youth. The vast process of cosmic change, with its infinite cycles of aggregation and dissolution, does but repeat on an overwhelming scale the familiar sequences of birth and death in animal species. Even the rising and setting of the heavenly bodies and the phases of the moon may, it is argued, result from a similar succession of perishing individuals, although we take them for different appearances of a single unalterable sphere.[207]

A similar vein of thought runs through the moral and religious philosophy of Lucretius. If we look on him as a reformer, we shall say that his object was to free life from the delusions with which it had been disfigured by ignorance and passion. If we look on him as an artist, we shall say that he instinctively sought to represent life in the pure and perfect beauty of its naked form. If we look on him as a poet, we shall say that he exhibits all the objects of false belief no longer in the independence of their fancied reality, but in their place among other vital phenomena, and in due subordination to the human consciousness whose power, even when it is bound by them, they reveal. But while the first alternative leaves him in the position of a mere imitator or expositor who brings home no lessons that Epicurus had not already enforced with far greater success, the other two, and above all the last, restore him to the position of an original genius, who, instead of deriving his intuitions from the Epicurean system, adopts just so much of that system as is necessary to give them coherence and shape. It may, no doubt, be urged, that were life reduced to the simple expression, the state of almost vegetative repose, demanded by Lucretius, denuded of love, of ambition, of artistic luxury, of that aspiration towards belief in and union with some central soul of things, which all religions, more or less distinctly embody, its value for imaginative purposes would be destroyed; and that the deepest lesson taught by his poem would not be how to enjoy existence with the greatest intensity, but how to abandon it with the least regret. Now it is just here that the wonderful power of poetry comes in, and does for once, under the form of a general exposition, what it has to do again and again under the easier conditions of individual presentation. For poetry is essentially tragic, and almost always excites the activity of our imagination, not by giving it the assured possession of realities, but by the strain resulting from their actual or their expected eclipse. If Homer and the Attic tragedians show us what is life, and what are the goods of life, it is not through experience of the things themselves, but through the form of the void and the outline of the shadow which their removal or obscuration has produced. So also in the universal tragedy of the Roman poet, where the actors are not persons, but ideas. Every belief is felt with more poignant intensity at the moment of its overthrow, and the world of illusion is compensated for intellectual extinction by imaginative persistence as a conscious creation, a memory, or a dream. There is no mythological picture so splendidly painted as those in which Lucretius has shown us Mavors pillowed on the lap of Venus, or led before us the Idaean mother in her triumphal car. No redeemer, credited with supernatural powers, has ever enjoyed such an apotheosis as that bestowed by his worshipper on the apostle of unbelief. Nowhere have the terrible and mysterious suggestions of mortality been marshalled with such effect as in the argument showing that death no more admits of experience than of escape. What love-inspired poet has ever followed the storm and stress of passion with such tenderness of sympathy or such audacity of disclosure, as he to whom its objects were disrobed of their divinity, for whom its fancied satisfaction was but the kindling to insaner effort of a fatally unquenchable desire? Instead of being 'compelled to teach a truth he would not learn,' Lucretius was enabled by the spirit of his own incomparable art to seize and fix for ever, in bold reversal of light and shade, those visions on which the killing light of truth had long before him already dawned.

The De Rerum Naturâ is the greatest of Roman poems, because it is just the one work where the abstract genius of Rome met with a subject combining an abstract form with the interest and inspiration of concrete reality; where negation works with a greater power than assertion; where the satire is directed against follies more wide-spread and enduring than any others; where the teaching in some most essential points can never be superseded; and where dependence on a Greek model left the poet free to contribute from his own imagination those elements to which the poetic value of his work is entirely due. By a curious coincidence, the great poet of mediaeval Italy attained success by the employment of a somewhat similar method. Dante represented, it is true, in their victorious combination, three influences against which Lucretius waged an unrelenting warfare—religion, the idealising love of woman, and the spiritualistic philosophy of Greece. Nevertheless, they resemble each other in this important particular, that both have taken an abstract theory of the world as the mould into which the burning metal of their imaginative conceptions is poured. Dante, however, had a power of individual presentation which Lucretius either lacked or had no opportunity of exercising; and therefore he approaches nearer to that supreme creativeness which only two races, the Greek and the English, have hitherto displayed on a very extended scale.

IX.

Returning once more to Epicurus, we have now to sum up the characteristic excellences and defects of his philosophy. The revival of the atomic theory showed unquestionable courage and insight. Outside the school of Democritus, it was, so far as we know, accepted by no other thinker. Plato never mentions it. Aristotle examined and rejected it. The opponents of Epicurus himself treated it as a self-evident absurdity.[208] Only Marcus Aurelius seems to have contemplated the possibility of its truth.[209]. But while to have maintained the right theory in the face of such universal opposition was a proof of no common discernment, we must remember that appropriating the discoveries of others, even when those discoveries are in danger of being lost through neglect, is a very different thing from making discoveries for one's self. No portion of the glory due to Leucippus and Democritus should be diverted to their arrogant successor. And it must also be remembered that the Athenian philosopher, by his theory of deflection, not only spoiled the original hypothesis, but even made it a little ridiculous.

The second service of Epicurus was entirely to banish the idea of supernatural interference from the study of natural phenomena. This also was a difficult enterprise in the face of that overwhelming theological reaction begun by Socrates, continued by Plato, and carried to grotesque consequences by the Stoics; but, here again, there can be no question of attributing any originality to the philosopher of the Garden. That there either were no gods at all, or that if there were they never meddled with the world, was a common enough opinion in Plato's time; and even Aristotle's doctrine of a Prime Mover excludes the notion of creation, providence, and miracles altogether. On the other hand, the Epicurean theory of idle gods was irrational in itself, and kept the door open for a return of superstitious beliefs.

The next and perhaps the most important point in favour of Epicureanism is its theory of pleasure as the end of action. Plato had left his idea of the good undefined; Aristotle had defined his in such a manner as to shut out the vast majority of mankind from its pursuit; the Stoics had revolted every instinct by altogether discarding pleasure as an end, and putting a purely formal and hollow perfection in its place. It must further be admitted that Epicurus, in tracing back justice to the two ideas of interest and contract, had hold of a true and fertile principle. Nevertheless, although ethics is his strongest ground, his usual ill-luck pursues him even here. It is where he is most original that he goes most astray. By reducing pleasure, as an end of action, to the mere removal of pain, he alters earlier systems of hedonism for the worse; and plays the game of pessimism by making it appear that, on the whole, death must be preferable to life, since it is what life can never be—a state of absolute repose. And by making self-interest, in the sense of seeking nothing but one's own pleasure or the means to it, the only rule of action, he endangers the very foundations of society. At best, the selfish system, as Coleridge has beautifully observed, 'stands in a similar relation to the law of conscience or universal selfless reason, as the dial to the sun which indicates its path by intercepting its radiance.'[210] Nor is the indication so certain as Coleridge admitted. A time may come when self-sacrifice shall be unnecessary for the public welfare, but we are not within a measurable distance of it as yet.

No word of commendation can be pronounced on the Epicurean psychology and logic. They are both bad in themselves, and inconsistent with the rest of the system. Were all knowledge derived from sense-impressions—especially if those impressions were what Epicurus imagined them to be—the atomic theory could never have been discovered or even conceived, nor could an ideal of happiness have been thought out. In its theory of human progress, Epicureanism once more shows to advantage;

although in denying all inventiveness to man, and making him the passive recipient of external impressions, it differs widely from the modern school which it is commonly supposed to have anticipated. And we may reasonably suspect that, here as elsewhere, earlier systems embodied sounder views on the same subject.

The qualities which enabled Epicurus to compete successfully with much greater thinkers than himself as the founder of a lasting sect, were practical rather than theoretical. Others before him had taught that happiness was the end of life; none, like him, had cultivated the art of happiness, and pointed out the fittest methods for attaining it. The idea of such an art was a real and important addition to the resources of civilisation. No mistake is greater than to suppose that pleasure is lost by being made an object of pursuit. To single out the most agreeable course among many alternatives, and, when once found, steadily to pursue it, is an aptitude like any other, and is capable of being brought to a high degree of perfection by assiduous attention and self-discipline.[211] No doubt the capacity for enjoyment is impaired by excessive self-consciousness, but the same is true of every other accomplishment during the earlier stages of its acquisition. It is only the beginner who is troubled by taking too much thought about his own proficiency; when practice has become a second nature, the professor of hedonism reaps his harvest of delight without wasting a thought on his own efforts, or allowing the phantom of pleasure in the abstract to allure him away from its particular and present realisation. And, granting that happiness as such can be made an object of cultivation, Epicurus was perfectly right in teaching that the removal of pain is its most essential condition, faulty as was (from a speculative point of view) his confusion of the condition with the thing itself. If the professed pleasure-seekers of modern society often fail in the business of their lives, it is from neglecting this salutary principle, especially where it takes the form of attention to the requirements of health. In assigning a high importance to friendship, he was equally well inspired. Congenial society is not only the most satisfying of enjoyments in itself, but also that which can be most easily combined with every other enjoyment. It is also true, although a truth felt rather than perceived by our philosopher, that speculative agreement, especially when speculation takes the form of dissent from received opinions, greatly increases the affection of friends for one another. And as theology is the subject on which unforced agreement seems most difficult, to eliminate its influence altogether was a valuable though purely negative contribution to unanimity of thought and feeling in the hedonistic sect.

An attempt has recently been made by M. Guyau to trace the influence of Epicurus on modern philosophy. We cannot but think the method of this able and lucid writer a thoroughly mistaken one. Assuming the recognition of self-interest as the sole or paramount instinct in human nature, to be the essence of what Epicurus taught, M. Guyau, without more ado, sets down every modern thinker who agrees with him on this one point as his disciple, and then adds to the number all who hold that pleasure is the end of action; thus making out a pretty long list of famous names among the more recent continuators of his tradition. A more extended study of ancient philosophy would have shown the French critic that moralists who, in other respects, were most opposed to Epicurus, agreed with him in holding that every man naturally and necessarily makes his own interest the supreme test of right conduct; and that only with the definition of welfare did their divergence begin. On the other hand, the selfish systems of modern times differ entirely from Epicureanism in their conception of happiness. With Hobbes, for instance, whom M. Guyau classes as an Epicurean, the ideal is not painlessness but power; the desires are, according to his view, naturally infinite, and are held in check, not by philosophical precepts but by mutual restraint; while, in deducing the special virtues, his standard is not the good of each individual, but the good of the whole—in other words, he is, to that extent, a Stoic rather than an Epicurean. La Rochefoucauld, who is offered as another example of the same tendency, was not a moralist at all; and as a psychologist he differs essentially from Epicurus in regarding vanity as always and everywhere the great motive to virtue. Had the Athenian sage believed this he would have despaired of making men happy; for disregard of public opinion, within the limits of personal safety, was, with him, one of the first conditions of a tranquil existence. Nor would he have been less averse from the system of Helvétius, another of his supposed disciples. The principal originality of Helvétius was to insist that the passions, instead of being discouraged—as all previous moralists, Epicurus among the number, had advised—should be deliberately stimulated by the promise of unlimited indulgence to those who distinguished themselves by important public services. Of Spinoza we need say nothing, for M. Guyau admits that he was quite as much inspired by Stoic as by Epicurean ideas. At the same time, the combination of these two ethical systems would have been much better illustrated by modern English utilitarianism, which M. Guyau regards as a development of Epicureanism alone. The greatest happiness of the greatest number is not an individual or self-interested, but a universal end, having, as Mill has shown, for its ultimate sanction the love of humanity as a whole, which is an essentially Stoic sentiment. It may be added that utilitarianism has no sympathy with the particular theory of pleasure, whether sensual or negative, adopted by Epicurus. In giving a high, or even the highest place to intellectual enjoyments, it agrees with the estimate of Plato and Aristotle, to which he was so steadily opposed. And in duly appreciating the positive side of all enjoyments, it returns to the earlier hedonism from which he stood so far apart.

The distinctive features of Epicureanism have, in truth, never been copied, nor are they ever likely to be copied, by any modern system. It arose, as we have seen, from a combination of circumstances which will hardly be repeated in the future history of thought. As the heat and pressure of molten granite turn sandstone into slate, so also the mighty systems of Plato and Aristotle, coming into contact with the irreligious, sensual, empirical, and sceptical side of Attic thought, forced it to assume that sort of laminated texture which characterises the theoretical philosophy of Epicurus. And, at the very same moment, the disappearance of all patriotism and public spirit from Athenian life allowed the older elements of Athenian character, its amiable egoism, its love of frugal gratifications, its aversion from purely speculative interests, to create a new and looser bond of social union among those who were indifferent to the vulgar objects of ambition, but whom the austerer doctrines of Stoicism had failed to attract.

CHAPTER III. THE SCEPTICS AND ECLECTICS: GREEK PHILOSOPHY IN ROME.

I.

The year 155 B.C. was signalised by an important event, if not in the history of ideas, at least in the history of their diffusion. This was the despatch of an embassy from the Athenian people to the Roman Senate, consisting of three philosophers, the heads of their respective schools—Carneades the Academician, Critolaus the Peripatetic, and Diogenes the Stoic. Philosophic teaching, once proscribed at Athens, had, at the time of which we are speaking, become her chief distinction, and the most honourable profession pursued within her precincts. It was, then, as natural that an important mission should be confided to the most eminent representatives of the calling in question as that high ecclesiastics should be similarly employed by Rome in later ages, or that German university towns should send professors to represent their interests in the imperial Diet. But the same fate that befalls an established religion had befallen an established philosophy. An attempt to impose restrictions on the liberty of teaching had, indeed, been successfully resisted, and the experiment was never repeated.[212] Nevertheless, the teachers themselves lost as much in true dignity as they gained in affluence and popular estimation. In all probability, the threat of death would not have induced Socrates to undertake the task which was, apparently, accepted without compulsion and as an honourable duty by his successors. The Athenians had made an unprovoked raid on the town of Oropus; the affair had been referred to arbitration; and the aggressors had been sentenced to pay a fine of 500 talents. It was to obtain a remission of this sentence that the three Scholarchs were sent on an embassy to the Roman Senate.

If the nature of their errand was not precisely calculated to win respect for the profession of the Athenian envoys, the subsequent proceedings of one among their number proved still less likely to raise it in the estimation of those whose favour they sought to win. Hellenic culture was, at that time, rapidly gaining ground among the Roman aristocracy; Carneades, who already enjoyed an immense reputation for eloquence and ingenuity among his own countrymen, used the opportunity offered by his temporary residence in the imperial city to deliver public lectures on morality; and such was the eagerness to listen that for a time the young nobles could think and talk of nothing else. The subject chosen was justice. The first lecture recapitulated whatever had been said in praise of that virtue by Plato and Aristotle. But it was a principle of the sect to which Carneades belonged that every affirmative proposition, however strongly supported, might be denied with equal plausibility. Accordingly, his second discourse was entirely devoted to upsetting the conclusions advocated in the first. Transporting the whole question, as would seem, from a private to a public point of view, he attempted to show, from the different standards prevailing in different countries, that there was no such thing as an immutable rule of right; and also that the greatest and most successful States had profited most by unscrupulous aggressions on their weaker neighbours—his most telling illustrations being drawn from the history of the Romans themselves. Then, descending once more to private life, the sceptical lecturer expatiated on the frequency of those cases in which justice is opposed to self-interest, and the folly of sacrificing one's own advantage to that of another. 'Suppose a good man has a runaway slave or an unhealthy house to sell, will he inform the buyer of their deficiencies, or will he conceal them? In the one case he will be a fool, in the other case he will be unjust. Again, justice forbids us to take away the life or property of another. But in a shipwreck, will not the just man try to save his life at another's expense by seizing the plank of which some weaker person than himself has got hold—especially if they are alone on the sea together? If he is wise he will do so, for to act otherwise would be to sacrifice his life. So also, in flying before the enemy, will he not dispossess a wounded comrade of his horse, in order to mount and escape on it himself? Here, again, justice is incompatible with self-preservation—that is to say, with wisdom!'[213]

At the time when Carneades delivered his lectures, the morality of Rome resembled that of Sparta during her great conflict with Athens, as characterised by one of the speakers in the Melian Dialogue. Scrupulously honourable in their dealings with one another, in their dealings with foreign nations her citizens notoriously identified justice with what was agreeable or advantageous to themselves. The arguments of the Academic philosopher must, therefore, have been doubly annoying to the leaders of the State, as a satire on its public policy and as a source of danger to the integrity of its private life. In this respect, old Cato was a type of the whole race. In all transactions with his fellow-citizens, and in every office undertaken on behalf of the community, his honesty was such that it became proverbial. But his absolute disregard of international justice has become equally proverbial through the famous advice, reiterated on every possible occasion, that an unoffending and unwarlike city should be destroyed, lest its existence should at some future time become a source of uneasiness to the mistress of the world. Perhaps it was a secret consciousness of his own inconsistency which prevented him from directly proposing that Carneades should not be allowed to continue his lectures. At any rate, the ex-Censor contented himself with moving that the business on which the Athenian envoys had come should be at once concluded, that they might return to their classes at Athens, leaving the youth of Rome to seek instruction as before from the wise conversation and example of her public men.[214] We are not told whether his speech on this occasion wound up with the usual formula, caeterum, Patres Conscripti, sententia mea est Carthaginem esse delendam; but as it is stated that from the year 175 to the end of his life, he never made a motion in the Senate that was not terminated by those words, we are entitled to assume that he did not omit them in the present instance. If so, the effect must have been singularly grotesque; although, perhaps, less so than if attention had been drawn to the customary phrase by its unexpected absence. At any rate, Carneades had an opportunity of carrying back one more illustration of ethical inconsistency wherewith to enliven his lectures on the 'vanity of dogmatising' and the absolute equilibrium of contradictory opinions.

It has been mentioned that Carneades was the head of the Academic school. In that capacity, he was the lineal inheritor of Plato's teaching. Yet a public apology for injustice, even when balanced by a previous panegyric on its opposite, might seem to be of all lessons the most alien from Platonism; and in a State governed by Plato's own laws, it would certainly have been punishable with death. To explain this anomaly is to relate the history of Greek scepticism, which is what we shall now attempt to do.

II.

In modern parlance, the word scepticism is often used to denote absolute unbelief. This, however, is a misapplication; and, properly speaking, it should be reserved, as it was by the Greeks, for those cases in which belief is simply withheld, or in which, as its etymology implies, the mental state connoted is a desire to consider of the matter before coming to a decision. But, of course, there are occasions when, either from prudence or politeness, absolute rejection of a proposition is veiled under the appearance of simple indecision or of a demand for further evidence; and at a time when to believe in certain theological dogmas was either dangerous or discreditable, the name sceptic may have been accepted on all hands as a convenient euphemism in speaking about persons who did not doubt, but denied them altogether. Again, taken in its original sense, the name sceptic is applicable to two entirely different, or rather diametrically opposite classes. The true philosopher is more slow to believe than other men, because he is better acquainted than they are with the rules of evidence, and with the apparently strong claims on our belief often possessed by propositions known to be false. To that extent, all philosophers are sceptics, and are rightly regarded as such by the vulgar; although their acceptance of many conclusions which the unlearned reject without examination, has the contrary effect of giving them a reputation for extraordinary credulity or even insanity. And this leads us to another aspect of scepticism—an aspect under which, so far from being an element of philosophy, it is one of the most dangerous enemies that philosophy has to face. Instead of regarding the difficulties which beset the path of enquiry as a warning against premature conclusions, and a stimulus to more careful research, it is possible to make them a pretext for abandoning enquiry altogether. And it is also possible to regard the divergent answers given by different thinkers to the same problem, not as materials for comparison, selection or combination, nor even as indications of the various directions in which a solution is not to be sought, but as a proof that the problem altogether passes the power of human reason to solve.

Were this intellectual despondency to issue in a permanent suspense of judgment, it would be bad enough; but practically its consequences are of a much more mischievous character. The human mind is so constituted that it must either go forward or fall back; in no case can it stand still. Accordingly, the lazy sceptic almost always ends by conforming to the established creeds and customs of his age or of the society in which he lives; thus strengthening the hands of authority in its conflict with the more energetic or courageous enquirers, whose object is to discover, by the unaided efforts of reason, some new and positive principle either of action or of belief. And the guardians of orthodoxy are so well aware of the profit to be reaped from this alliance that, when debarred from putting down their opponents by law or by public opinion, they anxiously foster false scepticism where it is already rampant, and endeavour to create it where it does not exist. Sometimes disinterested morality is the object of their attack, and at other times the foundations of inductive science. Their favourite formula is that whatever objections may be urged against their own doctrines, others equally strong may be urged against the results of free thought; whereas the truth is that such objections, being applicable to all systems alike, exactly balance one another, leaving the special arguments against irrationalism to tell with as much force as before. And they also lay great stress on the internal dissensions of their assailants—dissensions which only bring out into more vivid relief the one point on which all are agreed, that, whatever else may be true, the traditional opinions are demonstrably false.

As might be expected from the immense exuberance of their intellectual life, we find every kind of scepticism represented among the Greeks; and, as with their other philosophical tendencies, there is evidence of its existence previous to or independent of scientific speculation. Their very religion, though burdened with an enormous mass of fictitious legends, shows a certain unwillingness to transgress the more obvious laws of nature, not noticeable in the traditions of kindred or neighbouring races. Its tendency is rather to imagine supernatural causes for natural events, or to read a divine meaning into accidental occurrences, than to introduce impossibilities into the ordinary course of history. And some of its most marvellous stories are told in such a manner that the incredulous satire with which they were originally received is, by a beautiful play of irony, worked into the very texture of the narrative itself. For example, the Greeks were especially disinclined to believe that one of the lower animals could speak with a human voice, or that a dead man could be brought back to life—contradicted as both suppositions were by the facts of universal experience. So when the horse Xanthus replies to his master's reproaches, Homer adds that his voice was arrested by the Erinyes—that is to say, by the laws of nature; and we may suspect that nothing more is intended by his speech than the interpretation which Achilles would spontaneously put on the mute and pathetic gaze of the faithful steed. And when, to illustrate the wondrous medical skill of Asclêpius, it is related that at last he succeeded in restoring a dead man to life, the story adds that for this impious deed both the healer and his patient were immediately transfixed by a thunderbolt from heaven.[215] Another impossibility is to predict with any certainty the future fate of individuals, and here also—as has been already observed in a different connexion[216]—the Greeks showed their extreme scepticism with regard to any alleged contravention of a natural law, under the transparent disguise of stories about persons whom ambiguous predictions had lured to their fall.

It is even doubtful how far the Greek poets believed in the personality of their gods, or, what comes to the same thing, in their detachment from the natural objects in which a divine power was supposed to be embodied. Such a detachment is most completely realised when they are assembled in an Olympian council; but, as Hegel has somewhere observed, Homer never brings his gods together in this manner without presenting them in a ridiculous light—that is to say, without hinting that their existence must not be taken quite in earnest. And the existence of disembodied spirits seems to be similarly conceived by the great epic master. The life of the souls in Hades is not a continuance but a memory and a reflection of their life on earth. The scornful reply of Achilles to the congratulations of Odysseus implies, as it were, the consciousness of his own nonentity. By no other device could the irony of the whole situation, the worthlessness of a merely subjective immortality, be made so poignantly apparent.[217]

The characters in Homer are marked by this incredulous disposition in direct proportion to their general wisdom. When Agamemnon relates his dream to the assembled chiefs, Nestor dryly observes that if anyone of less authority had told them such a story they would have immediately rejected it as untrue. Hector's outspoken contempt for augury is well known; and his indifference to the dying words of Patroclus is equally characteristic. In the Odyssey, Alcinous pointedly distinguishes his guest from the common run of travellers, whose words deserve no credit. That Telemachus should tell who is his father, with the uncomplimentary reservation that he has only his mother's word for it, is evidently meant as a proof of the young man's precocious shrewdness; and it is with the utmost difficulty that Penelope herself is persuaded of her husband's identity. So in the Agamemnon of Aeschylus, nothing less than the report of an eye-witness will convince the Chorus of old men that Troy has really fallen.[218] Finally, to complete the list of examples afforded independently of philosophical reflection, Herodotus repeatedly expresses disbelief in the stories told him, or, what is more remarkable, holds his judgment in suspense with regard to their veracity.

Scepticism, as a philosophical principle, is alien from early Greek thought; but it is pervaded by a negative tendency exhibited in four different directions, all converging towards the later attitude of suspensive doubt. There are sharp criticisms on the popular mythology; there are protests against the ascription of reality to sensible appearances; there are contemptuous references on the part of some philosophers to the opinions held by others; and there are occasional lamentations over the difficulty of getting at any truth at all. The importance, however, of these last utterances has been considerably exaggerated both in ancient and modern times. For, in some instances, they are attributable solely to the distrust of sense-perception, and in others they seem to express nothing more than a passing mood against which we must set the dogmatic conclusions elsewhere enunciated with perfect confidence by the same thinkers.[219] At the same time, we have to note, as an illustration of the standing connexion between theological belief and that kind of scepticism which is shown by distrust in man's power of discovering the truth for himself, that the strongest expressions of such a distrust are to be found in the two most religious of the pre-Socratic thinkers, Xenophanes and Empedocles.

III.

A new period begins with the Greek Humanists. We use this term in preference to that of Sophists, because, as has been shown, in specially dealing with the subject, half the teachers known under the latter denomination made it their business to popularise physical science and to apply it to morality, while the other half struck out an entirely different line, and founded their educational system on the express rejection of such investigations; their method being, in this respect, foreshadowed by the greatest poet of the age, who concentrates all his attention on the workings of the human mind, and followed by its greatest historian, with whom a similar study takes the place occupied by geography and natural history in the work of Herodotus. This absorption in human interests was unfavourable alike to the objects and to the methods of previous enquiry: to the former, as a diversion from the new studies; to the latter, as inconsistent with the flexibility and many-sidedness of conscious mind. Hence the true father of philosophical scepticism was Protagoras. With him, for the first time, we find full expression given to the proper sceptical attitude, which is one of suspense and indifference as opposed to absolute denial. He does not undertake to say whether the gods exist or not. He regards the real essence of Nature as unknowable, on account of the relativity which characterises all sensible impressions. And wherever opinions are divided, he undertakes to provide equally strong arguments for both sides of the question. He also anticipates the two principal tendencies exhibited by all future scepticism in its relation to practice. One is its devotion to humanity, under the double form of exclusive attention to human interests, and great mildness in the treatment of human beings. The other is a disposition to take custom and public opinion, rather than any physical or metaphysical law, for the standard and sanction of morality. Such scepticism might for the moment be hostile to religion; but a reconciliation was likely to be soon effected between them.

The famous theses of Gorgias were quoted in a former chapter as an illustration of the tactics pursued by Greek Humanism in its controversy with physical science. They must be noticed again in the present connexion, on account of their bearing on the development of scepticism, and as having inaugurated a method of reasoning often employed in subsequent attacks, directed, not against the whole of knowledge, but against particular parts of it. The scepticism of Protagoras rested on the assumption that there is an external reality from the reaction of which with mind all our perceptions proceed. Neither of these two factors can be known apart from the other, and as both are in a constant flux, our knowledge of the resulting compound at one time does not show what it has been or will be at another time. But

Gorgias altogether denied the existence of any objective reality; and he attempted to disprove it by an analytical instead of a synthetic argument, laying down a series of disjunctive propositions, and upsetting the different alternatives in succession. Existence must be either something or nothing, or both together; and if something, it must be either finite or infinite, or both, and either one or many, or both. His argument against an infinite existence is altogether futile; but it serves to illustrate the undeveloped state of reflection at that period. The eternity of the world is confounded with its unlimited extension in space: and this hypothesis, again, is met by the transparent quibble that the world, not being in any one place, must be nowhere or not at all. And the alternative that the world has not always existed is refuted by the unproved assumption, which, apparently, no Greek philosopher ever thought of disputing, that nothing can begin without being caused by something else. Still, however contemptible such reasonings may seem, it is obvious that in them we have the first crude form of the famous antinomies by which Kant long afterwards sought to prove the impossibility of a world existing in space and time apart from a percipient subject, and which have since been used to establish in a more general way the unknowability of existence as such. It will also be observed that the sceptical arguments respectively derived from the relativity of thought and from the contradictions inherent in its ultimate products are run together by modern agnostics. But no reason that we can remember has ever been given to show that an idea is necessarily subjective because it is self-contradictory.

The second thesis of Gorgias was that, even granting the world to exist, it could not possibly be known. Here the reasoning is unexpectedly weak. Because all thoughts do not represent facts,—as, for example, our ideas of impossible combinations, like chariots running over the sea,—it is assumed that none do. But the problem how to distinguish between true and false ideas was raised, and it was round this that the fiercest battle between dogmatists and sceptics subsequently raged. And in the complete convertibility of consciousness and reality postulated by Gorgias, we may find the suggestion of a point sometimes overlooked in the automatist controversy—namely, that the impossibility, if any, of our acting on the material world reciprocally involves the impossibility of its acting on us, in so far as we are conscious beings. If thought cannot be translated into movement, neither can movement be translated into thought.

The third thesis maintains that, granting the world to exist and to be knowable, one man cannot communicate his knowledge to another; for, the different classes of sensations being heterogeneous, a visual or tactual impression on our consciousness cannot be conveyed by an auditory impression on the consciousness of someone else. This difficulty has been completely overcome by the subsequent progress of thought. We cannot, it is true, directly communicate more than a few sensations to one another; but by producing one we may call up others with which it has become associated through previous experience. And the great bulk of our knowledge has been analysed into relations of co-existence, succession, and resemblance, which are quite independent of the particular symbols employed to transmit them from one mind to another.[220]

The scepticism of Aristippus and the Cyrenaics mediated between the views of Protagoras and those of Gorgias, while marking an advance on both. According to this school, we know nothing beyond our own feelings, and it must be left undecided whether they are caused by an external reality or not. Nor can the feelings of one individual justify us in reasoning to the existence of similar feelings in the mind of another individual.[221] It might be objected that the arguments advanced in support of the latter assertion are suicidal, for they are derived from the abnormal states of consciousness accompanying particular diseases, or else from the divergences of taste exhibited by different individuals even when in good health,—an apparent admission that we are sufficiently well acquainted with the phenomena in question to institute a comparison between them, which, by hypothesis, is impossible. And this is, in fact, the method by which Mr. Herbert Spencer has endeavoured to upset the whole theory of subjective idealism, as involving at every step an assumption of the very realities that it professes to deny. But the Cyrenaic and the modern idealist have a perfect right to show that the assumptions of their adversaries are self-contradictory; and the readiest way of so doing is to reason from them as if they were true. The real answer to that extreme form of idealism which denies the possibility of making known our feelings to each other is that, our bodies being similarly constructed and responding to similar impressions by similar manifestations, I have the same sort of warrant for assuming that your states of consciousness are like mine that I have for assuming you to exist at all. The inference must, of course, be surrounded by proper precautions, such as are seldom used by unscientific reasoners. We must make sure that the structure is the same and that the excitement is the same, or that their differences, if any, are insignificant, before we can attribute the same value to the same manifestations of feeling on the part of different persons; but that this can be done, at least in the case of the elementary sensations, is shown by the easy detection of such anomalies as colour-blindness where they exist.

With Socrates and Plato, scepticism exhibits itself under two new aspects: as an accompaniment of religious belief, and as an element of constructive thought. Thus they represent both the good and the bad side of this tendency: the aspect under which it is a help, and the aspect under which it is a hindrance to scientific investigation. With both philosophers, however, the restriction or negation of human knowledge was a consequence rather than a cause of their theological convictions; nor do they seem to have appreciated its value as a weapon in the controversy with religious unbelief. When Socrates represented the irreconcilable divergence in the explanations of Nature offered by previous thinkers as a sufficient condemnation of their several pretensions, he did not set this fact against the arguments by which a Xenophanes had similarly endeavoured to overthrow the popular mythology; but he looked on it as a fatal consequence of their insane presumption in meddling with the secrets of the gods. On one occasion only, when explaining to Euthydêmus that the invisibility of the gods is no reason for doubting their existence, he argues, somewhat in Butler's style, that our own minds, whose existence we cannot doubt, are equally invisible.[222] And the Platonic Socrates makes it his business to demonstrate the universality of human ignorance, not as a caution against dogmatic unbelief, but as a glorification of the divine knowledge; though how we come to know that there is any such knowledge he leaves utterly unexplained.

In Plato's Parmenides we have to note the germ of a new dialectic. There it is suggested that we may overcome the difficulties attending a particular theory—in this instance the theory of self-existing ideas—by considering how much greater are the difficulties which would ensue on its rejection. The arguments advanced by Zeno the Eleatic against the reality of motion are mentioned as a case in point; and Plato proceeds to illustrate his proposed method by showing what consequences respectively follow if we first assume the existence, and then the non-existence of the One; but the whole analysis seems valueless for its immediate purpose, since the resulting impossibilities on either side are left exactly balanced; and Plato does not, like some modern metaphysicians, call in our affections to decide the controversy.

The method by which Plato eventually found his way out of the sceptical difficulty, was to transform it from a subjective law of thought into an objective law of things. Adopting the Heracleitean physics as a sufficient explanation of the material world, he conceived, at a comparatively early period of his mental evolution, that the fallaciousness of sense-impressions is due, not to the senses themselves, but to the instability of the phenomena with which they deal; and afterwards, on discovering that the interpretation of ideal relations was subject to similar perplexities, he assumed that, in their case also, the contradiction arises from a combination of Being with not-Being determining whatever differences prevail among the ultimate elements of things. And, finally, like Empedocles, he solved the problem of cognition by establishing a parallel between the human soul and the universe as a whole; the circles of the Same and the Other being united in the celestial orbits and also in the mechanism of the brain.[223]

It was by an analogous, though, of course, far more complicated and ingenious adjustment, that Hegel sought to overcome the agnosticism which Kant professed to have founded on a basis of irrefragable proof. With both philosophers, however, the sceptical principle was celebrating its supreme triumph at the moment of its fancied overthrow. The dogmatism of doubt could go no further than to resolve the whole chain of existence into a succession of mutually contradictory ideas.

If the synthesis of affirmation and negation cannot profitably be used to explain the origin of things in themselves, it has a real and very important function when limited to the subjective sphere, to the philosophy of practice and of belief. It was so employed by Socrates, and, on a much greater scale, by Plato himself. To consider every proposition from opposite points of view, and to challenge the claim of every existing custom on our respect, was a proceeding first instituted by the master, and carried out by the disciple in a manner which has made his investigations a model for every future enquirer. Something of their spirit was inherited by Aristotle; but, except in his logical treatises, it was overborne by the demands of a pre-eminently dogmatic and systematising genius. In criticising the theories of his predecessors, he has abundantly illustrated the power of dialectic, and he has enumerated its resources with conscientious completeness; but he has not verified his own conclusions by subjecting them to this formidable testing apparatus.

Meanwhile the scepticism of Protagoras had not been entirely absorbed into the systems of his rivals, but continued to exist as an independent tradition, or in association with a simpler philosophy. The famous school of Megara, about which, unfortunately, we have received very little direct information, was nominally a development of the Socratic teaching on its logical side, as the Cynic and Cyrenaic schools were on its ethical side, but like them also, it seems to have a more real connexion with the great impulse previously given to speculation by the Sophists. At any rate, we chiefly hear of the Megarians as having denied the possibility of definition, to which Socrates attached so much importance, and as framing questions not susceptible of a categorical answer,—an evident satire on the Socratic method of eliciting the truth by cross-examination.[224] What they really derived from Socrates seems to have been his mental concentration and independence of external circumstances. Here they closely resembled the Cynics, as also in their contempt for formal logic; but while Antisthenes found a sanction for his indifference and impassivity in the order of nature, their chief representative, Stilpo, achieved the same result by pushing the sceptical principle to consequences from which even the Cyrenaics would have shrunk. Denying the possibility of attaching a predicate to a subject, he seems, in like manner, to have isolated the mind from what are called its affections, or, at least, to have made this isolation his ideal of the good. Even the Stoics did not go to such a length; and Seneca distinguishes himself from the followers of Stilpo by saying, 'Our sage feels trouble while he overcomes it, whereas theirs does not feel it at all.'[225]

IV.

So far, the sceptical theory had been put forward after a somewhat fragmentary fashion, and in strict dependence on the previous development of dogmatic philosophy. With the Humanists it had taken the form of an attack on physical science; with the Megarians, of a criticism on the Socratic dialectic; with both, it had been pushed to the length of an absolute negation, logically not more defensible than the affirmations to which it was opposed. What remained was that, after being consistently formulated, its results should be exhibited in their systematic bearing on the practical interests of mankind. The twofold task was accomplished by Pyrrho, whose name has accordingly continued to be associated, even in modern times, with the profession of universal doubt. This remarkable man was a native of Elis, where a branch of the Megarian school had at one time established itself; and it seems likely that the determining impulse of his life was, directly or indirectly, derived from Stilpo's teaching. A contemporary of Alexander the Great, he accompanied the Macedonian army on its march to India, subsequently returning to his native city, where he died at an advanced age, about 275 B.C. The absurd stories about his indifference to material obstacles when out walking have been already mentioned in a former chapter, and are sufficiently refuted by the circumstances just related. The citizens of Elis are said to have shown their respect for the philosopher by exempting him from taxation, appointing him their chief priest—no inappropriate office for a sceptic of the true type—and honouring his memory with a statue, which was still pointed out to sightseers in the time of Pausanias.[226]

Pyrrho, who probably no more believed in books than in anything else, never committed his opinions to writing; and what we know of them is derived from the reports of his disciples, which, again, are only preserved in a very incomplete form by the compilers of the empire. According to these, Pyrrho began by declaring that the philosophic problem might be summed up in the three following questions: 'What is the nature of things? What should be our relation to them? What is the practical consequence of this determination?' Of its kind, this statement is probably the best ever framed, and might be accepted with equal readiness by every school of thought. But the scepticism of Pyrrho at once reveals itself in his answer to the first question. We know nothing about things in themselves. Every assertion made respecting them is liable to be contradicted, and neither of the two opposing propositions deserves more credence than the other. The considerations by which Pyrrho attempts to establish this proposition were probably suggested by the systems of Plato and Aristotle. The only possible avenues of communication with the external world are, he tells us, sense and reason. Of these the former was so universally discredited that he seems to have regarded any elaborate refutation of its claims as superfluous. What we perceive by our senses is the appearance, not the reality of things. This is exactly what the Cyrenaics had already maintained. The inadequacy of reason is proved by a more original method. Had men any settled principles of judgment, they would agree on questions of conduct, for it is with regard to these that they are best informed, whereas the great variety of laws and customs shows that the exact opposite is true. They are more hopelessly divided on points of morality than on any other.[227] It will be remembered that Pyrrho's fellow-townsman, Hippias, had, about a hundred years earlier, founded his theory of Natural Law on the arbitrary and variable character of custom. The result of combining his principles with those professed by Protagoras and Gorgias was to establish complete moral scepticism; but it would be a mistake to suppose that moral distinctions had no value for him personally, or that they were neglected in his public teaching.

Pyrrho

Timon, a celebrated disciple of Pyrrho, added another and, from the speculative point of view, a much more powerful argument, which, however, may equally have been borrowed from the master's lectures. Readers of the Posterior Analytics will remember how strongly Aristotle dwells on the necessity of starting with first principles which are self-evidently true. The chain of demonstration must have something to hang on, it cannot be carried back ad infinitum. Now, Timon would not admit of such a thing as first principles. Every assumption, he says, must rest on some previous assumption, and as this process cannot be continued for ever, there can be no demonstration at all. This became a very favourite weapon with the later Sceptics, and, still at the suggestion of Aristotle, they added the further 'trope' of compelling their adversaries to choose between going back ad infinitum and reasoning in a circle—in other words, proving the premises by means of the conclusion. Modern science would not feel much appalled by the sceptical dilemma. Its actual first principles are only provisionally assumed as ultimate, and it is impossible for us to tell how much farther their analysis may be pursued; while, again, their validity is guaranteed by the circular process of showing that the consequences deduced from them agree with the facts of experience. But as against those modern philosophers who, in adherence to the Aristotelian tradition, still seek to base their systems on first principles independent of any individual experience, the sceptical argument is unanswerable, and has even been strengthened by the progress of knowledge. To this day, thinkers of different schools cannot agree about the foundations of belief, and what to one seems self-evidently true, is to another either conceivably or actually false. To Mr. Herbert Spencer the persistence of force is a necessary truth; to Prof. Stanley Jevons its creation is a perfectly possible contingency; while to others, again, the whole conception of force, as understood by Mr. Spencer, is so absolutely unmeaning that they would decline to entertain any proposition about the Invariability of the objective reality which it is supposed to represent. And when the à priori dogmatist affects to treat the negations of his opponents as something that they do not think, but only think they think, they may, with perfect fairness, attribute his rejection of their beliefs—as, for example, free-will—to a similar subjective illusion. Moreover, the pure experimentalists can point to a circumstance not foreseen by the ancient sceptics, which is that propositions once generally regarded as incontrovertible by thinking men, are now as generally abandoned by them.

Having proved, to his satisfaction, that the nature of things is unknowable, Pyrrho proceeds to deal with the two remaining heads of the philosophic problem. To the question what should be our relation to a universe which we cannot reach, the answer is, naturally, one of total indifference. And the advantage to be derived from this attitude is, he tells us, that we shall secure the complete imperturbability wherein true happiness consists. The sceptical philosophy does not agree with Stilpo in denying the reality of actual and immediate annoyances, for it denies nothing; but it professes to dispel that very large amount of unhappiness which arises from the pursuit of fancied goods and the expectation of future calamities. In respect to the latter, what Pyrrho sought was to arrive by the exercise of reasoning at the tranquillity which unreasoning animals naturally enjoy. Thus, we are told that, when out at sea in a storm, he called the attention of the terrified passengers to a little pig which was quietly feeding in spite of the danger, and taught them that the wise man should attain to a similar kind of composure.

Various other anecdotes of more or less doubtful authenticity are related, showing that the philosopher could generally, though not always, act up to his own ideal of indifference. He lived with his sister, who was a midwife by profession, and patiently submitted to the household drudgery which she unsparingly imposed on him. Once, however, she succeeded in goading him into a passion; and on being rather inopportunely reminded of his professed principles by a bystander, the sceptic tartly replied that a wretched woman like that was no fit subject for a display of philosophical indifference. On another occasion, when taunted for losing his self-possession at the attack of a furious dog, he observed, with truth, that, after all, philosophers are human beings.[228]

Thus we find Pyrrho competing with the dogmatists as a practical moralist, and offering to secure the inward tranquillity at which they too aimed by an easier method than theirs. The last eminent representative of the sceptical school, Sextus Empiricus, illustrates its pretensions in this respect by the well-known story of Apelles, who, after vainly endeavouring to paint the foam on a horse's mouth, took the sponge which he used to wipe his easel, and threw it at the picture in vexation. The mixture of colours thus accidentally applied produced the exact effect which he desired, but at which no calculation could arrive. In like manner, says Sextus, the confusion of universal doubt accidentally resulted in the imperturbability which accompanies suspense of judgment as surely as a body is followed by its shadow.[229] There was, however, no accident about the matter at all. The abandonment of those studies which related to the external world was a consequence of the ever-increasing attention paid to human interests, and that these could be best consulted by complete detachment from outward circumstances, was a conclusion inevitably suggested by the negative or antithetical moment of Greek thought. Hence, while the individualistic and apathetic tendencies of the age were shared by every philosophical school, they had a closer logical connexion with the idealistic than with the naturalistic method; and so it is among the successors of Protagoras that we find them developed with the greatest distinctness; while their incorporation with Stoicism imposed a self-contradictory strain on that system which it never succeeded in shaking off. Epicureanism occupied a position midway between the two extremes; and from this point of view, we shall be better able to understand both its inherent weakness as compared with the other ancient philosophies, and the admiration which it has attracted from opposite quarters in recent years. To some it is most interesting as a revelation of law in Nature, to others as a message of deliverance to man—not merely a deliverance from ignorance and passion, such as its rivals had promised, but from all established systems, whether religious, political, or scientific. And unquestionably Epicurus did endeavour to combine both points of view in his theory of life. In seeking to base morality on a knowledge of natural law he resembles the Stoics. In his attacks on fatalism, in his refusal to be bound down by a rigorously scientific explanation of phenomena, in his failure to recognise the unity and power of Nature, and in his preference of sense to reason, he partially reproduces the negative side of Scepticism; in his identification of happiness with the tranquil and imperturbable self-possession of mind, in his mild humanism, and in his compliance with the established religion of the land, he entirely reproduces its positive ethical teaching. On the other hand, the two sides of his philosophy, so far from completing, interfere with and mar one another. Emancipation from the outward world would have been far more effectually obtained by a total rejection of physical science than by the construction of a theory whose details were, on any scientific principles, demonstrably untrue. The appeal to natural instinct as an argument for hedonism would, consistently followed out, have led to one of two conclusions, either of which is incompatible with the principle that imperturbability is the highest good. If natural instinct, as manifested by brutes, by children, and by savages, be the one sure guide of action, then Callicles was right, and the habitual indulgence of passion is wiser than its systematic restraint. But if Nature is to be studied on a more specific and discriminating plan, if there are human as distinguished from merely animal impulses, and if the higher development of these should be our rule of life, then Plato and Aristotle and the Stoics were right, and the rational faculties should be cultivated for their own sake, not because of the immunity from superstitious terrors which they secure. And we may add that the attendance on public worship practised by Epicurus agreed much better with the sceptical suspense of judgment touching divine providence than with its absolute negation, whether accompanied or not by a belief in gods who are indifferent to sacrifice and prayer.

It was, no doubt, for these and similar reasons that all the most vigorous intellects of Hellas ranged themselves either on the Stoic or on the Sceptic side, leaving the halfhearted compromise of Epicurus to those who could not think out any one theory consistently, or who, like the Romans at first, were not acquainted with any system but his. Henceforth, during a period of some centuries, the whole philosophic movement is determined by the interaction of these two fundamental forces. The first effect of their conflict was to impose on Scepticism an important modification, illustrating its essentially parasitic character. We have seen it, as a general tendency of the Greek mind, clinging to the very texture of mythology, accompanying the earliest systematic compilation of facts, aiding the humanistic attacks on physical science, associated with the first great religious reaction, operating as the dialectic of dialectic itself, and finally assuming the form of a shadowy morality, in rivalry with and imitation of ethical systems based on a positive and substantial doctrine. We have now to trace its metamorphosis into a critical system extending its ramifications in parallelism with the immense dogmatic structure of Stoicism, and simultaneously endeavouring to reach the same practical results by a more elastic adaptation to the infirmities of human reason and the uncertainties of sensible experience. As such, we shall also have to study its influence over the most plastic of Roman intellects, the great orator in whose writings Greek philosophy was reclothed with something of its ancient charm, so that many who were debarred from admission to the groves and porticoes of Athens have caught an echo of the high debates which once stirred their recesses, as they trod the shady slopes of Tusculum under his visionary guidance, or followed his searching eyes over the blue waters to Pompeii, while he reasoned on mind and its object, on sense and knowledge, on doubt and certainty, with Lucullus and Hortensius, on the sunlight Baian shore. It is the history of the New Academy that we shall now proceed to trace.

V.

When we last had occasion to speak of the Platonic school, it was represented by Polemo, one of the teachers from whose lessons Zeno the Stoic seems to have compiled his system. Under his superintendence, Platonism had completely abandoned the metaphysical traditions of its founder. Physics and dialectics had already been absorbed by Aristotelianism. Mathematics had passed into the hands of experts. Nothing remained but the theory of ethics; and, as an ethical teacher, Polemo was only distinguished from the Cynics by the elegance and moderation of his tone. Even this narrow standing-ground became untenable when exposed to the formidable competition of Stoicism. The precept, Follow Nature, borrowed by the new philosophy from Polemo, acquired a far deeper significance than he could give it, when viewed in the light of an elaborate physical system showing what Nature was, and whither her guidance led. But stone after stone had been removed from the Platonic superstructure and built into the walls of other edifices, only to bring its original foundation the more prominently into sight. This was the initial doubt of Socrates, widened into the confession of universal ignorance attributed to him by Plato in the Apologia. Only by returning to the exclusively critical attitude with which its founder had begun could the Academy hope to exercise any influence on the subsequent course of Greek speculation. And it was also necessary that the agnostic standpoint should be taken much more in earnest by its new representatives than by Socrates or Plato. With them it had been merely the preparation for a dogmatism even more self-confident than that of the masters against whom they fought; but if in their time such a change of front might seem compatible with the retention of their old strongholds, matters now stood on a widely different footing. Experience had shown that the purely critical position could not be abandoned without falling back on some one or other of the old philosophies, or advancing pretensions inconsistent with the dialectic which had been illustrated by their overthrow. The course marked out for Plato's successors by the necessities of thought might have been less evident had not Pyrrhonism suddenly revealed to them where their opportunities lay, and at the same time, by its extinction as an independent school, allowed them to step into the vacant place.

It was at this juncture that the voluntary withdrawal of an older fellow-pupil placed Arcesilaus at the head of the Academy. The date of his accession is not given, but we are told that he died 241 or 240 B.C. in the seventy-fifth year of his age. He must, therefore, have flourished a generation later than Zeno and Epicurus. Accomplished, witty, and generous, his life is described by some as considerably less austere than that of the excellent nonentities whom he succeeded. Yet its general goodness was testified to by no less an authority than his contemporary, the noble Stoic, Cleanthes. 'Do not blame Arcesilaus,' exclaimed the latter to an unfriendly critic; 'if he denies duty in his words, he affirms it in his deeds.' 'You don't flatter me,' observed Arcesilaus. 'It is flattering you,' rejoined Cleanthes, 'to say that your actions belie your words.'[230] It might be inferred from this anecdote that the scepticism of the new teacher, like that of Carneades after him, was occasionally exercised on moral distinctions, which, as then defined and deduced, were assuredly open to very serious criticism. Even so, in following the conventional standard of the age, he would have been acting in perfect consistency with the principles of his school. But, as a matter of fact, his attacks seem to have been exclusively aimed at the Stoic criterion of certainty. We have touched on this difficult subject in a former chapter, but the present seems a more favourable opportunity for setting it forth in proper detail.

The Stoics held, as Mr. Herbert Spencer, who resembles them in so many respects, now holds, that all knowledge is ultimately produced by the action of the object on the subject. Being convinced, however, that each single perception, as such, is fallible, they sought for the criterion of certainty in the repetition and combination of individual impressions; and, again like Mr. Spencer, but also in complete accordance with their dynamic theory of Nature, they estimated the validity of a belief by the degree of tenacity with which it is held. The various stages of assurance were carefully distinguished and arranged in an ascending series. First came simple perception, then simple assent, thirdly, comprehension, and finally demonstrative science. These mental acts were respectively typified by extending the forefinger, by bending it as in the gesture of beckoning, by clenching the fist, and by placing it, thus clenched, in the grasp of the other hand. From another point of view, they defined a true conviction as that which can only be produced by the action of a corresponding real object on the mind. This theory was complicated still further by the Stoic interpretation of judgment as a voluntary act; by the ethical significance which it consequently received; and by the concentration of all wisdom in the person of an ideal sage. The unreserved bestowal of belief is a practical postulate dictated by the necessities of life; but only he who knows what those necessities are, in other words only the wise man, knows when the postulate is to be enforced. In short, the criterion of your being right is your conviction that you are right, and this conviction, if you really possess it, is a sufficient witness to its own veracity. Or again, it is the nature of man to act rightly, and he cannot do so unless he has right beliefs, confirmed and clinched by the consciousness that they are right.

Arcesilaus left no writings, and his criticisms on the Stoic theory, as reported by Cicero and Sextus Empiricus, have a somewhat unsatisfactory appearance. By what we can make out, he seems to have insisted on the infallibility of the wise man to a much greater extent than the Stoics themselves, not allowing that there was any class of judgments in which he was liable to be mistaken. But just as the Stoics were obliged to accept suicide as an indispensable safeguard for the inviolability of their personal dignity and happiness, so also Arcesilaus had recourse to a kind of intellectual suicide for the purpose of securing immunity from error. The only way, according to him, in which the sage can make sure of never being mistaken is never to be certain about anything. For, granting that every mental representation is produced by a corresponding object in the external world, still different objects are connected by such a number of insensible gradations that the impressions produced by them are virtually indistinguishable from one another; while a fertile source of illusions also exists in the diversity of impressions produced by the same object acting on different senses and at different times. Moreover, the Stoics themselves admitted that the sage might form a mistaken opinion; it was only for his convictions that they claimed unerring accuracy, each of the two—opinion and conviction—being the product of a distinct intellectual energy. Here again, Arcesilaus employed his method of infinitesimal transitions, refusing to admit that the various cognitive faculties could be separated by any hard and fast line; especially as, according to the theory then held by all parties, and by none more strongly than the Stoics, intellectual conceptions are derived exclusively from the data of sense and imagination. We can see that the logic of Scepticism is, equally with that of the other Greek systems, determined by the three fundamental moments of Greek thought. There is first the careful circumscription of certainty; then there is the mediating process by which it is insensibly connected with error; and, lastly, as a result of this process, there is the antithetical opposition of a negative to an affirmative proposition on every possible subject of mental representation.[231]

To the objection that his suspensive attitude would render action impossible, Arcesilaus replied that any mental representation was sufficient to set the will in motion; and that, in choosing between different courses, probability was the most rational means of determination. But the task of reducing probable evidence to a system was reserved for a still abler dialectician, who did not appear on the scene until a century after his time. Arcesilaus is commonly called the founder of the Middle, Carneades the founder of the New Academy. The distinction is, however, purely nominal. Carneades founded nothing. His principles were identical with those of his predecessor; and his claim to be considered the greatest of the Greek sceptics is due to his having given those principles a wider application and a more systematic development. The Stoics regarded it as a special dispensation of providence that Chrysippus, the organising genius of their school, should have come between its two most formidable opponents, being thus placed in a position to answer the objections of the one and to refute by anticipation those of the other.[232] It might seem to less prejudiced observers that the thinker whose cause benefited most by this arrangement was Carneades. Parodying a well-known iambic, he used to say:

'Without Chrysippus I should not have been.'[233]

And, in fact, it was by a close study of that writer's voluminous treatises that he was able to cover the immense extent of ground which Scepticism thenceforward disputed with the dogmatic schools. Nor were his attacks directed against Stoicism only, but against all other positive systems past and present as well. What he says about the supposed foundation of knowledge is even now an unanswerable objection to the transcendental realism of Mr Herbert Spencer. States of consciousness speak for themselves alone, they do not include the consciousness of an external cause.[234] But the grounds on which he rests his negation of all certainty are still superficial enough, being merely those sensible illusions which the modern science of observation has been able either to eliminate altogether or to restrict within narrow and definable limits. That phenomena, so far from being necessarily referred to a cause which is not phenomenal, cannot be thought of at all except in relation to one another, and that knowledge means nothing more than a consciousness of this relation, was hardly perceived before the time of Hume.

Turning from sense to reason, Carneades attacks the syllogistic process on grounds already specified in connexion with the earlier Sceptics; and also on the plea that to prove the possibility of syllogism is itself to syllogise, and thus involves either a petitio principii or a regress ad infinitum.[235] Such a method is, of course, suicidal, for it disproves the possibility of the alleged disproof, a consideration which the Stoics did not fail to urge, and which the later Sceptics could only meet by extending the rule of suspense to their own arguments against argument.[236] Nevertheless the sceptical analysis detected some difficulties in the ordinary theory of logic, which have been revived in modern times, and have not yet received any satisfactory solution. Sextus Empiricus, probably copying an earlier authority, it may be Carneades himself, observes that, as the major premise of every syllogism virtually contains the minor, it is either superfluous, or assumes the proposition to be proved. Thus we argue that Socrates is an animal because he is a man, and all men are animals. But if we do not know this latter proposition to be true in the case of Socrates, we cannot be sure that it is true in any case; while if we know it to be true in his case, we do not need to begin by stating it in general terms. And he also attempts to show the impossibility of a valid induction by the consideration, since so often urged, that to generalise from a limited number of instances to a whole class is unsafe, for some of the unknown instances may be contradictory, while the infinite, or at least indefinite multiplicity of individuals precludes the possibility of their exhaustive enumeration.[237]

When the Academicians pass from the form to the matter of dogmatic philosophy, their criticisms acquire greater interest and greater weight. On this ground, their assaults are principally directed against the theology of their Stoic and Epicurean rivals. It is here in particular that Carneades reveals himself to us as the Hume of antiquity. Never has the case for agnosticism been more powerfully made out than by him or by the disciples whom he inspired. To the argument for the existence of supernatural beings derived from universal consent, he replies, first, that the opinion of the vulgar is worthless, and secondly, that men's beliefs about the gods are hopelessly at variance with one another, even the same divinity being made the subject of numberless discordant legends.[238] He reduces the polytheistic deification of natural objects to an absurdity by forcing it back through a series of insensible gradations into absolute fetichism.[239] The personification of mental qualities is similarly treated, until an hypothesis is provided for every passing mood.[240] Then, turning to the more philosophical deism of the Stoics, he assails their theory of the divine benevolence with instance after instance of the apparent malevolence and iniquity to be found in Nature; vividly reminding one of the facts adduced by Mr. Herbert Spencer in confutation of the similar views held by modern English theologians.[241] As against the whole theory of final causes, Carneades argues after a method which, though logically sound, could not then present itself with the authority which advancing science has more recently shown it to possess. 'What you Stoics,' he says, 'explain as the result of conscious purpose, other philosophers, like Strato for instance, explain with equal plausibility as the result of natural causation. And such is our ignorance of the forces at work in Nature that even where no mechanical cause can be assigned, it would be presumptuous to maintain that none can exist.[242] The reign of law does not necessarily prove the presence of intelligence; it is merely the evidence of a uniform movement quite consistent with all that we know about the working of unconscious forces.[243] To contend, with Socrates, that the human mind must be derived from a Universal Mind pervading all Nature would logically involve the transfer of every human attribute to its original source.[244] And to say that the Supreme Being, because it surpasses man, must possess an intelligence like his, is no more rational than to make the same assumption with regard to a great city because it is superior to an ant.'[245]

The materialism of his dogmatic contemporaries placed them at a terrible disadvantage when the sceptical successor of Plato went on to show that eternal duration is incompatible with whatever we know about the constitution of corporeal substance; and this part of his argument applied as much to the Epicurean as to the Stoic religion.[246] But even a spiritualistic monotheism is not safe from his dissolving criticism. According to Carneades, a god without senses has no experience of whatever pleasurable or painful feelings accompany sensation, and is therefore, to that extent, more ignorant than a man; while to suppose that he experiences painful sensations is the same as making him obnoxious to the diminished vitality and eventual death with which they are naturally associated. And, generally speaking, all sensation involves a modification of the sentient subject by an external object, a condition necessarily implying the destructibility of the former by the latter.[247] So also, moral goodness is an essentially relative quality, inconceivable without the possibility of succumbing to temptation, which we cannot attribute to a perfect Being.[248] In a word, whatever belongs to conscious life being relative and conditioned, personality is excluded from the absolute by its very definition.

As to the proofs of divine agency derived from divination, they are both irrational and weak. If all things are predetermined by God's providence, knowledge of the future is useless, and, therefore, cannot have been given to us. Moreover, no confidence can be placed in the alleged fulfilments of prophecy; probably most of them are fictitious and the remainder accidental. For the rest, good luck is distributed without regard to merit; and the general corruption of mankind shows that, from the Stoic point of view, human nature is a complete failure.[249]

Well may M. Havet say of the Academicians: 'ce sont eux et non les partisans d'Epicure qui sont les libres penseurs de l'antiquité ou qui l'auraient voulu être; mais ils ne le pouvaient pas.'[250] They could not, for their principles were as inconsistent with an absolute negation as with an absolute affirmation; while in practice their rule was, as we have said, conformity to the custom of the country; the consequence of which was that Sceptics and Epicureans were equally assiduous in their attendance at public worship. It is, therefore, with perfect dramatic appropriateness that Cicero puts the arguments of Carneades into the mouth of Cotta, the Pontifex Maximus; and, although himself an augur, takes the negative side in a discussion on divination with his brother Quintus. And our other great authority on the sceptical side, Sextus Empiricus, is not less emphatic than Cotta in protesting his devotion to the traditional religion of the land.[251]

We have seen with what freedom Carneades discussed the foundations of morality. It is now evident that in so doing he did not exceed the legitimate functions of criticism. No one at the present day looks on Prof. Bain and Mr. Henry Sidgwick as dangerous teachers because they have made it clear that to pursue the greatest happiness of the greatest number is not always the way to secure a maximum of happiness for oneself. The really dangerous method, as we now see, is to foster illusions in early life which subsequent experience must dispel.

With the introduction of practical questions, we pass to the great positive achievement of Carneades, his theory of probable evidence. Intended as an account of the process by which belief is adjusted to safe action rather than of the process by which it is brought into agreement with reality, his logic is a systematisation of the principles by which prudent men are unconsciously guided in common life. Carneades distinguishes three degrees of probability. The lowest is attached to simple perception. This arises when we receive the impression of an object without taking the attendant circumstances into account. The next step is reached when our first impression is confirmed by the similar impressions received from its attendant circumstances; and when each of these, again, bears the test of a similar examination our assurance is complete. The first belief is simply probable; the second is probable and uncontradicted; the third probable, uncontradicted, and methodically established. The example given by Sextus is that of a person who on seeing a coil of rope in a dark passage thinks that it may be a snake, and jumps over it, but on turning round and observing that it remains motionless feels inclined to form a different opinion. Remembering, however, that snakes are sometimes congealed by cold in winter, he touches the coil with his stick, and finally satisfies himself by means of this test that the image present to his mind does not really represent a snake. The circumstances to be examined before arriving at a definite judgment include such considerations as whether our senses are in a healthy condition, whether we are wide awake, whether the air is clear, whether the object is steady, and whether we have taken time enough to be sure that the conditions here specified are fulfilled. Each degree of probability is, again, divisible into several gradations according to the strength of the impressions received and the greater or less consilience of all the circumstances involved.[252]

The Academic theory of probability bears some resemblance to the Canonic of Epicurus, and may have been partially suggested by it. Both are distinguished from the Aristotelian and Stoic logic by the care with which they provide for the absence of contradictory evidence. In this point, however, the superiority of Carneades to Epicurus is very marked. It is not enough for him that a present impression should suggest a belief not inconsistent with past experience; in the true inductive spirit, he expressly searches for negative instances, and recommends the employment of experiment for this purpose. Still more philosophical is the careful and repeated analysis of attendant circumstances, a precaution not paralleled by anything in the slovenly method of his predecessor. Here the great value of scepticism as an element in mental training becomes at once apparent. The extreme fallibility of the intellectus sibi permissus had to be established before precautions could be adopted for its restraint. But the evidence accepted in proof of this fallibility has been very different at different times, and has itself given rise to more than one fallacious interpretation. With us it is, for the most part, furnished by experience. The circumstance that many demonstrable errors were formerly received as truths is quite sufficient to put us on our guard against untested opinions. With Bacon, it was not the erroneousness of previous systems, but their barrenness and immobility, which led him to question the soundness of their logic; and his doubts were confirmed by an analysis of the disturbing influences under which men's judgments are formed. The ancient Sceptics were governed entirely by à priori considerations. Finding themselves confronted by an immense mass of contradictory opinions, they argued that some of these must be false as all could not possibly be true. And an analysis of the human faculties led them, equally on à priori grounds, to the conclusion that these irreconcilable divergences were but the result and the reproduction of an interminable conflict carried on within the mind itself. They could not foresee how much time would do towards reducing the disagreement of educated opinion within a narrower compass. They did not know what the experience of experience itself would teach. And their criticisms on the logic and metaphysics of their opponents were rendered inconclusive, as against all certainty, by the extent to which they shared that logic and metaphysics themselves. Carneades, at least, seems to assume throughout that all existence is material, that there is a sharp distinction between subject and object in knowledge, and that there is an equally sharp distinction between sensation and reasoning in the processes by which knowledge is obtained. In like manner, his ethical scepticism all turns on the axiom, also shared by him with the Stoics, that for a man to be actuated by any motive but his own interest is mere folly.

Modern agnosticism occupies the same position with regard to the present foundation and possible future extension of human knowledge as was occupied by the ancient Sceptics with regard to the possibility of all knowledge. Its conclusions also are based on a very insufficient experience of what can be effected by experience, and on an analysis of cognition largely adopted from the system which it seeks to overthrow. Like Scepticism also, when logically thought out, it tends to issue in a self-contradiction, at one time affirming the consciousness of what is, by definition, beyond consciousness; and at another time dogmatically determining the points on which we must remain for ever ignorant. It may be that some problems, as stated by modern thinkers, are insoluble; but perhaps we may find our way our of them by transforming the question to be solved.

If, in the domain of pure speculation, contemporary agnosticism exaggerates the existing divergences, in ethics its whole effort is, contrariwise, to reduce and reconcile them. Such was also the tendency of Carneades. He declared that, in their controversy about the highest good, the difference between the Stoics and the Peripatetics was purely verbal. Both held that we are naturally framed for the pursuit of certain objects, and that virtuous living is the only means by which they can be attained. But while the disciples of Aristotle held that the satisfaction of our natural impulses remains from first to last the only end, the disciples of Zeno insisted that at some point—not, as would seem very particularly specified—virtuous conduct, which was originally the means towards this satisfaction, becomes substituted for it as the supreme and ultimate good.[253] That the point at issue was more important than it seemed is evident from its reproduction under another form in modern ethical philosophy. For, among ourselves, the controversy between utilitarianism and what, for want of a better name, we must call intuitionism, is gradually narrowing itself to the question whether the pursuit of another's good has or has not a higher value than the quantity of pleasure which accrues to him from it, plus the effects of a good example and the benefits that society at large is likely to gain from the strength which exercise gives to the altruistic dispositions of one of its members. Those who attribute an absolute value to altruism, as such, connect this value in some way or other with the spiritual welfare of the agent; and they hold that without such a gain to himself he would gradually fall back on a life of calculating selfishness or of unregulated impulse. Here we have the return from a social to an individual morality. The Stoics, conversely, were feeling their way from the good of the individual to that of the community; and they could only bridge the chasm by converting what had originally been a means towards self-preservation into an end in itself. This Carneades could not see. Convinced that happiness was both necessary and attainable, but convinced also that the systems which had hitherto offered it as their reward were logically untenable, he wished to place morality on the broad basis of what was held in common by all schools, and this seemed to be the rule of obedience to Nature's dictates,—a rule which had also the great merit of bidding men do in the name of philosophy what they already felt inclined to do without any philosophy at all. We are told, indeed, that he would not commit himself to any particular system of ethics; the inference, however, is not that he ignored the necessity of a moral law, but that he wished to extricate it from a compromising alliance with untenable speculative dogmas. Nevertheless his acceptance of Nature as a real entity was a survival of metaphysics; and his morality was, so far as it went, an incipient return to the traditions of the Old Academy.

VI.

We have now reached a point where Greek philosophy seems to have swung back into the position which it occupied three hundred years before, towards the close of the Peloponnesian War. The ground is again divided between naturalists and humanists, the one school offering an encyclopaedic training in physical science and exact philology, the other literary, sceptical, and limiting its attention to the more immediate interests of life; but both agreeing in the supreme importance of conduct, and differing chiefly as to whether its basis should or should not be sought in a knowledge of the external world. Materialism is again in the ascendant, to this extent at least, that no other theory is contemplated by the students of physical science; while the promise of a spiritualistic creed is to be found, if at all, in the school whose scepticism throws it back on the subjective sphere, the invisible and impalpable world of mind. The attitude of philosophy towards religion has, indeed, undergone a marked change; for the Stoic naturalists count themselves among the most strenuous supporters of beliefs and practices which their Sophistic predecessors had contemned, while the humanist criticism is cautiously guarded by at least an external conformity to established usage; but the Platonic doctrine of immortality has disappeared with the dogmatic spiritualism on which it rested; and faith in superior beings tends to dissociate itself from morality, or to become identified with a simple belief in the fixity of natural law.

Whenever naturalism and scepticism have thus stood opposed, the result has been their transformation or absorption into a new philosophy, combining the systematic formalism of the one with the introspective idealism of the other. In Greece such a revolution had already been effected once before by Plato; and a restoration of his system seemed the most obvious solution that could offer itself on the present occasion. Such was, in fact, the solution eventually adopted; what we have to explain is why its adoption was delayed so long. For this various reasons may be offered. To begin with, the speculative languor of the age was unfavourable to the rise of a new school. Greece was almost depopulated by the demands of foreign service; and at Alexandria, where a new centre of Hellenism had been created, its best energies were absorbed by the cultivation of positive science. It was, no doubt, in great part owing to the dearth of ability that ideas which, at an earlier period, would have been immediately taken up and developed, were allowed to remain stationary for a hundred years—the interval separating a Carneades from an Arcesilaus. The regular organisation of philosophical teaching was another hindrance to progress. A certain amount of property was annexed to the headships of the different schools, and served as an endowment, not of research but of contented acquiescence in the received traditions. Moreover, the jealousy with which the professors of rival doctrines would naturally regard one another, was likely to prevent their mutual approximation from going beyond certain not very close limits, and might even lead to a still severer definition of the characteristic tenets which still kept them apart. Another and deeper disturbing force lay in the dissensions which, at a very early stage of its development, had split the spiritualistic philosophy into two opposing tendencies respectively represented by Plato and Aristotle. Any thinker who wandered away from the principles either of Stoicism or of Scepticism was more likely to find himself bewildered by the conflicting claims of these two illustrious masters, than to discern the common ground on which they stood, or to bring them within the grasp of a single reconciling system. Finally, an enormous perturbation in the normal course of speculation was produced by the entrance of Rome on the philosophical scene. But before estimating the influence of this new force, we must follow events to the point at which it first becomes of calculable importance.

We have seen how Carneades, alike in his theory of probability and in his ethical eclecticism, had departed from the extreme sceptical standpoint. His successor, Clitomachus, was content with committing the doctrines of the master to writing. A further step was taken by the next Scholarch, Philo, who is known as the Larissaean, in order to distinguish him from his more celebrated namesake, the Alexandrian Jew. This philosopher asserted that the negations of the New Academy were not to be taken as a profession of absolute scepticism, but merely as a criticism on the untenable pretensions of the Stoa. His own position was that, as a matter of fact, we have some certain knowledge of the external world, but that no logical account can be given of the process by which it is obtained—we can only say that such an assurance has been naturally stamped on our minds.[254] This is the theory of intuitions or innate ideas, still held by many persons; and, as such, it marks a return to pure Platonism, having been evidently suggested by the semi-mythological fancies of the Meno and the Phaedrus. With Philo as with those Scotch professors who long afterwards took up substantially the same position, the leading motive was a practical one, the necessity of placing morality on some stronger ground than that of mere probability. Neither he nor his imitators saw that if ethical principles are self-evident, they need no objective support; if they are derivative and contingent, they cannot impart to metaphysics a certainty which they do not independently possess. The return to the old Academic standpoint was completed by a much more vigorous thinker than Philo, his pupil, opponent, and eventual successor, Antiochus. So far from attempting any compromise with the Sceptics, this philosopher openly declared that they had led the school away from its true traditions; and claimed for his own teaching the merit of reproducing the original doctrine of Plato.[255] In reality, he was, as Zeller has shown, an eclectic.[256] It is by arguments borrowed from Stoicism that he vindicates the certainty of human knowledge. Pushing the practical postulate to its logical conclusion, he maintains, not only that we are in possession of the truth, but also—what Philo had denied—that true beliefs bear on their face the evidence by which they are distinguished from illusions. Admitting that the senses are liable to error, he asserts the possibility of rectifying their mistakes, and of reasoning from a subjective impression to its objective cause. The Sceptical negation of truth he meets with the familiar argument that it is suicidal, for to be convinced that there can be no conviction is a contradiction in terms; while to argue that truth is indistinguishable from falsehood implies an illogical confidence in the validity of logical processes; besides involving the assumption that there are false appearances and that they are known to us as such, which would be impossible unless we were in a position to compare them with the corresponding truths.[257] For his own part, Antiochus adopted without alteration the empirical theory of Chrysippus, according to which knowledge is elaborated by reflection out of the materials supplied by sense. His physics were also those of Stoicism with a slight Peripatetic admixture, but without any modification of their purely materialistic character. In ethics he remained truer to the Academic tradition, refusing to follow the Stoics in their absolute isolation of virtue from vice, and of happiness from external circumstances, involving as it did the equality of all transgressions and the worthlessness of worldly goods. But the disciples of the Porch had made such large concessions to common sense by their theories of preference and of progress, that even here there was very little left to distinguish his teaching from theirs.[258]

Meanwhile a series of Stoic thinkers had also been feeling their way towards a compromise with Plato and Aristotle, which, so far as it went, was a step in the direction of spiritualism. We have seen, in a former chapter, how one of the great distinguishing marks of Stoicism, as compared with the systems immediately preceding it, was the substitution of a pervading monism for their antithesis between God and the world, between heaven and earth, between reason and sense. It will be remembered also that this monistic creed was associated with a return to the Heracleitean theory that the world is periodically destroyed by fire. Now, with reference to three out of these four points, Boêthus, a Stoic contemporary of Carneades, returned to the Aristotelian doctrine. While still holding to the materialism of his own school, including a belief in the corporeal nature of the divinity, he separated God from the world, and represented him as governing its movements from without; the world itself he maintained to be eternal; and in the mind of man he recognised reason or nous as an independent source of conviction. In his cosmology, Boêthus was followed by a more celebrated master, Panaetius, who also adopted the Aristotelian rationalism so far as to deny the continued existence of the soul after death, and to repudiate the belief in divination which Stoicism had borrowed from popular superstition; while in psychology he partially restored the distinction between life and mind which had been obliterated by his predecessors.[259] The dualistic theory of mind was carried still further by Posidonius, the most eminent Stoic of the first century B.C. This very learned and accomplished master, while returning in other points to a stricter orthodoxy, was led to admit the Platonic distinction between reason and passion, and to make it the basis of his ethical system.[260] But the Platonising tendencies of Posidonius had no more power than those of Antiochus to effect a true spiritualistic revival, since neither they nor any of their contemporaries had any genius for metaphysical speculation; while the increased attention paid to Aristotle did not extend to the fundamental principles of his system, which, even within the Peripatetic school, were so misconceived as to be interpreted in a thoroughly materialistic sense.[261]

A distinct parallelism may be traced in the lines of evolution along which we have accompanied our two opposing schools. While the Academicians were coming over to the Stoic theory of cognition, the Stoics themselves were moving in the same general direction, and seeking for an external reality more in consonance with their notions of certainty than the philosophy of their first teachers could supply. For, as originally constituted, Stoicism included a large element of scepticism, which must often have laid its advocates open to the charge of inconsistency from those who accepted the same principle in a more undiluted form. The Heracleitean flux adopted by Zeno as the physical basis of his system, was much better suited to a sceptical than to a dogmatic philosophy, as the use to which it was put by Protagoras and Plato sufficiently proved; and this was probably the reason why Boêthus and Panaetius partially discarded it in favour of a more stable cosmology. The dialectical studies of the school also tended to suggest more difficulties than they could remove. The comprehensive systematisation of Chrysippus, like that of Plato and Aristotle, had for its object the illustration of each topic from every point of view, and especially from the negative as well as from the positive side. The consequence was that his indefatigable erudition had collected a great number of logical puzzles which he had either neglected or found himself unable to solve. There would, therefore, be a growing inclination to substitute a literary and rhetorical for a logical training: and as we shall presently see, there was an extraneous influence acting in the same direction. Finally, the rigour of Stoic morality had been strained to such a pitch that its professors were driven to admit the complete ideality of virtue. Their sage had never shown himself on earth, at least within the historical period; and the whole world of human interests being, from the rational point of view, either a delusion or a failure, stood in permanent contradiction to their optimistic theory of Nature. The Sceptics were quite aware of this practical approximation to their own views, and sometimes took advantage of it to turn the tables on their opponents with telling effect. Thus, on the occasion of that philosophical embassy with an account of which the present chapter began, when a noble Roman playfully observed to Carneades, 'You must think that I am not a Praetor as I am not a sage, and that Rome is neither a city nor a state,' the great Sceptic replied, turning to his colleague Diogenes, 'That is what my Stoic friend here would say.'[262] And Plutarch, in two sharp attacks on the Stoics, written from the Academic point of view, and probably compiled from documents of a much earlier period,[263] charges them with outraging common sense by their wholesale practical negations, to at least as great an extent as the Sceptics outraged it by their suspense of judgment. How the ethical system of Stoicism was modified so as to meet these criticisms has been related in a former chapter; and we have just seen how Posidonius, by his partial return to the Platonic psychology, with its division between reason and impulse, contributed to a still further change in the same conciliatory sense.

VII.

We have now reached a point in history where the Greek intellect seems to be struck with a partial paralysis, continuing for a century and a half. During that period, its activity—what there is of it—is shown only in criticism and erudition. There is learning, there is research, there is acuteness, there is even good taste, but originality and eloquence are extinct. Is it a coincidence, or is it something more, that this interval of sterility should occur simultaneously with the most splendid period of Latin literature, and that the new birth of Greek culture should be followed by the decrepitude and death of the Latin muse? It is certain that in modern Europe, possessing as it does so many independent sources of vitality, the flowering-times of different countries rarely coincide; England and Spain, from the middle of the sixteenth to the middle of the seventeenth century, being the only instances that we can recall of two countries almost simultaneously reaching the highest point of their literary development. Possibly, during the great age of Latin literature, all the most aspiring Greeks found employment as tutors in Roman families; while the reading public of the West were too much absorbed by the masterpieces composed in their own language, or too elated with the consciousness of a new superiority, to encourage the rivalry of those from whom they had wrested not only poetical independence, but also, what till then had never been disputed with the Greeks, supreme dominion in the world of mind. It is, at any rate, significant that while Greek was the favourite language of Roman lovers in the time of Lucretius and again in the time of Juvenal, there are no allusions to its having been employed by them during the intermediate period.[264] Be this as it may, from the fall of the Republic to the time of Trajan, philosophy, like poetry and eloquence—or at least all philosophy that was positive and practical—became domiciled in Rome, and received the stamp of the Roman character. How Stoicism was affected by the change has been pointed out in a former chapter. What we have now to study is chiefly the reaction of Rome on the Greek mind, and its bearing on the subsequent development of thought.

This reaction had begun to make itself felt long before the birth of a philosophical literature in the Latin language. It may be traced to the time when the lecture-halls at Athens were first visited by Roman students, and Greek professors first received on terms of intimate companionship into the houses of Roman nobles. In each instance, but more especially in the latter, not only would the pupil imbibe new ideas from the master, but the master would suit his teaching to the tastes and capacities of the pupil. The result would be an intellectual condition somewhat resembling that which attended the popularisation of philosophy in Athens during the latter half of the fifth century B.C.; and all the more so as speculation had already spontaneously reverted to the Sophistic standpoint. The parallel will be still more complete if we take the word Sophist in its original and comprehensive sense. We may then say that while Carneades, with his entrancing eloquence and his readiness to argue both sides of a question, was the Protagoras of the new movement; Panaetius, the dignified rationalist and honoured friend of Laelius and the younger Scipio, its Prodicus; and Posidonius, the astronomer and encyclopaedic scholar, its Hippias, Phaedrus the Epicurean was its Anaxagoras or Democritus.

The Epicurean philosophy was, in fact, the first to gain a footing in Rome; and it thereby acquired a position of comparative equality with the other schools, to which it was not really entitled, but which it has ever since succeeded in maintaining. The new doctrine fell like a spark on a mass of combustible material. The Romans were full of curiosity about Nature and her workings; full of contempt for the degrading Etruscan superstitions which hampered them at every turn, and the falsity of which was proving too much even for the official gravity of their state-appointed interpreters; full of impatience at the Greek mythology which was beginning to substitute itself for the severe abstractions of their own more spiritual faith;[265] full of loathing for the Asiatic orgies which were being introduced into the highest society of their own city. Epicureanism offered them a complete and easily intelligible theory of the world, which at the same time came as a deliverance from supernatural terrors. The consequence was that its different parts were thrown out of perspective, and their relative importance almost reversed. Originally framed as an ethical system with certain physical and theological implications, it was interpreted by Lucretius, and apparently also by his Roman predecessors,[266] as a scientific and anti-religious system, with certain references to conduct neither very prominently brought forward nor very distinctly conceived. And we know from the contents of the papyrus rolls discovered at Herculaneum, that those who studied the system in its original sources paid particular attention to the voluminous physical treatises of Epicurus, as well as to the theological works of his successors. Nor was this change of front limited to Epicureanism, if, as we may suspect, the rationalistic direction taken by Panaetius was due, at least in part, to a similar demand on the side of his Roman admirers.

But what had happened once before when philosophy was taken up by men of the world, repeated itself on this occasion. Attention was diverted from speculative to ethical problems, or at least to issues lying on the borderland between speculation and practice, such as those relating to the criterion of truth and the nature of the highest good. On neither of these topics had Epicureanism a consistent answer to give, especially when subjected to the cross-examination of rival schools eager to secure Roman favour for their own doctrines. Stated under any form, the Epicurean morality could not long satisfy the conquerors of the world. To some of them it would seem a shameful dereliction of duty, to others an irksome restraint on self-indulgence, while all would be alienated by its declared contempt for the general interests of culture and ambition. Add to this that the slightest acquaintance with astronomy, as it was then taught in Hellenic countries, would be fatal to a belief in the Epicurean physics, and we shall understand that the cause for which Lucretius contended was already lost before his great poem saw the light.

The requirements which Epicureanism failed to meet, were, to a great extent, satisfied by Stoicism. This philosophy had, from a comparatively early period, won the favour of a select class, but had been temporarlly overshadowed by the popularity of its hedonistic and anti-religious rival, when a knowledge of the Greek systems first became diffused through Italy. The uncouth language of the early Stoics and the apparently unpractical character of their theories doubtless exercised a repellent effect on many who were not out of sympathy with their general spirit. These difficulties were overcome first by Panaetius, and then, to a still greater extent, by Posidonius, the elder contemporary and friend of Pompeius and Cicero, who was remarkable not only for his enormous learning but also for his oratorical talent.[267] It seems probable that the lessons of this distinguished man marked the beginning of that religious reaction which eventually carried all before it. We have already seen how he abandoned the rationalistic direction struck out by his predecessor, Panaetius; and his return to the old

Stoic orthodoxy may very well have responded to a revival of religious feeling among the educated Roman public, who by this time must have discovered that there were other ways of escaping from superstition besides a complete rejection of the supernatural.

The triumph of Stoicism was, however, retarded by the combined influence of the Academic and Peripatetic schools. Both claimed the theory of a morality founded on natural law as a doctrine of their own, borrowed from them without acknowledgment by the Porch, and restated under an offensively paradoxical form. To a Roman, the Academy would offer the further attraction of complete immunity from the bondage of a speculative system, freedom of enquiry limited only by the exigencies of practical life, and a conveniently elastic interpretation of the extent to which popular faiths might be accepted as true. If absolute suspense of judgment jarred on his moral convictions, it was ready with accommodations and concessions. We have seen how the scepticism of Carneades was first modified by Philo, and then openly renounced by Philo's successor, Antiochus. Roman influence may have been at work with both; for Philo spent some time in the capital of the empire, whither he was driven by the events of the first Mithridatic War; while Antiochus was the friend of Lucullus and the teacher of Cicero.[268]

VIII.

The greatest of Roman orators and writers was also the first Roman that held opinions of his own in philosophy. How much original thought occurs in his voluminous contributions to the literature of the subject is more than we can determine, the Greek authorities on which he drew being known almost exclusively through the references to them contained in his disquisitions. But, judging from the evidence before us, carefully sifted as it has been by

German scholars, we should feel disposed to assign him a foremost rank among the thinkers of an age certainly not distinguished either for fertility or for depth of thought. It seems clear that he gave a new basis to the eclectic tendencies of his contemporaries, and that this basis was subsequently accepted by other philosophers whose speculative capacity has never been questioned.

Cicero

Cicero describes himself as an adherent of the New Academy, and expressly claims to have reasserted its principles after they had fallen into neglect among the Greeks, more particularly as against his own old master Antiochus, whose Stoicising theory of cognition he agrees with Philo in repudiating.[269] Like Philo also, he bases certainty on the twofold ground of a moral necessity for acting on our beliefs,[270] and the existence of moral intuitions, or natural tendencies to believe in the mind itself;[271] or, perhaps, more properly speaking, on the single ground of a moral sense. This, as already stated, was unquestionably a reproduction of the Platonic ideas under their subjective aspect. But in his general views about the nature and limits of human knowledge, Cicero leaves the Academy behind him, and goes back to Socrates. Perhaps no two men of great genius could be more unlike than these two,—for us the most living figures in ancient history if not in all history,—the Roman being as much a type of time-servingness and vacillation as the Athenian was of consistency and resolute independence. Yet, in its mere external results, the philosophy of Socrates is perhaps more faithfully reproduced by Cicero than by any subsequent enquirer; and the differences between them are easily accounted for by the long interval separating their ages from one another. Each set out with the same eager desire to collect knowledge from every quarter; each sought above all things for that kind of knowledge which seemed to be of the greatest practical importance; and each was led to believe that this did not include speculations relating to the physical world; one great motive to the partial scepticism professed by both being the irreconcilable disagreement of those who had attempted an explanation of its mysteries. The deeper ground of man's ignorance in this respect was stated somewhat differently by each; or perhaps we should say that the same reason is expressed in a mythical form by the one and in a scientific form by the other. Socrates held that the nature of things is a secret which the gods have reserved for themselves; while, in Cicero's opinion, the heavens are so remote, the interior of the earth so dark, the mechanism of our own bodies so complicated and subtle, as to be placed beyond the reach of fruitful observation.[272] Nor did this deprivation seem any great hardship to either, since, as citizens of great and free states, both were pre-eminently interested in the study of social life; and it is characteristic of their common tendency that both should have been not only great talkers and observers but also great readers of ancient literature.[273]

With regard to ethics, there is, of course, a great difference between the innovating, creative genius of the Greek and the receptive but timid intelligence of the Roman. Yet the uncertainty which, in the one case, was due to the absence of any fixed system, is equally present in the other, owing to the embarrassment of having so many systems among which to choose. Three ethical motives were constantly present to the thoughts of Socrates: the utility of virtue, from a material point of view, to the individual; its social necessity; and its connexion with the dual constitution of man as a being composed of two elements whereof the one is infinitely superior to the other; but he never was able, or never attempted to co-ordinate them under a single principle. His successors tried to discover such a principle in the idea of natural law, but could neither establish nor apply it in a satisfactory manner. Cicero reproduces the Socratic elements, sometimes in their original dispersion and confusion, sometimes with the additional complication and perplexity introduced by the idea through which it had been hoped to systematise and reconcile them. To him, indeed, that idea was even more important than to the Greek moralists; for he looked on Nature as the common ground where philosophy and untrained experience might meet for mutual confirmation and support.[274] We have seen how he adopted the theory—as yet not very clearly formulated—of a moral sense, or general faculty of intuition, from Philo. To study and obey the dictates of this faculty, as distinguished from the depraving influence of custom, was his method of arriving at truth and right. But if, when properly consulted, it always gave the same response, a similar unanimity might be expected in the doctrines of the various philosophical schools; and the adhesion of Academicians, Peripatetics, and Stoics to the precept, Follow Nature, seemed to demonstrate that such an agreement actually existed. Hence Cicero over and over again labours to prove that their disputes were merely verbal, and that Stoicism in particular had borrowed its ethics wholesale from his own favourite sect. Yet from time to time their discrepancies would force themselves on his notice; and by none have the differences separating Stoicism from its rivals been stated with more clearness, concision, and point.[275] These relate to the absolute self-sufficingness of virtue, its unity, and the incompatibility of emotion with its exercise. But Cicero seems to have regarded the theory of preference and rejection as a concession to common sense amounting to a surrender of whatever was parodoxical and exclusive in the Stoic standpoint.[276] And with respect to the question round which controversy raged most fiercely, namely, whether virtue was the sole or merely the chief condition of happiness, Cicero, as a man of the world, considered that it was practically of no consequence which side prevailed.[277] It would be unfair to blame him for not seeing, what the stricter school felt rather than saw, that the happiness associated with goodness was not of an individual but of a social character, and therefore could not properly be compared with objects of purely individual desire, such as health, wealth, friends, and worldly fame.

But even taken in its mildest form, there were difficulties about Greek idealism which still remained unsolved. They may be summed up in one word, the necessity of subordinating all personal and passionate feelings to a higher law, whatever the dictates of that law may be. Of such self-suppression few men were less capable than Cicero. Whether virtue meant the extirpation or merely the moderation of desire and emotion, it was equally impossible to one of whom Macaulay has said, with not more severity than truth, that his whole soul was under the dominion of a girlish vanity and a craven fear.[278] Such weak and well-intentioned natures almost always take refuge from their sorrows and self-reproaches in religion; and probably the religious sentiment was more highly developed in Cicero than in any other thinker of the age. Here also a parallel with Socrates naturally suggests itself. The relation between the two amounts to more than a mere analogy; for not only was the intellectual condition of old Athens repeating itself in Rome, but the religious opinions of all cultivated Romans who still retained their belief in a providential God, were, to an even greater extent than their ethics, derived through Stoicism from the great founder of rational theology. Cicero, like Socrates, views God under the threefold aspect of a creator, a providence, and an informing spirit:—identical in his nature with the soul of man, and having man for his peculiar care. With regard to the evidence of his existence, the teleological argument derived from the structure of organised beings is common to both; the argument from universal belief, doubtless a powerful motive with Socrates, is more distinctly put forward by Cicero; and while both regard the heavenly luminaries as manifest embodiments of the divine essence, Cicero is led by the traditions of Plato, Aristotle, and the Stoics, to present the regularity of their movements as the most convincing revelation of a superhuman intelligence, and to identify the outermost starry sphere with the highest God of all.[279] Intimately associated with this view is his belief in the immortality of the soul, which he supposes will return after death to the eternal and unchangeable sphere whence it originally proceeded.[280] But his familiarity with the sceptical arguments of Carneades prevented Cicero from putting forward his theological beliefs with the same confidence as Socrates; while, at the same time, it enabled him to take up a much more decided attitude of hostility towards the popular superstitions from which he was anxious, so far as possible, to purify true religion.[281] To sum up: Cicero, like Kant, seems to have been chiefly impressed by two phenomena, the starry heavens without and the moral law within; each in its own way giving him the idea of unchanging and everlasting continuance, and both testifying to the existence of a power by which all things are regulated for the best. But the materialism of his age naturally prevented him from regarding the external order as a mere reflex or lower manifestation of the inward law by which all spirits feel themselves to be members of the same intelligible community.

We have illustrated the position of Cicero by reference to the master who, more than any other Greek philosopher, seems to have satisfied his ideal of perfect wisdom. We must now observe that nothing is better calculated to show how inadequate was the view once universally taken of Socrates, and still, perhaps, taken by all who are not scholars, than that it should be applicable in so many points to Cicero as well. For, while the influence of the one on human thought was the greatest ever exercised by a single individual, the influence of the other was limited to the acceleration of a movement already in full activity, and moreover tending on the whole in a retrograde direction. The immeasurable superiority of the Athenian lies in his dialectical method. It was not by a mere elimination of differences that he hoped to establish a general agreement, but by reasoning down from admitted principles, which were themselves to be the result of scientific induction brought to bear on a comprehensive and ever-widening area of experience. Hence his scepticism, which was directed against authority, tended as much to stimulate enquiry as that of the Roman declaimer, which was directed against reason, tended to deaden or to depress it. Hence, also, the political philosophy of Socrates was as revolutionary as that of his imitator was conservative. Both were, in a certain sense, aristocrats; but while the aristocracy of the elegant rhetorician meant a clique of indolent and incapable nobles, that of the sturdy craftsman meant a band of highly-trained specialists maintained in power by the choice, the confidence, and the willing obedience of an intelligent people. And while the religion of Cicero was a blind reliance on providence supplemented by priestcraft in this world, with the hope, if things came to the worst, of a safe retreat from trouble in the next; the religion of Socrates was an active co-operation with the universal mind, an attempt to make reason and the will of God prevail on earth, with the hope, if there was any future state, of carrying on in it the intellectual warfare which alone had made life worth living here. No less a contrast could be expected between the orator who turned to philosophy only for the occupation of a leisure hour, or for relief from the pangs of disappointed ambition, and the thinker who gave her his whole existence as the elect apostle and martyr of her creed.

IX.

We have seen what was the guiding principle of Cicero's philosophical method. By interrogating all the systems of his time, he hoped to elicit their points of agreement, and to utilise the result for the practical purposes of life. As actually applied, the effect of this method was not to reconcile the current theories with one another, nor yet to lay the foundation of a more comprehensive philosophy, but to throw back thought on an order of ideas which, from their great popularity, had been incorporated with every system in turn, and, for that very reason, seemed to embody the precise points on which all were agreed. These were the idea of Nature, the idea of mind or reason, and the idea of utility. We have frequently come across them in the course of the present work. Here it will suffice to recall the fact that they had been first raised to distinct consciousness when the results of early Greek thought were brought into contact with the experiences of Greek life, and more especially of Athenian life, in the age of Pericles. As originally understood, they gave rise to many complications and cross divisions, arising from what was considered to be their mutual incompatibility or equivalence.

Thus Nature was openly rejected by the sceptical Sophists, ignored by Socrates, and, during a long period of his career, treated with very little respect by Plato; reason, in its more elaborate forms, was slighted by the Cynics, and employed for its own destruction by the Megarians, in both cases as an enemy to utility; while to Aristotle the pure exercise of reason was the highest utility of any, and Nature only a lower manifestation of the same idealising process. At a later period, we find Nature accepted as a watchword by Stoics, Epicureans, and Sceptics alike, although, of course, each attached a widely different meaning to the term; the supremacy of reason, without whose aid, indeed, their controversies could not have been carried on, is recognised with similar unanimity; and each sect lays exclusive stress on the connexion of its principles with human happiness, thus making utility the foremost consideration in philosophy. Consequently, to whatever system a Roman turned, he would recognise the three great regulative conceptions of Greek thought, although frequently enveloped in a network of fine-spun distinctions and inferences which to him must have seemed neither natural nor reasonable nor useful. On the other hand, apart from such subtleties, he could readily translate all three into terms which seemed to show that, so far from being divided by any essential incompatibility, they did but represent different aspects of a single harmonious ideal. Nature meant simplicity, orderliness, universality, and the spontaneous consentience of unsophisticated minds. Reason meant human dignity, especially as manifested in the conquest of fear and of desire. And whatever was natural and reasonable seemed to satisfy the requirements of utility as well. It might seem also that these very principles were embodied in the facts of old Roman life and of Rome's imperial destiny. The only question was which school of Greek philosophy gave them their clearest and completest interpretation. Lucretius would have said that it was the system of Epicurus; but such a misconception was only rendered possible by the poet's seclusion from imperial interests, and, apparently, by his unacquaintance with the more refined forms of Hellenic thought. Rome could not find in Epicureanism the comprehensiveness, the cohesion, and the power which marked her own character, and which she only required to have expressed under a speculative form. Then came Cicero, with his modernised rhetorical version of what he conceived to be the Socratic philosophy. His teaching was far better suited than that of his great contemporary to the tastes of his countrymen, and probably contributed in no small degree to the subsequent discredit of Epicureanism; yet, by a strange irony, it told, to the same extent, in favour of a philosophy from which Cicero himself was probably even more averse than from the morality of the Garden. In his hands, the Academic criticism had simply the effect of dissolving away those elements which distinguished Stoicism from Cynicism; while his eclecticism brought into view certain principles more characteristic of the Cynics than of any other sect. The Nature to whose guidance he constantly appeals was, properly speaking, not a Socratic but a Sophistic or Cynic idea; and when the Stoics appropriated it, they were only reclaiming an ancestral possession. The exclusion of theoretical studies and dialectical subtleties from philosophy was also Cynic; the Stoic theology when purified, as Cicero desired that it should be purified, from its superstitious ingredients, was no other than the naturalistic monotheism of Antisthenes; and the Stoic morality without its paradoxes was little more than an ennobled Cynicism. The curve described by thought was determined by forces of almost mechanical simplicity. The Greek Eclectics, seeking a middle term between the Academy and the Porch, had fallen back on Plato; Cicero, pursuing the same direction, receded to Socrates; but the continued attraction of Stoicism drew him to a point where the two were linked together by their historical intermediary, the Cynic school. And, by a singular coincidence, the primal forms of Roman life, half godlike and half brutal, were found, better than anything in Hellenic experience, to realise the ideal of a sect which had taken Heracles for its patron saint. Had Diogenes searched the Roman Forum, he would have met with a man at every step.

Meanwhile the morality of Stoicism had enlisted a force of incalculable importance on its behalf. This was the life and death of the younger Cato. However narrow his intellect, however impracticable his principles, however hopeless his resistance to the course of history, Cato had merits which in the eyes of his countrymen placed him even higher than Caesar; and this impression was probably strengthened by the extraordinary want of tact which the great conqueror showed when he insulted the memory of his noblest foe. Pure in an age of corruption, disinterested in an age of greed, devotedly patriotic in an age of selfish ambition, faithful unto death in an age of shameless tergiversation, and withal of singularly mild and gentle character, Cato lived and died for the law of conscience, proving by his example that if a revival of old Roman virtue were still possible, only through the lessons of Greek philosophy could this miracle be wrought. And it was equally clear that Rome could only accept philosophy under a form harmonising with her ancient traditions, and embodying doctrines like those which the martyred saint of her republican liberties had professed.

The Roman reformers were satisfied to call themselves Stoics; and, in reviewing the Stoic system, we saw to what an extent they welcomed and developed some of its fundamental thoughts. But we have now to add that the current which bore them on had its source deeper down than the elaborate combinations of Zeno and Chrysippus, and entered into the composition of every other system that acted on the Roman intellect simultaneously with theirs. Thus whatever forces co-operated with Stoicism had the effect not of complicating but of simplifying its tendencies, by bringing into exclusive prominence the original impulse whence they sprang, which was the idea of Natural Law. Hence the form ultimately assumed by Roman thought was a philosophy of Nature, sometimes appearing more under a Stoic, and sometimes more under a Cynic guise. Everything in Roman poetry that is not copied from Greek models or inspired by Italian passion—in other words, its didactic, descriptive, and satiric elements—may be traced to this philosophy. Doubtless the inculcation of useful arts, the delight in beautiful scenery, the praises of rustic simplicity, the fierce protests against vice under all its forms, and the celebration of an imperial destiny, which form the staple of Rome's national literature, spring from her own deepest life; but the quickening power of Greek thought was needed to develope them into articulate expression.

There is, indeed, nothing more nobly characteristic of the Hellenic spirit, especially as organised by Socrates, than its capacity not only for communicating, but for awakening ideas; thus enabling all the nations among which it spread to realise the whole potential treasure of theoretical and practical energy with which they were endowed. And, from this point of view, we may say that what seems most distinctively proper to Rome—the triumphant consciousness of herself as a world-conquering and world-ruling power—came to her from Greece, and under the form of a Greek idea, the idea of providential destiny. It was to make his countrymen understand the fateful character and inevitable march of her empire that Polybius composed his great history; it was also by a Greek that the most successful of her early national epics was sung; and when at last her language was wrought into an adequate instrument of literary expression—thanks also to Greek rhetorical teaching,—and the culture of her children had advanced so far that they could venture to compete with the Greeks on their own ground, it was still only under forms suggested by Stoicism that Virgil could rewrite the story of his country's dedication to her predestined task.

That Virgil was acquainted with this philosophy and had accepted some of its principal conclusions is evident from a famous passage in the Sixth Aeneid,[282] setting forth the theory of a universal and all-penetrating soul composed of fiery matter, whence the particular souls of men and animals are derived, by a process likened to the scattering and germination of seeds; from another equally famous passage in the Fourth Eclogue,[283] describing the periodical recurrence of events in the same order as before; and also, although to a less extent, from his acceptance of the Stoic astronomy in the Georgics;[284] a circumstance which, by the way, renders it most unlikely that he looked up to Lucretius as an authority in physical science.[285] But even apart from this collateral evidence, one can see that the Aeneid is a Stoic poem. It is filled with the ideas of mutation and vicissitude overruled by a divinely appointed order; of the prophetic intimations by which that order is revealed; of the obedience to reason by which passion is subdued; and of the faith in divine goodness by which suffering is made easy to be borne. And there are also gleams of that universal humanity familiar to Stoicism, which read to some like an anticipation of the Christian or the modern spirit, but which really resemble them only as earlier manifestations of the same great philosophical movement.

This analogy with subsequent developments is aided, so far as it goes, by the admixture of a certain Platonic element with Virgil's Stoicism, shown chiefly by the references to an antenatal existence of the soul, introduced for the purpose of bringing Rome's future heroes on the scene. This, however, is the last example of an attempt on the part of a Roman writer to combine Plato's teaching with Stoicism.[286] At a time when the Romans were more conscious of their literary dependence on Greece than was the case after the Augustan age had reached its zenith, they were probably drawn by the beauty of its literary form to study a system which could otherwise interest them but little. Thus, not only is Cicero full of admiration for Plato—as, indeed, might be expected with so highly cultivated a disciple of the Academy—but Cato, according to the well-known story, spent his last hours reading and re-reading the Phaedo; and his nephew Brutus also occupied an intermediate position between the Old Academy and the Porch. The Roman love of simplification and archaism induced subsequent thinkers either to let Platonism drop altogether, or to study those elements in which it differed from the pure naturalistic doctrine under their Pythagorean form. It may even be doubted whether Virgil's psychology is not derived from Pythagoras rather than from Plato; Ovid, so far as he philosophises at all, is unquestionably a follower of the former;[287] and in the moral teaching of the Sextii, who flourished under Augustus, Pythagorean principles are blended with Stoicism.[288] It is another manifestation of the same effort to grasp every Greek doctrine by its roots, that Horace should proclaim himself the disciple of Aristippus rather than of Epicurus.[289] Even he, however, feels himself drawn with advancing years towards the nobler faith which was now carrying all before it.[290]

With Seneca and his contemporaries, Stoicism has shaken itself free from alien ingredients, and has become the accepted creed of the whole republican opposition, being especially pronounced in the writings of the two young poets, Persius and Lucan. But in proportion as naturalistic philosophy assumed the form of a protest against vice, luxury, inhumanity, despotism, and degradation, or of an exhortation to welcome death as a deliverance from those evils, in the same proportion did it tend to fall back into simple Cynicism; and on this side also it found a ready response, not only in the heroic fortitude, but also in the brutal coarseness and scurrility of the Roman character. Hence the Satires of the last great Roman poet, Juvenal, are an even more distinct expression of Cynic than the epic of Virgil had been of Stoic sentiment. Along with whatever was good and wholesome in Cynicism there is the shameless indecency of the Cynics, and their unquestioning acceptance of mendicancy and prostitution as convenient helps to leading a natural and easily contented life. And it may be noticed that the free-thinking tendencies which distinguished the Cynics from the Stoics are also displayed in Juvenal's occasional denunciations of superstition.

X.

Thus the final effect of its communion with the Roman mind was not so much to develop Greek philosophy any further, or to reconcile its warring sects with one another, as to aid in their decomposition by throwing them back on the earlier forms whence they had sprung. Accordingly we find that the philosophic activity of Hellas immediately before and after the Christian era—so far as there was any at all—consisted in a revival of the Pythagorean and Cynic schools, accompanied by a corresponding resuscitation of primitive Scepticism. This last takes the shape of a very distinct protest against the fashionable naturalism of the age, just as the scepticism of Protagoras and Gorgias—if our view be correct—had once been called forth by the naturalism of Prodicus and Hippias. The principal representative, if not the founder, of Neo-Scepticism was Aenesidêmus, who taught in Alexandria, when we are not informed, but probably after the middle of the first century A.D.[291] An avowed disciple of Pyrrho, his object was to reassert the sceptical principle in its original purity, especially as against the Academicians, whom he charged with having first perverted and then completely abandoned it.[292] Aenesidêmus would hear nothing of probabilities nor of moral certainties. He also claimed to distinguish himself from the Academicians by refusing to assert even so much as that nothing can be asserted; but it appears that, in this point, he had been fully anticipated by Arcesilaus and Carneades.[293] For the rest, his own Scepticism recalls the method of Gorgias and Protagoras much more distinctly than the method of the New Academy—a fresh illustration of the archaic and revivalist tendencies displayed by philosophy at this period. In other words, it is not against the reasoning processes that his criticisms are directed, but against the theory of causation on the objective side, and against the credibility of our immediate perceptions on the subjective side.[294] But, in both directions, he has worked out the difficulties of the old Sophists with a minuteness and a precision unknown to them; and some of his points have been found worth repeating in a different connexion by modern critics. Thus, in analysing the theory of causation, he draws attention to the plurality of causes as an obstacle to connecting any given consequent with one antecedent more than with another; to the illegitimate assumption that the laws inferred from experience hold good under unknown conditions; to the arbitrary assumption of hypothetical causes not evinced by experience; and to the absurdity of introducing a new difficulty for the purpose of explaining an old one.[295] With regard to causation itself, Aenesidêmus seems to have resolved it into action and reaction, thus eliminating the condition of antecedence and consequence, without which it becomes unintelligible.[296]

The Alexandrian Sceptic's general arguments against the possibility of knowledge resolve themselves into a criticism of what Sir W. Hamilton called Natural Realism, somewhat complicated and confused by a simultaneous attack on the theory of natural morality conceived as something eternal and immutable. They are summed up in the famous ten Tropes. Of these the first three are founded on the conflicting sensations produced by the same object when acting on different animals—as is inferred from the marked contrast presented by their several varieties of origin and structure,—on different men, and on the different senses of the same individual. The fourth, which has evidently an ethical bearing, enlarges on the changes in men's views caused by mental and bodily changes, according to their health, age, disposition, and so forth. The next five Tropes relate to circumstances connected with the objects themselves: their distance and position as regards the spectator, the disturbance produced in their proper action by external influences such as air and light, together with the various membranes and humours composing the organs of sense through which they are apprehended; their quantitative variation, involving as it does opposite effects on the senses, or as with medicines, on the health; the law of relativity, according to which many things are only known when taken in company with others, such as double and half, right and left, whole and part; comparative frequency or rarity of occurrence, as with comets, which, while really of much less importance than the sun, excite much more interest from their being so seldom seen. Finally, the tenth Trope is purely ethical, and infers the non-existence of a fixed moral standard from the divergent and even opposite customs prevailing among different nations.[297]

In his attacks on the prevalent theories of ethics, Aenesidêmus again reminds us both of Protagoras and of modern agnosticism. According to him, the general disagreement of mankind proves, among other things, that there is no definable highest good—it is neither virtue, nor pleasure, nor knowledge.[298] In the absence of any dogmatic teaching on the subject at the time when he lived, Protagoras could not give an opinion with regard to the summum bonum; but Plato's famous dialogue represents him as one who, from his point of view, would be unwilling to admit the possibility of introducing fixed principles into conduct; and in like manner, Mr. Herbert Spencer, while accepting the hedonistic principle, gives it such an extremely general signification that he is thrown back on the sceptical principle of leaving everyone free to follow his own inclinations, provided that, in so doing, he does not interfere with the liberty of others.

The parallel between Aenesidêmus and Protagoras would become still more complete were it true that the Alexandrian philosopher also sought to base his Scepticism on the Heracleitean theory of Nature, arguing that contradictory assertions are necessitated by the presence of contradictory properties in every object.

That Aenesidêmus held this view is stated as a fact by Sextus, whose testimony is here corroborated by Tertullian, or rather by Tertullian's informant, Soranus. We find, however, that Zeller, who formerly accepted the statement in question as true, has latterly seen reason to reject it. Aenesidêmus cannot, he thinks, have been guilty of so great an inconsistency as to base his Scepticism on the dogmatic physics of Heracleitus. And he explains the agreement of the ancient authorities by supposing that the original work of Aenesidêmus contained a critical account of the Heracleitean theory, that this was misinterpreted into an expression of his adhesion to it by Soranus, and that the blunder was adopted at second-hand by both Sextus and Tertullian.[299]

It is, at any rate, certain that the successors of Aenesidêmus adhered to the standpoint of Pyrrho. One of them, Agrippa, both simplified and strengthened the arguments of the school by reducing the ten Tropes to five. The earlier objections to human certainty were summed up under two heads: the irreconcilable conflict of opinions on all subjects; and the essential relativity of consciousness, in which the percipient and the perceived are so intimately united that what things in themselves are cannot possibly be discovered. The other three Tropes relate to the baselessness of reasoning. They were evidently suggested by Aristotle's remarks on the subject. The process of proof cannot be carried backwards ad infinitum, nor can it legitimately revolve in a circle. Thus much had already been admitted, or rather insisted on by the great founder of logic. But the Sceptics could not agree to Aristotle's contention, that demonstration may be based on first principles of self-evident certainty. They here fell back on their main argument; that the absence of general agreement on every point is fatal to the existence of such pretended axioms. A still further simplification was effected by the reduction of the five Tropes to two—that all reasoning rests on intuition, and that men's intuitions are irreconcilably at variance with one another.[300] As against true science, the sceptical Tropes are powerless, for the validity of its principles has nothing to do with their general acceptance. They are laid before the learner for his instruction, and if he chooses to regard them as either false or doubtful, the misfortune will be his and not theirs. But as against all attempts to constrain belief by an appeal to authority, the Tropes still remain invincible. Whether the testimony invoked be that of ancient traditions or of a supposed inward witness, there is always the same fatal objection that other traditions and other inward witnesses tell quite a different story. The task of deciding between them must, after all, be handed over to an impersonal reason. In other words, each individual must judge for himself and at his own risk, just as he does in questions of physical science.

We have already observed that Scepticism among the ancients was often cultivated in connexion with some positive doctrine which it indirectly served to recommend. In the case of its last supporters, this was the study of medicine on an empirical as opposed to a deductive method. The Sceptical contention is that we cannot go beyond appearances; the empirical contention is, that all knowledge comes to us from experience, and that this only shows us how phenomena are related to one another, not how they are related to their underlying causes, whether efficient or final. These allied points of view have been brought into still more intimate association by modern thought, which, as will be shown in the concluding chapter, has sprung from a modified form of the ancient Scepticism, powerfully aided by a simultaneous development of physical science. At the same time, the new school have succeeded in shaking off the narrowness and timidity of their predecessors, who were still so far under the influence of the old dogmatists as to believe that there was an inherent opposition between observation and reasoning in the methods of discovery, between facts and explanations in the truths of science, and between antecedence and causation in the realities of Nature. In this respect, astronomy has done more for the right adjustment of our conceptions than any other branch of knowledge; and it is remarkable that Sextus Empiricus, the last eminent representative of ancient Scepticism, and the only one (unless Cicero is to be called a Sceptic) whose writings are still extant, should expressly except astronomy from the destructive criticism to which he subjects the whole range of studies included in what we should call the university curriculum of his time.[301] We need not enter into an analysis of the ponderous compilation referred to; for nearly every point of interest which it comprises has already been touched on in the course of our investigation; and Sextus differs only from his predecessors by adding the arguments of the New Academy to those of Protagoras and Pyrrho, thus completing the Sceptical cycle. It will be enough to notice the singular circumstance that so copious and careful an enumeration of the grounds which it was possible to urge against dogmatism—including, as we have seen, many still employed for the same or other purposes,—should have omitted the two most powerful solvents of any. These were left for the exquisite critical acumen of Hume to discover. They relate to the conception of causation, and to the conception of our own personality as an indivisible, continuously existing substance, being attempts to show that both involve assumptions of an illegitimate character. Sextus comes up to the very verge of Hume's objection to the former when he observes that causation implies relation, which can only exist in thought;[302] but he does not ask how we come to think such a relation, still less does he connect it with the perception of phenomenal antecedence; and his attacks on the various mental faculties assumed by psychologists pass over the fundamental postulate of personal identity, thus leaving Descartes what seemed a safe foundation whereon to rebuild the edifice of metaphysical philosophy.

XI.

The effect aimed at by ancient Scepticism under its last form was to throw back reflection on its original starting-point. Life was once more handed over to the guidance of sense, appetite, custom, and art.[303] We may call this residuum the philosophy of the dinner-bell. That institution implies the feeling of hunger, the directing sensation of sound, the habit of eating together at a fixed time, and the art of determining time by observing the celestial revolutions. Even so limited a view contains indefinite possibilities of expansion. It involves the three fundamental relations that other philosophies have for their object to work out with greater distinctness and in fuller detail: the relation between feeling and action, binding together past, present, and future in the consciousness of personal identity; the relation of ourselves to a collective society of similarly constituted beings, our intercourse with whom is subject from the very first to laws of morality and of logic; and, finally, the relation in which we stand, both singly and combined, to that universal order by which all alike are enveloped and borne along, with its suggestions of a still larger logic and an auguster morality springing from the essential dependence of our individual and social selves on an even deeper identity than that which they immediately reveal. We have already had occasion to observe how the noble teaching of Plato and the Stoics resumes itself in a confession of this threefold synthesis; and we now see how, putting them at their very lowest, nothing less than this will content the claims of thought. Thus, in less time than it took Berkeley to pass from tar-water to the Trinity, we have led our Sceptics from their philosophy of the dinner-bell to a philosophy which the Catholic symbols, with their mythologising tendencies, can but imperfectly represent. And to carry them with us thus far, nothing more than one of their own favourite methods is needed. Wherever they attempt to arrest the progress of enquiry and generalisation, we can show them that no real line of demarcation exists. Let them once admit the idea of a relation connecting the elements of consciousness, and it will carry them over every limit except that which is reached when the universe becomes conscious of itself. Let them deny the idea of a relation, and we may safely leave them to the endless task of analysing consciousness into elements which are feelings and nothing more. The magician in the story got rid of a too importunate familiar by setting him to spin ropes of sand. The spirit of Scepticism is exorcised by setting it to divide the strands of reason into breadthless lines and unextended points.

What influence Scepticism exercised on the subsequent course of Greek thought is difficult to determine. If we are to believe Diogenes Laertius, who flourished in the second quarter of the third century A.D., every school except Epicureanism had at that time sunk into utter neglect;[304] and it is natural to connect this catastrophe with the activity of the Sceptics, and especially of Sextus Empiricus, whose critical compilation had appeared not long before. Such a conclusion would be supported by the circumstance that Lucian, writing more than fifty years earlier, directs his attacks on contemporary philosophy chiefly from the Sceptical standpoint; his Hermotimus in particular being a popularised version of the chief difficulties raised from that quarter. Still it remains to be shown why the criticism of the Greek Humanists, of Pyrrho, and of the New Academy should have produced so much more powerful an effect under their revived form than when they were first promulgated; and it may be asked whether the decline of philosophy should not rather be attributed to the general barbarisation of the Roman empire at that period.

We have also to consider in what relation the new Scepticism stood to the new Platonism by which, in common with every other school, it was eventually either displaced or absorbed. The answer usually given to this question is that the one was a reaction from the other. It is said that philosophy, in despair of being able to discover truth by reason, took refuge in the doctrine that it could be attained by supernatural revelation; and that this doctrine is the characteristic mark distinguishing the system of Plotinus from its predecessors. That a belief in the possibility of receiving divine communications was widely diffused during the last centuries of polytheism is, no doubt, established, but that it ever formed more than an adjunct to Neo-Platonism seems questionable; and there is no evidence that we are aware of to show that it was occasioned by a reaction from Scepticism. As a defence against the arguments of Pyrrho and his successors, it would, in truth, have been quite unavailing; for whatever objections applied to men's natural perceptions, would have applied with still greater force to the alleged supernatural revelation. Moreover, the mystical element of Neo-Platonism appears only in its consummation—in the ultimate union of the individual soul with the absolute One; the rest of the system being reasoned out in accordance with the ordinary laws of logic, and in apparent disregard of the Sceptical attacks on their validity.

The truth is that critics seem to have been misled by a superficial analogy between the spiritualistic revival accomplished by Plotinus, and the Romantic revival which marked the beginning of the present century. The two movements have, no doubt, several traits in common; but there is this great difference between them, that the latter was, what the former was not, a reaction against individualism, agnosticism, and religious unbelief. The right analogy will be found not by looking forward but by looking back. It will then be seen that the Neo-Platonists were what their traditional name implies, disciples of Plato, and not only of Plato but of Aristotle as well. They stood in the same relation to the systems which they opposed as that in which the two great founders of spiritualism had stood to the naturalistic and humanist schools of their time—of course with whatever modifications of a common standpoint were necessitated by the substitution of a declining for a progressive civilisation. Like Plato also, they were profoundly influenced by the Pythagorean philosophy, with its curious combination of mystical asceticism and mathematics. And, to complete the analogy, they too found themselves in presence of a powerful religious reaction, against the excesses of which, like him, they at first protested, although with less than his authority, and only, like him, to be at last carried away by its resistless torrent. It is to the study of this religious movement that we must now address ourselves, before entering on an examination of the latest form assumed by Greek philosophy among the Greeks themselves.

Note.—It does not enter into the plan of this work to study the educational and social aspects of Greek philosophy under the Roman Empire. Those who wish for information on the subject should consult Capes's Stoicism, Martha's Moralistes sous l'Empire Romain, Renan's Marc-Aurèle, chap, iii., Aubertin's Sénèque et Saint Paul, Havet's Christianisme et ses Origines, Vol. II., Gaston Boissier's Religion Romaine, Duruy's Histoire Romaine, chap, lxi., Friedländer's Darstellungen aus der Sittengeschichte Rom's, Vol. III., chap. v. (5th ed.), and Bruno Bauer's Christus und die Cäsaren.

CHAPTER IV.
THE RELIGIOUS REVIVAL.

I.

The result of recent enquiries into the state of civilisation under the Roman Empire during the first two centuries of its existence, has been to suggest conclusions in many respects at variance with those formerly entertained. Instead of the intellectual stagnation, the moral turpitude, and the religious indifference which were once supposed to have been the most marked characteristics of that period, modern scholars discern symptoms of active and fruitful thought, of purity and disinterestedness both in public and private life, but above all of a religious feeling which erred far more on the side of excess than on the side of defect. This change of view may be traced to various causes. A new class of investigators have made ancient history an object of special study. Fresh evidence has been brought to light, and a more discriminating as well as a more extended use has been made of the sources already available. And, perhaps, even greater importance is attributable to the principle now so generally accepted, that historical phenomena, like all other phenomena, are essentially continuous in their movement. The old theories assumed that the substitution of Christian for what is called Pagan civilisation was accompanied by a sudden break in men's habits and ideas. But the whole spirit of modern philosophy has prepared us to believe that such a break is not likely to have ever occurred. And a new survey of the period in question is leading us to the conviction that, as a matter of fact, it did not occur.

For a long time the history of the Roman Empire was written by the descendants of its most deadly enemies—by Christian ecclesiastics or by scholars trained under their influence, and by the inheritors of the northern races who overran and destroyed it. The natural tendency of both classes was to paint the vices of the old society in the most glaring colours, that by so doing they might exhibit the virtues of its conquerors and the necessity of their mission in stronger relief. In this respect, their task was greatly facilitated by the character of the authorities from whom their information was principally derived. Horace and Petronius, Seneca and Juvenal, Tacitus and Suetonius, furnished them with pictures of depravity which it was impossible to exaggerate, which had even to be toned down before they could be reproduced in a modern language. No allowance was made for the influence of a rhetorical training in fostering the cultivation of effect at the expense of truth, nor for the influence of aristocratic prejudice in securing a ready acceptance for whatever tended to the discredit of a monarchical government. It was also forgotten that the court and society of Rome could give no idea of the life led in the rest of Italy and in the provinces. Moreover, the contrast continually instituted or implied by these historians was not between the ancient civilisation and the state of things which immediately succeeded it, nor yet between the society of a great capital as it was then, and as it was in the historian's own time. The points selected for contrast were what was worst in Paganism and what is best in Christianity. The one was judged from the standpoint of courtiers and men of the world, embittered by disappointment and familiar with every form of depravity, the other was judged from the standpoint of experience acquired in a college quadrangle, a country parsonage, or a cathedral close. The modern writer knew little enough even about his own country, he knew next to nothing about what morality was in the Middle Ages, and nothing at all about what it still continues to be in modern Italy.

Even the very imperfect means of information supplied by the literature of the empire were not utilised to the fullest extent. It was naturally the writers of most brilliant genius who received most attention, and these, as it happened, were the most prejudiced against their contemporaries. Their observations, too, were put on record under the form of sweeping generalisations; while the facts from which a different conclusion might be gathered lay scattered through the pages of more obscure authorities, needing to be carefully sifted out and brought together by those who wished to arrive at a more impartial view of the age to which they relate.

Another noteworthy circumstance is that the last centuries of Paganism were on the whole marked by a steady literary decline. To a literary man, this meant that civilisation as a whole was retrograding, that it was an effete organism which could only be regenerated by the infusion of new life from without; while, conversely, the fresh literary productivity of mediaeval and modern Europe was credited to the complete renovation which Christianity and the Barbarians were supposed to have wrought. A closer study of Roman law has done much to correct this superficial impression. It has revealed the existence, in at least one most important domain, of a vast intellectual and moral advance continued down to the death of Marcus Aurelius. And the retrograde movement which set in with Commodus may be fairly attributed to the increased militarism necessitated by the encroachments of barbarism, and more directly to the infusion of barbarian elements into the territory of the empire, rather than to any spontaneous decay of Roman civilisation. The subsequent resuscitation of art and letters is another testimony to the permanent value and vitality of ancient culture. It was in those provinces which had remained least affected by the northern invasion, such as Venetia and Tuscany, that the free activity of the human intellect was first or most fruitfully resumed, and it was from the irradiation of still unconquered Byzantium that the light which re-awakened them was derived.

Another science which has only been cultivated on a large scale within comparatively recent years has confirmed the views suggested by jurisprudence. An enormous mass of inscriptions has been brought to light, deciphered, collated, and made available by transcription for the purposes of sedentary scholars. With the help of these records, fragmentary though they be, we have obtained an insight into the sentiments, beliefs, and social institutions of Pagan antiquity as it was just before the conversion of the Roman world to Christianity, such as literature alone could not supply. Literature and history, too, have told a somewhat different story when read over again in the light of these new discoveries. Finally, the whole mine of materials, new and old, has been worked by a class of enquirers who bring to their task qualities nearly unknown among the scholars of a former generation. These men are familiar with an immense range of studies lying outside their special subject, but often capable of affording it unexpected illustrations; they are free from theological prejudices; they are sometimes versed in the practical conduct of state affairs; and habits of wide social intercourse have emancipated them from the narrowing associations incident to a learned profession.

Perhaps no subject has gained so much from the application of the new historical method as that which we have now to study in its connexion with the progress of Greek philosophy. This is the religion of the Roman empire. On former occasions, we have had to observe how fruitful was the interaction between faith and reason in the early stages of Greek thought. We have now to show how the same process was continued on a greater scale during its later development and diffusion. The conditions and results of this conflict have sometimes been gravely misconceived. We have said that in more than one direction important advances were made under the empire. In the direction of pure rationalism, however, there was no advance at all, but, on the contrary, a continual loss of the ground formerly won. The polytheism which Christianity displaced turns out to have been far more vigorous and fertile than was once supposed, and in particular to have been supported by a much stronger body not only of popular sentiment, but, what at first seems very surprising, of educated conviction. We were formerly taught to believe that the faith of Homer and Aeschylus, of Pythagoras and Pheldlas, was In the last stage of decrepıtude when ıts destıned successor appeared, that it had long been abandoned by the philosophers, and was giving place in the minds of the vulgar to more exciting forms of superstition newly imported from the East. The undue preponderance given to purely literary sources of information is largely responsible for an opinion which now appears to have been mistaken. Among the great Roman writers, Lucretius proclaims himself a mortal enemy to religion; Ennius and Horace are disbelievers in providence; the attitude of Juvenal towards the gods and towards a future life is at least ambiguous, and that of Tacitus undecided; Cicero attacks the current superstitions with a vigour which has diverted attention from the essentially religious character of his convictions; Lucian, by far the most popular Greek writer of the empire, is notorious for his hostility to every form of theology. Among less known authors, the elder Pliny passionately denounces the belief in a divine guidance of life and in the immortality of the soul.[306] Taken alone, these instances would tend to prove that sceptical ideas were very widely diffused through Roman society, both before and after the establishment of the empire. Side by side, however, with the authorities just cited there are others breathing a very different spirit; and what we have especially to notice is that with the progress of time the latter party are continually gaining in weight and numbers. And this, as we shall now proceed to show, is precisely what might have been expected from the altered circumstances which ensued when the civilised world was subjected to a single city, and that city herself to a single chief.

II.

In the world of thought no less than in the world of action, the boundless license which characterised the last days of Roman republicanism was followed by a period of tranquillity and restraint. Augustus endeavoured to associate his system of imperialism with a revival of religious authority. By his orders a great number of ruinous temples were restored, and the old ceremonies were celebrated once more with all their former pomp. His efforts in this direction were ably seconded by the greatest poet and the greatest historian of the age. Both Virgil and Livy were animated by a warm religious feeling, associated, at least in the case of the latter, with a credulity which knew no bounds. With both, religion took an antiquarian form. They were convinced that Rome had grown great through faith in the gods, that she had a divine mandate to conquer the world, and that this supernatural mission might be most clearly perceived in the circumstances of her first origin.[307] It is also characteristic that both should have been provincials, educated in the traditions of a reverent conservatism, and sympathising chiefly with those elements in the constitution of Rome which brought her nearest to primitive Italian habits and ideas. Now it was not merely the policy, it was the inevitable consequence of imperialism to favour the provinces[308] at the expense of the capital, by depriving the urban population and the senatorial aristocracy of the political preponderance which they had formerly enjoyed. Here, as in most other instances, what we call a reaction did not mean a change in the opinions or sentiments of any particular persons or classes, but the advent of a new class whose ways of thinking now determined the general tone of the public mind.

One symptom of this reaction was the fashionable archaism of the Augustan age, the tendency to despise whatever was new in literature, and to exalt whatever was old. It is well known how feelingly Horace complains of a movement which was used to damage his own reputation as a poet;[309] but what seems to have escaped observation is, that this protest against the literary archaism of his contemporaries is only one symptom of a much profounder division between his philosophy and theirs. He was just as good a patriot as they were, but his sympathies were with the Hellenising aristocracy to which Lucretius and Cicero had belonged, not with the narrow-minded conservatism of the middle classes and the country people. He was a man of progress and free-thought, who accepted the empire for what it might be worth, a Roman Prosper Merimée or Sainte-Beuve, whose preference of order to anarchy did not involve any respect for superstitious beliefs simply because they were supported by authority. And this healthy common sense Is so much a part of his character, that he sometImes gives his mistresses the benefit of it, warning Leuconoe against the Babylonian soothsayers, and telling Phidyle that the gods should be approached not only with sacrifices but with clean hands.[310] Yet so strong was the spirit of the age, that the sceptical poet occasionally feels himself obliged to second or to applaud the work of restoration undertaken by Augustus, and to augur from it, with more or less sincerity, a reformation in private life.[311] And even the frivolous Ovid may be supposed to have had the same object in view when composing his Fasti.

The religious revival initiated by Augustus for his own purposes was soon absorbed and lost in a much wider movement, following independent lines and determined by forces whose existence neither he nor any of his contemporaries could suspect. Even for his own purposes, something more was needed than a mere return to the past. The old Roman faith and worship were too dry and meagre to satisfy the cravings of the Romans themselves in the altered conditions created for them by the possession of a world-wide empire; still less could they furnish a meeting-ground for all the populations which that empire was rapidly fusing into a single mass.

Augustus

But what was wanted might be trusted to evolve itself without any assistance from without, once free scope was given to the religious instincts of mankind. These had long been kept in abeyance by the creeds which they had originally called into existence, and by the rigid political organisation of the ancient city-state. Local patriotism was adverse to the introduction of new beliefs either from within or from without. Once the general interests of a community had been placed under the guardianship of certain deities with definite names and jurisdictions, it was understood that they would feel offended at the prospect of seeing their privileges invaded by a rival power; and were that rival the patron of another community, his introduction might seem like a surrender of national independence at the feet of an alien conqueror. So, also, no very active proselytism was likely to be carried on when the adherents of each particular religion believed that its adoption by an alien community would enable strangers and possible enemies to secure a share of the favour which had hitherto been reserved for themselves exclusively. And to allure away the gods of a hostile town by the promise of a new establishment was, in fact, one of the stratagems commonly employed by the general of the besieging army.[312]

If the Roman conquest did not altogether put an end to these sentiments, it considerably mitigated their intensity. The imperial city was too strong to feel endangered by the introduction of alien deities within its precincts. The subject states were relieved from anxiety with regard to a political independence which they had irrecoverably lost. Moreover, since the conquests of Alexander, vast aggregations of human beings had come into existence, to which the ancient exclusiveness was unknown, because they never had been cities at all in the ancient sense of the word. Such were Alexandria and Antioch, and these speedily became centres of religious syncretism. Rome herself, in becoming the capital of an immense empire, acquired the same cosmopolitan character. Her population consisted for the most part of emancipated slaves, and of adventurers from all parts of the world, many of whom had brought their national faiths with them, while all were ready to embrace any new faith which had superior attractions to offer. Another important agent in the diffusion and propagation of new religions was the army. The legions constituted a sort of migratory city, recruited from all parts of the empire, and moving over its whole extent. The dangers of a military life combined with its authoritative ideas are highly favourable to devotion; and the soldiers could readily adopt new modes for the expression of this feeling both from each other and from the inhabitants of the countries where they were stationed, and would in turn become missionaries for their dissemination over the most distant regions. That such was actually the case is proved by numerous religious inscriptions found in the neighbourhood of Roman camps.[313]

After considering by what agencies the seeds of religious belief were carried from place to place, we have to examine, what was even more important, the quality of the soil on which they fell. And here, to continue the metaphor, we shall find that the Roman plough had not only broken through the crust of particularist prejudice, but had turned up new social strata eminently fitted to receive and nourish the germs scattered over their surface by every breeze and every bird of passage, or planted and watered by a spiritual sower's hand. Along with the positive check of an established worship, the negative check of dissolving criticism had, to a great extent, disappeared with the destruction of the régime which had been most favourable to its exercise during the early stages of progress. The old city aristocracies were not merely opposed on patriotic grounds to free-trade in religion, but, as the most educated and independent class in the community, they were the first to shake off supernatural beliefs of every kind. We have grown so accustomed to seeing those beliefs upheld by the partisans of political privilege and attacked in the name of democratic principles, that we are apt to forget how very modern is the association of free-thought with the supremacy of numbers. It only dates from the French Revolution, and even now it is far from obtaining everywhere. Athens was the most perfectly organised democracy of antiquity, and in the course of this work we have repeatedly had occasion to observe how strong was the spirit of religious bigotry among the Athenian people. If we want rationalistic opinions we must go to the great nobles and their friends, to a Pericles, a Critias, or a Protagoras. There must also have been perfect intellectual liberty among the Roman nobles who took up Hellenic culture with such eagerness towards the middle of the second century B.C., and among those who, at a later period, listened with equanimity or approval to Caesar's profession of Epicureanism in a crowded senatorial debate. It was as much in order that the De Rerum Naturâ should have been written by a member of this class as that the Aeneid should proceed from the pen of a modest provincial farmer. In positive knowledge, Virgil greatly excelled Lucretius, but his beliefs were inevitably determined by the traditions of his ignorant neighbours. When civil war, proscription, delation, and, perhaps more than any other cause, their own delirious extravagance, had wrought the ruin of the Roman aristocracy, their places were taken by respectable provincials who brought with them the convictions without the genius of the Mantuan poet; and thenceforward the tide of religious reaction never ceased rising until the Crusades, which were its supreme expression, unexpectedly brought about a first revival of Hellenic culture. On that occasion, also, the first symptoms of revolt manifested themselves among the nobles; taking the form of Gnosticism in the brilliant courts of Languedoc, and, at a later period, of Epicureanism in the Ghibelline circles of Florentine society; while, conversely, when the Ciompi or poorer artisans of Florence rose in revolt against the rich traders, one of the first demands made by the successful insurgents was, that a preaching friar should be sent to give them religious instruction. At a still later period, the same opposition of intellectual interests continues to be defined by the same social divisions. Two distinct currents of thought co-operated to bring about the Protestant Reformation. One, which was religious and reactionary, proceeded from the people. The other, which was secularising, scholarly, and scientific, represented the tendencies of the upper classes and of those who looked to them for encouragement and support. Throughout the sixteenth and seventeenth centuries, many noble names are to be found among the champions of reason; and while speculative liberty is associated with the ascendency of the aristocratic party, superstition and intolerance are associated with the triumph of the people, whether under the form of a democracy or of a levelling despotism. So, also, the great emancipating movement of the eighteenth century was fostered by the descendants of the Crusaders, and, until after the Revolution, met with no response among the bourgeoisie or the people; indeed the reaction in favour of supernaturalism was begun by a child of the people, Rousseau. All this, as we have already observed, has been reversed in more recent times; but the facts quoted are enough to prove how natural it was that in the ancient world decay of class privileges should be equivalent to a strengthening of the influences which made for supernaturalism and against enlightened criticism.

III.

After the revolution which destroyed the political power of the old aristocracy, there came a further revolution the effect of which was to diminish largely its social predominance. We learn from the bitter sarcasms of Horace and Juvenal that under the empire wealth took the place of birth, if not, as those satirists pretend, of merit, as a passport to distinction and respect. Merely to possess a certain amount of money procured admission to the equestrian and senatorial orders; while a smaller pecuniary qualification entitled any Roman citizen to rank among the Honestiores as opposed to the Humiliores, the latter only being liable, if found guilty of certain offences, to the more atrocious forms of capital punishment, such as death by the wild beasts or by fire.[314] Even a reputation for learning was supposed to be a marketable commodity; and when supreme power was held by a philosopher, the vulgar rich could still hope to attract his favourable notice by filling their houses with books.[315] We also know from Juvenal, what indeed the analogy of modern times would readily suggest, that large fortunes were often rapidly made, and made by the cultivation of very sordid arts. Thus members of the most ignorant and superstitious classes were constantly rising to positions where they could set the tone of public opinion, or at least help to determine its direction.

The military organisation of the empire had the further effect of giving a high social status to retired centurions—men probably recruited from the most barbarous provincial populations, and certainly more remarkable for their huge size than for their mental gifts.[316] When one of these heroes heard a philosopher state that nothing can be made out of nothing, he would ask with a horse-laugh whether that was any reason for going without one's dinner.[317] On the other hand, when it came to be a question of supernatural agency, a man of this type would astonish the Jews themselves by his credulity. Imbued with the idea of personal authority, he readily fancied that anyone standing high in the favour of God could cure diseases from a distance by simply giving them the word of command to depart.[318]

A much more important factor in the social movement than those already mentioned was the ever-increasing influence of women. This probably stood at the lowest point to which it has ever fallen, during the classic age of Greek life and thought. In the history of Thucydides, so far as it forms a connected series of events, four times only during a period of nearly seventy years does a woman cross the scene. In each instance her apparition only lasts for a moment. In three of the four instances she is a queen or a princess, and belongs either to the half-barbarous kingdoms of northern Hellas or to wholly barbarous Thrace. In the one remaining instance— that of the woman who helps some of the trapped Thebans to make their escape from Plataea—while her deed of mercy will live for ever, her name is for ever lost.[319] But no sooner did philosophy abandon physics for ethics and religion than the importance of those subjects to women was perceived, first by Socrates, and after him by Xenophon and Plato. Women are said to have attended Plato's lectures disguised as men. Women formed part of the circle which gathered round Epicurus in his suburban retreat. Others aspired not only to learn but to teach. Arêtê, the daughter of Aristippus, handed on the Cyrenaic doctrine to her son, the younger Aristippus. Hipparchia, the wife of Crates the Cynic, earned a place among the representatives of his school. But all these were exceptions; some of them belonged to the class of Hetaerae; and philosophy, although it might address itself to them, remained unaffected by their influence. The case was widely different in Rome, where women were far more highly honoured than in Greece;[320] and even if the prominent part assigned to them in the legendary history of the city be a proof, among others, of its untrustworthiness, still that such stories should be thought worth inventing and preserving is an indirect proof of the extent to which feminine influence prevailed. With the loss of political liberty, their importance, as always happens at such a conjuncture, was considerably increased. Under a personal government there is far more scope for intrigue than where law is king; and as intriguers women are at least the equals of men. Moreover, they profited fully by the levelling tendencies of the age. One great service of the imperial jurisconsults was to remove some of the disabilities under which women formerly suffered. According to the old law, they were placed under male guardianship through their whole life, but this restraint was first reduced to a legal fiction by compelling the guardian to do what they wished, and at last it was entirely abolished. Their powers both of inheritance and bequest were extended; they frequently possessed immense wealth; and their wealth was sometimes expended for purposes of public munificence. Their social freedom seems to have been unlimited, and they formed combinations among themselves which probably served to increase their general influence.[321]

All these circumstances taken together would permit the Roman women to have opinions of their own if they liked, and would ensure a respectful hearing for whatever they had to say; while the men who had opinions to propagate would, for the same reason, be deeply interested in securing their adhesion. On the other hand, they received a good literary education, being sent apparently to the same schools as their brothers, and there made acquainted with, at least, the Latin poets.[322] Thus they would possess the degree of culture necessary for readily receiving and transmitting new impressions. And we know, as a matter of fact, that many Roman ladies entered eagerly into the literary movement of the age, sharing the studies of their husbands, discoursing on questions of grammar, freely expressing their opinion on the relative merits of different poets, and even attempting authorship on their own account.[323] Philosophy, as it was then taught, attracted a considerable share of their attention; and some great ladies were constantly attended by a Stoic professor, to whose lectures they listened seemingly with more patience than profit.[324] One of their favourite studies was Plato's Republic, according to Epictêtus, because it advocated a community of wives;[325] or, as we may more charitably suggest, because it admitted women to an equality with men. But there is no evidence to prove that their inquisitiveness ever went to the length of questioning the foundations of religious faith; and we may fairly reckon their increasing influence among the forces which were tending to bring about an overwhelming religious revival among the educated classes.

In this connexion, some importance must also be attributed to the more indirect influence exercised by children; These did not form a particularly numerous class in the upper ranks of Roman society; but, to judge by what we see in modern France, the fewer there were of them the more attention were they likely to receive; and their interests, which like those of the other defenceless classes had been depressed or neglected under the aristocratic régime, were favoured by the reforming and levelling movement of the empire. One of Juvenal's most popular satires is entirely devoted to the question of their education; and, in reference to this, the point of view most prominently put forward is the importance of the examples which are offered to them by their parents. Juvenal, himself a free-thinker, is exceedingly anxious that they should not be indoctrinated with superstitious opinions; but we may be sure that a different order of considerations would equally induce others to give their children a careful religious training, and to keep them at a distance from sceptical influences; while the spontaneous tendency of children to believe in the supernatural would render it easier to give them moral instruction under a religious form.

To complete our enumeration of the forces by which a new public opinion was being created, we must mention the slaves. Though still liable to be treated with great barbarity, the condition of this class was considerably ameliorated under the empire. Their lives and, in the case of women, their chastity, were protected by law; they were allowed by custom to accumulate property; they had always the hope of liberty before their eyes, for emancipations were frequent and were encouraged by the new legislation; they often lived on terms of the closest intimacy with their masters, and were sometimes educated enough to converse with them on subjects of general interest. Now a servile condition is more favourable than any other to religious ideas. It inculcates habits of unquestioning submission to authority; and by the miseries with which it is attended immensely enhances the value of consolatory beliefs, whether they take the form of faith in divine protection during this life, or of a compensation for its afflictions in the next. Moreover, a great majority of the Roman slaves came from those Eastern countries which were the native land of superstition, and thus served as missionaries of Oriental cults and creeds in the West, besides furnishing apt disciples to the teachers who came from Asia with the express object of securing converts to their religion in Rome. The part played by slaves in the diffusion of Christianity is well known; what we have to observe at present is that their influence must equally have told in favour of every other supernaturalist belief, and, to the same extent, against the rationalism of writers like Horace and Lucian.

Thus Roman civilisation, even when considered on its liberal, progressive, democratic side, seems to have necessarily favoured the growth and spread of superstition, because the new social strata which it turned up were less on their guard against unwarranted beliefs than the old governing aristocracies with their mingled conservatism and culture. But this was not all; and on viewing the empire from another side we shall find that under it all classes alike were exposed to conditions eminently inconsistent with that individual independence and capacity for forming a private judgment which had so honourably distinguished at least one class under the republican régime. If imperialism was in one sense a levelling and democratic system, in another sense it was intensely aristocratic, or rather timocratic. Superiorities of birth, race, age, and sex were everywhere tending to disappear, only that they might be replaced by the more ignoble superiorities of brute-force, of court-favour, and of wealth. The Palace set an example of caprice on the one side and of servility on the other which was faithfully followed through all grades of Roman society, less from a spirit of imitation than because circumstances were at work which made every rich man or woman the centre of a petty court consisting of voluntary dependents whose obsequiousness was rewarded by daily doles of food and money, by the occasional gift of a toga or even of a small farm, or by the hope of a handsome legacy. Before daybreak the doors of a wealthy house were surrounded by a motley crowd, including not only famished clients but praetors, tribunes, opulent freedmen, and even ladies in their litters; all come nominally for the purpose of paying their respects to the master, but in reality to receive a small present of money. At a later hour, when the great man went abroad, he was attended by a troop of poor hangers-on, who, after trudging about for hours in his train and accompanying him home in the afternoon, often missed the place at his table which their assiduities were intended to secure. Even when it came, the invitation brought small comfort, as only the poorest food and the worst wine were set before the client, while he had the additional vexation of seeing his patron feasting on the choicest dishes and the most delicious vintages; and this was also the lot of the domestic philosopher whom some rich men regarded as an indispensable member of their retinue.[326] Of course those who wished for a larger share of the patron's favours could only hope to win it by unstinted tokens of admiration, deference, or assent; and probably many besides the master of thirty legions in the well-known story were invariably allowed to be right by the scholars with whom they condescended to dispute.

Besides the attentions lavished on every wealthy individual, those who had no children were especially courted, and that too by others who were as well off as themselves with the object of being remembered in their wills. So advantageous a position, indeed, did these orbi, as they were called, occupy, that among the higher classes there was extreme unwillingness to marry; although, as an encouragement to population, the father of three children enjoyed several substantial privileges. This circumstance, again, by preventing the perpetuation of wealthy families, and allowing their property to pass into the hands of degraded fortune-hunters, rendered impossible the consolidation of a new aristocracy which might have reorganised the traditions of liberal culture, and formed an effectual barrier against the downward pressure of despotism on the one side and the inroads of popular superstition on the other.

As a last illustration of the extent to which authority and subordination were pushed in Roman society, it may be mentioned that the better class of slaves were permitted to keep slaves for their own service. But whether the institution of slavery as a whole should be reckoned among the conditions favourable to authoritative beliefs is doubtful, as it was an element common to every period of antiquity. Perhaps, however paradoxical such an assertion may seem, the very frequency of emancipation gave increased strength to the feeling of dependence on an overruling personal power. A freedman could not forget that the most important event in his life was due, not to any natural law, but to the will or the caprice of a master; and this reflection must have confirmed his faith in the divine beings of whom he and his master were fellow-slaves.

IV.

We have now to show what new beliefs gained most ground, and what old beliefs were most successfully revived, through the combination of favourable conditions, an analysis of which has been attempted in the preceding pages. Among the host of creeds which at this period competed with one another for the favour of the rich or for the suffrages of the poor, there were some that possessed a marked advantage over their rivals in the struggle for existence. The worship of Nature considered as imaging the vicissitudes of human life, could not fail to be the most popular of any. All who desired a bond of sympathy uniting them with their fellow-subjects over the whole empire, and even with the tribes beyond its frontiers, might meet on this most universal ground. All who wished to combine excitement with devotion were attracted by the dramatic representation of birth and death, of bereavement and sorrow and searching, of purification through suffering, and triumphant reunion with the lost objects of affection in this or in another world. Inquisitive or innovating minds were gratified by admission to secrets a knowledge of which was believed to possess inestimable value. And the most conservative could see in such celebrations an acknowledgment, under other forms, of some divinity which had always been reverenced in their own home, perhaps even the more authentic reproduction of adventures already related to them as dim and uncertain traditions of the past. More than one such cultus, representing under the traits of personal love and loss and recovery, the death of vegetation in winter and its return to life in spring, was introduced from the East, and obtained a wide popularity through the empire. Long before the close of the republic, the worship of Cybele was established in Rome with the sanction of the Senate. Other Asiatic deities of a much less respectable character, Astarte and the so-called Syrian goddess, though not officially recognised, enjoyed a celebrity extending to the remotest corners of the western world.[327] Still greater and more universal was the veneration bestowed on Isis and Serapis. From the prince to the peasant, from the philosopher to the ignorant girl, all classes united in doing homage to their power. Their mysteries were celebrated in the mountain valleys of the Tyrol, and probably created as much excitement among the people of that neighbourhood as the Ammergau passion-play does at present.[328] An inscription has been discovered describing in minute detail an offering made to Isis by a Spanish matron in honour of her little daughter. It was a silver statue richly ornamented with precious stones, resembling, as our authority observes, what would now be presented to the Madonna,[329] who indeed is probably no more than a Christian adaptation of the Egyptian goddess. And Plutarch, or another learned and ingenious writer whose work has come down to us under his name, devotes a long treatise to Isis and Osiris, in which the mythical history of the goddess is as thickly covered with allegorical interpretations as the statue dedicated to her by the Spanish lady was with emeralds and pearls.

Another form of naturalistic religion, fitted for universal acceptance by its appeals to common experience, was the worship of the Sun. It was probably as such that Mithras, a Syro-Persian deity, obtained a success throughout the Roman empire which at one time seemed to balance the rising fortunes of Christianity. Adoration of the heavenly bodies was, indeed, very common during this period, and was probably connected with the extreme prevalence of astrological superstition. It would also harmonise perfectly with the still surviving Olympian religion of the old Hellenic aristocracy, and would profit by the support which philosophy since the time of Socrates had extended to this form of supernaturalist belief. But, perhaps, for that very reason the classes which had now become the ultimate arbiters of opinion, felt less sympathy with Mithras-worship and other kindred cults than with the Egyptian mysteries. These had a more recognisable bearing on their own daily life, and, like the Chthonian religions of old Greece, they included a reference to the immortality of the soul. Moreover, the climate of Europe, especially of western Europe, does not permit the sun to become an object of such excessive adoration as in southern Asia. Mithras-worship, then, is an example of the expansive force exhibited by Oriental ideas rather than of a faith which really satisfied the wants of the Roman world.

A far higher place must be assigned to Judaism among the competitors for the allegiance of Europe. The cosmopolitan importance at one time assumed by this religion has been considerably obscured, owing to the subsequent devolution of its part to Christianity. It is, however, by no means impossible that, but for the diversion created by the Gospel, and the disastrous consequences of their revolt against Rome, the Jews might have won the world to a purified form of their own monotheism. A few significant circumstances are recorded showing how much influence they had acquired, even in Rome, before the first preaching of Christianity. The first of these is to be found in Cicero's defence of Flaccus. The latter was accused of appropriating part of the annual contributions sent to the temple at Jerusalem; and, in dealing with this charge, Cicero speaks of the Jews, who were naturally prejudiced against his client, as a powerful faction the hostility of which he is anxious not to provoke.[330] Some twenty years later, a great advance has been made. Not only must the material interests of the Jews be respected, but a certain conformity to their religious prescriptions is considered a mark of good breeding, In one of his most amusing satires, Horace tells us how, being anxious to shake off a bore, he appeals for help to his friend Aristius Fuscus, and reminds him of some private business which they had to discuss together. Fuscus sees his object, and being mischievously determined to defeat it, answers: 'Yes, I remember perfectly, but we must wait for some better opportunity; this is the thirtieth Sabbath, do you wish to insult the circumcised Jews?' 'I have no scruples on that point,' replies the impatient poet. 'But I have,' rejoins Fuscus,—'a little weak-minded, one of the many, you know—excuse me, another time.'[331] Nor were the Jews content with the countenance thus freely accorded them. The same poet elsewhere intimates that whenever they found themselves in a majority, they took advantage of their superior strength to make proselytes by force.'[332] And they pursued the good work to such purpose that a couple of generations later we find Seneca bitterly complaining that the vanquished had given laws to the victors, and that the customs of this abominable race were established over the whole earth.[333] Evidence to the same effect is given by Philo Judaeus and Josephus, who inform us that the Jewish laws and customs were admired, imitated, and obeyed over the whole earth.[334] Such assertions might be suspected of exaggeration, were they not, to a certain extent, confirmed by the references already quoted, to which others of the same kind may be added from later writers showing that it was a common practice among the Romans to abstain from work on the Sabbath, and even to celebrate it by praying, fasting, and lighting lamps, to visit the synagogues, to study the law of Moses, and to pay the yearly contribution of two drachmas to the temple at Jerusalem.[335]

Then as now, Judaism seems to have had a much greater attraction for women than for men; and this may be accounted for not only by the greater credulity of the female sex, which would equally predispose them in favour of every other new religion, but also by their natural sympathy with the domestic virtues which are such an amiable and interesting feature in the Jewish character. Josephus tells us that towards the beginning of Nero's reign nearly all the women of Damascus were attached to Judaism;[336] and he also mentions that Poppaea, the mistress and afterwards the wife of Nero, used her powerful influence for the protection of his compatriots, though whether she actually became a proselyte, as some have supposed, is doubtful.[337] According to Ovid, the synagogues were much visited by Roman women, among others, apparently, by those of easy virtue, for he alludes to them as resorts which the man of pleasure in search of a conquest will find it advantageous to frequent.[338]

The monotheism of the Jehovist religion would seem to have marked it out as the natural faith of a universal empire. Yet, strange to say, it was not by this element of Judaism that proselytes were most attracted. Our authorities are unanimous in speaking of the sabbath-observance as the most distinguishing trait of the Jews themselves, and the point in which they were most scrupulously imitated by their adherents; while the duty of contributing to the maintenance of the temple apparently stood next in popular estimation. But if this be true, it follows that the liberation of the spiritualistic element in Judaism from its ceremonial husk was a less essential condition to the success of Christianity than some have supposed. What the world objected to in Judaism was not its concrete, historical, practical side, but its exclusiveness, and the hatred for other nations which it was supposed to breed. What the new converts wished was to take the place of the Jews, to supersede them in the divine favour, not to improve on their law. It was useless to tell them that they were under no obligation to observe the sabbath, when the institution of a day of rest was precisely what most fascinated them in the history of God's relations with his chosen people. And it was equally useless to tell them that the hour had come when the Father should not be worshipped any more at Jerusalem but everywhere in spirit and in truth, when Jerusalem had become irrevocably associated in their minds with the establishment of a divine kingdom on this earth. Thus, while the religion of the Middle Ages reached its intensest expression in armed pilgrimages to Palestine, the religion of modern Puritanism has embodied itself by preference in the observance of what it still delights to call the sabbath.

It must not be supposed that the influx of Asiatic religions into Europe was attended by any loss of faith in the old gods of Greece and Italy, or by any neglect of their worship. The researches of Friedländer have proved the absolute erroneousness of such an idea, widely entertained as it has been. Innumerable monuments are in existence testifying to the continued authority of the Olympian divinities, and particularly of Jupiter, over the whole extent of the Roman empire. Ample endowments were still devoted to the maintenance of their service; their temples still smoked with sacrifices; their litanies were still repeated as a duty which it would have been scandalous to neglect; in all hours of public and private danger their help was still implored, and acknowledged by the dedication of votive offerings when the danger was overcome; it was still believed, as in the days of Homer, that they occasionally manifested themselves on earth, signalising their presence by works of superhuman power.[339] Nor was there anything anomalous in this peaceable co-existence of the old with the new faiths. So far back as we can trace the records both of Greek and Roman polytheism, they are remarkable for their receptive and assimilative capacity. Apollo and Artemis were imported into Greece from Lycia, Heracles and Aphrodite from Phoenicia, Dionysus and Ares probably from Thrace. Roman religion under its oldest form included both a Latin or Sabine and an Etruscan element; at a subsequent period it became Hellenised without losing anything of its grave and decorous character. In Greece, the elastic system of divine relationships was stretched a little further so as to make room for the new comers. The same system, when introduced into Roman mythology, served to connect and enliven what previously had been so many rigid and isolated abstractions. With both, the supreme religious conception continued to be what it had been with their Aryan ancestors, that of a heavenly Father Jove; and the fashionable deities of the empire were received into the pantheon of Homer and Hesiod as recovered or adopted children of the same Olympian sire. The danger to Hellenistic polytheism was not from another form of the same type, but from a faith which should refuse to amalgamate with it on any terms; and in the environment created by Roman imperialism with its unifying and cosmopolitan character, such a faith, if it existed anywhere, could not fail in the long-run to supersede and extinguish its more tolerant rivals. But the immediate effect produced by giving free play to men's religious instincts was not the concentration of their belief on a single object, or on new to the exclusion of old objects, but an extraordinary abundance and complexity of supernaturalism under all its forms. This general tendency, again, admits of being decomposed into two distinct currents, according as it was determined by the introduction of alien superstitions from without, or by the development of native and popular superstition from within. But, in each case, the retrogressive movement resulted from the same political revolution. At once critical and conservative, the city-aristocracies prevented the perennial germs of religious life from multiplying to any serious extent within the limits of their jurisdiction, no less vigilantly than they prohibited the importation of its completed products from abroad. We have now to study the behaviour of these germs when the restraint to which they had formerly been subjected was lightened or withdrawn.

V.

The old religions of Greece and Italy were essentially oracular. While inculcating the existence of supernatural beings, and prescribing the modes according to which such beings were to be worshipped, they paid most attention to the interpretation of the signs by which either future events in general, or the consequences of particular actions, were supposed to be divinely revealed. Of these intimations, some were given to the whole world, so that he who ran might read, others were reserved for certain favoured localities, and only communicated through the appointed ministers of the god. The Delphic oracle in particular enjoyed an enormous reputation both among Greeks and barbarians for guidance afforded under the latter conditions; and during a considerable period it may even be said to have directed the course of Hellenic civilisation. It was also under this form that supernatural religion suffered most injury from the great intellectual movement which followed the Persian wars. Men who had learned to study the constant sequences of Nature for themselves, and to shape their conduct according to fixed principles of prudence or of justice, either thought it irreverent to trouble the god about questions on which they were competent to form an opinion for themselves, or did not choose to place a well-considered scheme at the mercy of his possibly interested responses.

Delphic oracle

That such a revolution occurred about the middle of the fifth century B.C., seems proved by the great change of tone in reference to this subject which one perceives on passing from Aeschylus to Sophocles. That anyone should question the veracity of an oracle is a supposition which never crosses the mind of the elder dramatist. A knowledge of augury counts among the greatest benefits conferred by Prometheus on mankind, and the Titan brings Zeus himself to terms by his acquaintance with the secrets of destiny. Sophocles, on the other hand, evidently has to deal with a sceptical generation, despising prophecies and needing to be warned of the fearful consequences brought about by neglecting their injunctions.

Probably few contributed so much to the change as Socrates, notwithstanding his general piety and the credulity which he exhibited on this particular point. For his ethical and dialectical training, combined with that careful study of facts which he so earnestly recommended, went very far towards making a consultation of the oracle superfluous; and he did actually impress on his auditors the duty of dispensing with its assistance in all cases except those where a knowledge of the future was necessary and could not be otherwise obtained.[340] Even so superstitious a believer as Xenophon improved on his master's lessons in this respect, and instead of asking the Pythia whether he should take service with the younger Cyrus—as Socrates had advised—simply asked to what god he should sacrifice before starting on the expedition. Towards the beginning of our era, as is well known, the Greek oracles had fallen into complete neglect and silence.

But all this time the popular belief in omens had continued unaffected, and had apparently even increased. The peculiar Greek feeling known as Deisidaimonia is first satirised by Theophrastus, who defines it as cowardice with regard to the gods, and gives several amusing instances of the anxiety occasioned by its presence—all connected with the interpretation of omens—such as Aristophanes could hardly have failed to notice had they been usual in his time. Nor were such fancies confined to the ignorant classes. Although the Stoics cannot be accused of Deisidaimonia, they gave their powerful sanction to the belief in divination, as has been already mentioned in our account of their philosophy. It would seem that whatever authority the great oracular centres had lost was simply handed over to lower and more popular forms of the same superstition.

In Rome, as well as in Greece, rationalism took the form of disbelief in divination. Here at least the Epicurean, the Academician, and, among the Stoics, the disciple of Panaetius, were all agreed. But as the sceptical movement began at a much later period in Rome than in the country where it first originated, so also did the supernaturalist reaction come later, the age of Augustus in the one corresponding very nearly with the age of Alexander in the other. Virgil and Livy are remarkable for their faith in omens; and although the latter complains of the general incredulity with which narratives of such events were received, his statements are to be taken rather as an index of what people thought in the age immediately preceding his own, than as an accurate description of contemporary opinion. Certainly nothing could be farther from the truth than to say that signs and prodigies were disregarded by the Romans under the empire. Even the cool and cautious Tacitus feels himself obliged to relate sundry marvellous incidents which seemed to accompany or to prefigure great historical catastrophes; and the more credulous Suetonius has transcribed an immense number of such incidents from the pages of older chroniclers, besides informing us of the extreme attention paid even to trifling omens by Augustus.[341]

Meanwhile the recognised methods for looking into futurity continued to enjoy their old popularity, and that which relied on indications afforded by the entrails of sacrifices was practised with unabated confidence down to the time of Julian.[342] Even faith in natural law, where it existed, accommodated itself to the prevalent superstition by taking the form of astrology; and it is well known what reliance the emperor Tiberius, for his time a singularly enlightened man, placed on predictions derived from observation of the starry heavens.

Subsequently, with the revival of Hellenism, the Greek oracles broke silence, and regained even more than their ancient reputation, as the increased facilities for locomotion now rendered them accessible from the remotest regions.[343] Sometimes the miraculous character of their responses resulted in the conversion of hardened infidels. In this connexion, the following anecdote is related by Plutarch. A certain governor of Cilicia entertained serious doubts about the gods, and was still further confirmed in his impiety by the Epicureans who surrounded him. This man, for the purpose of throwing discredit on the famous oracle of Mopsus, sent a freedman to consult it, bearing a sealed letter containing a question with whose purport neither he nor any one else except the sender was acquainted. On arriving at the oracle, the messenger was admitted to pass a night within the temple, which was the method of consultation usually practised there. In his sleep a beautiful figure appeared to him, and after uttering the words 'a black one,' immediately vanished. On hearing this answer the governor fell on his knees in consternation, and, opening the sealed tablet, showed his friends the question which it contained, 'Shall I sacrifice a white or a black bull to thee?' The Epicureans were confounded; while the governor offered up the prescribed sacrifice, and became thenceforward a constant adorer of Mopsus.[344]

Nothing, as Friedländer observes, shows so well what intense credulity prevailed at this time, with reference to phenomena of a marvellous description, as the success obtained by a celebrated impostor, Alexander of Abonuteichus, whose adventurous career may still be studied in one of Lucian's liveliest pieces. Here it will be enough to mention that Alexander was a clever charlatan of imposing figure, winning manners, and boundless effrontery, who established himself in Abonuteichus, a small town in Paphlagonia, on the southern shore of the Black Sea, where he made a trade of giving oracles in the name of Asclêpius. The god of healing was represented for the occasion by a large tame serpent fitted with a human head made of painted canvas and worked by horsehair strings. Sometimes the oracular responses were delivered by the mouth of the god himself. This was managed with the help of a confederate who spoke through a tube connected with the false head. Such direct communications were, however, only granted as an exceptional favour and for a high price. In most instances the answer was given in writing, and the fee charged for it only amounted to a shilling of our money. Alexander had originally fixed on Abonuteichus, which was his native place and therefore well known to him, as the seat of his operations, on account of the extraordinary superstition of its inhabitants; but the people of the adjacent provinces soon showed themselves to be nowise behind his fellow-townsmen in their credulity. The fame of the new oracle spread over all Asia Minor and Thrace; and visitors thronged to it in such numbers as sometimes to produce a scarcity of provisions. The prophet's gross receipts rose to an average of 3,000l. a year, and the office of interpreting his more ambiguous responses became so lucrative that the two exegêtes employed for this purpose paid each a talent a year (240l.) for the privilege of exercising it.

It was from the Epicureans, of whom we are told that there were a considerable number in these parts, that the most serious opposition to the impostor proceeded; but he contrived to silence their criticisms by denouncing them to the fanatical multitude as 'atheists and Christians.' Towards Epicurus himself Alexander nourished an undying hatred; and when the oracle was consulted with regard to that philosopher's fate, it made answer that he was 'bound in leaden chains and seated in a morass.' The κύριαι δόξαι, or summary of the Epicurean creed, he publicly burned and threw its ashes into the sea; and one unfortunate town which contained a large school of Epicureans he punished by refusing its inhabitants access to the oracle. On the other hand, according to Lucian, he was on the best of terms with the disciples of Plato, Chrysippus, and Pythagoras.[345]

At last tidings of the oracle made their way to Italy and Rome, where they created intense excitement, particularly among the leading men of the state. One of these, Rutilianus, a man of consular dignity and well known for his abject superstition, threw himself head-foremost into the fashionable delusion. He sent off messenger after messenger in hot haste to the shrine of Asclêpius; and the wily Paphlagonian easily contrived that the reports which they carried back should still further inflame the curiosity and wonder of his noble devotee. But, in truth, no great refinement of imposture was needed to complete the capture of such a willing dupe. One of his questions was, what teacher should he employ to direct the studies of his son? Pythagoras and Homer were recommended in the oracular response. A few days afterwards, the boy died, much to the discomfiture of Alexander, whose enemies took the opportunity of triumphing over what seemed an irretrievable mistake. But Rutilianus himself came to the rescue. The oracle, he said, clearly foreshadowed his son's death, by naming teachers who could only be found in the world below. Finally, on being consulted with regard to the choice of a wife, the oracle promptly recommended the daughter of Alexander and the Moon; for the prophet professed to have enjoyed the favours of that goddess in the same circumstances as Endymion. Rutilianus, who was at this time sixty years old, at once complied with the divine injunction, and celebrated his marriage by sacrificing whole hecatombs to his celestial mother-in-law.

With so powerful a protector, Alexander might safely bid his enemies defiance. The governor of Bithynia had to entreat Lucian, whose life had been threatened by the impostor, to keep out of harm's way. 'Should anything happen to you,' he said, 'I could not afford to offend Rutilianus by bringing his father-in-law to justice.' Even the best and wisest man then living yielded to the prevalent delusion. Marcus Aurelius, who was at that time fighting with the Marcomanni, was induced to act on an oracle from Abonuteichus, promising that if two lions were thrown into the Danube a great victory would be the result. The animals made their way safely to the opposite bank; but were beaten to death with clubs by the barbarians, who mistook them for some outlandish kind of wolf or dog; and the imperial army was shortly afterwards defeated with a loss of 20,000 men.[346] Alexander helped himself out of the difficulty with the stale excuse that he had only foretold a victory, without saying which side should win. He was not more successful in determining the duration of his own life, which came to an end before he had completed seventy years, instead of lasting, as he had prophesied, for a hundred and fifty. This miscalculation, however, seems not to have impaired his reputation, for even after his death it was believed that a statue of him in the market-place of Parium in Mysia had the power of giving oracles.[347]

VI.

Another wide-spread superstition was the belief in prophetic or premonitory dreams. This was shared by some even among those who rejected supernatural religion,—a phenomenon not unparalleled at the present day. Thus the elder Pliny tells us how a soldier of the Praetorian Guard in Rome was cured of hydrophobia by a remedy revealed in a dream to his mother in Spain, and communicated by her to him. The letter describing it was written without any knowledge of his mishap, and arrived just in time to save his life.[348] And Pliny was himself induced by a dream to undertake the history of the Roman campaigns in Germany.[349] Religious believers naturally put at least equal confidence in what they imagined to be revelations of the divine will. Galen, the great physician, often allowed himself to be guided by dreams in the treatment of his patients, and had every reason to congratulate himself on the result. The younger Pliny, Suetonius, Dion Cassius, and the emperors Augustus and Marcus Aurelius, were all influenced in a similar manner; and among these Dion, who stands last in point of time, shows by his repeated allusions to the subject that superstition, so far from diminishing, was continually on the increase.[350]

It was natural that the best methods of interpreting so useful a source of information should be greatly sought after, and that they should be systematised in treatises expressly devoted to the subject. One such work, the Oneirocritica of Artemidôrus, is still extant. It was composed towards the end of the second century, as its author tells us, at the direct and repeated command of Apollo. According to Artemidôrus, the general belief in prophecy and in the existence of providence must stand or fall with the belief in prophetic dreams. He looked on the compilation of his work as the fulfilment of a religious mission, and his whole life was devoted to collecting the materials for it. His good faith is, we are told, beyond question, his industry is enormous, and he even exercises considerable discrimination in selecting and elucidating the phenomena which are represented to us as manifestations of a supernatural interest in human affairs. Thus his beliefs may be taken as a fair gauge of the extent to which educated opinion had at that time become infected with vulgar superstition.[351]

Dreams, like oracles, were occasionally employed for the conversion of infidels. An incident of the kind is related by Aelian, a writer who flourished early in the third century, and who is remarkable, even in that age, for his bigoted orthodoxy. A certain man named Euphronius, he tells us, whose delight was to study the blasphemous nonsense of Epicurus, fell very ill of consumption, and sought in vain for help from the skill of the physicians. He was already at death's door, when, as a last resource, his friends placed him in the temple of Asclêpius. There he dreamed that a priest came to him and said, 'This man's only chance of salvation is to burn the impious books of Epicurus, knead the ashes up with wax, and use the mixture as a poultice for his chest and stomach.' On awakening, he followed the divine prescription, was restored to health, and became a model of piety for the rest of his life. The same author gives us a striking instance of prayer answered, also redounding to the credit of Asclêpius, the object of whose favour is, however, on this occasion not a human being but a fighting-cock. The scene is laid at Tanagra, where the bird in question, having had his foot hurt, and evidently acting under the influence of divine inspiration, joins a choir who are singing the praises of Asclêpius, contributing his share to the sacred concert, and, to the best of his ability, keeping time with the other performers. 'This he did, standing on one leg and stretching out the other, as if to show its pitiable condition. So he sang to his saviour as far as the strength of his voice would permit, and prayed that he might recover the use of his limb.' The petition is granted, whereupon our hero claps his wings and struts about 'with outstretched neck and nodding crest like a proud warrior, thus proclaiming the power of providence over irrational animals.'[352]

Aelian mentions other remarkable examples of the piety displayed by brutes. 'Elephants worship the sun, stretching out their trunks to it like hands when it rises while men doubt the existence of the gods, or at least their care for us.' 'There is an island in the Black Sea, sacred to Heracles, where the mice touch nothing that belongs to the god. When the grapes which are intended to be used for his sacrifices begin to ripen, they quit the island in order to escape the temptation of nibbling at them, coming back when the vintage is over. Hippo, Diagoras, Herostratus, and other enemies of the gods would, no doubt, spare these grapes just as little as anything else that was consecrated to their use.'[353]

It is, perhaps, characteristic of the times that Aelian's stories should redound more especially to the credit of Asclêpius and Heracles, who were not gods of the first order, but demi-gods or deified mortals. Their worship, like that of the Nature-powers connected with earth rather than with heaven, belongs particularly to the popular religion, and seems to have been repressed or restrained in societies organised on aristocratic principles. And as more immediate products of the forces by which supernaturalist beliefs are created and maintained, such divinities would profit by the free scope now given to popular predilections. In their case also, as with the earth-goddesses Dêmêtêr and Isis, a more immediate and affectionate relation might be established between the believer and the object of his worship than had been possible in reference to the chief Olympian gods. Heracles had lived the life of a man, his activity had been almost uniformly beneficent, and so he was universally invoked, as a helper and healer, in the sick-chamber no less than on the storm-tost ship.[354] Asclêpius was still more obviously the natural refuge of those who were afflicted with any bodily disease, and, in a time of profound peace, this was of all calamities the most likely to turn men's thoughts towards a supernatural protector. Hence we find that where, apart from Christianity, the religious enthusiasm of the second century reaches its intensest expression, which is in the writings of the celebrated rhetor Aristeides, Asclêpius comes in for the largest share of devotional feeling. During an illness which continued through thirteen years, Aristeides sought day and night for help and inspiration from the god. It came at last in the usual form of a prescription communicated through a dream. Both on this and on other occasions, the excitement of an overwrought imagination combined with an exorbitant vanity made the sophist believe himself to be preferred above all other men as an object of the divine favour. At one time he would see himself admitted in his dreams to an exchange of compliments with Asclêpius; at other times he would convert the most ordinary incidents into signs of supernatural protection. Thus his foster-sister having died on the day of his own recovery from a dangerous epidemic, it was revealed to him in a dream that her life had been accepted as a ransom for his. We are told that the monks of the Middle Ages could not refrain from expressing their indignant contempt for the insane credulity of Aristeides, in marginal notes on his orations; but the last-mentioned incident, at least, is closely paralleled by the well-known story that a devout lady was once permitted to redeem the life of Pius IX. by the sacrifice of her own.[355]

Besides this increasing reverence paid to the deified mortals of ancient mythology, the custom of bestowing divine honours on illustrious men after or even before their death, found new scope for its exercise under the empire. Among the manifestations of this tendency, the apotheosis of the emperors themselves, of course, ranks first. We are accustomed to think of it as part of the machinery of despotism, surrounded by official ceremonies and enforced by cruel punishments; but, in fact, it first originated in a spontaneous movement of popular feeling; and in the case of Marcus Aurelius at least, it was maintained for a whole century, if not longer, by the mere force of public opinion. And many prophecies (which, as usual, came true) were made on the strength of revelations received from him in dreams.[356] But a much stronger proof of the prevalent tendency is furnished by the apotheosis of Antinous. In its origin this may be attributed to the caprice of a voluptuous despot; but its perpetuation long after the motives of flattery or of fear had ceased to act, shows that the worship of a beautiful youth, who was believed to have given his life for another, satisfied a deep-seated craving of the age. It is possible that, in this and other instances, the deified mortal may have passed for the representative or incarnation of some god who was already believed to have led an earthly existence, and might therefore readily revisit the scene of his former activity. Thus Antinous constantly appears with the attributes of Dionysus; and Apollonius of Tyana, the celebrated Pythagorean prophet of the first century, was worshipped at Ephesus in the time of Lactantius under the name of Heracles Alexicacus, that is, Heracles the defender from evil.[357]

VII.

We now pass to a form of supernaturalism more characteristic than any other of the direction which men's thoughts were taking under the Roman empire, and more or less profoundly connected with all the other religious manifestations which have hitherto engaged our attention. This is the doctrine of immortality, a doctrine far more generally accepted in the first centuries of the Christian era, but quite apart from Christian influence, than is supposed by most persons. Here our most trustworthy information is derived from the epigraphic monuments. But for them, we might have continued to believe that public opinion on this subject was faithfully reflected by a few sceptical writers, who were, in truth, speaking only for themselves and for the numerically insignificant class to which they belonged. Not that the Inscriptions all point one way and the books another way. On the contrary, there are epitaphs most distinctly repudiating the notion of a life beyond the grave, just as there are expressions let fall by men of learning which show that they accepted it as true. As much might be expected from the divisions then prevailing in the speculative world. Of all philosophical systems, Epicureanism was, at this time, the most widely diffused: its adherents rejected the belief in another world as a mischievous delusion; and many of them seem to have carefully provided that their convictions should be recorded on their tombs. The monument of one such philosopher, dedicated to eternal sleep, is still extant; others are dedicated to safe repose; others, again, speak of the opposite belief as a vain imagination. A favourite epitaph with persons of this school runs as follows:—'I was nothing and became, I was and am no more, so much is true. To speak otherwise is to lie, for I shall be no more.'[358] Sometimes, from the depths of their unconsciousness, the dead are made to express indifference to the loss of existence. Sometimes, in what was popularly believed to be the spirit of Epicureanism, but was, in reality, most alien to it, they exhort the passer-by to indulge his appetites freely, since death is the end of all.

It must further be noted that disbelief in a future life, as a philosophical principle, was not confined to the Epicureans. All philosophers except the Platonists and Pythagoreans were materialists; and no logical thinker who had once applied his mind to the subject could accept such an absurdity as the everlasting duration of a complex corporeal substance, whether consisting of gaseous or of fiery matter. A majority of the Stoics allowed the soul to continue its individual existence until, in common with the whole world, it should be reabsorbed into the elemental fire; but others looked forward to a more speedy extinction, without ceasing on that account to consider themselves orthodox members of the school. Of these the most remarkable instance is Marcus Aurelius. The great emperor was not blind to what seemed the enormous injustice of death, and did not quite see his way to reconciling it with the Stoic belief in a beneficent providence; but the difficulty of finding room for so many ghosts, and perhaps also the Heracleitean dogma of perpetual transformation, led him to renounce whatever hope he may at one time have cherished of entering on a new existence in some better world.[359] A similar consequence was involved in the principles of the Peripatetic philosophy; and Alexander of Aphrodisias, the famous Aristotelian commentator, who flourished about 200 A.D., affirms the perishable nature of the soul on his own account, and, with perfect justice, attributes the same belief to Aristotle himself.[360]

Among the scientific and literary men who were not pledged to any particular school, we find the elder Pliny rejecting the belief in immortality, not only as irrational but as the reverse of consolatory. It robs us, he declares, of Nature's most especial boon, which is death, and doubles the pangs of dissolution by the prospect of continued existence elsewhere.[361]

Quintilian leaves the question undecided;[362] Tacitus expresses himself doubtfully;[363] and Galen, whose great physiological knowledge enabled him to see how fallacious were Plato's arguments, while his philosophical training equally separated him from the materialists, also refuses to pronounce in favour of either side.[364] What Juvenal thought is uncertain; but, from his general tone, we may conjecture that he leant to the negative side.[365]

Against these we have to set the confident expressions of belief in a future life employed by all the Platonists and Pythagoreans, and by some of the Stoic school. But their doctrines on the subject will be most advantageously explained when we come to deal with the religious philosophy of the age as a whole. What we have now to examine is the general condition of popular belief as evinced by the character of the funereal monuments erected in the time of the empire. Our authorities are agreed in stating that the majority of these bear witness to a wide-spread and ever-growing faith in immortality, sometimes conveyed under the form of inscriptions, sometimes under that of figured reliefs, sometimes more naïvely signified by articles placed in the tomb for use in another world. 'I am waiting for my husband,' is the inscription placed over his dead wife by one who was, like her, an enfranchised slave. Elsewhere a widow 'commends her departed husband to the gods of the underworld, and prays that they will allow his spirit to revisit her in the hours of the night.'[366] 'In death thou art not dead,' are the words deciphered on one mouldering stone. 'No,' says a father to a son whom he had lost in Numidia, 'thou hast not gone down to the abode of the Manes but risen to the stars of heaven.' At Doxato, near Philippi in Macedonia, 'a mother has graven on the tomb of her child: "We are crushed by a cruel blow, but thou hast renewed thy being and art dwelling in the Elysian fields."'[367] This conception of the future world as a heavenly and happy abode where human souls are received into the society of the gods, recurs with especial frequency in the Greek epitaphs, but is also met with in Latin-speaking countries. And, considering how great a part the worship of departed spirits plays in all primitive religions, just such a tendency might be expected to show itself at such a time, if, as we have contended, the conditions of society under the empire were calculated to set free the original forces by which popular faith is created. It seems, therefore, rather arbitrary to assume, as Friedländer does,[368] that the movement in question was entirely due to Platonic influence,—especially considering that there are distinct traces of it to be found in Pindar;—although at the same time we may grant that it was powerfully fostered by Plato's teaching, and received a fresh impulse from the reconstitution of his philosophy in the third century of our era.

Side by side, however, with these exalted aspirations, the old popular belief in a subterranean abode of souls survived under its very crudest forms; and here also modern explorations have brought to light very surprising evidence of the strength with which the grotesque idea of Charon the Stygian ferryman still kept its hold on the imagination of uneducated people. Originally peculiar to Greece, where it still exists under a slightly altered form, this superstition penetrated into the West at a comparatively early period. Thus in the tombs of Campania alone many hundred skeletons have been found with bronze coins in their mouths, placed there to pay their passage across the Styx; and explorations at Praeneste show that this custom reaches back to the middle of the fourth century B.C. We also learn from Lucian that, in his time, the old animistic beliefs were entertained to the extent of burning or burying the clothes, ornaments, and other appurtenances of deceased persons along with their bodies, under the idea that the owners required them for use in the other world; and it is to such deposits that our museums of classical antiquity owe the greater part of their contents.[369]

When the belief in a future life assumes the form last mentioned, it is, as we have said, simply a survival of the most primitive animism, not testifying to any religious reaction at the time when it can be proved to have flourished. It is introduced in the present connexion merely to show what ideas were current among those classes to whose opinions Roman civilisation was gradually giving irresistible weight. How the minds of the richer and more educated classes were affected by this underlying stratum, is shown by the nature of the figured representations with which their last abodes were ornamented. Everyone has been made tolerably familiar with these through the sculptured sarcophagi preserved in our museums; but, from their symbolical character, the significance of the reliefs with which they are decorated is not obvious at first sight; and some of the mythical adventures thus embodied may have been wrought without any reference to the destination of the dark and narrow chamber which they enclosed, or may even have been intended to divert the imagination from sad thoughts by the luxuriance of rushing life and joy and victory which they displayed; but after making every possible deduction on this score, there remain many others offering a deeper source of consolation to the bereaved survivor by the pictured promise of future reunion with those whom he had loved and lost. One favourite subject is the visit of Diana to the sleeping Endymion, by which is clearly foreshadowed an awakening to divine felicity from the sleep of death. The rape of Proserpine, followed by her restoration to the upper world, conveys a similar intention; as also does the fate of Adonis, since he too was believed to have risen from the dead. The marriage of Bacchus and Ariadne unquestionably symbolises the exchange of an earthly for a heavenly life; and the scenes of Bacchic revelry with which the interior of some tombs is decorated, were, to the imagination of those who designed them, no unbecoming image of the joys awaiting a blessed soul in its celestial abode. An inscription of which we have already quoted the opening words expresses in terms that hope of companionship with the joyous band of Dionysus at which the plastic representations can but mutely hint. 'Now in a flowery meadow,' says the mourning mother of Doxato to her child, 'the priestess marked with a sacred seal is enrolling thee in the troop of Bacchus, where the Naiads that bear the sacred baskets claim thee as their fellow to lead the solemn procession by the light of torches.' At the same time, a tenderer or graver note is often struck. The stories of Admêtus and Alcestis, of Protesilaus and Laodameia, point to a renewal of conjugal love beyond the grave. What were formerly supposed to be scenes representing the eternal farewell of husband and wife are, in the opinion of modern archaeologists, pictures of their restoration to each other's arms. Rising higher still, Achilles among the daughters of Lycomêdes probably typifies the liberation of an immortal spirit from the seductions of sense. The labours of Heracles recall his apotheosis, and seem to show that a life of noble effort shall be rewarded hereafter. The battle of the Amazons is an allegory of strife with and triumph over the temptations of earthly delight. Another often-recurring theme, the hunting of the Calydonian boar, may mean the soul's victory over death; but this explanation is offered only as a conjecture of the present writer's.

A remarkable circumstance connected with the evidence afforded by the figured monuments is its progressive character. According to M. Ravaisson, 'As time goes on, the indications of belief in a future life, instead of becoming fainter, grow clearer and more distinct. More and more exalted ideas are formed of the soul's destiny, and ever increasing honours are paid to the dead. Moreover, these ideas and practices are extended so as to cover a greater number of individuals. At first it would seem that the only persons whose fate excites any interest are kings and heroes, the children or the descendants of the gods; in the course of time many others, and at last all, or nearly all, are admitted to a share in the same regard. The ancient principle that happiness is reserved for those who resemble the gods remains unchanged; but the notion of what constitutes resemblance to the gods, or in other words perfection, gradually becomes so modified, that all men may aspire to reach it.'[370]

We are here in presence of a phenomenon like that to which attention was invited in an early chapter of this work.[371] The belief in immortality, entertained under a gloomy and repulsive form by the uneducated, is taken up by the higher classes, brought into contact with their more generous ideas, broadened, deepened, purified, and finally made the basis of a new religion. Nevertheless, in the present instance at least, all was not clear gain; and the faith which smiles on us from storied sarcophagus and mural relief, or pleads for our sympathy in epitaphs more enduring than the hope which they enshrine, had also its grotesque and hideous side, for an expression of which we must turn to literature again.

Once credited with a continued existence, the departed spirit would not remain in the Hades or the Elysium provided for it by the justice or the piety, of the survivor, but persisted in returning to this world and manifesting a most uncomfortable interest in its affairs; or, even if willing to remain at rest, it was liable to be dragged back by incantations, and compelled to reveal the secrets of futurity at the bidding of an unprincipled magician. What science and good feeling combined have proved unable to keep down among ourselves, naturally raged with unmitigated virulence at a time when the primitive barbarism and superstition were only covered over by a crust of culture which at many points was growing thinner every day. Among Latin writers, the younger Pliny, Suetonius, and Apuleius, among Greek writers, Plutarch, Pausanias, Maximus Tyrius, Philostratus, and Dion Cassius, afford unequivocal evidence of their belief and the belief of their contemporaries in ghostly apparitions; and Lucian, while rejecting ghost-stories on his own account, speaks as if they were implicitly accepted even in philosophical circles.[372] Still more abundant is the evidence proving the frequency of attempts made to evoke spirits by means of magical incantations. Horace's Canidia boasts that she can raise the dead even after their bodies have been burned.[373] Lucan describes the process of conjuring up a ghost at length; and it is thought that he inserted the whole scene in his poem as a satire on the emperor Nero, who is known to have been addicted to such practices, as were also his successors, Didius Julianus, Caracalla, and Elagabalus. And that the same art was cultivated by private persons is clear from the allusions made to it by Quintilian, Apuleius, Tertullian, and Heliodôrus.[374]

VIII.

We have now to consider how the philosophy of the empire was affected by the atmosphere of supernaturalism which surrounded it on every side. Of the Epicureans it need only be said that they were true to their trust, and upheld the principles of their founder so long as the sect itself continued to exist. But we may reckon it as a first consequence of the religious reaction, that, after Lucretius, Epicureanism failed to secure the adhesion of a single eminent man, and that, even as a popular philosophy, it suffered by the competition of other systems, among which Stoicism long maintained the foremost place. We showed in a former chapter how strong a religious colouring was given to their teaching by the earlier Stoics, especially Cleanthes. It would appear, however, that Panaetius discarded many of the superstitions accepted by his predecessors, possibly as a concession to that revived Scepticism which was so vigorously advocated just before his time; and it was under the form imposed on it by this philosopher that Stoicism first gained acceptance in Roman society; if indeed the rationalism of

Panaetius was not itself partly determined by his intercourse with such liberal minds as Laelius and the younger Scipio. But Posidonius, his successor, already marks the beginning of a reactionary movement; and, in Virgil, Stoical opinions are closely associated with an unquestioning acceptance of the ancient Roman faith.

The attitude of Seneca is much more independent; he is full of contempt for popular superstition, and his god is not very distinguishable from the order of Nature. Yet his tendency towards clothing philosophical instruction in religious terms deserves notice, as a symptom of the superior facility with which such terms lent themselves to didactic purposes. Acceptance of the universal order became more intelligible under the name of obedience to a divine decree; the unity of the human race and the obligations resulting therefrom impressed themselves more deeply on the imaginations of those who heard that men are all members of one body; the supremacy of reason over appetite became more assured when its dictates were interpreted as the voice of a god within the soul.[375]

The religious tendency of Seneca's philosophy appears rather in his psychology than in his metaphysics, in the stress which he lays on human immortality rather than in his discussions on creation and divine providence. His statements on this subject are not, indeed, very consistent, death being sometimes spoken of as the end of consciousness, and at other times, as the beginning of a new life, the 'birthday of eternity,' to quote a phrase afterwards adopted by Christian preachers. Nor can we be absolutely certain that the promised eternity is not merely another way of expressing the soul's absorption into and identification with the fiery element whence it was originally derived. This, however, is an ambiguity to be met with in other doctrines of a spiritual existence after death, nor is it entirely absent from the language even of Christian theologians. What deserves attention is that, whether the future life spoken of by Seneca be taken in a literal or in a figurative sense, it is equally intended to lead our thoughts away from the world of sensible experience to a more ideal order of things; and, to that extent, it falls in with the more general religious movement of the age. Whether Zeller is, for that reason, justified in speaking of him as a Platonising Stoic seems more questionable; for the Stoics always agreed with Plato in holding that the soul is distinct from and superior to the body, and that it is consubstantial with the animating principle of Nature. The same circumstances which were elsewhere leading to a revival of Platonism, equally tended to develope this side of Stoicism, but it seems needless to seek for a closer connexion between the two phenomena.[376]

On passing from Seneca to Epictêtus, we find that the religious element has received a considerable accession of strength, so considerable, indeed, that the simple progress of time will not altogether account for it. Something is due to the superior devoutness of the Eastern mind—Epictêtus was a Phrygian,—and still more to the difference in station between the two philosophers. As a noble, Seneca belonged to the class which was naturally most inclined to adopt an independent attitude towards the popular beliefs; as a slave, Epictêtus belonged to the class which was naturally most amenable to their authority. It was, however, no accident that philosophy should, at a distance of only a generation, be represented by two such widely contrasted individuals; for the whole tendency of Roman civilisation was, as we have seen, to bring the Oriental element and the servile element of society into ever-increasing prominence. Nothing proves the ascendency of religious considerations in the mind of Epictêtus more strongly than his aversion from the physical enquiries which were eagerly prosecuted by Seneca. Nature interests him solely as a manifestation of divine wisdom and goodness. As a consequence of this intensified religious feeling, the Stoic theory of natural law is transformed, with Epictêtus, into an expression of filial submission to the divine will, while the Stoic teleology becomes an enumeration of the blessings showered by providence on man. In the latter respect, his standpoint approaches very near to that of Socrates, who, although a free-born Athenian citizen, belonged, like him, to the poorer classes, and sympathised deeply with their feeling of dependence on supernatural protection,—a remark which also applies to the humble day-labourer Cleanthes. Epictêtus also shares the idea, characteristic of the

Platonic rather than of the Xenophontic Socrates, that the philosopher is entrusted with a mission from God, without which it would be perilous for him to undertake the office of a teacher, and which, in the discharge of that office, he should keep constantly before his eyes. But the dialectical element which with Socrates had furnished so strong a counterpoise to the authoritative and traditional side of his philosophy, is almost entirely wanting in the discourses of his imitator, and the little of it which he admits is valued only as a means of silencing the Sceptics. On the other hand, the weakness and insignificance of human nature, considered on the individual side, are abundantly illustrated, and contemptuous diminutives are habitually used in speaking of its component parts.[378] It would seem that the attitude of prostration before an overwhelming external authority prevented Epictêtus from looking very favourably on the doctrine of individual immortality; and even if he accepted that doctrine, which seems in the highest degree improbable, it held a much less important place in his thoughts than in those of Cicero and Seneca. It would seem, also, that the Stoic materialism was betraying its fundamental incompatibility with a hope originally borrowed from the idealism of Plato. Nor was this renunciation inconsistent with the ethical dualism which drew a sharp line of distinction between flesh and spirit in the constitution of man, for the superiority of the spirit arose from its identity with the divine substance into which it was destined to be reabsorbed after death.[379]

If, in the philosophy of Epictêtus, physics and morality become entirely identified with religion, religion, on the other hand, remains entirely natural and moral. It is an offering not of prayer but of praise, a service less of ceremonies and sacrifices than of virtuous deeds, a study of conscience rather than of prophecy, a faith not so much in supernatural portents as in providential law.[380] But in arriving at Marcus Aurelius, we have overstepped the line which divides rational religion from superstition. Instances of the good emperor's astonishing credulity have already been given and need not be repeated. They are enough to show that his lavish expenditure on public worship was dictated by something more than a regard for established customs. We know, indeed, that the hecatombs with which his victories were celebrated gave occasion to profane merriment even in the society of that period. On one occasion, a petition was passed from hand to hand, purporting to be addressed to the emperor by the white oxen, and deprecating his success on the ground that if he won they were lost.[381] Yet the same Marcus Aurelius, in speaking of his predecessor Antoninus, expressly specifies piety without superstition as one of the traits in his character which were most deserving of imitation.[382] And, undoubtedly, the mental condition of those who were continually in an agony of fear lest they should incur the divine displeasure by some purely arbitrary act or omission, or who supposed that the gods might be bribed into furthering their iniquitous enterprises, was beyond all comparison further removed from true wisdom than the condition of those who believed themselves to be favoured by particular manifestations of the divine beneficence, perhaps as a recompense for their earnest attempts to lead a just and holy life. We may conclude, then, that philosophy, while injuriously affected by the supernaturalist movement, still protected its disciples against the more virulent forms of superstition, and by entering into combination with the popular belief, raised it to a higher level of feeling and of thought. It was not, however, by Stoicism that the final reconciliation of ancient religion with philosophy could be accomplished, but by certain older forms of speculation which we now proceed to study.

In the preceding chapter we attempted to show that the tendency of Roman thought, when brought into contact with the Greek systems, was to resolve them into their component elements, or to throw them back on their historical antecedents. As a result of this dissolving process, the Stoicism of the second century split up into a number of more or less conflicting principles, each of which received exclusive prominence according to the changeful mood of the thinker who resorted to philosophy for consolation or for help. Stoicism had originally embraced the dynamism of Heracleitus, the teleology of Socrates, the physical morality of Prodicus and his Cynic successors, the systematising dialectic of Aristotle, the psychism of Plato and the Pythagoreans, and, to a certain extent, the superstitions of popular mythology. With Epictêtus, we find the Cynic and the Socratic elements most clearly developed, with Marcus Aurelius, the Socratic and the Heracleitean, the latter being especially strong in the meditations written shortly before his death. In the eastern provinces of the empire, Cynicism was preached as an independent system of morality, and obtained great success by its popular and propagandist character. Dion Chrysostom, a much-admired lecturer of the second century, speaks with enthusiasm of its most famous representative Diogenes, and recounts, with evident gusto, some of the most shameless actions attributed, perhaps falsely, to that eccentric philosopher.[383] And the popular rhetorician Maximus Tyrius, although a professed Platonist, places the Cynic life above every other.[384] But the traditions of Cynicism were thoroughly opposed to the prevalent polytheism; and its whole attitude was calculated to repel rather than to attract minds penetrated with the enthusiastic spirit of the age. To all such the Neo-Pythagorean doctrine came as a welcome revelation.

After its temporary adoption by the Academy, Pythagoreanism had ceased to exist as an independent system, but continued to lead a sort of underground life in connexion with the Orphic and Dionysiac mysteries. When or where it reappeared under a philosophical form cannot be certainly determined. Zeller fixes on the beginning of the first century B.C. as the most probable date, and on Alexandria as the most probable scene of its renewed speculative activity.[385] Some fifty years later, we find Pythagorean teachers in Rome, and traces of their influence are plainly discernible in the Augustan literature. Under its earliest form, the new system was an attempt to combine mathematical mysticism with principles borrowed from the Stoic and other philosophies; or perhaps it was simply a return to the poetical syncretism of Empedocles. Although composed of fire and air, the soul is declared to be immortal; and lessons of holiness are accompanied by an elaborate code of rules for ceremonial purification. The elder Sextius, from whom Seneca derived much of his ethical enthusiasm, probably belonged to this school. He taught a morality apparently identical with that of Stoicism in every point except the inculcation of abstinence from animal food.[386] To this might be added the practice of nightly self-confession—an examination from the moral point of view of how one's whole day has been spent,—were we certain that the Stoics did not originate it for themselves.[387]

The alliance between Neo-Pythagoreanism and Stoicism did not last long. Their fundamental principles were too radically opposed to admit of any reconciliation, except what could be effected by the absorption of both into a more comprehensive system. And Roman Stoicism, at least, was too practical, too scientific, too sane, to assimilate what must have seemed a curious amalgam of mathematical jugglery and dreamy asceticism; while the reputation of belonging to what passed for a secret society would be regarded with particular dread in the vicinity of the imperial court,—it was, in fact, for this particular reason that the elder Seneca persuaded his son to renounce the vegetarian diet which Sotion had induced him to adopt,—and the suspicious hostility of the public authorities may have had something to do with the speedy disappearance of Neo-Pythagoreanism from Rome.[388] On the other hand, so coarsely materialistic and utilitarian a doctrine as that of the Porch, must have been equally repulsive to the spiritualism which, while it discerned a deep kinship permeating all forms of animal existence, saw in the outward conditions of that existence only the prison or the tomb where a heaven-born exile lay immured in expiation of the guilt that had driven him from his former and well-nigh forgotten abode. Hence, after Seneca, we find the two schools pursuing divergent directions, the naturalism of the one becoming more and more contrasted with the spiritualism of the other. It has been mentioned how emphatically Marcus Aurelius rejected the doctrine of a future life, which, perhaps, had been brought under his notice as a tenet of the Neo-Pythagoreans. The latter, on their side, abandoned the Stoic cosmology for the more congenial metaphysics of Plato, which they enriched with some elements from Aristotle's system, but without in the least acknowledging their obligations to those two illustrious masters. On the contrary, they professed to derive their hidden wisdom from certain alleged writings of Pythagoras and his earlier disciples, which, with the disregard for veracity not uncommon among mystics, they did not scruple to forge wholesale. As a consequence of their unfortunate activity, literature was encumbered with a mass of worthless productions, of which many fragments still survive, mixed, perhaps, with some genuine relics of old Italiote speculation, the extrication of which is, however, a task of almost insuperable difficulty.

It is only as a religious philosophy that Neo-Pythagoreanism can interest us here. Considered in this light, the principles of its adherents may be summed up under two heads. First, they taught the separate existence of spirit as opposed to matter. Unlike the Stoics, they distinguished between God and Nature, although they were not agreed as to whether their Supreme Being transcended the world or was immanent in it. This, however, did not interfere with their fundamental contention, for either alternative is consistent with his absolute immateriality. In like manner, the human soul is absolutely independent of the body which it animates; it has existed and will continue to exist for ever. The whole object of ethics, or rather of religion, is to enforce and illustrate this independence, to prevent the soul from becoming attached to its prison-house by indulgence in sensual pleasures, to guard its habitation against defiling contact with the more offensive forms of material impurity. Hence their recommendation of abstinence from wine, from animal food, and from marriage, their provisions for personal cleanliness, their use of linen instead of woollen garments, under the idea that a vegetable is purer than an animal tissue. The second article of the Pythagorean creed is that spirit, being superior to matter, has the power of interfering with and controlling its movements, that, being above space and time, it can be made manifest without any regard to the conditions which they ordinarily impose. To what an extent this belief was carried, is shown by the stories told of Pythagoras, the supposed founder of the school, and Apollonius of Tyana, its still greater representative in the first century of our era. Both were credited with an extraordinary power of working miracles and of predicting future events; but, contrary to the usual custom of mythologers, a larger measure of this power was ascribed to the one who lived in a more advanced stage of civilisation, and the composition of whose biography was separated by a comparatively short interval from the events which it professes to relate.[389]

IX.

The most important result of the old Pythagorean teaching was, that it contributed a large element—somewhat too large, indeed,—to Plato's philosophy. Neo-Pythagoreanism bears precisely the same relation to that revived Platonism which was the last outcome of ancient thought. It will be remembered that the great controversy between Stoicism and Scepticism, which for centuries divided the schools of Athens, and was passed on by them to Cicero and his contemporaries, seemed tending towards a reconciliation based on a return to the founder of the Academy, when, from whatever cause, Greek speculation came to a halt, which continued until the last third of the first century after Christ. At that epoch, we find a great revival of philosophical interest, and this revival seems to have been maintained for at least a hundred years, that is to say, through the whole of what is called the age of the Antonines. In the struggle for existence among the rival sects which ensued, Platonism started with all the advantages that a great inheritance and a great name could bestow. At the commencement of this period, we find the Academy once more professing to hold the doctrines of its founder in their original purity and completeness. Evidently the sober common-sense view of Antiochus had been discarded, and Plato's own writings were taken as an authoritative standard of truth. A series of industrious commentators undertook the task of elucidating their contents. Nor was it only in the schools that their influence was felt. The beauty of their style must have strongly recommended the Dialogues to the attention of literary men. Plutarch, the most considerable Greek writer of his time, was a declared Platonist. So also was the brilliant African novelist, Apuleius, who flourished under Marcus Aurelius. Celsus, the celebrated anti-Christian controversialist, and Maximus, the Tyrian rhetorician, professed the same allegiance; and the illustrious physiologist Galen shows traces of Platonic influence. Platonism, as first constituted, had been an eminently religious philosophy, and its natural tendencies were still further strengthened at the period of its revival by the great religious reaction which we have been studying in the present chapter; while, conversely, in the struggle for supremacy among rival systems, its affinities with the spirit of the age gave it an immense advantage over the sceptical and materialistic philosophies, which brought it into still closer sympathy with the currents of popular opinion. And its partisans were drawn even further in the same direction by the influence of Neo-Pythagoreanism, representing, as this did, one among the three or four leading principles which Plato had attempted to combine.

The chief theological doctrines held in common by the two schools, were the immortality of the soul and the existence of daemons. These were supposed to form a class of spiritual beings, intermediate between gods and men, and sharing to some extent in the nature of both. According to Plutarch, though very long-lived, they are not immortal; and he quotes the famous story about the death of Pan in proof of his assertion;[390] but, in this respect, his opinion is not shared by Maximus Tyrius[391], who expressly declares them to be immortal; and, indeed, one hardly sees how the contrary could have been maintained consistently with Platonic principles; for, if the human soul never dies, much less can spirits of a higher rank be doomed to extinction. As a class, the daemons are morally imperfect beings, subject to human passions, and capable of wrong-doing. Like men also, they are divided into good and bad. The former kind perform providential and retributive offices on behalf of the higher gods, inspiring oracles, punishing crime, and succouring distress. Those who permit themselves to be influenced by improper motives in the discharge of their appointed functions, are degraded to the condition of human beings. The bad and morose sort are propitiated by a gloomy and self-tormenting worship.[392] By means of the imperfect character thus ascribed to the daemons, a way was found for reconciling the purified theology of Platonism with the old Greek religion. To each of the higher deities there is attached, we are told, a daemon who bears his name and is frequently confounded with him. The immoral or unworthy actions narrated of the old gods were, in reality, the work of their inferior namesakes. This theory was adopted by the Fathers of the Church, with the difference, however, that they altogether suppressed the higher class of Platonic powers, and identified the daemons with the fallen angels of their own mythology. This is the reason why a word which was not originally used in a bad sense has come to be synonymous with devil.

It was in perfect accordance with the spirit of Greek philosophy, and more particularly of Platonism, that a connecting link should be interposed between earth and heaven, the human and the divine, especially when, as at this time, the supreme creator had come to be isolated in solitary splendour from the rest of existence; but it would be a mistake to suppose that the daemons were invented for the purpose to which they were applied. We find them mentioned by Hesiod;[393] and they probably represent an even older phase of religious thought than the Olympian gods, being, in fact, a survival of that primitive psychism which peopled the whole universe with life and animation. This becomes still clearer when we consider that they are described, both under their earliest and their latest Greek form, as being, in part at least, human souls raised after death to a higher sphere of activity. Among these, Maximus Tyrius includes the demi-gods of mythology, such as Asclêpius and Heracles, who, as we have seen, were objects of particular veneration under the empire.[394] Thus daemon-worship combined three different elements or aspects of the supernaturalist movement:—the free play given to popular imagination by the decay or destruction of the aristocratic organisation of society and religion, the increasing tendency to look for a perpetuation and elevation of human existence, and the convergence of philosophical speculation with popular faith.

Daemonism, however, does not fill a very great place in the creed of Plutarch; and a comparison of him with his successors shows that the saner traditions of Greek thought only gradually gave way to the rising flood of ignorance and unreason. It is true that, as a moralist, the philosopher of Chaeronea considered religion of inestimable importance to human virtue and human happiness; while, as a historian, he accepted stories of supernatural occurrences with a credulity recalling that of Livy and falling little short of Dion Cassius. Nor did his own Platonistic monotheism prevent him from extending a very generous intellectual toleration to the different forms of polytheism which he found everywhere prevailing.[395] In this respect, he and probably all the philosophers of that and the succeeding age, the Epicureans, the Sceptics, and some of the Cynics alone excepted, offer a striking contradiction to one of Gibbon's most celebrated epigrams. To them the popular religions were not equally false but equally true, and, to a certain extent, equally useful. Where Plutarch drew the line was at what he called Deisidaimonia, the frightful mental malady which, as already mentioned, began to afflict Greece soon after the conquests of Alexander. It is generally translated superstition, but has a much narrower meaning. It expresses the beliefs and feelings of one who lives in perpetual dread of provoking supernatural vengeance, not by wrongful behaviour towards his fellow-men, nor even by intentional disrespect towards a higher power, but by the neglect of certain ceremonial observances; and who is constantly on the look-out for heaven-sent prognostications of calamities, which, when they come, will apparently be inflicted from sheer ill-will, Plutarch has devoted one of his most famous essays to the castigation of this weakness. He deliberately prefers atheism to it, showing by an elaborate comparison of instances that the former—with which, however, he has no sympathy at all—is much less injurious to human happiness, and involves much less real impiety, than such a constant attribution of meaningless malice to the gods. One example of Deisidaimonia adduced by Plutarch is Sabbatarianism, especially when carried, as it had recently been by the Jews during the siege of Jerusalem, to the point of entirely suspending military operations on the day of rest.[396] That the belief in daemons, some of whom passed for being malevolent powers, might yield a fruitful crop of new superstitions, does not seem to have occurred to Plutarch; still less that the doctrine of future torments of which, following Plato's example, he was a firm upholder, might prove a terror to others besides offenders against the moral law,—especially when manipulated by a class whose interest it was to stimulate the feeling in question to the utmost possible intensity.

When we pass from Plutarch to Maximus Tyrius and Apuleius, the darkness grows perceptibly thicker, and is no longer broken by the lucida tela diei with which the Theban thinker had combated at least one class of mistaken beliefs. These writers are so occupied with developing the positive aspects of supernaturalism—daemonology, divination, and thaumaturgy—that they can find no place for a protest against its extravagances and perversions; nor is their mysticism balanced by those extensive applications of philosophy to real life, whether under the form of biography or of discourses on practical morality, which enabled Plutarch's mind to preserve an attitude of comparative sobriety and calmness. Hence while Maximus is absolutely forgotten, and Apuleius remembered only as an amusing story-teller, Plutarch has been perhaps the most successful interpreter between Greek humanity and modern thought. His popularity is now rapidly declining, but the influence exercised by his writings on characters differing so much from one another and from his own as those of Montaigne, Rousseau, and Wordsworth, suffices to prove, if any proof be needed, how deep and wide were the sympathies which they once evoked.

What progress devotional feeling had made during the interval which separated Apuleius from Plutarch and his school, may be illustrated by a comparison of the terms which they respectively employ in reference to the Egyptian Isis. The author of the treatise on Isis and Osiris identifies the goddess with the female or material, as distinguished from the formative principle in Nature; which, to say the least of it, is not giving her a very exalted rank in the scheme of creation. Apuleius, on the other hand, addresses her, or makes his hero address her, in the following enthusiastic language:—

Holy everlasting Saviour of the human race! Bounteous nurse of mortals! Tender mother of the afflicted! Not for a day or night nor even for one little moment dost thou relax thy care for men, driving away the storms of life and stretching forth to them the right hand of deliverance, wherewith thou dost unravel even the tangled threads of fate, soothe the storms of fortune, and restrain the hurtful courses of the stars. The gods above adore thee, the gods below respect; thou dost cause the heavens to roll, the sun to shine; the world thou rulest, and treadest Tartarus under foot. To thee the stars reply, for thee the seasons come again; in thee the deities rejoice, and thee the elements obey. At thy nod the breezes blow, the clouds drop fatness, the seeds germinate and seedlings spring. But my wit is small to celebrate thy praises, my fortune poor to pay thee sacrifices, the abundance of my voice does not suffice to tell what I think of thy majesty, nor would a thousand tongues nor an unwearied and everlasting flow of speech. Therefore what alone religion joined to poverty can achieve, I will provide: an image of thy divine countenance and most holy godhead, guarded for perpetual contemplation within the recesses of my heart.[397]

Doubtless the cool intellect of a Greek and the fervid temperament of an African would always have expressed themselves in widely different accents. What we have to note is that the one was now taking the place of the other because the atmosphere had been heated up to a point as favourable to passion as it was fatal to thought.

After Apuleius, Platonism, outside the lecture rooms of Athens, becomes identified with Pythagoreanism, and both with dogmatic theology. In this direction, philosophy was feeling its way towards a reconciliation with two great Oriental religions, Hebrew monotheism and Medo-Persian dualism. The first advances had come from religion. Aristobulus, an Alexandrian Jew (B.C. 160), was apparently the first to detect an analogy between the later speculations of Plato and his own hereditary faith. Both taught that the world had been created by a single supreme God. Both were penetrated with the purest ethical ideas. Both associated sensuality and idolatry in the same vehement denunciations. The conclusion was obvious. What had been supernaturally revealed to the chosen people could not have been discovered elsewhere by a simple exercise of human reason. Plato must have borrowed his wisdom from Moses.[398] At a later period, the celebrated Philo, following up the clue thus furnished, proceeded to evolve the whole of Greek philosophy from the Pentateuch. An elaborate system of allegorical interpretation, borrowed from the Stoics, was the instrument with which he effected his enterprise. The result was what might have been foreseen—a complete Hellenisation of Hebrew religion. Circumscription, antithesis, and mediation were, as we know, the chief moments of Greek thought. Philo rearranged his monotheistic system according to the scheme which they supplied. He first determined the divine unity with such logical precision as to place God out of relation to the world. Then, in the true Greek spirit, he placed at the other end of his metaphysical scale matter—the shifting, formless, shadowy residuum left behind when every ideal element has been thought away from the world. So conceived, matter became, what it had been to Plato, the principle of all evil, and therefore something with which God could not possibly be brought into contact. Accordingly, the process of creation is made intelligible by the interposition of a connecting link in the shape of certain hypostasised divine attributes or forces, represented as at the same time belonging to and distinct from the divine personality. Of these the most important are the goodness to which the world owes its origin, and the power by which it is governed. Both are united in the Logos or Word.

This last idea—which, by the way, was derived not from Plato but from the Stoics—sums up in itself the totality of mediatorial functions by which God and the world are put into communication with one another. In like manner, Plato had interposed a universal soul between his Ideas and the world of sensible appearances, and had pointed to an arrangement of the Ideas themselves by which we could ascend in thought to a contemplation of the absolute good. There seems, however, to be a difference between the original Hellenic conception and the same conception as adapted to Oriental ways of thinking. With Plato, as with every other Greek philosopher, a mediator is introduced not for the purpose of representing the supreme ideal to us nor of transmitting our aspirations to it, but of guiding and facilitating our approach to it, of helping us to a perfect apprehension and realisation of its meaning. With Philo, on the contrary, the relation of the Logos to God is much the same as that of a Grand Vizier to an Oriental Sultan. And, from this point of view, it is very significant that he should compare it to the high-priest who lays the prayers of the people before the eternal throne, especially when we couple this with his declaration that the Logos is the God of us imperfect beings, the first God being reserved for the contemplation of those who are wise and perfect.[399]

Such a system was likely to result, and before long actually did result, in the realisation of the Logos on earth, in the creation of an inspired and infallible Church, mediating between God and man; while it gave increased authority and expansive power to another superstition which already existed in Philo's time, and of which his Logos doctrine was perhaps only the metaphysical sublimation,—the superstition that the divine Word has been given to mankind under the form of an infallible book. From another point of view, we may discern a certain connexion between the idea that God would be defiled by any immediate contact with the material world, and the Sabbatarianism which was so rife among Gentiles as well as among Jews at that period. For such a theory of the divine character readily associates itself with the notion that holiness excludes not only material industry but any interest the scope of which is limited to our present life.

That Philo's interpretation of Platonism ultimately reacted on Greek thought seems certain, but at what date his influence began to tell, and how far it reached, must remain undecided. Plutarch speaks of God's purity and of his transcendent elevation above the universe in language closely resembling that of the Alexandrian Jew, with whose opinions he may have been indirectly acquainted.[400] We have already seen how the daemons were employed to fill up the interval thus created, and what serious concessions to popular superstition the belief in their activity involved. Still Plutarch does not go so far as to say that the world was not created by God. This step was taken by Numenius, a philosopher who flourished about the middle of the second century, and who represents the complete identification of Platonism with Pythagoreanism, already mentioned as characteristic of the period following that date. Numenius is acquainted with Philo's speculations, and accepts his derivation of Platonism from the Pentateuch. 'What,' he asks, 'is Plato but a Moses writing in the Attic dialect?'[401] He also accepts the theory that the world was created by a single intermediate agent, whom, however, he credits with a much more distinct and independent personality than Philo could see his way to admitting. And he regards the human soul as a fallen spirit whose life on earth is the consequence of its own sinful desires. From such fancies there was but a single step to the more thorough-going dualism which looks on the material world as entirely evil, and as the creation of a blind or malevolent power. This step had already been taken by Gnosticism. The system so called summed up in itself, more completely, perhaps, than any other, all the convergent or conflicting ideas of the age. Greek mythology and Greek philosophy, Zoroastrianism, Judaism, and Christianity each contributed an element to the fantastic and complicated scheme propounded by its last great representative, Valentinus. This teacher pitches his conception of the supreme God even higher than Philo, and places him, like Plato's absolute Good, outside the sphere of being. From him—or it—as from a bottomless gulf proceed a vast series of emanations ending in the Demiurgus or creator of the visible world, whose action is described, in language vividly recalling the speculations of certain modern metaphysicians, as an enormous blunder. For, according to Gnosticism, the world is not merely infected with evil by participation in a material principle, it is evil altogether, and a special intervention of the higher powers is needed in order to undo the work of its delirious author.[402] Here we have a particular side of Plato's philosophy exaggerated and distorted by contact with Zoroastrian dualism. In the Statesman there is a mythical description of two alternate cycles, in one of which the world is governed by a wise providence, while in the other things are abandoned to themselves, and move in a direction the reverse of that originally imposed on them. It is in the latter cycle that Plato supposes us to be moving at present.[403] Again, after having been long content to explain the origin of evil by the resistance of inert matter to the informing power of ideal goodness, Plato goes a step further in his latest work, the Laws, and hazards the hypothesis of an evil soul actively counterworking the beneficent designs of God.[404] And we find the same idea subsequently taken up by Plutarch, who sees in it the most efficient means for exonerating God from all share in the responsibility for physical disorder and moral wrong.[405] But both master and disciple restricted the influence of their supposed evil soul within very narrow limits, and they would have repudiated with horror such a notion as that the whole visible world is a product of folly or of sin.

Gnostic pessimism marks the extreme point of aberration to which Greek thought was drawn by the attraction of Oriental superstition. How it was rescued from destruction by a new systematisation of its ancient methods and results will be explained in another chapter.

X.

In conclusion, a few words may profitably be devoted to the question whether the rationalistic movement of our own age is likely to be followed by such another supernaturalist reaction as that which made itself so powerfully felt during the first centuries of Roman imperialism. There is, no doubt, a certain superficial resemblance between the world of the Caesars and the world in which we live. Everywhere we see aristocracies giving way to more centralised and equitable forms of government, the authority of which is sometimes concentrated in the hands of a single absolute ruler. Not only are the interests and wishes of the poorer and less educated classes consulted with increasing anxiety, but the welfare of women is engrossing the attention of modern legislators to an even greater extent than was the case with the imperial jurists. Facilities for travelling, joined to the far-reaching combinations of modern statesmanship and modern strategy, are every day bringing Europe into closer contact with the religious life of Asia. The decay of traditional and organised theology is permitting certain forms of spontaneous and unorganised superstition to develope themselves once more, as witness the wide diffusion of spiritism, which is probably akin to the demonology and witchcraft of earlier ages, and would, no doubt, be similarly persecuted by the priests,—who, as it is, attribute spiritualistic manifestations to diabolical agency,—had they sufficient power for the purpose. Lastly, corresponding to the syncretism of the Roman empire, we may observe a certain mixture and combination of religious principles, Catholic ideas being avowedly adopted by even the most latitudinarian

Protestants, and Protestant influences entering into Catholicism, much more imperceptibly it is true, but probably to an equal extent.

The analogy between modern Europe and the Roman empire is, however, as we have already hinted, merely superficial. It has been shown in the course of our analysis that to ensure the triumph of superstition in the old world something more was necessary than the destruction of aristocratic government. Every feeling of liberty—except the liberty to die—and almost every feeling of self-respect had to be crushed out by the establishment of an authoritative hierarchy extending from the Emperor down to the meanest slaves, before the voice of Hellenic reason could be hushed. But among ourselves it is rather of the opposite fault—of too great independence and individualism—that complaints are heard. If we occasionally see a hereditary monarch or a popular minister invested with despotic power, this phenomenon is probably due to the circumstances of a revolutionary period, and will in course of time become more and more exceptional. Flatterers, parasites, and will-hunters are not an increasing but a diminishing class. Modern officers, as a body, show none of that contempt for reasoning and amenability to superstition which characterised the Roman centurions; in France, military men are even distinguished for their deadly hatred of priests. And, what is more important than any other element in our comparison, the reserves which modern civilisation is bringing to the front are of a widely different intellectual stature and equipment from their predecessors under Augustus and the Antonines. Since the reorganisation of industry by science, millions of working-men have received an education which prepares them to understand the universality of law much better than the literary education given to their social superiors, which, indeed, bears a remarkable resemblance to the rhetorical and sophistical training enjoyed by the contemporaries of Maximus Tyrius and Apuleius. If as much cannot be said of the middle classes, they are at any rate far more enlightened than Roman provincials, and are likely to improve still further with the spread of education—another peculiarly modern phenomenon. On this point we have, indeed, something better to argue from than à priori probabilities. We see before our eyes the rationalistic movement advancing pari passu with the democratic movement, and, in some countries, overtly aided by it. To say that this alliance has been provoked by an accidental and temporary association of monarchy and aristocracy with Church establishments, is a superficial explanation. The paid advocates of delusion know well where their interest lies. They have learned by experience that democracy means the education of the people, and that the education of the people means the loss of their own prestige. And they know also that, in many cases, the people are already sufficiently educated to use political power, once they have obtained it, for the summary destruction of organised and endowed superstition. What has been said of popular influence applies equally to the influence of women. When they were either not educated at all or only received a literary education, every improvement in their position was simply so much ground gained for superstition. The prospect is very different now. Women are beginning to receive a training like that of men, or rather a training superior to what all but a very few men have hitherto enjoyed. And the result is that, wherever this experiment has been tried, they have flung aside traditional beliefs once supposed to be a necessity of their nature even more decisively and disdainfully than have the professors by whom they are taught.

Once more, there was a cause of intellectual degeneration at work in the ancient world, which for us has almost ceased to exist. This was the flood of barbarism which enveloped and corrupted, long before it overwhelmed, the Hellenised civilisation of Rome. But if the danger of such an inundation is for ever removed, are we equally secure against the contagion of that intellectual miasma which broods over the multitudinous barbarian populations among whom we in turn are settling as conquerors and colonists? Anyone choosing to maintain the negative might point to the example of a famous naturalist who, besides contributing largely to the advancement of his own special science, is also distinguished for high general culture, but whom long residence in the East Indies has fitted to be the dupe of impostures which it is a disgrace even for men and women of fashion to accept. Experience, however, teaches us that, so far at least, there is little danger to be dreaded from this quarter. Instead of being prone to superstition, Anglo-Indian society is described as prevailingly sceptical or even agnostic; and, in fact, the study of theology in its lowest forms is apt to start a train of reflection not entirely conducive to veneration for its more modern developments. For the rest, European enlightenment seems likely to spread faster and farther among the conquered, than Oriental darkness among the conquering race.

So far, we have only considered belief in its relation to the re-distribution of political, social, and national forces. But behind all such forces there is a deeper and more perennial cause of intellectual revolution at work. There is now in the world an organised and ever-growing mass of scientific truths, at least a thousand times greater and a thousand times more diffused than the amount of positive knowledge possessed by mankind in the age of the Antonines. What those truths can do in the future may be inferred from what they have already done in the past. Even the elementary science of Alexandria, though it could not cope with the supernaturalist reaction of the empire, proved strong enough, some centuries later, to check the flood of Mahometan fanaticism, and for a time to lead captivity captive in the very strongholds of militant theological belief. When, long afterwards, Jesuitism and Puritanism between them threatened to reconquer all that the humanism of the Renaissance had won from superstition, when all Europe from end to end was red with the blood or blackened with the death-fires of heretics and witches, science, which had meanwhile been silently laying the foundations of a new kingdom, had but to appear before the eyes of men, and they left the powers of darkness to follow where she led. When the follies and excesses of the Revolution provoked another intellectual reaction, her authority reduced it to a mere mimicry and shadow of the terrible revenges by which analogous epochs in the past history of opinion had been signalised. And this was at a time when the materials of reaction existed in abundance, because the rationalistic movement of the eighteenth century had left the middle and lower classes untouched. At the present moment, Catholicism has no allies but a dispirited, half-sceptical aristocracy; and any appeal to other quarters would show that her former reserves have irrevocably passed over to the foe. What is more, she has unconsciously been playing the game of rationalism for fifteen centuries. By waging a merciless warfare on every other form of superstition, she has done her best to dry up the sources of religious belief. Those whom she calls heathens and pagans lived in an atmosphere of supernaturalism which rendered them far less apt pupils of philosophy than her own children are to-day. It was harder to renounce what she took away than it will be to renounce what she has left, when the truths of science are seen by all, as they are now seen by a few, to involve the admission that there is no object for our devotion but the welfare of sentient beings like ourselves; that there are no changes in Nature for which natural forces will not account; and that the unity of all existence has, for us, no individualisation beyond the finite and perishable consciousness of man.

CHAPTER V.
THE SPIRITUALISM OF PLOTINUS.

I.

Among the most interesting of Plutarch's religious writings is one entitled On the Delays in the Divine Vengeance.

PLOTINUS

As might be expected from the name, it deals with a problem closely akin to that which ages before had been made the subject of such sublime imagery and such inconclusive reasoning by the author of the Book of Job. What troubled the Hebrew poet was the apparently undeserved suffering of the just. What the Greek moralist feels himself called on to explain is the apparent prosperity and impunity of the wicked. He will not for a moment admit that crime remains unavengeful; his object is to show why the retribution does not follow directly on the deed. And, in order to account for this, he adduces a number of very ingenious reasons. By acting deliberately rather than in blind anger, the gods wish to read us a useful lesson in patience and forbearance. Sometimes their object is to give the sinner an opportunity for repentance and amendment; or else they may be holding him in reserve for the performance of some beneficial work. At other times, their justice is delayed only that it may be manifested by some signal and striking form of retribution. In many cases, the final stroke has been preceded by long years of secret torment; and even where no suffering seems to be inflicted, the pangs of remorse may furnish a sufficient expiation. Or again, vengeance may be reserved for a future generation. Some persons hold that to visit the sins of the fathers on the children is unjust, but in this they are profoundly mistaken. Members of the same family and citizens of the same state are connected as parts of one organic whole; sharing in the benefits which accrue from the good deeds of their predecessors, it is right that they should also share in the responsibility for their crimes. Moreover, the posterity of the wicked inherit a sinful disposition which, as the gods can clearly foresee, would betray itself in overt acts were they not cut off in their youth. And it is equally an error to suppose that the original wrongdoers remain unaffected by the retribution which befalls their descendants. On the contrary, they witness it from the next world, where it adds poignancy to their remorse, and entails on them fresh penalties over and above those which they have already been doomed to suffer.

Thus with Plutarch, as with his master Plato, a future world is the grand court of appeal from the anomalies and inequalities of this world; and, following the example of the Gorgias and the Republic, he reserves to the last a terrible picture of the torments held in store for those who have not expiated their transgressions on earth, describing them as they are supposed to have been witnessed by a human soul temporarily separated from the body for the purpose of viewing and reporting on this final manifestation of divine justice. It would appear, however, from the narrative in question that future punishments are not eternal. After a more or less protracted period of expiation, the immortal soul is restored to the upper world, under whatever embodiment seems most appropriate to its former career. Among those whose turn has arrived for entering on a new existence at the moment when Plutarch's visitor makes his descent to hell, is the soul of Nero. The wicked Emperor has just been condemned to assume the form of a viper, when a great light shines forth, and from the midst of the light a voice is heard crying: 'Let him reappear under the guise of a song-bird haunting the neighbourhood of marshes and meres; for he has already paid the penalty of his guilt, and the gods owe him some kindness for having liberated Greece, the best and most beloved by them of all the nations that he ruled.'

It would seem from this singular and touching expression of gratitude that the deathless idealism of Hellas found in Nero's gift of a nominal liberty ample compensation for the very real and precious works of art of which she was despoiled on the occasion of his visit to her shores. At first sight, that visit looks like nothing better than a display of triumphant buffoonery on the one side and of servile adulation on the other. But, in reality, it was a turning-point in the history of civilisation, the awakening to new glories of a race in whom life had become, to all outward appearance, extinct. For more than a whole century the seat of intellectual supremacy had been established in Rome; and during the same period Rome herself had turned to the West rather than to the East for renovation and support. Caesar's conquests were like the revelation of a new world; and three times over, when the two halves of the divided empire came into collision, the champion who commanded the resources of that world had won. Henceforth it was to her western provinces and to her western frontiers that Rome looked for danger, for aggrandisement, or for renown. In Horace's time, men asked each other what the warlike Cantabrians were planning; and the personal presence of Augustus himself was needed before those unruly Iberians could be subdued. His adopted sons earned their first laurels at the expense of Alpine mountaineers. His later years are filled with German campaigns; and the great disaster of Varus must have riveted attention more closely than any victory to what was passing between the Rhine and the Elbe. Under Claudius, the conquest of Britain opened a new source of interest in the West, and, like Germany before, supplied a new title of triumph to the imperial family. Half the literary talent in Rome, the two Senecas, Lucan, and at a later period Martial and Quintilian, came from Spain, as also did Trajan, whose youth fall in this period.

With Nero's visit to Greece in 66 the reaction begins. When, a few years later, the empire was disputed between a general from Gaul and a general from Syria, it was the candidate of the Eastern legions who prevailed; the revolt of Judaea drew attention to Eastern affairs; and the great campaigns of Trajan must have definitely turned the tide of public interest in that direction, notwithstanding the far-sighted protest of Tacitus. On more peaceful ground, Hadrian's Asiatic tours and his protracted residence in Athens completed the work inaugurated by Nero. In his reign, the intellectual centre of gravity is definitely transferred to Greece; and Roman literature, after its last blaze of splendour under Trajan, becomes extinct, or survives only in forms borrowed from the sophistical rhetoric of the East.

Plutarch, who was twenty-one when Nero declared his country free, was the first leader in the great Hellenist revival, without, at the same time, entirely belonging to it. He cared more for the matter than for the form of antiquity, for the great deeds and greater thoughts of the past than for the words in which they were related and explained. Hence, by the awkwardness and heaviness of his style, he is more akin to the writers of the Alexandrian period than to his immediate successors. On the one side, he opens the era of classical idealism; on the other, he closes that of encyclopaedic erudition. The next generation bore much the same relation to Plutarch that the first Sophists bore to Hecataeus and Herodotus. Addressing themselves to popular audiences, they were obliged to study perspicuity and elegance of expression, at the risk, it is true, of verbosity and platitude. Such men were Dion Chrysostom, Herôdes Atticus, Maximus Tyrius, and Aristeides. But the old models were imitated with more success by writers who lived more entirely in the past. Arrian reproduced the graceful simplicity of Xenophon in his narrative of the campaigns of Alexander and his reports of the lectures of Epictêtus. Lucian composed dialogues ranking with the greatest masterpieces of lighter Attic literature. The felicity of his style and his complete emancipation from superstition may probably be traced to the same source—a diligent study of the ancient classics. It is certain that neither as a writer nor as a critic does he represent the average educated taste of his own times. So far from giving polytheism its deathblow, as he was formerly imagined to have done, he only protested unavailingly against its restoration.

Not only oratory and literature, but philosophy and science were cultivated with renewed vigour. The line between philosophy and sophisticism was not, indeed, very distinctly drawn. Epictêtus severely censures the moral teachers of his time for ornamenting their lectures with claptrap rhetoric about the battle of Thermopylae or flowery descriptions of Pan and the Nymphs.[406] And the professed declaimers similarly drew on a store of philosophical commonplaces. This sort of popular treatment led to the cultivation of ethics and theology in preference to logic and metaphysics, and to an eclectic blending of the chief systems with one another. A severer method was inculcated in the schools of Athens, especially after the endowment of their professors by Marcus Aurelius; but, in practice, this came to mean what it means in modern universities, the substitution of philology for independent enquiry. The question was not so much what is true as what did Plato or Aristotle really think. Alexandrian science showed something of the same learned and traditional character in the works of Ptolemy; but the great name of Galen marks a real progress in physiology, as well as a return to the principles of Hippocrates.

Thus, so far as was possible in such altered circumstances, did the Renaissance of the second century reproduce the intellectual environment from which Plato's philosophy had sprung. In literature, there was the same attention to words rather than to things; sometimes taking the form of exact scholarship, after the manner of Prodicus; sometimes of loose and superficial declamation, after the manner of Gorgias. There was the naturalism of Hippias, elaborated into a system by the Stoics, and practised as a life by the new Cynics. There was the hedonism of Aristippus, inculcated under a diluted form by the Epicureans. There was the old Ionian materialism, professed by Stoics and Epicureans alike. There was the scepticism of Protagoras, revived by Aenesidêmus and his followers. There was the mathematical mysticism of the Pythagoreans, flourishing in Egypt instead of in southern Italy. There was the purer geometry of the Alexandrian Museum, corresponding to the school of Cyrênê. On all sides, there was a mass of vague moral preaching, without any attempt to exhibit the moral truths which we empirically know as part of a comprehensive metaphysical philosophy. And, lastly, there was an immense undefined religious movement, ranging from theologies which taught the spirituality of God and of the human soul, down to the most irrational and abject superstition. We saw in the last chapter how, corresponding to this environment, there was a revived Platonism, that Platonism was in fact the fashionable philosophy of that age, just as it afterwards became the fashionable philosophy of another Renaissance thirteen centuries later. But it was a Platonism with the backbone of the system taken out. Plato's thoughts all centred in a carefully considered scheme for the moral and political regeneration of society. Now, with the destruction of Greek independence, and the absorption everywhere of free city-states into a vast military empire, it might seem as if the realisation of such a scheme had become altogether impracticable. The Republic was, indeed, at that moment realising itself under a form adapted to the altered exigencies of the time; but no Platonist could as yet recognise in the Christian Church even an approximate fulfilment of his master's dream. Failing any practical issue, there remained the speculative side of Plato's teaching. His writings did not embody a complete system, but they offered the materials whence a system could be framed. Here the choice lay between two possible lines of construction; and each had, in fact, been already attempted by his own immediate disciples. One was the Pythagorean method of the Old Academy, what Aristotle contemptuously called the conversion of philosophy into mathematics. We saw in the last chapter how the revived Platonism of the first and second centuries entered once more on the same perilous path, a path which led farther and farther away from the true principles of Greek thought, and of Plato himself when his intellect stood at its highest point of splendour. Neo-Pythagorean mysticism meant an unreconciled dualism of spirit and matter; and as the ultimate consequence of that dualism, it meant the substitution of magical incantations and ceremonial observances for the study of reason and virtue. Moreover, it readily allied itself with Oriental beliefs, which meant a negation of natural law that the Greeks could hardly tolerate, and, under the form of Gnostic pessimism, a belief in the inherent depravity of Nature that they could not tolerate at all.

The other alternative was to combine the dialectical idealism of Plato with the cosmology of early Greek thought, interpreting the two worlds of spirit and Nature as gradations of a single series and manifestations of a single principle. This was what Aristotle had attempted to do, but had not done so thoroughly as to satisfy the moral wants of his own age, or the religious wants of the age when a revived Platonism was seeking to organise itself into a system which should be the reconciliation of reason and faith. Yet the better sort of Platonists felt that this work could not be accomplished without the assistance of Aristotle, whose essential agreement with their master, as against Stoicism, they fully recognised. Their mistake was to assume that this agreement extended to every point of his teaching. Taken in this sense, their attempted harmonies were speedily demolished by scholars whose professional familiarity with the original sources showed them how strongly Aristotle himself had insisted on the differences which separated him from the Academy and its founder.[407] To identify the two great spiritualist philosophers being impossible, it remained to show how they could be combined. The solution of such a problem demanded more genius than was likely to be developed in the schools of Athens. An intenser intellectual life prevailed in Alexandria, where the materials of erudition were more abundantly supplied, and where contact with the Oriental religions gave Hellenism a fuller consciousness of its distinction from and superiority to every other form of speculative activity. And here, accordingly, the fundamental idea of Neo-Platonism was conceived.

II.

Plotinus is not only the greatest and most celebrated of the Neo-Platonists, he is also the first respecting whose opinions we have any authentic information, and therefore the one who for all practical purposes must be regarded as the founder of the school. What we know about his life is derived from a biography written by his disciple Porphyry. This is a rather foolish performance; but it possesses considerable interest, both on account of the information which it was intended to supply, and also as affording indirect evidence of the height to which superstition had risen during the third century of our era. Plotinus gave his friends to understand that he was born in Egypt about 205 A.D.; but so reluctant was he to mention any circumstance connected with his physical existence, that his race and parentage always remained a mystery. He showed somewhat more communicativeness in speaking of his mental history, and used to relate in after-life that at the age of twenty-eight he had felt strongly attracted to the study of philosophy, but remained utterly dissatisfied with what the most famous teachers of Alexandria had to tell him on the subject. At last he found in Ammonius Saccas the ideal sage for whom he had been seeking, and continued to attend his lectures for eleven years. At the end of that period, he joined an eastern expedition under the Emperor Gordian, for the purpose of making himself acquainted with the wisdom of the Persians and Indians, concerning which his curiosity seems to have been excited by Ammonius. But his hopes of further enlightenment in that quarter were not fulfilled. The campaign terminated disastrously; the emperor himself fell at the head of his troops in Mesopotamia, and Plotinus had great difficulty in escaping with his life to Antioch. Soon afterwards he settled in Rome, and remained there until near the end of his life, when ill-health obliged him to retire to a country seat in Campania, the property of a deceased friend, Zêthus. Here the philosopher died, in the sixty-sixth year of his age.

Plotinus seems to have begun his career as a public teacher soon after taking up his residence in Rome. His lectures at first assumed the form of conversations with his private friends. Apparently by way of reviving the traditions of Socrates and Plato, he encouraged them to take an active part in the discussion: but either he did not possess the authority of his great exemplars, or the rules of Greek dialogue were not very strictly observed in Rome; for we learn from the report of an eye-witness that interruptions were far too frequent, and that a vast amount of nonsense was talked.[408]

Afterwards a more regular system of lecturing was established, and papers were read aloud by those who had any observations to offer, as in our own philosophical societies.

The new teacher gathered round him a distinguished society, comprising not only professional philosophers, but also physicians, rhetors, senators, and statesmen. Among the last-mentioned class, Rogatianus, who filled the office of praetor, showed the sincerity of his conversion by renouncing the dignities of his position, surrendering his worldly possessions, limiting himself to the barest necessaries of life, and allowing himself to be dependent even for these on the hospitality of his friends. Thanks to this asceticism, he recovered the use of his hands and feet, which had before been completely crippled with gout.[409]

The fascination exercised by Plotinus was not only intellectual, but personal. Singularly affable, obliging, and patient, he was always ready to answer the questions of his friends, even laying aside his work in order to discuss the difficulties which they brought to him for solution. His lectures were given in Greek; and although this always remained to him a foreign language, the pronunciation and grammar of which he never completely mastered, his expressions frequently won admiration by their felicity and force; and the effect of his eloquence was still further heightened by the glowing enthusiasm which irradiated his whole countenance, naturally a very pleasing one, during the delivery of the more impressive passages.[410]

As might be expected, the circle of admirers which surrounded Plotinus included several women, beginning with his hostess Gemina and her daughter. He also stood high in the favour of the Emperor Galienus and his consort Salonina; so much so, indeed, that they were nearly persuaded to let him try the experiment of restoring a ruined city in Campania, and governing it according to Plato's laws.[411] Porphyry attributes the failure of this project to the envy of the courtiers; Hegel, with probably quite as much reason, to the sound judgment of the imperial ministers.[412]

Our philosopher had, however, abundant opportunity for showing on a more modest scale that he was not destitute of practical ability. So high did his character stand, that many persons of distinction, when they felt their end approaching, brought their children to him to be taken care of, and entrusted their property to his keeping. As a result of the confidence thus reposed in him, his house was always filled with young people of both sexes, to whose education and material interests he paid the most scrupulous attention, observing that as long as his wards did not make a profession of philosophy, their estates and incomes ought to be preserved unimpaired. It is also mentioned that, although frequently chosen to arbitrate in disputes, he never made a single enemy among the Roman citizens—a piece of good fortune which is more than one could safely promise to anyone similarly circumstanced in an Italian city at the present day.[413]

Plotinus possessed a remarkable power of reading the characters and even the thoughts of those about him. It is said, probably with some exaggeration, that he predicted the future fate of all the boys placed under his care. Thus he foretold that a certain Polemo, in whom he took particular interest, would devote himself to love and die young; which proved only too true, and may well have been anticipated by a good observer without the exercise of any supernatural prescience. As another instance of his penetration, we are told that a valuable necklace having been stolen from a widow named Chione, who lived in his house with her family, the slaves were all led into the presence of Plotinus that he might single out the thief. After a careful scrutiny, the philosopher put his finger on the guilty individual. The man at first protested his innocence, but was soon induced by an application of the whip to confess, and, what was a much more valuable verification of his accuser's insight, to restore the missing article. Porphyry himself could testify from personal experience to his friend's remarkable power of penetration. Being once about to commit suicide, Plotinus divined his intention, and told him that it proceeded, not from a rational resolution, but from a fit of the blues, as a remedy for which he prescribed change of scene, and this did in fact have the desired effect.[414]

Previous to his forty-ninth year, Plotinus wrote nothing. At that age he began to compose short essays on subjects which suggested themselves in the course of his oral teaching. During the next ten years, he produced twenty-one such papers, some of them only a page or two in length. At the end of that period, he made the acquaintance of his future editor and biographer, Porphyry, a young student of Semitic extraction, whose original name was Malchus. The two soon became fast friends; and whatever speculative differences at first divided them were quickly removed by an amicable controversy between Porphyry and another disciple named Amelius, which resulted in the unreserved adhesion of the former to the doctrine of their common master.[415] The literary activity of Plotinus seems to have been powerfully stimulated by association with the more methodical mind of Porphyry. During the five years[416] of their personal intercourse he produced nineteen essays, amounting altogether to three times the bulk of the former series. Eight shorter pieces followed during the period of failing health which preceded his death, Porphyry being at that time absent in Sicily, whither he had retired when suffering from the fit of depression already mentioned.

Porphyry observes that the first series of essays show the immaturity of youth—a period which he extends to what is generally considered the sufficiently ripe age of fifty-nine;—the second series the full-grown power of manhood; and the last the weakness of declining years. The truth is that his method of criticism, at least in this instance, was to judge of compositions as if their merit depended on their length, and perhaps also with reference to the circumstance whether their subject had or had not been previously talked over with himself. In point of fact, the earlier pieces include some of the very best things that Plotinus ever wrote; and, taking them in the order of their composition, they form a connected exposition of Neo-Platonic principles, to which nothing of importance was ever added. This we shall attempt to show in the most effectual manner possible by basing our own account of Neo-Platonism on an analysis of their contents; and we strongly recommend them to the attention of all Greek scholars who wish to make themselves acquainted with Plotinus at first hand, but have not leisure to wade through the whole of his works. It may also be mentioned that the last series of essays are distinguished by the popular character of their subjects rather than by any evidence of failing powers, one of them, that on Providence,[417] being remarkable for the vigour and eloquence of its style.

By cutting up some of the longer essays into parts, Porphyry succeeded, much to his delight, in bringing the whole number up to fifty-four, which is a product of the two perfect numbers six and nine. He then divided them into six volumes, each containing nine books—the famous Enneads of Plotinus. His principle of arrangement was to bring together the books in which similar subjects were discussed, placing the easier disquisitions first. This disposition has been adhered to by subsequent editors, with the single exception of Kirchhoff, who has printed the works of Plotinus according to the order in which they were written.[418] Porphyry's scrupulous information has saved modern scholars an incalculable amount of trouble, but has not, apparently, earned all the gratitude it deserved, to judge by Zeller's intimation that the chronological order of the separate pieces cannot even now be precisely determined.[419] Unfortunately, what could have been of priceless value in the case of Plato and Aristotle, is of comparatively small value in the case of Plotinus. His system must have been fully formed when he began to write, and the dates in our possession give no clue to the manner in which its leading principles were evolved.[420]

Such, so far as they can be ascertained, are the most important facts in the life of Plotinus. Interwoven with these, we find some legendary details which vividly illustrate the superstition and credulity of the age. It is evident from his childish talk about the numbers six and nine that Porphyry was imbued with Pythagorean ideas. Accordingly, his whole account of Plotinus is dominated by the wish to represent that philosopher under the guise of a Pythagorean saint. We have already alluded to the manner in which he exalts his hero's remarkable sagacity into a power of supernatural prescience and divination. He also tells us, with the most unsuspecting good faith, how a certain Alexandrian philosopher whose jealousy had been excited by the success of his illustrious countryman, endeavoured to draw down the malignant influences of the stars on the head of Plotinus, but was obliged to desist on finding that the attack recoiled on himself.[421] On another occasion, an Egyptian priest, by way of exhibiting his skill in magic, offered to conjure up the daemon or guardian spirit of Plotinus. The latter readily consented, and the Temple of Isis was chosen for the scene of the operations, as, according to the Egyptian, no other spot sufficiently pure for the purpose could be found in Rome. The incantations were duly pronounced, when, much to the admiration of those present, a god made his appearance instead of the expected daemon. By what particular marks the divinity of the apparition was determined, Porphyry omits to mention. The philosopher was congratulated by his countryman on the possession of such a distinguished patron, but the celestial visitor vanished before any questions could be put to him. This mishap was attributed to a friend 'who, either from envy or fear, choked the birds which had been given him to hold,' and which seem to have played a very important part in the incantation, though what it was, we do not find more particularly specified.[422]

Another distinguished compliment was paid to Plotinus after his death by no less an authority than the Pythian Apollo, who at this period had fully recovered the use of his voice. On being consulted respecting the fate of the philosopher's soul, the god replied by a flood of bombastic twaddle, in which the glorified spirit of Plotinus is described as released from the chain of human necessity and the surging uproar of the body, swimming stoutly to the storm-beaten shore, and mounting the heaven-illumined path, not unknown to him even in life, that leads to the blissful abodes of the immortals.[423]

In view of such tendencies, one hardly knows how much confidence is to be placed in Porphyry's well-known picture of his master as one who lived so entirely for spiritual interests that he seemed ashamed of having a body at all. We are told that, as a consequence of this feeling, he avoided the subject of his past life, refused to let his portrait be painted, neglected the care of his health, and rigorously abstained from animal food, even when it was prescribed for him under the form of medicine.[424] All this may be true, but it is not very consistent with the special doctrines of Plotinus as recorded in his writings, nor should it be allowed to influence our interpretation of them. In his personal character and conduct he may have allowed himself to be carried away by the prevalent asceticism and superstition of the age; in his philosophy he is guided by the healthier traditions of Plato and Aristotle, and stands in declared opposition to the mysticism which was a negation of Nature and of life.

How far Plotinus was indebted to Ammonius Saccas for his speculative ideas is another question with respect to which the Pythagoreanising tendencies of his biographer may possibly have contributed to the diffusion of a serious misconception. What Porphyry tells us is this. Before leaving Alexandria, Plotinus had bound himself by a mutual agreement with two of his fellow-pupils, Herennius and Origines (not the Christian Father, but a pagan philosopher of the same age and name), to keep secret what they had learned by listening to the lectures of Ammonius. Herennius, however, soon broke the compact, and Origines followed his example. Plotinus then considered that the engagement was at an end, and used the results of his studies under Ammonius as the basis of his conversational lectures in Rome, the substance of which, we are left to suppose, was subsequently embodied in his published writings. But, as Zeller has pointed out, this whole story bears a suspicious resemblance to what is related of the early Pythagorean school. There also the doctrines of the master were regarded by his disciples as a mystery which they pledged themselves to keep secret, and were only divulged through the infidelity of one among their number, Philolaus. And the same critic proves by a careful examination of what are known to have been the opinions of Origines and Longinus, both fellow-pupils of Plotinus, that they differed from him on some points of essential importance to his system. We cannot, therefore, suppose that these points were included in the teaching of their common master, Ammonius.[425] But if this be so, it follows that Plotinus was the real founder of the Neo-Platonic school; and, in all cases, his writings remain the great source whence our knowledge of its first principles is derived.

III.

In point of style, Plotinus is much the most difficult of the ancient philosophers, and, in this respect, is only surpassed by a very few of the moderns. Even Longinus, who was one of the most intelligent critics then living, and who, besides, had been educated in the same school with our philosopher, could not make head or tail of his books when copies of them were sent to him by Porphyry, and supposed, after the manner of philologists, that the text must be corrupt, much to the disgust of Porphyry, who assures us that its accuracy was unimpeachable.[426] Probably politeness prevented Longinus from saying, what he must have seen at a glance, that Plotinus was a total stranger to the art of literary composition. We are told that he wrote as fast as if he were copying from a book; but he had never mastered even the elements of the Greek language; and the weakness of his eyesight prevented him from reading over what he had written. The mistakes in spelling and grammar Porphyry corrected, but it is evident that he has made no alterations in the general style of the Enneads; and this is nearly as bad as bad can be—disjointed, elliptical, redundant, and awkward. Chapter follows chapter and paragraph succeeds to paragraph without any fixed principle of arrangement; the connexion of the sentences is by no means clear; some sentences are almost unintelligible from their extreme brevity, others from their inordinate length and complexity. The unpractised hand of a foreigner constantly reveals itself in the choice and collocation of words and grammatical inflections. Predicates and subjects are huddled together without any regard to the harmonies of number and gender, so that even if false concords do not occur, we are continually annoyed by the suggestion of their presence.[427]

But even the most perfect mastery of Greek would not have made Plotinus a successful writer. We are told that before taking up the pen he had thoroughly thought out his whole subject; but this is not the impression produced by a perusal of the Enneads. On the contrary, he seems to be thinking as he goes along, and to be continually beset by difficulties which he has not foreseen. The frequent and disorderly interruptions by which his lectures were at one time disturbed seem to have made their way into his solitary meditations, breaking or tangling the thread of systematic exposition at every turn. Irrelevant questions are constantly intruding themselves, to be met by equally irrelevant answers. The first mode of expressing an idea is frequently withdrawn, and another put in its place, which is, in most cases, the less intelligible of the two; while, as a general rule, when we want to know what a thing is, Plotinus informs us with indefatigable prolixity what it is not.

Nevertheless, by dint of pertinacious repetition, the founder of Neo-Platonism has succeeded in making the main outlines, and to a great extent the details, of his system so perfectly clear that probably no philosophy is now better understood than his. In this respect, Plotinus offers a remarkable contrast to the two great thinkers from whom his ideas are principally derived. While Plato and Aristotle construct each particular sentence with masterly clearness, the general drift of their speculations is by no means easy to ascertain; and, even now, critics take diametrically opposite views of the interpretation which is to be put on their teaching with regard to several most important points. The expositors of Neo-Platonism, on the contrary, show a rare unanimity in their accounts of its constitutive principles. What they differ about is its origin and its historical significance. And these are points on which we too shall have to enter, since all the ancient systems are interesting to us chiefly as historical phenomena, and Neo-Platonism more so than any other. Plotinus effected a vast revolution in speculative opinion, but he effected it by seizing on the thoughts of others rather than by any new thoughts or even new developments or applications of his own.

Whether Plotinus was or was not the disciple of Ammonius, it is beyond all doubt that he considered himself the disciple of Plato. There are more than a hundred references to that philosopher in the Enneads, against less than thirty references to all the other ancient thinkers put together;[428] and, what is more remarkable, in only about half of them is he mentioned by name. The reader is expected to know that 'he' always means Plato. And it is an article of faith with Plotinus that his master cannot be mistaken; when the words of oracular wisdom seem to contradict one another, there must be some way of harmonising them. When they contradict what he teaches himself, the difficulty must be removed by skilful interpretation; or, better still, it must be discreetly ignored.[429] On the other hand, when a principle is palpably borrowed from Aristotle, not only is its derivation unacknowledged, but we are given to understand by implication that it belongs to the system which Aristotle was at most pains to controvert.[430]

But numerous as are the obligations, whether real or imaginary, of the Alexandrian to the Athenian teacher, they range over a comparatively limited field. What most interests a modern student in Platonism—its critical preparation, its conversational dialectic, its personal episodes, its moral enthusiasm, its political superstructure—had apparently no interest for Plotinus as a writer. He goes straight to the metaphysical core of the system, and occupies himself with re-thinking it in its minutest details. Now this was just the part which had either not been discussed at all, or had been very insufficiently discussed by his predecessors. It would seem that the revival of Platonic studies had followed an order somewhat similar to the order in which Plato's own ideas were evolved. The scepticism of the Apologia had been taken up and worked out to its last consequences by the New Academy. The theory of intuitive knowledge, the ethical antithesis between reason and passion, and the doctrine of immortality under its more popular form, had been resumed by the Greek and Roman Eclectics. Plutarch busied himself with the erotic philosophy of the Phaedrus and the Symposium, as also did his successor, Maximus Tyrius. In addition to this, he and the other Platonists of the second century paid great attention to the theology adumbrated in those dialogues, and in the earlier books of the Republic. But meanwhile Neo-Pythagoreanism had intervened to break the normal line of development, and, under its influence, Plutarch passed at once to the mathematical puzzles of the Timaeus. With Plato himself the next step had been to found a state for the application of his new principles; and such was the logic of his system, that the whole stress of adverse circumstances could not prevent the realisation of a similar scheme from being mooted in the third century; while, as we have seen, something more remotely analogous to it was at that very time being carried out by the Christian Church. Plato's own disappointed hopes had found relief in the profoundest metaphysical speculations; and now the time has come when his labours in this direction were to engage the attention hitherto absorbed by the more popular or literary aspects of his teaching.

Now it was by this side of Platonism that Aristotle also had been most deeply fascinated. While constantly criticising the ideal theory, he had, in truth, accepted it under a modified form. His universal classification is derived from the dialectic method. His psychology and theology are constructed on the spiritualistic basis of the Academy, and out of materials which the founder of the Academy had supplied. It was therefore natural that Plotinus should avail himself largely of the Stagirite's help in endeavouring to reproduce what a tradition of six centuries had obscured or confused. To reconcile the two Attic masters was, as we know, a common school exercise. Learned commentators had, indeed, placed their disagreement beyond all dispute. But there remained the simpler course of bringing their common standpoint into greater prominence, and combining their theories where this seemed possible without too openly renouncing the respect due to what almost all considered the superior authority of Plato. To which of the two masters Neo-Platonism really owed most is a question that must be postponed until we have made ourselves acquainted with the outlines of the system as they appear in the works of Plotinus.

IV.

It has been already mentioned how large a place was given to erotic questions by the literary Platonists of the second century. Even in the school of Plotinus, Platonic love continued to be discussed, sometimes with a freedom which pained and disgusted the master beyond measure.[431] His first essay was apparently suggested by a question put to him in the course of some such debate.[432] The subject is beauty. In his treatment of it, we find our philosopher at once rising superior to the indecorous frivolities of his predecessors. Physical beauty he declares to be the ideal element in objects, that which they have received from the creative soul, and which the perceptive soul recognises as akin to her own essence. Love is nothing but the excitement and joy occasioned by this discovery. But to understand the truer and higher forms of beauty, we must turn away from sensible perceptions, and study it as manifested in wise institutions, virtuous habits, and scientific theories. The passionate enthusiasm excited by the contemplation of such qualities as magnanimity, or justice, or wisdom, or valour can only be explained by assuming that they reveal our inmost nature, showing us what we were destined for, what we originally were, and what we have ceased to be. For we need only enumerate the vices which make a soul hideous—injustice, sensuality, cowardice, and the like—to perceive that they are foreign to her real nature, and are imposed on her by contamination with the principle of all evil, which is matter. To be brave means not to dread death, because death is the separation of the soul from the body. Magnanimity means the neglect of earthly interests. Wisdom means the elevation of our thoughts to a higher world. The soul that virtue has thus released becomes pure reason, and reason is just what constitutes her intrinsic beauty. It is also what alone really exists; without it all the rest of Nature is nothing. Thus foul is opposed to fair, as evil to good and false to true. Once more, as the soul is beautiful by participation in reason, so reason in its turn depends on a still higher principle, the absolute good to which all things aspire, and from which they are derived—the one source of life, of reason, and of existence. Behind all other loves is the longing for this ultimate good; and in proportion to its superiority over their objects is the intensity of the passion which it inspires, the happiness which its attainment and fruition must bestow. He who would behold this supreme beauty must not seek for it in the fair forms of the external world, for these are but the images and shadows of its glory. It can only be seen with the inward eye, only found in the recesses of our own soul. To comprehend the good we must be good ourselves; or, what is the same thing, we must be ourselves and nothing else. In this process of abstraction, we first arrive at pure reason, and then we say that the ideas of reason are what constitutes beauty. But beyond reason is that highest good of which beauty is merely the outward vesture, the source and principle from which beauty springs.

It is evident that what Plotinus says about beauty and love was suggested by the well-known passages on the same subject in the Phaedrus and the Symposium. His analysis of aesthetic emotion has, however, a much more abstract and metaphysical character than that of his great model. The whole fiction of an antenatal existence is quietly let drop. What the sight of sensible beauty awakens in a philosophic soul is not the memory of an ideal beauty beheld in some other world, but the consciousness of its own idealising activity, the dominion which it exercises over unformed and fluctuating matter. And, in all probability, Plato meant no more than this—in fact he hints as much elsewhere,[433]—but he was not able or did not choose to express himself with such unmistakable clearness.

Again, this preference for mythological imagery on the part of the more original and poetical thinker seems to be closely connected with a more vivid interest in the practical duties of life. With Plotinus, the primal beauty or supreme good is something that can be isolated from all other beauty and goodness, something to be perceived and enjoyed in absolute seclusion from one's fellow-men. God is, indeed, described as the source and cause of all other good. But neither here nor elsewhere is there a hint that we should strive to resemble him by becoming, in our turn, the cause of good to others. Platonic love, on the contrary, first finds its reality and truth in unremitting efforts for the enlightenment and elevation of others, being related to the transmission of spiritual life just as the love inspired by visible beauty is related to the perpetuation and physical ennoblement of the race.

This preference of pure abstract speculation to beneficent action may be traced to the influence of Aristotle. Some of the most enthusiastic expressions used by Plotinus in speaking of his supreme principle seem to have been suggested by the Metaphysics and the last book of the Nicomachean Ethics. The self-thinking thought of the Stagirite does not, indeed, take the highest rank with him. But it is retained in his system, and is only relegated to a secondary place because, for reasons which we shall explain hereafter, it does not fulfil equally well with Plato's Idea of Good, the condition of absolute and indivisible unity, without which a first principle could not be conceived by any Greek philosopher. But this apparent return to the standpoint of the Republic really involves a still wider departure from its animating spirit. In other words, Plotinus differs from Aristotle as Aristotle himself had differed from Plato; he shares the same speculative tendency, and carries it to a greater extreme.

We have also to note that Plotinus arrives at his Absolute by a method apparently very different from that pursued by either of his teachers. Plato's primal beauty is, on the face of it, an abstraction and generalisation from all the scattered and imperfect manifestations of beauty to be met with in our objective experience. And Aristotle is led to his conception of an eternal immaterial thought by two lines of analysis, both starting from the phenomena of external Nature. The problem of his Physics is to account for the perpetuity of motion. The problem of his Metaphysics is to explain the transformation of potential into actual existence. Plotinus, on the other hand, is always bidding us look within. What we admire in the objective world is but a reflex of ourselves. Mind is the sole reality; and to grasp this reality under its highest form, we must become like it. Thus the more we isolate our own personality and self-identity from the other interests and experiences of life, the more nearly do we approach to consciousness of and coalescence with the supreme identity wherein all things have their source.

But on looking at the matter a little more closely, we shall find that Plotinus only set in a clearer light what had all along been the leading motive of his predecessors. We have already observed that Plato's whole mythological machinery is only a fanciful way of expressing that independent experience which the mind derives from the study of its own spontaneous activity. And the process of generalisation described in the Symposium is really limited to moral phenomena. Plato's standpoint is less individualistic than that of Plotinus in so far as it involves a continual reference to the beliefs, experiences, and wants of other men; but it is equally subjective, in the sense of interpreting all Nature by the analogies of human life. There are even occasions when his spiritualism goes the length of inculcating complete withdrawal from the world of common life into an ideal sphere, when he seems to identify evil with matter, when he reduces all virtue to contempt for the interests of the body, in language which his Alexandrian successor could adopt without any modification of its obvious meaning.[434]

So also with Aristotle. As a naturalist, he is, indeed, purely objective; but when he offers a general explanation of the world, the subjective element introduced by Protagoras and Socrates at once reappears. Simple absolute self-consciousness is for him the highest good, the animating principle of Nature, the most complete reality, and the only one that would remain, were the element of nonentity to disappear from this world. The utter misconception of dynamic phenomena which marks his physics and astronomy can only be accounted for by his desire to give life the priority over mechanical motion, and reason the priority over life. Thus his metaphysical method is essentially identical with the introspective method recommended by Plotinus, and, if fully worked out, might have led to the same results.

We cannot, then, agree with Zeller, when he groups the Neo-Platonists together with the other post-Aristotelian schools, on the ground that they are all alike distinguished from Plato and Aristotle by the exclusive attention which they pay to subjective and practical, as opposed to scientific and theoretical interests. It seems to us that such distinctions are out of relation to the historical order in which the different systems of Greek philosophy were evolved. It is not in the substance of their teaching, but in their diminished power of original speculation, that the thinkers who came after Aristotle offer the strongest contrast to their predecessors. In so far as they are exclusively practical and subjective, they follow the Humanists and Socrates. In so far as they combine Socratic tendencies with physical studies, they imitate the method of Plato and Aristotle. Their cosmopolitan naturalism is inherited from the Cynics in the first instance, more remotely from the physiocratic Sophists, and, perhaps, in the last resort, from Heracleitus. Their religion is traceable either to Pythagoras, to Socrates, or to Plato. Their scepticism is only a little more developed than that of Protagoras and the Cyrenaics. But if we seek for some one principle held in common by all these later schools, and held by none of the earlier schools, we shall seek for it in vain. The imitative systems are separated from one another by the same fundamental differences as those which divide the original systems. Now, in both periods, the deepest of all differences is that which divides the spiritualists from the materialists. In both periods, also, it is materialism that comes first. And in both, the transition from one doctrine to the other is marked by the exclusive prominence given to subjective, practical, sceptical, or theological interests in philosophy; by the enthusiastic culture of rhetoric in general education; and by a strong religious reaction in the upper ranks of society.

Thus we can quite agree with Zeller when he observes[435] that Neo-Platonism only carried out a tendency towards spiritualism which had been already manifesting itself among the later Stoics, and had been still further developed by the Neo-Pythagoreans. But what does this prove? Not what Zeller contends for, which is that Neo-Platonism stands on the same ground with the other post-Aristotelian systems, but simply that a recurrence of the same intellectual conditions was being followed by a recurrence of the same results. Now, as before, materialism was proving its inadequacy to account for the facts of mental experience. Now, as before, morality, after being cut off from physical laws, was seeking a basis in religious or metaphysical ideas. Now, as before, the study of thoughts was succeeding to the study of words, and the methods of popular persuasion were giving place to the methods of dialectical demonstration. Of course, the age of Plotinus was far inferior to the age of Plato in vitality, in genius, and in general enlightenment, notwithstanding the enormous extension which Roman conquest had given to the superficial area of civilisation, as the difference between the Enneads and the Dialogues would alone suffice to prove. But this does not alter the fact that the general direction of their movement proceeds in parallel lines.

In saying that the post-Aristotelian philosophers were not original thinkers, we must guard against the supposition that they contributed nothing of value to thought. On the contrary, while not putting forward any new theories, they generalised some of the principles borrowed from their predecessors, worked out others in minute detail, and stated the arguments on both sides of every controverted point with superior dialectic precision. Thus, while materialism had been assumed as self-evidently true by the pre-Socratic schools, it was maintained by the Stoics and Epicureans on what seemed to be grounds of experience and reason. And, similarly, we find that Plotinus, having arrived at the consciousness that spiritualism is the common ground on which Plato and Aristotle stand, the connecting trait which most completely distinguishes them from their successors, proceeds in his second essay[436] to argue the case against materialism more powerfully than it had ever been argued before, and with nearly as much effect as it has ever been argued since.

V.

Our personality, says the Alexandrian philosopher, cannot be a property of the body, for this is composed of parts, and is in a state of perpetual flux. A man's self, then, is his soul; and the soul cannot be material, for the ultimate elements of matter are inanimate, and it is inconceivable that animation and reason should result from the aggregation of particles which, taken singly, are destitute of both; while, even were it possible, their disposition in a certain order would argue the presence of an intelligence controlling them from without. The Stoics themselves admit the force of these considerations, when they attribute reason to the fiery element or vital breath by which, according to them, all things are shaped. They do, indeed, talk about a certain elementary disposition as the principle of animation, but this disposition is either identical with the matter possessing it, in which case the difficulties already mentioned recur, or distinct from it, in which case the animating principle still remains to be accounted for.

Again, to suppose that the soul shares in the changes of the body is incompatible with the self-identity which memory reveals. To suppose that it is an extended substance is incompatible with its simultaneous presence, as an indivisible whole, at every point to which its activity reaches; as well as with the circumstance that all our sensations, though received through different organs, are referred to a common centre of consciousness. If the sensorium is a fluid body it will have no more power of retaining impressions than water; while, if it is a solid, new impressions will either not be received at all, or only when the old impressions are effaced.

Passing from sensation to thought, it is admitted that abstract conceptions are incorporeal: how, then, can they be received and entertained by a corporeal substance? Or what possible connexion can there be between different arrangements of material particles and such notions as temperance and justice? This is already a sufficiently near approach to the language of modern philosophy. In another essay, which according to the original arrangement stands third, and must have been composed immediately after that whence the foregoing arguments are transcribed, there is more than an approach, there is complete coincidence.[437] To deduce mind from atoms is, says Plotinus, if we may so speak, still more impossible than to deduce it from the elementary bodies. Granting that the atoms have a natural movement downwards, granting that they suffer a lateral deflection and so impinge on one another, still this could do no more than produce a disturbance in the bodies against which they strike. But to what atomic movement can one attribute psychic energies and affections? What sort of collision in the vertical line of descent, or in the oblique line of deflection, or in any direction you please, will account for the appearance of a particular kind of reasoning or mental impulse or thought, or how can it account for the existence of such processes at all? Here, of course, Plotinus is alluding to the Epicureans; but it is with the Stoic and other schools that he is principally concerned, and we return to his attack on their psychology.

The activities of the soul are thought, sensation, reasoning, desire, attention, and so forth: the activities of body are heat, cold, impact, and gravitation; if to these we add the characteristics of mind, the latter will have no special properties by which it can be known. And even in body we distinguish between quantity and quality; the former, at most, being corporeal, and the latter not corporeal at all. Here Plotinus just touches the idealistic method of modern spiritualism, but fails to follow it any further. He seems to have adopted Aristotle's natural realism as a sufficient theory of external perception, and to have remained uninfluenced by Plato's distrust of sensible appearances.

After disposing of the Stoic materialism, according to which the soul, though distinct from the body, is, equally with it, an extended and resisting substance, our philosopher proceeds to discuss the theories which make it a property or function of the body. The Pythagorean notion of the soul as a harmony of the body is met by a reproduction of the well-known arguments used against it in Plato's Phaedo. Then comes the Aristotelian doctrine that the soul is the entelechy—that is to say, the realised purpose and perfection—of the physical organism to which it belongs. This is an idea which Aristotle himself had failed to make very clear, and the inadequacy of which he had virtually acknowledged by ascribing a different origin to reason, although this is counted as one of the psychic faculties. Plotinus, at any rate, could not appreciate an explanation which, whatever else it implied, certainly involved a considerable departure from his own dualistic interpretation of the difference between spirit and matter. He could not enter into Aristotle's view of the one as a lower and less concentrated form of the other. The same arguments which had already been employed against Stoicism are now turned against the Peripatetic psychology. The soul as a principle, not only of memory and desire, but even of nutrition, is declared to be independent of and separable from the body. And, finally, as a result of the whole controversy, its immortality is affirmed. But how far this immortality involves the belief in a prolongation of personal existence after death, is a point which still remains uncertain. We shall return to the question in dealing with the religious opinions of Plotinus.

Closely connected with the materialism of the Stoics, and equally adverse to the principles of Plato and Aristotle, was their fatalism. In opposition to this, Plotinus proceeds to develop the spiritualistic doctrine of free-will.[438] In the previous discussion, we had to notice how closely his arguments resemble those employed by more modern controversialists. We have here to point out no less wide a difference between the two. Instead of presenting free-will as a fact of consciousness which is itself irreconcilable with the dependence of mental on material changes, our philosopher, conversely, infers that the soul must be free both from the conditions of mechanical causation and from the general interdependence of natural forces, because it is an individual substance.[439] In truth, the phenomena of volition were handled by the ancient philosophers with a vagueness and a feebleness offering the most singular contrast to their powerful and discriminating grasp of other psychological problems. Of necessarianism, in the modern sense, they had no idea. Aristotle failed to see that, quite apart from external restraints, our choice may conceivably be determined with the utmost rigour by an internal motive; nor could he understand that the circumstances which make a man responsible for his actions do not amount to a release of his conduct from the law of universal causation. In this respect, Plato saw somewhat deeper than his disciple, but created fresh confusion by identifying freedom with the supremacy of reason over irrational desire.[440] Plotinus generally adopts the Platonist point of view. According to this, the soul is free when she is extricated from the bonds of matter, and determined solely by the conditions of her spiritual existence. Thus virtue is not so much free as identical with freedom; while, contrariwise, vice means enslavement to the affections of the body, and therefore comes under the domain of material causation.[441] Yet, again, in criticising the fatalistic theories which represent human actions as entirely predetermined by divine providence, he protests against the ascription of so much that is evil to so good a source, and insists that at least the bad actions of men are due to their own free choice.[442]

In vindicating human freedom, Plotinus had to encounter a difficulty exceedingly characteristic of his age. This was the astrological superstition that everything depended on the stars, and that the future fate of every person might be predicted by observing their movements and configurations at the time of his birth. Philosophers found it much easier to demolish the pretensions of astrology by an abstract demonstration of their absurdity, than to get rid of the supposed facts which were currently quoted in their favour. That fortunes could be foretold on the strength of astronomical calculations with as much certainty as eclipses, seems to have been an accepted article of belief in the time of Plotinus, and one which he does not venture to dispute. He is therefore obliged to satisfy himself with maintaining that the stars do not cause, but merely foreshow the future, in the same manner as the flight of birds, to the prophetic virtue of which he also attaches implicit credence. All parts of Nature are connected by such an intimate sympathy, that each serves as a clue to the rest; and, on this principle, the stars may be regarded as the letters of a scripture in which the secrets of futurity are revealed.[443]

How much originality there may be in the anti-materialistic arguments of Plotinus we cannot tell. He certainly marks a great advance on Plato and Aristotle, approximating, in this respect, much more closely than they do to the modern standpoint. The indivisibility and permanence of mind had, no doubt, been strongly insisted on by those teachers, in contrast with the extended and fluctuating nature of body. But they did not, like him, deduce these characteristics from a direct analysis of consciousness as such. Plato inferred the simplicity and self-identity of mind from the simplicity and self-identity of the ideas which it contemplates. Aristotle went a step further, or perhaps only expressed the same meaning more clearly, when he associated immateriality with the identity of subject and object in thought.[444] Moreover, both Plato and Aristotle seem to have rested the whole spiritualistic case on objective rather than on subjective considerations; although, as we have seen, the subjective interest was what dominated all the while in their thoughts. Starting with the analogy of a living body, Plato argues, both in the Phaedrus and in the Laws, that soul must everywhere be the first cause of motion, and therefore must exist prior to body.[445] The elaborate scientific analysis of Aristotle's Physics leads up to a similar conclusion; and the ontological analysis of the Metaphysics starts with the distinction between Form and Matter in bodies, to end with the question of their relative priority, and of the objective machinery by which they are united. Plotinus, too, sometimes refers to mind as the source of physical order; but this is rather in deference to his authorities than because the necessity of such an explanation seemed to him, as it did to them, the deepest ground of a spiritualistic philosophy. On the other hand, his psychological arguments for the immateriality of the soul are drawn from a wider area of experience than theirs, feeling being taken into account no less than thought; instead of restricting himself to one particular kind of cognition for evidence of spiritual power, he looks for it in every manifestation of living personality.

In criticising the Stoic system as a whole, the New Academy and the later Sceptics had incidentally dwelt on sundry absurdities which followed from the materialistic interpretation of knowledge; and Plotinus evidently derived some of his most forcible objections from their writings; but no previous philosopher that we know of had set forth the whole case for spiritualism and against materialism with such telling effect. And what is, perhaps, more important than any originality in detail, is the profound insight shown in choosing this whole question of spiritualism versus materialism for the ground whereon the combined forces of Plato and Aristotle were to fight their first battle against the naturalistic system which had triumphed over them five centuries before. It was on dialectical and ethical grounds that the controversy between Porch and Academy, on ethical and religious grounds that the controversy between Epicureanism and all other schools of philosophy, had hitherto been conducted. Cicero and Plutarch never allude to their opponents as materialists. Only once, in his polemic against Colôtes, does Plutarch observe that neither a soul nor anything else could be made out of atoms, but this is because they are discrete, not because they are extended.[446] For the rest, his method is to trip up his opponents by pointing out their inconsistencies, rather than to cut the ground from under their feet by proving that their theory of the universe is wrong.

Under such guidance as this. Platonism had made but little way. We saw, in the concluding sections of the last chapter and in the opening section of the present chapter, that it profited by the religious and literary revival of the second century, just as it was to profit long afterwards by the greater revival of the fifteenth century, so much so as to become the fashionable philosophy of the age. Yet, even in that period of its renewed splendour, the noblest of contemporary thinkers was not a Platonist but a Stoic; and although it would be unfair to measure the moral distance between the Porch and the Academy by the interval which separates an Aurelius from an Apuleius, still it would seem as if naturalism continued to be the chosen creed of strenuous and dutiful endeavour, while spiritualism was drifting into an alliance with hysterical and sensuous superstition. If we may judge by the points which Sextus Empiricus selects for controversial treatment, Stoicism was still the reigning system in his time, that is to say, about the beginning of the third century; and if, a generation later, it had sunk into neglect, every rival school, except that of Epicurus, was in exactly the same condition. Thus the only advance made was to substitute one form of materialism for another, until Neo-Platonism came and put an end to their disputes by destroying the common foundation on which they stood; while, at the same time, it supplied a completely organised doctrine round which the nobler elements of the Hellenic revival could rally for a last stand against the foes that were threatening it from every side.

VI.

We have seen how Plotinus establishes the spiritualistic basis of his philosophy. We have now to see how he works out from it in all directions, developing the results of his previous enquiries into a complete metaphysical system. It will have been observed that the whole method of reasoning by which materialism was overthrown, rested on the antithesis between the unity of consciousness and the divisibility of corporeal substance. Very much the same method was afterwards employed by Cartesianism to demonstrate the same conclusion. But with Descartes and his followers, the opposition between soul and body was absolute, the former being defined as pure thought, the latter as pure extension. Hence the extreme difficulty which they experienced in accounting for the evident connexion between the two. The spiritualism of Plotinus did not involve any such impassable chasm between consciousness and its object. According to him, although the soul is contained in or depends on an absolutely self-identical unity, she is not herself that unity, but in some degree shares the characters of divisibility and extension.[117] If we conceive all existence as bounded at either extremity by two principles, the one extended and the other inextended, then soul will still stand midway between them; not divided in herself, but divided in respect to the bodies which she animates. Plotinus holds that such an assumption is necessitated by the facts of sensation. A feeling of pain, for example, is located in a particular point of the body, and is, at the same time, apprehended as my feeling, not as some one else's. A similar synthesis obtains through the whole of Nature. The visible universe consists of many heterogeneous parts, held together by a single animating principle. And we can trace the same qualities and figures through a multitude of concrete individuals, their essential unity remaining unbroken, notwithstanding the dispersion of the objects in which they inhere.

Here Plotinus avowedly follows the teaching of Plato, who, in the Timaeus, describes Being or Substance as composed by mingling the indivisible and unchanging with the divisible and corporeal principle.[448] And, although there is no express reference, we know that in placing soul between the two, he was equally following Plato. It is otherwise in the next essay, which undertakes to give a more explicit analysis of psychical phenomena.[449] The soul, we are told, consists, like external objects, of two elements related to one another as Form and Matter. These are reason and sense. The office of the former is, primarily, to enlighten and control the latter. Plato had already pointed to such a distinction; but Aristotle was the first to work it out clearly, and to make it the hinge of his whole system. It is, accordingly, under the guidance of Aristotle that Plotinus proceeds in what he has next to say. Just as there is a soul of the world corresponding to our soul, so also, he argues, there must be a universal objective Reason outside and above the world. In speaking of this Reason, we shall, for clearness' sake, in general call it by its Greek name, Nous. Nous, according to Aristotle, is the faculty by which we apprehend abstract ideas; it is self-thinking thought; and, as such, it is the prime mover of Nature. Plotinus adopts the first two positions unreservedly, and the third to a certain extent; while he brings all three into combination with the Platonic theory of ideas. It had always been an insuperable difficulty in the way of Plato's teaching that it necessitated, or seemed to necessitate, the unintelligible notion of ideas existing without any mind to think them. For a disciple of Aristotle, the difficulty ceases to exist if the archetypal essences assumed by Plato are conceived as residing in an eternal Nous. But, on the other hand, how are we to reconcile such an accommodation with Aristotle's principle, that the Supreme Intelligence can think nothing but itself? Simply by generalising from the same master's doctrine that the human Nous is identical with the ideas which it contemplates. Thought and its object are everywhere one. Thus, according to Plotinus, the absolute Nous embraces the totality of archetypes or forms which we see reflected and embodied in the material universe. In thinking them, it thinks itself, not passing from one to the other as in discursive reasoning, nor bringing them into existence by the act of thought, but apprehending them as simultaneously present realities.

To explain how the Nous could be identical with a number of distinct ideas was a difficult problem. We shall have to show at a more advanced stage of our exposition how Plotinus endeavoured to solve it with the help of Plato's Sophist. In the essay where his theory is first put forward, he cuts the knot by asserting that each idea virtually contains every other, while each in its actual and separate existence is, so to speak, an independent Nous. But correlation is not identity; and to say that each idea thinks itself is not to explain how the same subject can think, and in thinking be identical with all. The personal identity of the thinking subject still stands in unreconciled opposition to the multitude of thoughts which it entertains, whether successively or in a single intuition. Of two things one: either the unity of the Nous or the diversity of its ideas must be sacrificed. Plotinus evades the alternative by a kind of three-card trick. Sometimes his ideal unity is to be found under the notion of convergence to a common centre, sometimes under the notion of participation in a common property, sometimes under the notion of mutual equivalence.

The confusion was partly inherited from Aristotle. When discussing the psychology of that philosopher, we showed that his active Nous is no other than the idea of which we are at any moment actually conscious. Our own reason is the passive Nous, whose identity is lost in the multiplicity of objects with which it becomes identified in turn. But Aristotle was careful not to let the personality of God, or the supreme Nous, be endangered by resolving it into the totality of substantial forms which constitute Nature. God is self-conscious in the strictest sense. He thinks nothing but himself. Again, the subjective starting-point of Plotinus may have affected his conception of the universal Nous. A single individual may isolate himself from his fellows in so far as he is a sentient being; he cannot do so in so far as he is a rational being. His reason always addresses itself to the reason of some one else—a fact nowhere brought out so clearly as in the dialectic philosophy of Socrates and Plato. Then, when an agreement has been established, their minds, before so sharply divided, seem to be, after all, only different personifications of the same universal spirit. Hence reason, no less than its objects, comes to be conceived as both many and one. And this synthesis of contradictories meets us in modern German as well as in ancient Greek philosophy.

After his preliminary analysis of Nous, we find Plotinus working out in two directions from the conception so obtained.[450] He begins by explaining in what relation the human soul stands to the universal reason. To him, personally, it seemed as if the world of thought into which he penetrated by reflecting on his own inmost essence, was so much the real home of his soul that her presence in a bodily habitation presented itself as a difficulty requiring to be cleared up. In this connexion, he refers to the opinions of the Pythagoreans, who looked on our earthly life as an unmixed evil, a punishment for some sin committed in a former stage of existence. Their views seem to have been partly shared by Plato. Sometimes he calls the body a prison and a tomb into which the soul has fallen from her original abode. Yet, in his Timaeus, he glorifies the visible world, and tells us that the universal soul was divinely appointed to give it life and reason; while our individual souls have also their part to play in perfecting the same providential scheme.

It is to the second theory that Plotinus evidently leans. However closely his life may have been conformed to the Pythagorean model—a point with respect to which we have nothing better than the very prejudiced statements of Porphyry to rely on—there is no trace of Pythagorean asceticism in his writings. Hereafter we shall see how hostile he was to Gnostic pessimism. In the preceding essay, he had already specified admiration for physical beauty as a first and necessary step in the soul's ascent to a contemplation of spiritual realities;[451] and now it is under the guidance of Plato's later speculations that he proceeds to account for her descent from that higher world to the restraints of matter and of sense.

With regard to the universal soul of Nature, there is, indeed, no difficulty at all. In giving a sensible realisation to the noetic ideas, she suffers no degradation or pollution by contact with the lower elements of matter. Enthroned on the outer verge of the cosmos, she governs the whole course of Nature by a simple exercise of volition, and in the enjoyment of a felicity which remains undisturbed by passion or desire. But just as we have seen the supreme Nous resolving itself into a multitude of individual intelligences, so also does the cosmic soul produce many lesser or partial souls of which our own is one. Now these derivative souls cannot all be equal, for that would be to defeat the purpose of creation, which is to realise all the possibilities of creation from the highest to the lowest. Thus each has an office corresponding to her place in the scale of perfection.[452] We may say of the human soul that she stoops to conquer. Her mission is to cope with the more recalcitrant forms of matter. It is to the struggle with their impurities that the troubles and passions of our life are due. By yielding to earthly temptations, we suffer a second fall, and one much more real than the first; by overcoming them, as is perfectly in our power to do, we give scope and exercise to faculties which would otherwise have remained dormant and unknown. Moreover, our soul retains the privilege of returning to her former abode, enriched by the experience acquired in this world, and with that clearer perception of good which the knowledge of its opposite alone can supply. Nay, paradoxical as the assertion may seem, she has not entirely descended to earth, but remains in partial communication with the noetic world by virtue of her reasoning faculty; that is to say, when its intuitions are not darkened and disturbed by the triumph of sensuous impressions over the lower soul. On this and on many other occasions, Plotinus betrays a glimmering consciousness that his philosophy is purely subjective, and that its attempted transcendentalism is, in truth, a projection of psychological distinctions into the external world. Starting with the familiar division of human nature into body, soul, and spirit (or reason), he endeavours to find an objective counterpart for each. Body is represented by the material universe, soul by the animating principle of Nature, reason by the extramundane Nous. Under these three heads is comprised the totality of real existence; but existence itself has to be accounted for by a principle lying above and beyond it, which has still to be obtained by an effort of abstraction from the data that self-consciousness supplies.[453]

In his very first essay, Plotinus had hinted at a principle higher and more primordial than the absolute Nous, something with which the soul is connected by the mediation of Nous, just as she herself mediates between Nous and the material world. The notion of such a supreme principle was derived from Plato. In the sixth and seventh books of the Republic, we are told that at the summit of the dialectic series stands an idea to grasp which is the ultimate object of all reasoning. Plato calls this the Idea of Good, and describes it as holding a place in the intellectual world analogous to that held by the sun in the physical world. For, just as the sun brings all visible things into being, and also gives the light by which they are seen, so also the Good is not only that by which the objects of knowledge are known, but also that whence their existence is derived, while at the same time itself transcending existence in dignity and power.[454]

In a former part of this work[455] we found reason to believe that Plato's supreme good is no other than the Idea of Sameness which occurs in the Sophist and in the Timaeus, where it is correlated with the Idea of Difference; and we also concluded that the divine creator of the last-named dialogue is intended to represent it under a more concrete and popular form.[456] We may, perhaps, also discover it in the Limit of the Philêbus; and if we are to believe what Aristotle tells us about the later teaching of Plato, it seems to have finally coalesced with the Pythagorean One, which combines with the unlimited Dyad to form first number, and then everything else, just as the Same combines with the Different to form existence in the Timaeus.[457]

For the Platonic Idea of Good, Aristotle had substituted his own conception of self thinking thought, as the absolute on which all Nature hangs: and we have seen how Plotinus follows him to the extent of admitting that this visible universe is under the immediate control of an incorporeal Reason, which also serves as a receptacle for the Platonic Ideas. But what satisfied Aristotle does not fully satisfy him. The first principle must be one, and Nous fails to answer the conditions of absolute unity, Even self-thinking thought involves the elementary dualism of object and subject. Again, as Plotinus somewhat inconsistently argues, Nous, being knowledge, must cognise something simpler than itself.[458] Or, perhaps, what he means is that in Nous, which is its product, the first principle becomes self-conscious. Consciousness means a check on the outflow of energy due to the restraining action of the One, a return to and reflection on itself of the creative power.[459]

If the necessity of the One is proved by the inward differentiation of what seemed most simple, it is also proved by the integration of what seems most divided. In his next essay, our philosopher wanders off from the investigation of what he has just begun, by abruptly starting the question whether all souls are one.[460] This question is, however, most intimately connected with his main theme. He answers it in the affirmative. Strictly personal as our feelings seem, we are, in reality, one with each other, through our joint participation in the world-soul. Love and sympathy among human beings are solely due to this connexion. Plotinus mentions, as another evidence of its reality, the secret affinities called into play even at a great distance by magical spells—an allusion very characteristic of his age.[461] What prevents us from more fully perceiving the unity of all souls is the separateness of the bodies with which they are associated. Matter is the principle of individuation. But even within the soul there is a division between the rational and the irrational part, concentration being the characteristic of the one and dispersion of the other. The latter is fitted by its divided nature for presiding over the bodily functions of sensation and nutrition; and with the dissolution of the body it returns to the unity of the higher soul. There are two ways in which we can account for this pervading unity. It is either as products or as portions of the universal soul that all particular souls are one. Plotinus combines both explanations. The world-soul first gives birth to an image of itself, and then this is subdivided into as many partial souls as there are bodies requiring animation.

On extending our survey still wider, we find that the existence of a thing everywhere depends on its unity.[462] All bodies perish by dissolution, and dissolution means the loss of unity. Health, beauty, and virtue are merely so many different kinds of harmony and unison. Shall we then say that soul, as the great unifying power in Nature, is the One of which we are in search? Not so; for preceding investigations have taught us that soul is only an agent for transmitting ideas received from a higher power; and the psychic faculties themselves are held together by a unifying principle for which we have to account. Neither is the whole sum of existence the One, for its very name implies a plurality of parts. And the claims of the Nous to that distinction have been already disproved. In short, nothing that exists can be the One, for, as we have seen, unity is the cause of existence and must therefore precede it.

'What then,' asks Plotinus, 'is the One? No easy question to answer for us whose knowledge is based on ideas, and who can hardly tell what ideas are, or what is existence itself. The farther the soul advances in this formless region, where there is nothing for her to grasp, nothing whose impress she can receive, the more does her footing fail her, the more helpless and desolate does she feel. Oftentimes she wearies of such searching and is glad to leave it all and to descend into the world of sense until she finds rest on the solid earth, as the eyes are relieved in turning from small objects to large. For she does not know that to be one herself is to have gained the object of her search, for then she is no other than that which she knows. Nevertheless it is only by this method that we can master the philosophy of the One. Since, then, what we seek is one, and since we are considering the first principle of all things and the Good, he who enters on this quest must not place himself afar from the things that are first by descending to the things that are last, but he must leave the objects of sense, and, freed from all evil, ascend to the first principle of his own nature, that by becoming one, instead of many, he may behold the beginning and the One. Therefore he must become Reason, trusting his soul to Reason for guidance and support, that she may wakefully receive what it sees, and with this he must behold the One, not admitting any element of sense, but gazing on the purest with pure Reason and with that which in Reason is first. Should he who addresses himself to this enterprise imagine that the object of his vision possesses magnitude or form or bulk, then Reason is not his guide, for such perceptions do not belong to its nature but to sense and to the opinion which follows on sense. No; we must only pledge Reason to perform what it can do. Reason sees what precedes, or what contains, or what is derived from itself. Pure are the things in it, purer still those which precede, or rather, that which precedes it. This is neither reason nor anything that is; for whatever is has the form of existence, whereas this has none, not even an ideal form. For the One, whose nature is to generate all things, cannot be any of those things itself. Therefore it is neither substance, nor quality, nor reason, nor soul; neither moving nor at rest, not in place, not in time, but unique of its kind, or rather kindless, being before all kind, before motion and before rest, for these belong to being, and are that to which its multiplicity is due. Why, then, if it does not move, is it not at rest? Because while one or both of these must be attributed to being, the very act of attribution involves a distinction between subject and predicate, which is impossible in the case of what is absolutely simple.'[463]

The One cannot, properly speaking, be an object of knowledge, but is apprehended by something higher than knowledge. This is why Plato calls it ineffable and indescribable. What we can describe is the way to the view, not the view itself. The soul which has never been irradiated with the light of that supreme splendour, nor filled with the passionate joy of a lover finding rest in the contemplation of his beloved, cannot be given that experience in words. But the beatific vision is open to all. He from whom it is hidden has only himself to blame. Let him break away from the restraints of sense and place himself under the guidance of philosophy, that philosophy which leads from matter to spirit, from soul to Nous, from Nous to the One.

Plotinus himself, we are told, reached the climax of complete unification several times in his life, Porphyry only once, in the sixty-eighth year of his age. Probably the condition so denominated was a species of hypnotic trance. Its importance in the Neo-Platonic system has been considerably exaggerated, and on the strength of this single point some critics have summarily disposed of Plotinus and his whole school as unreasoning mystics. Mysticism is a vague word capable of very various applications. In the present instance, we presume that it is used to express a belief in the existence of some method for the discovery of truth apart from tradition; observation, and reasoning. And, taken in this sense, the Neo-Platonic method of arriving at a full apprehension of the One would be considered an extreme instance of mysticism. We must bear in mind, however, that Plotinus arrives at an intellectual conception of absolute unity by the most strictly logical process. It makes no difference that his reasoning is unsound, for the same criticism applies to other philosophers who have never been accused of mysticism. It may be said that after leading us up to a certain point, reason is replaced by intuition. Rather, what the ultimate intuition does is not to take the place of logic, but to substitute a living realisation for an abstract and negative conception. Moreover, the intuition is won not by forsaking logic, but by straining its resources to the very utmost. Again, one great characteristic of mysticism, as ordinarily understood, is to deny the truth of common observation and reasoning. Now Plotinus never goes this length. As we have already remarked, he does not even share Plato's distrust of sensible impressions, but rather follows the example of Aristotle in recognising their validity within a certain sphere. Nor does he mention having received any revelations of divine truth during his intercourse with the absolute One. This alone marks an immense difference between his ecstasies—if such they can be called—and those of the Christian mystics with whom he is associated by M. Barthélemy Saint-Hilaire.[464]

It may be said that the One is itself a mystical conception, involving a reversal of all our ordinary beliefs. The universe is a vast multiplicity of objects, held together, if you will, by some secret bond of union possibly related to the personal unity of consciousness, but still neither lost nor confused in its identity. Precisely; but Plotinus himself fully admits as much. His One is the cause of existence, not existence itself. He knows just as well as we do, that the abstract idea of unity has no reality apart from the mind. But if so, why should he associate it, in the true mystical style, with the transports of amorous passion? The question is pertinent, but it might be addressed to other Greek systems as well. We must remember that Plotinus is only commenting and enlarging on Plato. In the Republic also, the Idea of Good is described as transcending the existence and the knowledge which it produces,[465] and in the Symposium, the absolute self beautiful, which seems to be the Good under another name, is spoken of in terms not less passionately enthusiastic than any applied by Plotinus to the vision of the One.[466] Doubtless the practical sense of the great Attic master did not desert him even here: the object of all thought, in its widest sweep and in its highest flight, is to find room for every possible expansion of knowledge, for every possible elevation of life. Plotinus was a stranger to such broad views; but in departing from Plato, as usual he follows Aristotle. The absolute self-thinking thought of the Stagirite is, when we examine it closely, only one degree less chimerical than the Neo-Platonic unification. For it means consciousness of self without the correlative consciousness of a not-self, and as such, according to Aristotle, it affords an eternal felicity equal or superior to the best and happiest moments of our sensitive human life. What Plotinus does is to isolate personal identity from reason and, as such, to make it at once the cause and the supreme ideal of existence. This involves two errors: first a false abstraction of one subjective phenomenon from the sum total of conscious life; and, secondly, an illegitimate generalisation of this abstraction into an objective law of things. But in both errors, Aristotle had preceded him, by dissociating reason from all other mental functions, and by then attributing the whole cosmic movement to the love which this isolated faculty of reason, in its absolute self-existence, for ever inspires. And he also set the example of associating happiness, which is an emotional state, with an intellectual abstraction from which emotion is necessarily excluded.

Again, the Stoics, Epicureans, and Sceptics all pass for being absolute rationalists. Yet their common ideal of impassive self-possession, when worked out to its logical consequences, becomes nearly indistinguishable from the self-simplification of Plotinus. All alike exhibit the Greek tendency towards endless abstraction—what we have called the analytical moment of Greek thought, working together with the moments of antithesis and circumscription. The sceptical isolation of man from Nature, the Epicurean isolation of the individual from the community, the Stoic isolation of will from feeling, reached their highest and most abstract expression in the Neo-Platonic isolation of pure self-identity from all other modes of consciousness and existence combined.

In estimating the intellectual character of Plotinus, we must also remember that the theory of the absolute One occupies a relatively small place in his speculations; while, at a rough computation, the purely mystical portions of his writings—by which we understand those in which allusion is made to personal and incommunicable experiences of his own—do not amount to more than one per cent. of the whole. If these have attracted more attention than all the rest put together, the reason probably is that they offer an agreeable relief to the arid scholasticism which fills so much of the Enneads, and that they are the only very original contribution made by Plotinus to Greek literature. But the significance of a writer must not always be measured by his most original passages, and this is eminently true of our philosopher. His great merit was to make the spiritualism of Plato and Aristotle more intelligible and interesting than it had been before, and to furnish reason with a rallying-point when it was threatened with utter destruction by the religious revival of the empire.

VII.

So far our investigation has been analytical. We have seen Plotinus acquire, one after another, the elements out of which his system has still to be constructed. The first step was to separate spirit from matter. They are respectively distinguished as principles of union and of division. The bodies given to us in experience are a combination of the two, a dispersion of form over an infinitely extended, infinitely divisible, infinitely changeful substratum. Our own souls, which at first seemed so absolutely self-identical, present, on examination, a similarly composite character. A fresh analysis results in the separation of Nous or Reason from the lower functions of conscious life. And we infer by analogy that the soul in Nature bears the same relation to a transcendent objective Nous. Nous is essentially pure self-consciousness, and from this self-consciousness the world of Ideas is developed. Properly speaking, Ideas are the sole reality: sensible forms are an image of them impressed on matter through the agency of the world-soul. But Nous, or the totality of Ideas, though high, is not the highest. All that has hitherto occupied us, Nature, Soul, and Reason, is pervaded by a fundamental unity, without which nothing could exist. But Soul is not herself this unity, nor is Reason. Self-consciousness, even in its purest expression, involves a duality of object and subject. The notion of Being is distinct from the notion of oneness. The principle represented by the latter, as the cause of all things, must itself transcend existence. At the same time, it is revealed to us by the fact of our own personal identity. To be united with oneself is to be united with the One.

Thus we have, in all, five gradations: the One, Nous, Soul, the sensible world, and, lastly, unformed Matter. Taken together, the first three constitute a triad of spiritual principles, and, as such, are associated in a single group by Plotinus.[467] Sometimes they are spoken of as the Alexandrian Trinity. But the implied comparison with the Trinity of Catholicism is misleading. With Neo-Platonism, the supreme unity is, properly speaking, alone God and alone One. Nous is vastly inferior to the first principle, and Soul, again, to Nous. Possibly the second and third principles are personal; the first most certainly is not, since self-consciousness is expressly denied to it by Plotinus. Nor is it likely that the idea of a supernatural triad was suggested to Neo-Platonism by Christianity. Each of the three principles may be traced to its source in Greek philosophy. This has been already shown in the case of the One and of the Nous. The universal soul is to be found in Plato's Timaeus; it is analogous, at least in its lower, divided part, to Aristotle's Nature; and it is nearly identical with the informing spirit of Stoicism. As to the number three, it was held in high esteem long before the Christian era, and was likely to be independently employed for the construction of different systems at a time when belief in the magical virtue of particular numbers was more widely diffused than at any former period of civilised history.

From another point of view, as we have already observed with Kirchner, the fundamental triad assumed by Plotinus is body, soul, and spirit. Under their objective aspect of the sensible universe, the world-soul, and the Nous, these three principles constitute the sum of all reality. Take away plurality from Nous and there remains the One. Take away soul from body and there remains unformed matter. These are the two transcendent principles between which the others extend, and by whose combination in various proportions they are explained. It is true that Plotinus himself does not allude to the possibility of such an analysis, but it exhibits, better than any other, the natural order of his dialectic.

Plotinus passes by an almost insensible transition from the more elementary and analytical to the more constructive portion of his philosophy. This naturally falls into two great divisions, the one speculative and the other practical. It has to be shown by what necessity and in what order the great cosmic principles are evolved from their supreme source; and it has also to be shown in what way this knowledge is connected with the supreme interests of the human soul. The moral aspect of Neo-Platonism is not at first very clearly distinguished from its metaphysical aspect; and both find their most general solution in the same line of thought that has led us up to a contemplation of the ultimate One. For the successive gradations of our ascent represent, in an inverted order, the steps of creative energy by which all things are evolved from their primal source; while they directly correspond to the process of purification through which every soul must pass in returning from the exile of her separate and material existence to the happiness of identification with God. And here we at once come on the fundamental contradiction of the system. What we were so carefully taught to consider as one and nothing more, must now be conceived as the first cause and the supreme good. Plotinus does, indeed, try to evade the difficulty by saying that his absolute is only a cause in relation to other things, that it is not so much good as the giver of good, that it is only one in the sense of not being many.[468] But after making these reservations, he continues to use the old terms as confidently as if they stood for the ideas usually associated with them. His fundamental error was to identify three distinct methods of connecting phenomena, in thought, with each other or with ourselves. We may view things in relation to their generating antecedents, in relation to other things with which they are associated by resemblance or juxtaposition, or in relation to the satisfaction of our own wants. These three modes of reference correspond to Aristotle's efficient, formal, and final causes; but the word causation should be applied only to the first. Whether their unfortunate confusion both by Aristotle and by his successors was in any appreciable degree due to their having been associated by him under a common denomination, may reasonably be doubted. It is rather more probable that the same name was given to these different conceptions in consequence of their having first become partially identified in thought. Social arrangements, which have a great deal to do with primitive speculation, would naturally lead to such an identification. The king or other chief magistrate stands at the head of the social hierarchy and forms the bond of union among its members; he is the source of all authority; and his position, or, failing that, his favour, is regarded as the supreme good. Religion extends the same combination of attributes to her chief God; and philosophy, following on the lines of religion, employs it to unify the methods of science and morality.

All existence, according to Plotinus, proceeds from the One, which he also calls God. But God does not create the world by a conscious exercise of power; for, as we have seen, every form of consciousness is excluded from his definition. Neither does it proceed from him by emanation, for this would imply a diminution of his substance.[469] It is produced by an overflow of his infinite power.[470] Our philosopher tries to explain and defend this rather unintelligible mode of derivation by the analogy of physical substances and their actions. Light is constantly coming from the sun without any loss to the luminary itself.[471] And all things are, in like manner, constantly communicating their proper virtue to others while remaining unaltered themselves. Here we have a good example of the close connexion between science and abstract speculation. People often talk as if metaphysics was something beyond the reach of verification. But some metaphysical theories admit, at any rate, of disproof, in so far as they are founded on false physical theories. Had Plotinus known that neither the sun nor anything else in Nature can produce force out of nothing, he would, very probably, have hesitated to credit the One with such a power.

In reasoning up from the world to its first cause, we were given to understand that the two were related to one another as contradictory opposites. The multiple must proceed from the simple, and existence from that which does not exist. But the analogies of material production now suggest a somewhat different view. What every power calls into existence is an image of itself, but the effect is never more than a weakened and imperfect copy of its original. Thus the universe appears as a series of diminishing energies descending in a graduated scale from the highest to the lowest. Here, again, bad science makes bad philosophy. Effects are never inferior to their causes, but always exactly equal, the effect being nothing else than the cause in another place or under another form. This would be obvious enough, did not superficial observation habitually confound the real cause with the sum of its concomitants. What we are accustomed to think of as a single cause is, in truth, a whole bundle of causes, which do not always converge to a single point, and each of which, taken singly, is, of course, inferior to the whole sum taken together. Thus when we say that the sun heats the earth, this is only a conventional way of speaking. What really does the work is a relatively infinitesimal part of the solar heat separately transmitted to us through space. Once neglect this truth, and there is no reason why effects should not exceed as well as fall short of their causes in any assignable proportion. Such an illusion is, in fact, produced when different energies converge to a point. Here it is the consequent and not the antecedent which is confounded with the sum of its concomitants, as when an explosion is said to be the effect of a spark.

Of course we are speaking of causation as exercised under the conditions of time, space, matter, and motion. It is then identical with the transmission of energy and obeys the laws of energy. And to talk about causation under any other conditions than these is utter nonsense. But Plotinus and other philosophers exclude the most essential of the conditions specified from their enquiries into the ultimate origin of things. We are expressly informed that the genesis of Nous from the One, and of Soul from Nous, must not be conceived as taking place in time but in eternity.[472] Unfortunately those who make such reservations are not consistent. They continue to talk about power, causation, priority, and so forth, as if these conceptions were separable from time. Hence they have to choose between making statements which are absolutely unintelligible and making statements which are absolutely untrue.

Perhaps the processes of logic and mathematics may be adduced as an exception. It may be contended that the genus is prior to the species, the premise to the conclusion, the unit to the multiple, the line to the figure, in reason though not in time. And Plotinus avails himself to the fullest extent of mathematical and logical analogies in his transcendental constructions. His One is the starting-point of numeration, the centre of a circle, the identity involved in difference; and under each relation it claims an absolute priority, of which causal power is only the most general expression. We have already seen how a multitude of archetypal Ideas spring from the supreme Nous as from their fountain-head. Their production is explained, on the lines of Plato's Sophist, as a process of dialectical derivation. By logically analysing the conception of self-consciousness, we obtain, first of all, Nous itself, or

Reason, as the subject, and Existence as the object of thought. Subject and object, considered as the same with one another, give us Identity; considered as distinct, they give us Difference. The passage from one to the other gives Motion; the limitation of thought to itself gives Rest. The plurality of determinations so obtained gives number and quantity, their specific difference gives quality, and from these principles everything else is derived.[473] It might seem as if, here at least, we had something which could be called a process of eternal generation—a causal order independent of time. But, in reality, the assumed sequence exists only in our minds, and there it takes place under the form of time, not less inevitably than do the external re-arrangements of matter and motion. Thus in logic and mathematics, such terms as priority, antecedence, and evolution can only be used to signify the order in which our knowledge is acquired; they do not answer to causal relations existing among things in themselves. And apart from these two orders—the objective order of dynamical production in space and time, and the subjective order of intelligibility in thought—there is no kind of succession that we can conceive. Eternal relations, if they exist at all, must be relations of co-existence, of resemblance, or of difference, continued through infinite time. Wherever there is antecedence, the consequent can only have existed for a finite time.

Some may think that we have pushed this point at unnecessary length. But the Neo-Platonic method is not quite so obsolete as they, perhaps, suppose. Whenever we repeat the Nicene and Athanasian Creeds, we are expressing our religious belief in the language of the Alexandrian schools, thus pledging ourselves to metaphysical dogmas which we can neither explain nor defend. Such terms as sonship and procession have no meaning except when applied to relations conceived under the form of time; and to predicate eternity of them is to reduce them to so much unintelligible jargon.

An energy continually advancing through successive gradations, and diminishing as it advances—such, as we have seen, is the conception of existence offered by Plotinus. We have seen, also, how to explain the genesis of one principle from another without the aid of supernatural volition or of mechanical causation, he is compelled to press into the service every sort of relationship by which two objects can be connected, and to invest it with a dynamical significance which only the phenomena of matter and motion can possess. But what he chiefly relies on for guidance in this tortuous labyrinth of timeless evolution, is the old Greek principle that contraries are generated from one another. And with him, as with the earlier thinkers, all contraries reduce themselves, in the last analysis, to the four great antitheses of the One and the Many, Being and not-Being, the Same and the Other, Rest and Motion. It matters nothing that he should have followed Plato to the extent of co-ordinating five of these terms as supreme archetypal Ideas, immediately resulting from the self-consciousness of Nous, and themselves producing all other forms of existence. They are used, quite independently of that derivation, to explain the connexion of the various creative principles with one another. Nous is deduced from its first cause as Being from not-Being, as the Many from the One, as Difference from Identity, and as Motion from Rest.[474] To explain the generation of Soul from Nous is a more difficult problem. The One had originally been defined as the antithetical cause of Nous, and therefore the latter could easily be accounted for by simply reversing the analytical process; whereas Nous had not been defined as the cause of Soul, but as the model whence her creative Ideas are derived. Soul, in fact, is not opposed to anything; she is the connecting link between sense and spirit. In this strait, Plotinus seems to think that the antithesis between Rest and Motion is the best fitted to express the nature of her descent from the higher principle; and on one occasion he illustrates the relation of his three divine substances to one another by the famous figure of a central point representing the One, a fixed circle round that point representing the Nous, and outside that, again, a revolving circle representing the Soul.[475] Still, the different parts of the system are very awkwardly pieced together at this juncture; for the creative energy of the Nous has already been invoked to account for the Ideas or partial intelligences into which it spontaneously divides; and one does not understand how it can be simultaneously applied to the production of something that is not an Idea at all.

Fresh difficulties arise in explaining the activity which the Soul, in her turn, exerts. As originally conceived, her function was sufficiently clear. Mediating between two worlds, she transforms the lower one into a likeness of the higher, stamping on material objects a visible image of the eternal Ideas revealed to her by a contemplation of the Nous. And, as a further elaboration of this scheme, we were told that the primary soul generates an inferior soul, which, again, subdivides itself into the multitude of partial souls required for the animation of different bodily organisms. But now that our philosopher has entered on a synthetic construction of the elements furnished by his preliminary analysis, he finds himself confronted by an entirely new problem. For his implied principle is that each hypostasis must generate the grade which comes next after it in the descending series of manifestations, until the possibilities of existence have been exhausted. But in developing and applying the noetic Ideas, the Soul, apparently, finds a pre-existing Matter ready to hand. Thus she has to deal with something lower than herself, which she did not create, and which is not created by the Forms combined with it in sensible experience. We hear of a descent from thought to feeling, and from feeling to simple vitality,[476] but in each instance the depth of the Soul's fall is measured by the extent to which she penetrates into the recesses of a substance not clearly related to her nor to anything above her.

Plotinus is driven by this perplexity to reconsider the whole theory of Matter.[477] He takes Aristotle's doctrine as the groundwork of his investigation. According to this, all existence is divided into Matter and Form. What we know of things—in other words, the sum of their differential characteristics—is their Form. Take away this, and the unknowable residuum is their Matter. Again, Matter is the vague indeterminate something out of which particular Forms are developed. The two are related as Possibility to Actuality, as the more generic to the more specific substance through every grade of classification and composition. Thus there are two Matters, the one sensible and the other intelligible. The former constitutes the common substratum of bodies, the other the common element of ideas.[478] The general distinction between Matter and Form was originally suggested to Aristotle by Plato's remarks on the same subject; but he differs from his master in two important particulars. Plato, in his Timaeus, seems to identify Matter with space.[479] So far, it is a much more positive conception than the ὕλη of the Metaphysics. On the other hand, he constantly opposes it to reality as something non-existent; and he at least implies that it is opposed to absolute good as a principle of absolute evil.[480] Thus while the Aristotelian world is formed by the development of Power into Actuality, the Platonic world is composed by the union of Being and not-Being, of the Same and the Different, of the One and the Many, of the Limit and the Unlimited, of Good and Evil, in varying proportions with each other.

Plotinus, as we have said, starts with the Aristotelian account of Matter; but by a process of dialectical manipulation, he gradually brings it into almost complete agreement with Plato's conception; thus, as usual, mediating between and combining the views of his two great authorities. In the first place, he takes advantage of Aristotle's distinction between intelligible and sensible Matter, to strip the latter of that positive and vital significance with which it had been clothed in the Peripatetic system. In the world of Ideas, there is an element common to all specific forms, a fundamental unity in which they meet and inhere, which may without impropriety be called their Matter. But this Matter is an eternal and divine substance, inseparably united with the fixed forms which it supports, and, therefore, something which, equally with them, receives light and life and thought from the central source of being. It is otherwise with sensible Matter, the common substance of the corporeal elements. This is, to use the energetic expression of our philosopher, a decorated corpse.[481] It does not remain constantly combined with any form, but is for ever passing from one to another, without manifesting a particular preference for any. As such, it is the absolute negation of Form, and can only be conceived, if at all, by thinking away every sensible quality. Neither has it any quantity, for quantity means magnitude, and magnitude implies definite figure. Aristotle opposed to each particular form a corresponding privation, and placed Matter midway between them. Plotinus, on the other hand, identifies Matter with the general privation of all forms. It is at this point that he begins to work his way back to the Platonic notion of Matter as simple extension. There must, after all, be something about Matter which enables it to receive every kind of quality and figure,—it must have some sort of mass or bulk, not, indeed, in any definite sense, but with an equal capacity for expansion and for contraction. Now, says Plotinus, the very indeterminateness of Matter is precisely the capacity for extension in all directions that we require. 'Having no principle of stability, but being borne towards every form, and easily led about in all directions, it acquires the nature of a mass.'[482]

Henceforth, whatever our philosopher says about Matter will apply to extension and to extension alone. It cannot be apprehended by sight, nor by hearing, nor by smell, nor by taste, for it is neither colour, nor sound, nor odour, nor juice. Neither can it be touched, for it is not a body, but it becomes corporeal on being blended with sensible qualities. And, in a later essay, he describes it as receiving all things and letting them depart again without retaining the slightest trace of their presence.[483] Why then, it may be asked, if Plotinus meant extension, could he not say so at once, and save us all this trouble in hunting out his meaning? There were very good reasons why he should not. In the first place, he wished to express himself, so far as possible, in Aristotelian phraseology, and this was incompatible with the reduction of Matter to extension. In the next place, the idea of an infinite void had been already appropriated by the Epicureans, to whose system he was bitterly opposed. And, finally, the extension of ordinary experience had not the absolute generality which was needed in order to bring Matter into relation with that ultimate abstraction whence, like everything else, it has now to be derived.

As a result of the preceding analysis, Plotinus at last identifies Matter with the Infinite—not an infinite something, but the Infinite pure and simple, apart from any subject of which it can be predicated. We started with what seemed a broad distinction between intelligible and sensible Matter. That distinction now disappears in a new and more comprehensive conception; and, at the same time, Plotinus begins to see his way towards a restatement of his whole system in clearer terms. 'The Infinite is generated from the infinity or power or eternity of the One; not that there is infinity in the One, but that it is created by the One.'[484] With the first outrush of energy from the primal fount of things, Matter begins to exist. But no sooner do movement and difference start into life, than they are restrained and bent back by the presence of the One; and this reflection of power or being on itself constitutes the supreme self-consciousness of Nous.[485] Whether the subsequent creation of Soul involves a fresh production of energy, or whether a portion of the original stream, which was called into existence by the One, escapes from the restraining self-consciousness of Nous and continues its onward flow—this Plotinus does not say. What he does say is that Soul stands to Nous in the relation of Matter to Form, and is raised to perfection by gazing back on the Ideas contained in Nous, just as Nous itself had been perfected by returning to the One.[486] But while the two higher principles remain stationary, the Soul, besides giving birth to a fresh stream of energy, turns towards her own creation and away from the fountain of her life. And, apparently, it is only by this condescension on her part that the visible world could have been formed.[487] We can explain this by supposing that as the stream of Matter departs more and more from the One, its power of self-reflection continually diminishes, and at length ceases altogether. It is thus that the substratum of sensible objects must, as we have seen, be conceived under the aspect of a passive recipient for the forms imposed on it by the Soul; and just as those forms are a mere image of the noetic Ideas, so also, Plotinus tells us, is their Matter an image of the intelligible Matter which exists in the Nous itself; only the image realises the conception of a material principle more completely than the archetype, because of its more negative and indeterminate nature, a diminution of good being equivalent to an increase of evil.[488]

Still Plotinus gives no clear answer to the question whence comes this last and lowest Matter. He will not say that it is an emanation from the Soul, nor yet will he say that it is a formless residue of the element out of which she was shaped by a return to the Nous. In truth, he could not make up his mind as to whether the Matter of sensible objects was created at all. He oscillates between unwillingness to admit that absolute evil can come from good, and unwillingness to admit that the two are co-ordinate principles of existence. And, as usual, where ideas fail him, he helps himself out of the difficulty with metaphors. The Soul must advance, and in order to advance she must make a place for herself, and that there may be a place there must be body. Or, again, while remaining fixed in herself, she sends out a great light, and by the light she sees that there is darkness beyond its extreme verge, and moulds its formless substance into shape.[489]

The ambiguities and uncertainties which Plotinus exhibits in theorising on the origin of Matter, are due not only to the conflicting influences of Plato and Aristotle, but also to another influence quite distinct from theirs. This is the Stoic cosmology. While utterly repudiating the materialism of the Stoics, Plotinus evidently felt attracted by their severe monism, and by the consistent manner in which they derived every form of existence from the divine substance. They too recognised a distinction between Form and Matter, the active and the passive principle in Nature, but they supposed that the one, besides being penetrated and moulded by the other, had also been originally produced by it. Such a theory was well suited to the energetic and practical character of Stoic morality, with its aversion from mere contemplation, its immediate bearing on the concrete interests of life. Man was conceived as an intelligent force, having for his proper function to bring order out of chaos, 'to make reason and the will of God prevail,' and this ideal appeared to be reflected in the dynamic constitution of Nature. With Plotinus, on the other hand, as with Aristotle, theory and not practice was the end of life, or rather, as he himself expressed it, practice was an inferior kind of theorising, an endeavour to set before oneself in outward form what should properly be sought in the noetic world where subject and object are one.[490] Accordingly, while accepting the Stoic monism, he strove to bring it into close agreement with Aristotle's cosmology, by substituting contemplation for will as the creative principle in all existence, no less than as the ideal of happiness for man.

We have seen how, in accordance with this view, each principle is perfected by looking back on its source.[491] Thus the activity of the world-soul, so far as it is exercised for the benefit of what comes after and falls beneath her, is an anomaly only to be accounted for by her inferior place in the system of graduated descent; or else by the utter impotence of Matter, which is incapable of raising itself into Form by a spontaneous act of reflection, and can only passively receive the images transmitted to it from above, without being able to retain even these for any time. Nay, here also, what looks like creative energy admits of being assimilated more or less closely to an exercise of idealising thought. It is really for her own sake that the Soul fills what lies beyond her with life and light, not, like Plato's Soul, from pure disinterested joy in the communication and diffusion of good. It is because she recoils with horror from darkness and nonentity that she shapes the formless substance into a residence for herself, on the model of the imperial palace whence she came. Thus the functions of sensation, nutrition, and reproduction are to be regarded as so many modes of contemplation. In the first, the Soul dwells on the material images which already exist; in the second and third, she strives to perpetuate and multiply them still further. And the danger is that she may become so enthralled by her own creation as to forget the divine original after which it is formed.[492] Should she yield to the snare, successive transmigrations will sink her lower and lower into the depths of animalism and material darkness. To avoid this degradation, to energise with the better part of our nature, is to be good. And with the distinction between good and evil, we pass from the metaphysical to the ethical portion of the system.

VIII.

All virtue, with Plotinus, rests on the superiority of the soul to the body. So far, he follows the common doctrine of Plato and Aristotle. But in working out the distinction, he is influenced by the individualising and theoretic philosophy of the latter rather than by the social and practical philosophy of the former. Or, again, we may say that with him the intellectualism of Aristotle is heightened and warmed by the religious aspirations of Plato, strengthened and purified by the Stoic passionlessness, the Stoic independence of external goods. In his ethical system, the virtues are arranged in an ascending scale. Each grade reproduces the old quadripartite division into Wisdom, Courage, Temperance and Justice, but in each their respective significance receives a new interpretation. As civic virtues, they continue to bear the meaning assigned to them in Plato's Republic. Wisdom belongs to reason, Courage to passionate spirit, Temperance to desire, while Justice implies the fulfilment of its appropriate function by each.[493] But all this only amounts to the restriction of what would otherwise be unregulated impulse, the imposition of Form on Matter, the supremacy of the soul over the body; whereas what we want is to get rid of matter altogether. Here also, Plato sets us on the right track when he calls the virtues purifications. From this point of view, for the soul to energise alone without any interference, is Wisdom; not to be moved by the passions of the body is Temperance; not to dread separation from the body is Courage; and to obey the guidance of reason is Justice.[494] Such a disposition of the soul is what Plato means by flying from the world and becoming like God. Is this enough? No, it is not. We have, so far, been dealing only with the negative conditions of good, not with good itself. The essential thing is not purification, but what remains behind when the work of purification is accomplished. So we come to the third and highest grade of virtue, the truly divine life, which is a complete conversion to reason. Our philosopher endeavours to fit this also into the framework of the cardinal virtues, but not without imposing a serious strain on the ordinary meaning of words. Of Wisdom nothing need be said, for it is the same as rationality. Justice is the self-possession of mind, Temperance the inward direction towards reason, Courage the impassivity arising from resemblance to that which is by nature impassive.[495]

Plotinus is careful to make us understand that his morality has neither an ascetic nor a suicidal tendency. Pleasures are to be tolerated under the form of a necessary relief and relaxation; pains are to be removed, but if incurable, they are to be patiently borne; anger is, if possible, to be suppressed, and, at any rate, not allowed to exceed the limits of an involuntary movement; fear will not be felt except as a salutary warning. The bodily appetites will be restricted to natural wants, and will not be felt by the soul, except, perhaps, as a transient excitement of the imagination.[496] Whatever abstinences our philosopher may have practised on his own account, we find no trace of a tendency towards self-mortification in his writings, nothing that is not consistent with the healthiest traditions of Greek spiritualism as originally constituted by the great Athenian school.

While not absolutely condemning suicide, Plotinus restricts the right of leaving this world within much narrower limits than were assigned to it by the Stoics. In violently separating herself from the body, the soul, he tells us, is acting under the influence of some evil passion, and he intimates that the mischievous effects of this passion will prolong themselves into the new life on which she is destined to enter.[497] Translated into more abstract language, his meaning probably is that the feelings which ordinarily prompt to suicide, are such as would not exist in a well-regulated mind. It is remarkable that Schopenhauer, whose views of life were, on other points, the very reverse of those held by Plotinus, should have used very much the same argument against self-destruction. According to his theory, the will to life, which it should be our principal business to conquer, asserts itself strongly in the wish to escape from suffering, and only delays the final moment of peaceful extinction by rushing from one phase of existence to another. And in order to prove the possibility of such a revival, Schopenhauer was obliged to graft on his philosophy a theory of metempsychosis, which, but for this necessity, would certainly never have found a place in it at all. In this, as in many other instances, an ethical doctrine is apparently deduced from a metaphysical doctrine which has, in reality, been manufactured for its support. All systems do but present under different formulas a common fund of social sentiment. A constantly growing body of public opinion teaches us that we do not belong to ourselves, but to those about us, and that, in ordinary circumstances, it is no less weak and selfish to run away from life than to run away from death.

Plotinus follows up his essay on the Virtues by an essay on Dialectic.[498] As a method for attaining perfection, he places dialectic above ethics; and, granting that the apprehension of abstract ideas ranks higher than the performance of social duties, he is quite consistent in so doing. Not much, however, can be made of his few remarks on the subject. They seem to be partly meant for a protest against the Stoic idea that logic is an instrument for acquiring truth rather than truth itself, and also against the Stoic use or abuse of the syllogistic method. In modern phraseology, Plotinus seems to view dialectic as the immanent and eternal process of life itself, rather than as a collection of rules for drawing correct inferences from true propositions, or from propositions assumed to be true. We have seen how he regarded existence in the highest sense as identical with the self-thinking of the absolute Nous, and how he attempted to evolve the whole series of archetypal Ideas contained therein from the simple fact of self-consciousness. Thus he would naturally identify dialectic with the subjective reproduction of this objective evolution; and here he would always have before his eyes the splendid programme sketched in Plato's Republic.[499] His preference of intuitive to discursive reasoning has been quoted by Ritter as a symptom of mysticism. But here, as in so many instances, he follows Aristotle, who also held that simple abstraction is a higher operation, and represents a higher order of real existence than complex ratiocination.[500]

The ultimate stage of perfection is, of course, the identification of subject and object, the ascent from the Nous to the One. But, on this point, Plotinus never added anything essential to what has already been quoted from the analytical portion of his enquiry, and the essay containing that passage is accordingly placed last in Porphyry's arrangement of his works.

Our account of Neo-Platonism has, with the exception of a few illustrations, been derived exclusively from the earlier essays of Plotinus. His subsequent writings are exceedingly obscure and tedious, and they add little by way either of development or defence to the outlines which he had sketched with a master's hand. Whatever materials they may supply for a better appreciation, whether of his philosophy or of his general character as a thinker, will most profitably find their place in the final survey of both which we shall now attempt to give.

IX.

Every great system of philosophy may be considered from four distinct points of view. We may ask what is its value as a theory of the world and of human life, measured either by the number of new truths which it contains, or by the stimulus to new thought which it affords. Or we may consider it from the aesthetic side, as a monumental structure interesting us not by its utility, but by its beauty and grandeur. Under this aspect, a system may be admirable for its completeness, coherence, and symmetry, or for the great intellectual qualities exhibited by its architect, although it may be open to fatal objections as a habitation for human beings, and may fail to reproduce the plan on which we now know that the universe is built. Or, again, our interest in the work may be purely historical and psychological; we may look on it as the product of a particular age and a particular mind, as summing up for us under their most abstract form the ideas and aspirations which at any given moment had gained possession of educated opinion. Or, finally, we may study it as a link in the evolution of thought, as a result of earlier tendencies, and an antecedent of later developments. We propose to make a few remarks on the philosophy of Plotinus, or, what is the same thing, on Neo-Platonism in general, from each of these four points of view.

In absolute value, Neo-Platonism stands lowest as well as last among the ancient schools of thought. No reader who has followed us thus far will need to be reminded how many valuable ideas were first brought to light, or reinforced with new arguments and illustrations by the early Greek thinkers, by the Sophists and Socrates, by Plato and Aristotle, by the Stoics, Epicureans, and Sceptics, and by the moralists of the Roman empire. On every subject of speculation that can be started, we continue to ask, like Plotinus himself, what the 'blessed ancients' had to say about it;[501] not, of course, because they lived a long time ago, but because they came first, because they said what they had to say with the unique charm of original discovery, because they were in more direct contact than we are, not, indeed, with the facts, but with the phenomena of Nature and life and thought. It is true that we have nothing more to learn from them, for whatever was sound in their teaching has been entirely absorbed into modern thought, and combined with ideas of which they did not dream. But until we come to Hume and his successors, there is nothing in philosophical literature that can be compared to their writings for emancipating and stimulating power; and, perhaps, when the thinkers of the last and present centuries have become as obsolete as Bacon and Descartes are now, those writings will continue to be studied with unabating zeal. Neo-Platonism, on the other hand, is dead, and every attempt made to galvanise it into new life has proved a disastrous failure. The world, that is to say the world of culture, will not read Plotinus and his successors, will not even read the books that are written about them by scholars of brilliant literary ability like MM. Vacherot and Jules Simon in France, Steinhart and Kirchner in Germany.[502]

We have not far to seek for the cause of this fatal condemnation. Neo-Platonism is nothing if not a system, and as a system it is false, and not only false but out of relation to every accepted belief. In combining the dialectic of Plato with the metaphysics of Aristotle and the physics of Stoicism, Plotinus has contrived to rob each of whatever plausibility it once possessed. The Platonic doctrine of Ideas was an attempt to express something very real and important, the distinction between laws and facts in Nature, between general principles and particular observations in science, between ethical standards and everyday practice in life. The eternal Nous of Aristotle represented the upward struggle of Nature through mechanical, chemical, and vital movements to self-conscious thought. The world-soul of Stoicism represented a return to monism, a protest against the unphilosophical antithesis between God and the world, spirit and matter, necessity and free-will. Plotinus attempts to rationalise the Ideas by shutting them up in the Aristotelian Nous, with the effect of severing them still more hopelessly from the real world, and, at the same time, making their subjective origin still more flagrantly apparent than before. And along with the Stoic conception of a world-soul, he preserves all those superstitious fancies about secret spiritual sympathies and affinities connecting the different parts of Nature with one another which the conception of a transcendent Nous, as originally understood by Aristotle, had at least the merit of excluding. Finally, by a tremendous wrench of abstraction, the unity of existence is torn away from existence itself, and the most relative of all conceptions is put out of relation to the thought which, in the very same breath, it is declared to condition, and to the things which it is declared to create.

Again, on the practical side, by combining Plato with Aristotle and both with Stoicism, Plotinus contrives to eliminate what is most valuable in each. If, in the Republic, the Good was placed above all existence, this was only that we might transform existence into its image. If Aristotle placed the theoretical above the ethical virtues, he assigned no limits but those of observation and reasoning to the energising of theoretic power. If the Stoics rested morality on the absolute isolation of the human will, they deduced from this principle not only the inwardness of virtue, but also the individualisation of duty, the obligation of beneficence, and the forgiveness of sin. But with Plotinus, Reason has no true object of contemplation outside its own abstract ideas, and the self-realisation of Stoicism means a barren consciousness of personal identity, from which every variety of interest and sympathy is excluded: it is not an expansion of our own soul into coincidence with the absolute All, but a concentration of both into a single point, a flight of the alone to the alone;[503] and only in this utter solitude does he suppose that the Platonic Good is finally and wholly possessed.

Nor, with a single exception, is the fundamental untruth of the system redeemed by any just and original observations on points of detail such as lie so thickly scattered over the pages of other metaphysicians, both in ancient and modern literature. The single exception is the refutation of materialism to which attention has been already directed. Apart from this, the Enneads do not contain one single felicitous or suggestive idea, nothing that can enlarge the horizon of our thoughts, nothing that can exalt the purpose of our lives.

If, however, we pass to the second point of view, and judge Neo-Platonism according to the requirements, not of truth or of usefulness, but of beauty, our first verdict of utter condemnation will be succeeded by a much more favourable opinion. Plotinus has used the materials inherited from his predecessors with unquestionable boldness and skill; and the constructive power exhibited in the general plan of his vast system is fully equalled by the close reasoning with which every detail is elaborated and fitted into its proper place. Nothing can be imagined more imposing than this wondrous procession of forms defiling from the unknown to the unknown—from the self-developing consciousness of Reason as it breaks and flames and multiplies into a whole universe of being and life and thought, ever returning, by the very law of their production, to the source whence they have sprung—onward and outward on the wings of the cosmic Soul, through this visible world, where they reappear as images of intellectual beauty in the eternal revolutions of the starry spheres above, in the everlasting reproduction of organic species below, in the loveliest thoughts and actions of the loveliest human souls—till the utmost limits of their propagation and dispersion have been reached, till the last faint rays of existence die out in the dark and void region that extends to infinity beyond. Nothing in the realm of abstractions can be more moving than this Odyssey of the human soul, wakened by visions of earthly loveliness to a consciousness of her true destiny, a remembrance of her lost and forgotten home; then abandoning these for the possession of a more spiritual beauty, ascending by the steps of dialectic to a contemplation of the archetypal Ideas that lie folded and mutually interpenetrated in the bosom of the eternal Reason where thought and being are but the double aspect of a single absolute reality; seeking farther and higher, beyond the limits of existence itself, for a still purer unity, and finding in the awful solitude of that supreme elevation that the central source of all things does not lie without but within, that only in returning to self-identity does she return to the One; or, again, descending to the last confines of light and life that she may prolong their radiation into the formless depths of matter, projecting on its darkness an image of the glory whose remembrance still attends her in her fall.

Still more impressive, if we consider the writings of Plotinus on their personal side, and as a revelation of their author's mind, is the high and sustained purity, the absolute detachment and disinterestedness by which they are characterised throughout. No trace of angry passion, no dallying with images of evil, interferes to mar their exalted spirituality from first to last. While the western world was passing through a period of horror and degradation such as had never been known before, the philosopher took refuge in an ideal sphere, and looked down on it all with no more disturbance to his serenity than if he had been the spectator of a mimic performance on the stage.[504] This, indeed, is one of the reasons why the Enneads are so much less interesting, from a literary point of view, than the works of the Roman Stoics. It is not only that we fail to find in them any allusions even of the faintest kind to contemporary events or to contemporary life and manners, such as abound in Seneca and Epictêtus, but there is not the slightest reference to the existence of such a thing as the Roman empire at all. One or two political illustrations occur, but they are drawn from old Greek city life, and were probably suggested by Plato or

Aristotle.[505] But this tremendous blank is so perfectly in keeping with the whole spirit of Neo-Platonism as to heighten instead of lowering its aesthetic effect. In studying the philosophy of the preceding centuries, to whatever school it may belong, we have the image of death always before our eyes; and to fortify us against its terrors, we are continually called upon to remember the vanity of life. This is the protest of thought against the world, just as in Lucian and Sextus we hear the protest of the world against thought. At last the whole bitter strife comes to an end, the vision of sense passes away,

And leaves us with Plotinus and pure souls.

Here we need no deliverance from troubles and indignities which are not felt; nor do we need to be prepared for death, knowing that we can never die. The world will no longer look askance at us, for we have ceased to concern ourselves about its reformation. No scepticism can shake our convictions, for we have discovered the secret of all knowledge through the consciousness of that which is eternal in ourselves. Thus the world of outward experience has dropped out of our thoughts, because thought has orbed into a world of its own.

X.

In the foregoing remarks we have already passed from the purely aesthetic to the historical or psychological view of Neo-Platonism—that is, the view which considers a philosophy in reference to the circumstances of its origin. Every speculative system reflects, more or less fully, the spirit of the age in which it was born; and the absence of all allusion to contemporary events does not prove that the system of Plotinus was an exception to this rule. It only proves that the tendency of the age was to carry away men's thoughts from practical to theoretical interests. We have already characterised the first centuries of Roman imperialism as a period of ever-increasing religious reaction; and in this reaction we attempted to distinguish between the development of supernaturalist beliefs which were native to Greece and Italy, and the importation of beliefs which had originated in the East. We saw also how philosophy shared in the general tendency, how it became theological and spiritualistic instead of ethical and naturalistic, how its professors were converted from opponents into upholders of the popular belief. Now, according to some critics, Neo-Platonism marks another stage in the gradual substitution of faith for reason, of authority for independent thought; the only question being whether we should interpret it as a product of Oriental mysticism, or as a simple sequence of the same movement which had previously led from Cicero to Seneca, from Seneca to Epictêtus, from Epictêtus to Marcus Aurelius.

Of these views, the first is taken by Ritter, and adopted with some modifications by M. Vacherot in his Histoire de l'École d'Alexandrie. It is also unreservedly accepted by Donaldson in his continuation of Müller's History of Greek Literature, and is probably held at this moment by most Englishmen who take any interest in the subject at all. The second view—according to which Neo-Platonism is, at least in its main features, a characteristic although degenerate product of Greek thought—is that maintained by Zeller. As against the Orientalising theory, it seems to us that Zeller has thoroughly proved his case.[506] It may be doubted whether there is a single idea in Plotinus which can be shown to have its exact counterpart in any of the Hindoo or other Asiatic systems whence he is supposed to have drawn; and, as our own analysis has abundantly shown, he says nothing that cannot be derived, either directly or by a simple and easy process of evolution, from Plato, Aristotle, and the Stoics. On the other hand, has not Zeller gone much too far in treating Neo-Platonism as a product of the great religious reaction which unquestionably preceded and accompanied its appearance? Has he not altogether underrated its importance as a purely speculative system, an effort towards the attainment of absolute truth by the simple exercise of human reason? It seems to us that he has, and we shall offer some grounds for venturing to differ from his opinion.

To appreciate the labours of Plotinus, we must, first of all, compare his whole philosophic method with that of his predecessors. Now, Zeller himself has shown quite clearly that in reach of thought, in power of synthesis, in accuracy of reasoning, not one of these can be compared to the founder of Neo-Platonism for a single moment.[507] We may go still further and declare with confidence that no philosopher of equal speculative genius had appeared in Hellas since Chrysippus, or, very possibly, since Aristotle. The only ground for disputing his claims to take rank with the great masters of Hellenic thought seems to be that his system culminates on the objective side in something which lies beyond existence, and on the subjective side in a mystical ecstasy which is the negation of reason. We have shown, however, that if the One is represented as transcending reality, so also is the Idea of Good which corresponds to it in Plato's scheme; and that the One is reached if not grasped by a process of reasoning which, although unsound, still offers itself as reasoning alone, and moves in complete independence of any revelation or intuition such as those to which the genuine systems of mysticism so freely resort.

It cannot be too often repeated that the One in no way conflicts with the world of real existence, but, on the contrary, creates and completes it. Now, within that world, with which alone reason is properly concerned, Plotinus never betrays any want of confidence in its power to discover truth; nor, contrary to what Zeller assumes, does he seem to have been in the least affected by the efforts of the later Sceptics to invalidate its pretensions in this respect.[508] Their criticism was, in fact, chiefly directed against Stoicism, and did not touch the spiritualistic position at all. That there can be no certain knowledge afforded by sensation, or, speaking more generally, by the action of an outward object on an inward subject, Plotinus himself fully admits or rather contends.[509] But while distrusting the ability of external perception, taken alone, to establish the existence of an external object by which it is caused, he expressly claims such a power for reason or understanding.[510] For him, as for Aristotle, and probably for Plato also, the mind is one with its real object; in every act of cognition the idea becomes conscious of itself. We do not say that Scepticism is powerless against such a theory as this, but, in point of fact, it was a theory which the ancient Sceptics had not attacked, and their arguments no more led Plotinus to despair of reason, than the similar arguments of Protagoras and Gorgias had led Plato and Aristotle to despair of it six centuries before. If Sextus and his school contributed anything to the great philosophical revolution of the succeeding age, it was by so weakening the materialistic systems as to render them less capable of opposing the spiritualistic revival when it came.

Unquestionably Plotinus was influenced by the supernaturalistic movement of his age, but only as Plato had been influenced by the similar reaction of his time; and just as the Athenian philosopher had protested against the superstitions which he saw gaining ground, so also did the Alexandrian philosopher protest, with far less vigour it is true, but still to some extent, against the worse extravagances universally entertained by his contemporaries. Among these, to judge by numerous allusions in his writings, astrology and magic held the foremost place. That there was something in both, he did not venture to deny, but he constantly endeavours to extenuate their practical significance and to give a more philosophical interpretation to the alleged phenomena on which they were based.

Towards the old polytheism, his attitude, without being hostile, is perfectly independent. We can see this even in his life, notwithstanding the religious colouring thrown over it by Porphyry. When invited by his disciple Amelius to join in the public worship of the gods, he proudly answered, 'It is their business to come to me, not mine to go to them.'[511] In allegorising the old myths, he handles them with as much freedom as Bacon, and evidently with no more belief in their historical character.[512] In giving the name of God to his supreme principle, he is careful to exclude nearly every attribute associated with divinity even in the purest forms of contemporary theology. Personality, intelligence, will, and even existence, are expressly denied to the One. Although the first cause and highest good of all things, it is so not in a religious but in an abstract, metaphysical sense. The Nous with its ideal offspring and the world-soul are also spoken of as gods; but their personality, if they have any, is of the most shadowy description, and there is no reason for thinking that Plotinus ever worshipped them himself or intended them to be worshipped by his disciples. Like Aristotle, he attributes animation and divinity to the heavenly bodies, but with such careful provisions against an anthropomorphic conception of their nature, that not much devotional feeling is likely to have mingled with the contemplation of their splendour. Finally, we arrive at the daemons, those intermediate spirits which play so great a part in the religion of Plutarch and the other Platonists of the second century. With regard to these, Plotinus repeats many of the current opinions as if he shared them; but his adhesion is of an extremely tepid character; and it may be doubted whether the daemons meant much more for him than for Plato.[513]

The immortality of the soul is a subject on which idealistic philosophers habitually express themselves in terms of apparently studied ambiguity, and this is especially true of Plotinus. Here, as elsewhere, he repeats the opinions and arguments of Plato, but with certain developments which make his adhesion to the popular belief in a personal duration after death considerably more doubtful than was that of his master. One great difficulty in the way of Plato's doctrine, as commonly understood, is that it attributes a permanence to individuals, which, on the principles of his system, should belong only to general ideas. Now, at first sight, Plotinus seems to evade this difficulty by admitting everlasting ideas of individuals no less than of generic types.[514] A closer examination, however, shows that this view is even more unfavourable than Plato's to the hope of personal immortality. For either our real self is independent of our empirical consciousness, which is just what we wish to have preserved, or, as seems more probable, the eternal existence which it enjoys is of an altogether ideal character, like that which Spinoza also attributed to the human soul, and which, in his philosophy, certainly had nothing to do with a prolongation of individual consciousness beyond the grave. As Madame de Staël observes of a similar view held at one time by Schelling, 'cette immortalité-là ressemble terriblement à la mort.' And when, in addition to his own theory of individual ideas, we find Plotinus adopting the theory of the Stoics, that the whole course of mundane affairs periodically returns to its starting-point and is repeated in the same order as before,[515] we cannot help concluding that human immortality in the popular sense must have seemed as impossible to him as it did to them. We must, therefore, suppose that the doctrine of metempsychosis and future retributions which he unquestionably professes, applies only to certain determinate cycles of psychic life; or that it was to him, what it had probably been to Plato, only a figurative way of expressing the essential unity of all souls, and the transcendent character of ethical distinctions.[516]

In this connexion we may deal with the question whether the philosophy of Plotinus is properly described as a pantheistic system. Plotinus was certainly not a pantheist in the same sense as Spinoza and Hegel. With him, the One and the All are not identical; although impersonal and unconscious, his supreme principle is not immanent in the universe, but transcends and creates it: the totality of things are dependent on it, but it is independent of them. Even were we to assume that the One is only ideally distinct from the existence which it causes, still the Nous would remain separate from the world-soul, the higher Soul from Nature, and, within the sphere of Nature herself, Matter would continue to be perpetually breaking away from Form, free-will would be left in unreconciled hostility to fate. Once, and once only, if we remember rightly, does our philosopher rise to the modern conception of the universe as an absolute whole whose parts are not caused but constituted by their fundamental unity, and are not really separated from one another in Nature, but only ideally distinguished in our thoughts. And he adds that we cannot keep up this effort of abstraction for long at a time; things escape from us, and return to their original unity.[517] With Plotinus himself, however, the contrary was true: what he could not keep up was his grasp on the synthetic unity of things. And he himself supplies us with a ready explanation why it should be so, when he points to the dividing tendency of thought as opposed to the uniting tendency of Nature. What he and the other Hellenic thinkers wanted above all, was to make the world clear to themselves and to their pupils, and this they accomplished by their method of serial classification, by bringing into play what we have often spoken of as the moments of antithesis, mediation, and circumscription, Stoicism also had just touched the pantheistic idea, only to let it go again. After being nominally identified with the world, the Stoic God was represented as a designing intelligence, like the Socratic God—an idea wholly alien from real pantheism.

If Plotinus rose above the vulgar superstitions of the West, while, at the same time, using their language for the easier expression of his philosophical ideas, there was one more refined superstition of mixed Greek and Oriental origin which he denounced with the most uncompromising vigour. This was

Gnosticism, as taught by Valentinus and his school. Towards the close of our last chapter, we gave some account of the theory in question. It was principally as enemies of the world and maligners of its perfection that the Gnostics made themselves offensive to the founder of Neo-Platonism. To him, the antithesis of good and evil was represented, not by the opposition of spirit and Nature, but by the opposition between his ideal principle through all degrees of its perfection, and unformed Matter. Like Plato, he looked on the existing world as a consummate work of art, an embodiment of the archetypal Ideas, a visible presentation of reason. But in the course of his attack on the Gnostics,[518] other points of great interest are raised, showing how profoundly his philosophy differed from theirs, how entirely he takes his stand on the fixed principles of Hellenic thought. Thus he particularly reproaches his opponents for their systematic disparagement of Plato, to whom, after all, they owe whatever is true and valuable in their metaphysics.[519] He ridicules their belief in demoniacal possession, with its wholly gratuitous and clumsy employment of supernatural agencies to account for what can be sufficiently explained by the operation of natural causes.[520] And, more than anything else, he severely censures their detachment of religion from morality. On this last point, some of his remarks are so striking and pertinent that they deserve to be quoted.

Above all, he exclaims, we must not fail to notice what effect this doctrine has on the minds of those whom they have persuaded to despise the world and all that it contains. Of the two chief methods for attaining the supreme good, one has sensual pleasure for its end, the other virtue, the effort after which begins and ends with God. Epicurus, by his denial of providence, leaves us no choice but to pursue the former. But this doctrine [Gnosticism], involving as it does a still more insolent denial of divine order and human law, laughs to scorn what has always been the accepted ideal of conduct, and, in its rage against beauty, abolishes temperance and justice—the justice that is associated with natural feeling and perpetuated by discipline and reason—along with every other ennobling virtue. So, in the absence of true morality, they are given over to pleasure and utility and selfish isolation from other men—unless, indeed, their nature is better than their principles. They have an ideal that nothing here below can satisfy, and so they put off the effort for its attainment to a future life, whereas they should begin at once, and prove that they are of divine race by fulfilling the duties of their present state. For virtue is the condition of every higher aspiration, and only to those who disdain sensual enjoyment is it given to understand the divine. How far our opponents are from realising this is proved by their total neglect of ethical science. They neither know what virtue is, nor how many virtues there are, nor what ancient philosophy has to teach us on the subject, nor what are the methods of moral training, nor how the soul is to be tended and cleansed. They tell us to look to God; but merely saying this is useless unless they can tell us what the manner of the looking is to be. For it might be asked, what is to prevent us from looking to God, while at the same time freely indulging our sensual appetites and angry passions. Virtue perfected, enlightened, and rooted in the soul, will reveal God to us, but without it he will remain an empty name.[521]

Even M. Vacherot, with all his anxiety to discover an Oriental origin for Neo-Platonism, cannot help seeing that this attack on the Gnostics was inspired by an indignant reaction of Greek philosophy against the inroads of Oriental superstition, and that the same character belongs more or less to the whole system of its author. But, so far as we are aware, Kirchner is the only critic who has fully worked out this idea, and exhibited the philosophy of Plotinus in its true character as a part of the great classical revival, which after producing the literature of the second century reached its consummation in a return to the idealism of Plato and Aristotle.[522]

Neo-Platonism may itself furnish us with no inapt image of the age in which it arose. Like the unformed Matter about which we have been hearing so much, the consciousness of that period was in itself dark, indeterminate and unsteady, uncreative, unspontaneous, unoriginating, but with a receptive capacity which enabled it to seize, reflect, and transmit the power of living Reason, the splendour of eternal thought.

XI.

In fixing the relation of Plotinus to his own age, we have gone far towards fixing his relation to all ages, the place which he occupies in the development of philosophy as a connected whole. We have seen that as an attempt to discover the truth of things, his speculations are worthless and worse than worthless, since their method no less than their teaching is false. Nevertheless, Wisdom is justified of all her children. Without adding anything to the sum of positive knowledge, Plotinus produced an effect on men's thoughts not unworthy of the great intellect and pure life which he devoted to the service of philosophy. No other thinker has ever accomplished a revolution so immediate, so comprehensive, and of such prolonged duration. He was the creator of Neo-Platonism, and Neo-Platonism simply annihilated every school of philosophy to which it was opposed. For thirteen centuries or more, the three great systems which had so long divided the suffrages of educated minds—Stoicism, Epicureanism, and Scepticism—ceased to exist, and were allowed to lapse into such complete oblivion that only a few fragments of the works in which they were originally embodied have been preserved. And Plotinus was enabled to do this by the profound insight which led him to strike less at any particular doctrine held by his opponents than at the common foundation on which they all stood, the materialism openly professed by the Stoics and Epicureans, and assumed by the Sceptics as the necessary presupposition of every dogmatic philosophy. It is true that the principle which he opposed to theirs was not of his own origination, although he stated it more powerfully than it had ever been stated before. But to have revived the spiritualism of Plato and Aristotle in such a way as to win for it universal acceptance, was precisely his greatest merit. It is also the only one that he would have claimed for himself. As we have already mentioned, he professed to be nothing more than the disciple of Plato. And although Aristotelian ideas abound in his writings, still not only are they overbalanced by the Platonic element, but Plotinus might justly have contended that they also belong, in a sense, to Plato, having been originally acquired by a simple development from his teaching.

We have said that the founder of Neo-Platonism contrived to blend the systems of his two great authorities in such a manner as to eliminate much of the relative truth which is contained in each of them taken by itself. It has been reserved for modern thought to accomplish the profounder synthesis which has eliminated their errors in combining their truths. Yet, perhaps, no other system would have satisfied the want of the time so well as that constructed by Plotinus out of the materials at his disposal. Such as it was, that system held its ground as the reigning philosophy until all independent thinking was suppressed by Justinian, somewhat more than two and a half centuries after its author's death. Even then it did not become extinct, but reappeared in Christian literature, in the writings attributed to Dionysius the Areopagite, and again in the daring speculations of Erigena, the father of mediaeval philosophy, to pass under more diluted forms into the teaching of the later Schoolmen, until the time arrived for its renewed study in the original sources as an element of the Platonic revival in the fifteenth century. All this popularity proves, as we say, that Plotinus suited his own age and other ages which reproduced the same general intellectual tendencies. But the important thing was that he made Plato and Aristotle more interesting, and thus led men to study their writings more eagerly than before. The true reign of those philosophers does not begin until we reach the Middle Ages, and the commanding position which they then enjoyed was due, in great measure, to the revolution effected by Plotinus.

But when Neo-Platonism, as a literature and a system, had given way to the original authorities from which it was derived, its influence did not, on that account, cease to be felt. In particular, Plotinus gave currency to a certain interpretation of Plato's teaching which has been universally accepted until a comparatively recent period, perhaps one may say until the time of Schleiermacher. We have seen how many elements of Platonism he left out of sight; and, thanks to his example, followed as it naturally was by Catholic theologians, the world was content to leave them out of sight as well. The charming disciple of Socrates whom we all know and love—the literary and dramatic artist, the brilliant parodist, the sceptical railleur from the shafts of whose irony even his own theories are not safe, the penetrating observer of human life, the far-seeing critic and reformer of social institutions—is a discovery of modern scholarship. Not as such did the master of idealism appear to Marsilio Ficino and Michael Angelo, to Lady Jane Grey and Cudworth and Henry More, to Berkeley and Hume and Thomas Taylor, to all the great English poets from Spenser to Shelley; not as such does he now appear to popular imagination; but as a mystical enthusiast, a dreamer of dreams which, whether they be realised or not in some far-off sphere, are, at any rate, out of relation to the world of sensuous experience and everyday life. So absolute, indeed, is the reaction from this view that we are in danger of rushing to the contrary extreme, of forgetting what elements of truth the Plotinian interpretation contained, and substituting for it an interpretation still more one-sided, still more inadequate to express the scope and splendour of Plato's thoughts. Plato believed in truth and right and purity, believed in them still more profoundly than Plotinus; and his was a more effectual faith precisely because he did not share the sterile optimism of his Alexandrian disciple, but worked and watched for the realisation of what, as yet, had never been realised.[523]

Finally, by the form which he gave to Platonism, Plotinus has had a large share in determining the direction of modern metaphysics. Although, as we have seen, not, properly speaking, a pantheist himself, he showed how the ideal theory could be transformed into a pantheistic system, and pantheism it immediately became when the peculiar limitations and subtleties of Greek thought had ceased to dominate over the western mind, and when the restraints of Catholic orthodoxy had been removed or relaxed. The stream of tendency in this direction runs all through the Middle Ages, and acquires new volume and momentum at the Renaissance, until, by a process which will be analysed in the next chapter, it reaches its supreme expansion in the philosophy of Spinoza. Then, after a long pause, it is taken up by Kant's successors, and combined with the subjective idealism of modern psychology, finally passing, through the intervention of Victor Cousin and Sir William Hamilton, into the philosophy of Mr. Herbert Spencer.

The last-named thinker would, no doubt, repudiate the title of pantheist; and it is certain that, under his treatment, pantheism has reverted, by a curious sort of atavism, to something much more nearly resembling the original doctrine of the Neo-Platonic school. Mr. Spencer tells us that the world is the manifestation of an unknowable Power. Plotinus said nearly the same, although not in such absolutely self-contradictory terms.[524] Mr. Spencer constantly assumes, by speaking of it in the singular number, that the creative Power of which we know nothing is one; having, apparently, convinced himself of its unity by two methods of reasoning. First, he identifies the transcendent cause of phenomena with the absolute, which is involved in our consciousness of relation; leaving it to be inferred that as relativity implies plurality, absoluteness must imply unity. And, secondly, from the mutual convertibility of the physical forces, he infers the unity of that which underlies force. Plotinus also arrives at the same result by two lines of argument, one à posteriori, and derived from the unity pervading all Nature; the other à priori, and derived from the fancied dependence of the Many on the One. Even in his use of the predicate Unknowable without a subject, Mr. Spencer has been anticipated by Damascius, one of the last Neo-Platonists, who speaks of the supreme principle as τὸ ἄγνωστον.[525] And the same philosopher anticipates the late Father Dalgairns in suggesting the very pertinent question, how, if we know nothing about the Unknowable, we know that it is unknowable.

Nor is this all. Besides the arguments from relativity and causation, Mr. Spencer has a third method for arriving at his absolute. He thinks away all the determinations imposed by consciousness on its objects, and identifies the residual substance with the ultimate reality of things. Now, this residue, as we have seen, exactly corresponds to the Matter, whether intelligible or sensible, of Aristotle and Plotinus. As such, it stands in extreme antithesis to the One, and yet there is a near kinship between them. Probably, according to Plotinus, and certainly according to Proclus,[526] Matter is a direct product of the One, whose infinite power it reflects. All existence is formed by the union, in varying proportions, of these two principles. Above all, both are unknowable. Thus it was natural that in the hands of less subtle analysts than the Greeks they should coalesce into a single substance. And, as a matter of fact, they have so coalesced in the systems of Giordano Bruno, of Spinoza, and finally of Mr. Spencer.

Here we imagine an impatient reader exclaiming, 'How can Mr. Herbert Spencer, who knows, if possible, even less of Greek philosophy than of his own Unknowable, have derived that principle from the Greeks?' Well, we have already traced the genealogy by which the two systems of agnosticism are connected. And some additional light will be thrown on the question if we consider that the form of Neo-Platonism was largely determined by the manner in which Plotinus brought the spiritualistic conceptualism of Plato and Aristotle into contact with the dynamic materialism of the Stoics; and that the form of Mr. Spencer's philosophy has been similarly determined by bringing the idealism of modern German thought into contact with the mechanical evolutionism of modern science. Thus, under the influence of old associations, has pantheism been metamorphosed into a crude agnosticism, which faithfully reproduces the likeness of its original ancestors, the Plotinian Matter and the Plotinian One.

XII.[527]

The history of Neo-Platonism, subsequently to the death of Plotinus, decomposes itself into several distinct tendencies, pursuing more or less divergent lines of direction. First of all, it was drawn into the supernaturalist movement against which it had originally been, in part at least, a reaction and a protest. One sees from the life of its founder how far his two favourite disciples, Amelius and Porphyry, were from sharing his superiority to the superstitions of the age. Both had been educated under Pythagorean influences, which were fostered rather than repressed by the new philosophy. With Porphyry, theoretical interests are, to a great extent, superseded by practical interests; and, in practice, the religious and ascetic predominates over the purely ethical element. Still, however great may have been his aberrations, they never went beyond the limits of Hellenic tradition.

Although of Syrian extraction, his attitude towards Oriental superstition was one of uncompromising hostility; and in writing against Christianity, his criticism of the Old Testament seems to have closely resembled that of modern rationalism. But with Porphyry's disciple, Iamblichus, every restraint is thrown aside, the wildest Oriental fancies are accepted as articles of belief, and the most senseless devotional practices are inculcated as means towards the attainment of a truly spiritual life.

Besides the general religious movement which had long been in action, and was daily gaining strength from the increasing barbarisation of the empire, there was, at this juncture, a particular cause tending to bring Greek philosophy into close alliance with the mythology which it had formerly rejected and denounced. This was the rapid rise and spread of Christianity. St Augustine has said that of all heathen philosophers none came nearer to the Christian faith than the Neo-Platonists.[528] Nevertheless, it was in them that the old religion found its only apologists and the new religion its most active assailants. We have already alluded to the elaborate polemic of Porphyry. Half a century later, the same principles could boast of a still more illustrious champion. The emperor Julian was imbued with the doctrines of Neo-Platonism, and was won back to the ancient faith by the teaching of its professors.

What seems to us the reactionary attitude of the spiritualist school was dictated by the circumstances of its origin. A product of the great classical revival, its cause was necessarily linked with the civilisation of ancient Greece, and of that civilisation the worship of the old gods seemed to form an integral element. One need only think of the Italian Renaissance, with its predilection for the old mythology, to understand how much stronger and more passionate this feeling must have been among those to whom Greek literature still spoke in a living language, whose eyes, wherever they turned, still rested on the monuments, unrivalled, undesecrated, unfallen, unfaded, of Greek religious art. Nor was polytheism what some have imagined it to have been at this period, merely a tradition, an association, a dream, drawing shadowy sustenance from the human works and human thoughts which it had once inspired. To Plotinus and Proclus, as formerly to Socrates and Plato and Aristotle, the luminaries of day and night blazed down from heaven as animated and immortal witnesses of its truth. It was not simply that the heavens declared the glory of God; to the pious beholder, they were visibly inhabited by glorious gods, and their constellated fires were, as Plotinus said, a scripture in which the secrets of destiny might be read. The same philosopher scornfully asks the Gnostics, who, in this respect, were indistinguishable from the Christians, whether they were so infatuated as to call the worst men their brothers, while refusing that title to the sun; and at a much later period, notwithstanding the heavy penalties attached to it, the worship of the heavenly bodies continued to be practised by the profoundest thinkers and scholars of the Neo-Platonic school.[529] Moreover, polytheism, by the very weakness and unfixity of its dogmas, gave a much wider scope to independent speculation than could be permitted within the limits of the Catholic Church, just because Catholicism itself constituted a philosophical system in which all the great problems of existence were provided with definite and authoritative solutions.

The final defeat of polytheism proved, in some respects, an advantage to Neo-Platonism, by compelling it to exchange theological controversy for studies which could be prosecuted, at least for a time, without giving umbrage to the dominant religion. At Alexandria the new spiritualism was associated, on genuinely Platonic principles, with the teaching of geometry by the noble and ill-fated Hypatia. In all the Neo-Platonic schools, whether at Rome, at Alexandria, at Constantinople, or at Athens, the writings of Plato and Aristotle were attentively studied, and made the subject of numerous commentaries, many of which are still extant. This return to the two great masters of idealism was, as we have already said, the most valuable result of the metaphysical revival, and probably contributed more than any other cause to the preservation of their works amidst the general wreck of ancient philosophical literature. Finally, efforts were made to present the doctrine of Plotinus under a more popular or a more scientific form, and to develope it into systematic completeness.

Driven by Christian intolerance from every other centre of civilisation, Greek philosophy found a last refuge in Athens, where it continued to be taught through the whole of the fifth century and the first quarter of the sixth. During that period, all the tendencies already indicated as characteristic of Neo-Platonism exhibited themselves once more, and contributed in about equal degrees to the versatile activity of its last original representative, Proclus (410-485). This remarkable man offers one of the most melancholy examples of wasted power to be found in the history of thought. Endowed with an enormous faculty for acquiring knowledge, a rare subtlety in the analysis of ideas, and an unsurpassed genius for their systematic arrangement, he might, under more favourable auspices, have been the Laplace or Cuvier of his age. As it was, his immense energies were devoted to the task of bringing a series of lifeless abstractions into harmony with a series of equally lifeless superstitions. A commentator both on Euclid and on Plato, he aspired to present transcendental dialectic under the form of mathematical demonstration. In his Institutes of Theology, he offers proofs equally elaborate and futile of much that had been taken for granted in the philosophy of Plotinus. Again, where there seems to be a gap in the system of his master, he fills it up by inserting new figments of his own. Thus, between the super-essential One and the absolute Nous, he interposes a series of henads or unities, answering to the multiplicity of intelligences or self-conscious Ideas which Plotinus had placed within the supreme Reason, or to the partial souls which he had placed after the world-soul. In this manner, Proclus, following the usual method of Greek thought, supplies a transition from the creative One to the Being which had hitherto been regarded as its immediate product; while, at the same time, providing a counterpart to the many lesser gods with which polytheism had surrounded its supreme divinity. Finally, as Plotinus had arranged all things on the threefold scheme of a first principle, a departure from that principle, and a subsequent reunion with it, Proclus divides the whole series of created substances into a succession of triads, each reproducing, on a small scale, the fundamental system of an origin, a departure, and a return. And he even multiplies the triads still further by decomposing each separate moment into a secondary process of the same description. For example, Intelligence as a whole is divided into Being, Life, and Thought, and the first of these, again, into the Limit, the Unlimited, and the absolute Existence (οὐσία), which is the synthesis of both. The Hegelian system is, as is well known, constructed on a similar plan; but while with Hegel the logical evolution is a progress from lower to higher and richer life, with Proclus, as with the whole Neo-Platonic school, and, indeed, with almost every school of Greek thought, each step forward is also a step downward, involving a proportionate loss of reality and power.

Thus Proclus was to Plotinus what Plotinus himself had been to Plato and Aristotle: that is to say, he stood one degree further removed from the actual truth of things and from the spontaneity of original reflection. And what we have said about the philosophic position of the master may be applied, with some modification, to the claims of his most eminent disciple. From a scientific point of view, the system, of Proclus is a mere mass of wearisome rubbish; from an aesthetic point of view it merits our admiration as the most comprehensive, the most coherent, and the most symmetrical work of the kind that antiquity has to show. It would seem that just as the architectural skill of the Romans survived all their other great gifts, and even continued to improve until the very last—the so-called temple of Minerva Medica being the most technically perfect of all their monuments—so also did the Greek power of concatenating ideas go on developing itself as long as Greece was permitted to have any ideas of her own.

The time arrived when this last liberty was to be taken away. In the year 529, Justinian issued his famous decree prohibiting the public teaching of philosophy in Athens, and confiscating the endowments devoted to the maintenance of its professors. It is probable that this measure formed part of a comprehensive scheme for completing the extirpation of paganism throughout the empire. For some two centuries past, the triumph of Christianity had been secured by an unsparing exercise of the imperial authority, as the triumph of Catholicism over heresy was next to be secured with the aid of the Frankish sword. A few years afterwards, the principal representatives of the Neo-Platonic school, including the Damascius of whom we have already spoken, and Simplicius, the famous Aristotelian commentator, repaired to the court of Khosru Nuschirvan, the King of Persia, with the intention of settling in his country for the rest of their lives. They were soon heartily sick of their adopted home. Khosru was unquestionably an enlightened monarch, greatly interested in Hellenic culture, and sincerely desirous of diffusing it among his people. It is also certain that Agathias, our only authority on this subject, was violently prejudiced against him. But it may very well be, as stated by that historian[530] that Khosru by no means came up to the exaggerated expectations formed of him by the exiled professors. He had been described to them as the ideal of a Platonic ruler, and, like inexperienced bookmen, they accepted the report in good faith. They found that he cared a great deal more for scientific questions about the cause of the tides and the modifications superinduced on plants and animals by transference to a new environment, than about the metaphysics of the

One.[531] Moreover, the immorality of Oriental society and the corruption of Oriental government were something for which they were totally unprepared. Better, they thought, to die at once, so that it were but on Roman soil, than to live on any conditions in such a country as Persia. Khosru was most unwilling to lose his guests, but on finding that they were determined to leave him, he permitted them to depart, and even made it a matter of express stipulation with the imperial government that they should be allowed to live in their old homes without suffering any molestation on account of their religious opinions.[532]

Simplicius continued to write commentaries on Aristotle after his return, and was even succeeded by a younger generation of Platonic expositors; but before the end of the sixth century paganism was extinct, and Neo-Platonism, as a separate school of philosophy, shared its fate. It will be the object of our next and concluding chapter to show that the disappearance of the old religion and the old methods of teaching did not involve any real break in the continuity of thought, and that modern speculation has been, through the greater part of its history, a reproduction of Greek ideas in new combinations and under altered names.

CHAPTER VI.
GREEK PHILOSOPHY AND MODERN THOUGHT.

I.

Adequately to exhibit the relation of Greek philosophy to modern thought would require a volume. The object of the present discussion is merely to show in what ways that relation has been most clearly manifested, and what assistance it may afford us in solving some important problems connected with the development of metaphysical and moral speculation.

Historians often speak as if philosophy took an entirely fresh start at different epochs of its existence. One such break is variously associated with Descartes, or Bacon, or some one of their Italian predecessors. In like manner, the introduction of Christianity, coupled with the closing of the Athenian schools by Justinian, is considered, as once was the suppression of the West-Roman Caesarate by Odoacer, to mark the beginning of a new régime. But there can be no more a real break in the continuity of intellectual than in the continuity of political history, beyond what sleep or inactivity may simulate in the life of the organic aggregate no less than in the life of the organic individual. In each instance, the thread is taken up where it was dropped. If the rest of the world has been advancing meanwhile, new tendencies will come into play, but only by first attaching themselves to older lines of movement. Sometimes, again, what seems to be a revolution is, in truth, the revival or liberation of an earlier movement, through the decay or destruction of beliefs which have hitherto checked its growth. Thus the systems of Plato and Aristotle, after carrying all before them for a brief period, were found unsuitable, from their vast comprehension and high spirituality, to the undeveloped consciousness of their age, and were replaced by popularised versions of the sceptical or naturalistic philosophies which they had endeavoured to suppress. And when these were at length left behind by the forward movement of the human mind, speculative reformers spontaneously reverted to the two great Socratic thinkers for a better solution of the problems in debate. After many abortive efforts, a teacher appeared possessing sufficient genius to fuse their principles into a seemingly coherent and comprehensive whole. By combining the Platonic and Aristotelian spiritualism with a dynamic element borrowed from Stoicism, Plotinus did for an age of intellectual decadence what his models had done in vain for an age of intellectual growth. The relation in which he stood to Stoicism, Epicureanism, and Scepticism, reproduced the relation in which they stood to the various physical and sophistic schools of their time; but the silent experience of six centuries won for him a much more enduring success.

Neo-Platonism was the form under which Greek philosophy passed into Christian teaching; and the transition was effected with less difficulty because Christianity had already absorbed some of its most essential elements from the original system of Plato himself. Meanwhile the revival of spiritualism had given an immense impulse to the study of the classic writings whence it was drawn; and the more they were studied the more prominently did their antagonism on certain important questions come into view. Hence, no sooner did the two systems between which Plotinus had established a provisional compromise come out victorious from their struggle with materialism, than they began to separate and draw off into opposing camps. The principal subject of dispute was the form under which ideas exist. The conflicting theories of Realism and Nominalism are already set forth with perfect clearness by Porphyry in his introduction to the Organon; and his statement of the case, as Victor Cousin has pointed out, gave the signal for a controversy forming the central interest of Scholasticism during the entire period of its duration.

Now, it is a remarkable fact, and one as yet not sufficiently attended to, that a metaphysical issue first raised between the Platonists and Aristotle, and regarded, at least by the latter, as of supreme importance for philosophy, should have been totally neglected at a time when abundant documents on both sides were open to consultation, and taken up with passionate eagerness at a time when not more than one or two dialogues of Plato and two or three tracts of Aristotle continued to be read in the western world. Various explanations of this singular anomaly may be offered. It may be said, for instance, that after every moral and religious question on which the schools of Athens were divided had been closed by the authoritative ruling of Catholicism, nothing remained to quarrel over but points too remote or too obscure for the Church to interfere in their decision; and that these were accordingly seized upon as the only field where human intelligence could exercise itself with any approach to freedom. The truth, however, seems to be that to take any interest in the controversy between Realism and Nominalism, it was first necessary that European thought as a whole should rise to a level with the common standpoint of their first supporters. This revolution was effected by the general adoption of a monotheistic faith.

Moreover, the Platonic ideas were something more than figments of an imaginative dialectic. They were now beginning to appear in their true light, and as what Plato had always understood them to be—no mere abstractions from experience, but spiritual forces by which sensuous reality was to be reconstituted and reformed. The Church herself seemed something more than a collection of individuals holding common convictions and obeying a common discipline; she was, like Plato's own Republic, the visible embodiment of an archetype laid up in Heaven.[533] And the Church's teaching seemed also to assume the independent reality of abstract ideas. Does not the Trinity involve belief in a God distinct from any of the Divine Persons taken alone? Do not the Fall, the Incarnation, and the Atonement become more intelligible if we imagine an ideal humanity sinning with the first Adam and purified by becoming united with the second Adam? Such, at least, seems to have been the dimly conceived metaphysics of St. Paul, whatever may now be the official doctrine of Rome. It was, therefore, in order that, during the first half of the Middle Ages, from Charlemagne to the Crusades, Realism should have been the prevailing doctrine; the more so because Plato's Timaeus, which was studied in the schools through that entire period, furnishes its readers with a complete theory of the universe; while only the formal side of Aristotle's philosophy is represented by such of his logical treatises as were then known to western Christendom.

Yet Realism concealed a danger to orthodoxy which was not long in making itself felt. Just as the substantiality of individuals disappeared in that of their containing species, so also did every subordinate species tend to vanish in the summum genus of absolute Being. Now such a conclusion was nothing less than full-blown pantheism; and pantheism was, in fact, the system of the first great Schoolman, John Scotus Erigena; while other Realists were only prevented from reaching the same goal by the restraint either of Christian faith or of ecclesiastical authority. But if they failed to draw the logical consequences of their premises, it was drawn for them by others; and Abélard did not fail to twit his opponents with the formidable heresy implied in their realistic principles.[534] As yet, however, the weight of authority inclined towards Plato's side; and the persecution suffered by

Abélard himself, as compared with the very mild treatment accorded to his contemporary, Gilbert de la Porrée, when each was arraigned on a charge of heresy, shows that while the Nominalism of the one was an aggravation, the Realism of the other was an extenuation of his offence.[535]

So matters stood when the introduction of Aristotle's entire system into western Europe brought about a revolution comparable to that effected two centuries later by the complete recovery of ancient literature. It was through Latin translations from the Arabic, accompanied by Arabic commentaries, that the Peripatetic philosophy was first revealed in its entirety; and even Albertus Magnus, living in the thirteenth century, seems to have derived his knowledge of the subject from these exclusively. But a few years after the capture of Constantinople by the Crusaders in 1204, the Greek manuscripts of Aristotle were brought to Paris; and, towards the middle of the century, a new Latin version was made from these under the supervision of St. Thomas Aquinas.[536] The triumph of Aristotle was now, at least for a time, secured. For, while in the first period of the Middle Ages we find only a single great name, that of Abélard, among the Nominalists, against a strong array of Realists, in the second period the proportions are reversed, and Realism has only a single worthy champion, Duns Scotus, to pit against Albertus, Aquinas, and William of Ockham, each of them representing one of the principal European nations.[537] The human intellect, hitherto confined within the narrow bounds of logic, now ranged over physics, metaphysics, psychology, and ethics; and although all these subjects were studied only at second-hand, and with very limited opportunities for criticism, still the benefit received must have been immense. The priceless service of the later Schoolmen is to have appropriated and successfully upheld, against Platonism on the one hand and theological mysticism on the other, a philosophy which, however superficial, took in the whole range of natural phenomena, derived all knowledge from external observation, and set an example of admirable precision in the systematic exposition of its results. If no positive addition was made to that vast storehouse of facts and ideas, the blame does not lie with Aristotle's method, but with the forcible suppression of free mental activity by the Church, or its diversion to more profitable fields by the study of Roman jurisprudence. Even as it was, Aristotle contributed largely to the downfall of ecclesiastical authority in two ways: directly by accustoming men to use their reason, and indirectly by throwing back mysticism on its proper office—the restoration of a purely personal religion.

But before the dissolving action of Nominalism had become fully manifest, its ascendency was once more challenged; and this time, also, the philosophical impulse came from Constantinople. Greek scholars, seeking help in the West, brought with them to Florence the complete works of Plato; and these were shortly made accessible to a wider public through the Latin translation of Ficino. Their influence seems at first to have told in favour of mysticism, for this was the contemporary tendency to which they could be most readily affiliated; and, besides, in swinging back from Aristotle's philosophy to the rival form of spiritualism, men's minds naturally reverted, in the first instance, to what had once linked them together—the system of Plotinus. Thus Platonism was studied through an Alexandrian medium, and as the Alexandrians had looked at it, that is to say, chiefly under its theological and metaphysical aspects. As such, it became the accepted philosophy of the Renaissance; and much of what we most admire in the literature—at least the English literature—of that period, is directly traceable to Platonic influence. That the Utopia of Sir Thomas More was inspired by the Republic and the Critias is, of course, obvious; and the great part played by the ideal theory in Spenser's Faery Queen, though less evident, is still sufficiently clear. As Mr. Green observes in his History of the English People (II., p. 413), 'Spenser borrows, in fact, the delicate and refined forms of the Platonic philosophy to express his own moral enthusiasm....

Justice, Temperance, Truth are no mere names to him, but real existences to which his whole nature clings with a rapturous affection.' Now it deserves observation, as illustrating a great revolution in European thought, that the relation of Plato to the epic of the English Renaissance is precisely paralleled by the relation of Aristotle to the epic of mediaeval Italy. Dante borrows more than his cosmography from the Stagirite. The successive circles of Hell, the spirals of Purgatory, and the spheres of Paradise, are a framework in which the characters of the poem are exhibited, not as individual actors whom we trace through a life's history, but as types of a class and representatives of a single mental quality, whether vicious or virtuous. In other words, the historical arrangement of all previous poems is abandoned in favour of a logical arrangement. For the order of contiguity in time is substituted the order of resemblance and difference in idea. How thoroughly Aristotelian, indeed, were the lines within which mediaeval imagination moved is proved by the possibility of tracing them in a work utterly different from Dante's—the Decameron of Boccaccio. The tales constituting this collection are so arranged that each day illustrates some one special class of adventures; only, to make good Aristotle's principle that earthly affairs are not subject to invariable rules, a single departure from the prescribed subject is allowed in each decade; while during one entire day the story-tellers are left free to choose a subject at their own discretion.

Now what distinguishes Spenser from Dante is that, while he also disposes his inventions according to an extremely artificial and abstract schematism, with him, as with Plato, abstractions acquire a separate individual existence, being, in fact, embodied as so many persons; while Dante, following Aristotle, never separates his from the concrete data of experience. And it may be noted that, in this respect at least, English literature has not deserted the philosophy which presided over its second birth. It has ever since been more prone to realise abstractions than any other literature, whether under the form of allegories, parables, or mere casual illustrations drawn from material objects. Even at this day, English writers crowd their pages with dazzling metaphors, which to Continental readers must have sometimes a rather barbaric effect.

Another and profounder characteristic of Plato, as distinguished from Aristotle, is his thorough-going opposition of reality to appearance; his distrust of sensuous perception, imagination, and opinion; his continual appeal to a hidden world of absolute truth and justice. We find this profounder principle also grasped and applied to poetical purposes in our Elizabethan literature, not only by Spenser, but by a still greater master—Shakespeare. It is by no means unlikely that Shakespeare may have looked into a translation of the Dialogues; at any rate, the intellectual atmosphere he breathed was so saturated with their spirit that he could easily absorb enough of it to inspire him with the theory of existence which alone gives consistency to his dramatic work from first to last. For the essence of his comedies is that they represent the ordinary world of sensible experience as a scene of bewilderment and delusion, where there is nothing fixed, nothing satisfying, nothing true; as something which, because of its very unreality, is best represented by the drama, but a drama that is not without mysterious intimations of a reality behind the veil. In them we have the

Fallings from us, vanishings,

Blank misgivings of a creature

Moving about in worlds not realised;

while in his tragedies we have the realisation of those worlds—the workings of an eternal justice which alone remains faithful to one purpose through the infinite flux of passion and of sense.

Besides the revival of Platonism, three causes had conspired to overthrow the supremacy of Aristotle. The literary Renaissance with its adoration for beauty of form was alienated by the barbarous dialect of Scholasticism; the mystical theology of Luther saw in it an ally both of ecclesiastical authority and of human reason; and the new spirit of passionate revolt against all tradition attacked the accepted philosophy in common with every other branch of the official university curriculum. Before long, however, a reaction set in. The innovators discredited themselves by an extravagance, an ignorance, a credulity, and an intolerance worse than anything in the teaching which they decried. No sooner was the Reformation organised as a positive doctrine than it fell back for support on the only model of systematic thinking at that time to be found. The Humanists were conciliated by having the original text of Aristotle placed before them; and they readily believed, what was not true, that it contained a wisdom which had eluded mediaeval research. But the great scientific movement of the sixteenth century contributed, more than any other impulse, to bring about an Aristotelian reaction. After winning immortal triumphs in every branch of art and literature, the Italian intellect threw itself with equal vigour into the investigation of physical phenomena. Here Plato could give little help, whereas Aristotle supplied a methodised description of the whole field to be explored, and contributions of extraordinary value towards the understanding of some, at least, among its infinite details. And we may measure the renewed popularity of his system not only by the fact that Cesalpino, the greatest naturalist of the age, professed himself its adherent, but also by the bitterness of the criticisms directed against it, and the involuntary homage offered by rival systems which were little more than meagre excerpts from the Peripatetic ontology and logic.

II.

Of all testimonies to the restored supremacy of Aristotelianism, there is none so remarkable as that afforded by the thinker who, more than any other, has enjoyed the credit of its overthrow. To call Francis Bacon an Aristotelian will seem to most readers a paradox. Such an appellation would, however, be much nearer the truth than were the titles formerly bestowed on the author of the Novum Organum. The notion, indeed, that he was in any sense the father of modern science is rapidly disappearing from the creed of educated persons. Its long continuance was due to a coalition of literary men who knew nothing about physics and of physicists who knew nothing about philosophy or its history. It is certain that the great discoveries made both before and during Bacon's lifetime were the starting-point of all future progress in the same direction. It is equally certain that Bacon himself had either not heard of those discoveries or that he persistently rejected them. But it might still be contended that he divined and formulated the only method by which these and all other great additions to human knowledge have been made, had not the delusion been dispelled by recent investigations, more especially those of his own editors, Messrs. Ellis and Spedding. Mr. Spedding has shown that Bacon's method never was applied to physical science at all. Mr. Ellis has shown that it was incapable of application, being founded on a complete misconception of the problem to be solved. The facts could in truth, hardly have been other than what they are. Had Bacon succeeded in laying down the lines of future investigation, it would have been a telling argument against his own implied belief that all knowledge is derived from experience. For, granting the validity of that belief, a true theory of discovery can only be reached by an induction from the observed facts of scientific practice, and such facts did not, at that time, exist in sufficient numbers to warrant an induction. It would have been still more extraordinary had he furnished a clue to the labyrinth of Nature without ever having explored its mazes on his own account. Even as it is, from Bacon's own point of view the contradiction remains. If ever any system was constructed à priori the Instauratio Magna was. But there is really no such thing as à priori speculation. Apart from observation, the keenest and boldest intellect can do no more than rearrange the materials supplied by tradition, or give a higher generalisation to the principles of other philosophers. This was precisely what Bacon did. The wealth of aphoristic wisdom and ingenious illustration scattered through his writings belongs entirely to himself; but his dream of using science as an instrument for acquiring unlimited power over Nature is inherited from the astrologers, alchemists, and magicians of the Middle Ages; and his philosophical system, with which alone we are here concerned, is partly a modification, partly an extension, of Aristotle's. An examination of its leading features will at once make this clear.

Bacon begins by demanding that throughout the whole range of experience new facts should be collected on the largest scale, in order to supply materials for scientific generalisation. There can be no doubt that he is here guided by the example of Aristotle, and of Aristotle alone. Such a storehouse of materials is still extant in the History of Animals, which evidently suggested the use of the word 'History' in this sense to Bacon, and which, by the way, is immensely superior to anything that he ever attempted in the same line. The facts on which Aristotle's Politics is based were contained in another vast descriptive work of the same kind, now unhappily lost. Even the Stagirite's more systematic treatises comprise a multitude of observations, catalogued according to a certain order, but not reduced to scientific principles. What Bacon did was to carry out, or to bid others carry out, the plan so suggested in every department of enquiry. But if we ask by what method he was guided in his survey of the whole field to be explored, how he came by a complete enumeration of the sciences, arranged according to their logical order,—the answer is still that he borrowed it from the Peripatetic encyclopaedia.

One need only compare the catalogue of particular histories subjoined to the Parasceve,[538] with a table of Aristotle's works, to understand how closely Bacon follows in the footsteps of his predecessor. We do, indeed, find sundry subjects enumerated on which the elder student had not touched; but they are only such as would naturally suggest themselves to a man of comprehensive intelligence, coming nearly two thousand years after his original; while they are mostly of no philosophical value whatever. Bacon's merit was to bring the distinction between the descriptive sciences and the theoretical sciences into clearer consciousness, and to give a view of the former corresponding in completeness to that already obtained of the latter.

The methodical distinction between the materials for generalisation and generalisation itself, is derived from the metaphysical distinction between Matter and Form in Nature.[539] This distinction is the next great feature of Bacon's philosophy, and it is taken, still more obviously than the first, from Aristotle, the most manifest blots of the original being faithfully reproduced in the copy. The Forms of simple substances were, according to the Stagirite, their sensible qualities. The Forms of aggregates were the whole complex of their differential characteristics. And although the formal cause or idea of a thing was carefully discriminated from its efficient and final causes, it was found impossible, in practice, to keep the three from running into one. Again, the distinction between single concepts and the judgments created by putting two concepts together, although clearly conveyed by the logical distinction between terms and propositions, was no sooner perceived than lost sight of, thanks to the unfortunate theory of essential predication. For it was thought that the import of universal propositions consisted either in stating the total concept to which a given mark belonged, or in annexing a new mark to a given concept. Hence, in Aristotle's system, the study of natural law means nothing but the definition and classification of natural types; and, in harmony with this idea, the whole universe is conceived as an arrangement of concentric spheres, each receiving its impulse from that immediately above it. Precisely the same confusion of Form, Cause, and Law reigns throughout Bacon's theory of Nature. We do, indeed, find mention made of axiomata or general propositions to a greater extent than in the Organon, but they are never clearly distinguished from Forms, nor Forms from functions.[540] And although efficient and material causes are assigned to physics, while formal and final causes are reserved for metaphysics—an apparent recognition of the wide difference between the forces which bring a thing into existence and the actual conditions of its stability,—this arrangement is a departure from the letter rather than from the spirit of Aristotle's philosophy. For the efficient causes of the De Augmentis answer roughly to the various kinds of motion discussed in the Physics and in the treatise On Generation and Corruption; while its Forms are, as we have seen, identified with natural causes or laws in the most general sense.

According to Bacon, the object of science is to analyse the complex of Forms making up an individual aggregate into its separate constituents; the object of art, to superinduce one or more such Forms on a given material. Hence his manner of regarding them differs in one important respect from Aristotle's. The Greek naturalist was, before all things, a biologist. His interest lay with the distinguishing characteristics of animal species. These are easily discovered by the unassisted eye; but while they are comparatively superficial, they are also comparatively unalterable. The English experimenter, being primarily concerned with inorganic bodies, whose properties he desired to utilise for industrial purposes, was led to consider the attributes of an object as at once penetrating its inmost texture, and yet capable of being separated from it, like heat and colour for instance. But, like every other thinker of the age, if he escapes from the control of Aristotle it is only to fall under the dominion of another Greek master—in this instance, Democritus. Bacon had a great admiration for the Atomists, and although his inveterate Peripatetic proclivities prevented him from embracing their theory as a whole, he went along with it so far as to admit the dependence of the secondary on the primary qualities of matter; and on the strength of this he concluded that the way to alter the properties of an object was to alter the arrangement of its component particles.

The next step was to create a method for determining the particular configuration on which any given property of matter depends. If such a problem could be solved at all, it would be by some new system of practical analysis. Bacon did not see this because he was a Schoolman, emancipated, indeed, from ecclesiastical authority, but retaining a blind faith in the power of logic. Aristotle's Organon had been the great storehouse of aids to verbal disputation; it should now be turned into an instrument for the more successful prosecution of physical researches. What definitions were to the one, that Forms should be to the other; and both were to be determined by much the same process. Now Aristotle himself had emphatically declared that the concepts out of which propositions are constructed were discoverable by induction and by induction alone. With him, induction meant comparing a number of instances, and abstracting the one circumstance, if any, in which they agreed. When the object is to establish a proposition inductively, he has recourse to a method of elimination, and bids us search for instances which, differing in everything else, agree in the association of two particular marks.[541] In the Topics he goes still further and supplies us with a variety of tests for ascertaining the relation between a given predicate and a given subject. Among these, Mill's Methods of Difference, Residues, and Concomitant Variations are very clearly stated.[542]

But he does not call such modes of reasoning Induction. So far as he has any general name for them at all, it is Dialectic, that is, Syllogism of which the premises are not absolutely certain; and, as a matter of nomenclature, he seems to be right. There is, undoubtedly, a process by which we arrive at general conclusions from the comparison of particular instances; but this process in its purity is nothing more nor less than induction by simple enumeration. All other reasoning requires the aid of universal propositions, and is therefore, to that extent, deductive. The methods of elimination or, as they are now called, of experiment, involve at every step the assumption of general principles duly specified in the chapter of Mill's Logic where they are analysed. And wherever we can rise immediately from, a single instance to a general law, it is because the examination of that single instance has been preceded by a chain of deductive reasoning.

The confusion of Induction, properly so called, and Elimination under a single name, is largely due to the bad example set by Bacon. He found it stated in the Analytics that all concepts and general propositions are established either by syllogism or by induction; and he found some very useful rules laid down in the Topics, not answering to what he understood by the former method; he therefore summarily dubbed them with the name of Induction, which they have kept ever since, to the incalculable confusion of thought.

In working out his theory of logic, the point on which Bacon lays most stress is the use of negative instances. He seems to think that their application to reasoning is an original discovery of his own. But, on examination, no more seems to be meant by it than that, before accepting any particular theory, we should consider what other explanations of the same fact might conceivably be offered. In other words, we should follow the example already set by Aristotle and nearly every other Greek philosopher after Socrates. But this is not induction; it is reasoning down from a disjunctive proposition, generally assumed without any close scrutiny, with the help of sundry conditional propositions, until we reach our conclusion by a sort of exhaustive process. Either this, that, or the other is the explanation of something. But if it were either that or the other, so and so would follow, which is impossible; therefore it must be this. No other logic is possible in the infancy of enquiry; but one great advantage of experiment and mathematical analysis is to relieve us from the necessity of employing it.

The value of experimentation as such had, however, scarcely dawned on Bacon. His famous Prerogative Instances are, in the main, a guide to simple observation, supplemented rather than replaced by direct interference with the phenomena under examination, comparable to that moderate use of the rack which he would have countenanced in criminal procedure. There was, perhaps, a deeper meaning in Harvey's remark that Bacon wrote about Nature like a Lord Chancellor than the great physiologist himself suspected. To Bacon the statesman, science was something to be largely endowed out of the public treasury in the sure hope that it would far more than repay the expenditure incurred, by inventions of priceless advantage to human life. To Bacon the lawyer, Nature was a person in possession of important secrets to be wrested from her by employing every artifice of the spy, the detective, the cross-examiner, and the inquisitorial judge; to Bacon the courtier, she was a sovereign whose policy might be discovered, and, if need be, controlled, by paying judicious attention to her humours and caprices. And, for this very reason, he would feel drawn by a secret affinity to the Aristotelian dialectic, derived as it was through Socrates and Plato from the practice of the Athenian law-courts and the debates of the Athenian assembly. No doubt the Topics was intended primarily for a manual of debate rather than of scientific enquiry; and the English Chancellor showed true philosophic genius in his attempt to utilise it for the latter purpose. Nevertheless the adaptation proved a mistake. It was not without good grounds that the Socratic dialectic had been reserved exclusively by its great founder, and almost exclusively by his successors, for those human interests from the discussion of which it was first derived. And the discoverers, who in Bacon's own lifetime were laying the foundations of physical science, employed a method totally different from his, because they started with a totally different conception of the universe. To them it was not a living whole, a Form of Forms, but a sum of forces to be analysed, isolated, and recombined, in fact or in idea, with a sublime disregard for the conditions under which they were presented to ordinary experience. That very extension of human power anticipated by Bacon came in a manner of which he had never dreamed. It was gained by studying, not the Forms to which he attached so much importance, but the modes of motion which he had relegated to a subordinate place in his classification of natural causes [543]

It has been said that, whatever may be the value of his logic, Bacon recalled men from the construction of baseless theories to the study of facts. But, here also, he merely echoes Aristotle, who said the same thing long before him, with much greater terseness, and with the superior authority of one who teaches by example as well as by precept; while the merit of reviving Aristotle's advice when it had fallen into oblivion belongs to another Bacon, the author of the Opus Majus; the merit of acting on it, to the savants of the Renaissance, to such men as Vesalius, Cesalpino, and Tycho Brahe.

But, towards the close of the sixteenth century, the time for amassing observations was past, no further progress being possible until the observations already recorded were interpreted aright. The just instinct of science perceived this; and for nearly a century after Cesalpino no addition of any magnitude was made to what Bacon called 'History,' while men's conceptions of natural law were undergoing a radical transformation.[544] To choose such a time for developing the Aristotelian philosophy was peculiarly unfortunate; for that philosophy had become, both on its good and on its bad side, an obstacle to progress, by encouraging studies which were not wanted, and by fostering a spirit of opposition to the Copernican astronomy.

The mere fact that Aristotle himself had pronounced in favour of the geocentric system did not count for much. The misfortune was that he had constructed an entire physical philosophy in harmony with it; that he had linked this to his metaphysics; and that the sensible experience on whose authority he laid so much stress, seemed to testify in its behalf. The consequence was that those thinkers who, without being professed Aristotelian partisans, still remained profoundly affected by the Peripatetic spirit, could not see their way to accepting a theory with which all the hopes of intellectual progress were bound up. These considerations will enable us to understand the attitude of Bacon towards the new astronomy; while, conversely, his position in this respect will serve to confirm the view of his character set forth in the preceding pages. The theory, shared by him with Aristotle, that Nature is throughout composed of Form and Matter reached its climax in the supposition that the great elementary bodies are massed together in a series of concentric spheres disposed according to some principle of graduation, symmetry, or contrast; and this seemed incompatible with any but a geocentric arrangement. It is true that Bacon quarrelled with the particular system maintained by Aristotle, and, under the guidance of Telesio, fell back on a much cruder form of cosmography; but his mind still remained dominated by the fancied necessity of conceiving the universe under the form of a stratified sphere; and those who persist in looking on him as the apostle of experience will be surprised to find that he treated the subject entirely from an à priori point of view. The truth is that Bacon exemplified, in his own intellectual character, every one of the fundamental fallacies which he has so picturesquely described. The unwillingness to analyse sensible appearances into their ideal elements was his Idol of the Tribe; the thirst for material utilities was his Idol of the Den: the uncritical acceptance of Aristotle's metaphysics, his Idol of the Theatre; and the undefined notions associated with induction, his Idol of the Market.

III.

We may consider it a fortunate circumstance that the philosophy of Form,—that is to say, of description, definition, classification, and sensuous perception, as distinguished from mathematical analysis and deductive reasoning,—was associated with a demonstrably false cosmology, as it thus became much more thoroughly discredited than would otherwise have been possible. At this juncture, the first to perceive and point out how profoundly an acceptance of the Copernican theory must affect men's beliefs about Nature and the whole universe, was Giordano Bruno; and this alone would entitle him to a great place in the history of philosophy. Thc conception of a single finite world surrounded by a series of eternal and unchangeable crystal spheres must, he said, be exchanged for the conception of infinite worlds dispersed through illimitable space. Once grant that the earth has a double movement round its own axis and round the sun, and Aristotle's whole system of finite existence collapses at once, leaving the ground clear for an entirely different order of ideas.[545] But, in this respect, whatever was established by the new science had already been divined by a still older philosophy than Aristotle's, as Bruno himself gladly acknowledged,[546] and the immediate effect of his reasoning was to revive the Atomic theory. The assumption of infinite space, formerly considered an insuperable objection to that theory, now became one of its chief recommendations; the arguments of Lucretius regained their full force, while his fallacies were let drop; Atomism seemed not only possible but necessary; and the materialism once associated with it was equally revived. But Aristotelianism, as we have seen, was not alone in the field, and on the first symptoms of a successful revolt, its old rival stood in readiness to seize the vacant throne. The question was how far its claim would be supported, and how far disputed by the new invaders. It might be supposed that the older forms of Greek philosophy, thus restored to light after an eclipse of more than a thousand years, would be no less hostile to the poetic Platonism than to the scientific Aristotelianism of the Renaissance. Such, however, was not the case; and we have to show how an alliance was established between these apparently opposite lines of thought, eventually giving birth to the highest speculation of the following century.

Bruno himself acted as a mediator between the two philosophies. His sympathies with Platonism were strongly pronounced, he looked with admiration on its mediaeval supporters, especially David of Dinan; and regretted the time when Oxford was a focus of realistic teaching, instead of being what he found her, devoted to the pedantic humanism of the Renaissance.[547] He fully accepted the pantheistic conclusions towards which Platonism always tended; but in proclaiming an absolute principle whence all specific differences are evolved, he is careful to show that, while it is neither Form nor Matter in the ordinary sense, it may be called Matter in the more refined signification attached to that term by Plotinus and, indeed, by Aristotle himself. There is a common substance underlying all abstract essences, just as there is a common substance left behind when the sensible qualities of different bodies are stripped off; and both are, at bottom, the same. Thus monism became the banner round which the older forms of Greek speculation rallied in their assault on Aristotle's philosophy, though what monism implied was as yet very imperfectly understood.

Meanwhile a new and powerful agency was about to interpose with decisive effect in the doubtful struggle. This was the study of mathematics. Revived by the Arabians and never wholly neglected during the Middle Ages, it had profited by the general movement of the Renaissance, and was finally applied to the cosmical problem by Galileo. In this connexion, two points of profound philosophical interest must be noted. The first is that, even in its fall, the Aristotelian influence survived, to some extent, both for good and for evil. To Aristotle belongs the merit of having been the first to base astronomy on physics. He maintains the earth's immobility on experimental no less than on speculative grounds. A stone thrown straight up in the air returns to its starting-point instead of falling to the west of it; and the absence of stellar parallax seems to show that there is no change in our position relatively to the heavenly bodies. After satisfying himself, on empirical considerations, that the popular astronomy is true, he proceeds to show that it must be true, by considerations on the nature of matter and motion, which, although mistaken, are conceived in a genuinely scientific spirit. Now Galileo saw that, to establish the Copernican system, he must first grapple with the Peripatetic physics, and replace it by a new dynamical theory. This, which he could hardly have effected by the ordinary mathematical methods, he did by borrowing the analytical method of Atomism and applying it to the measurement of motion. The law of falling bodies was ascertained by resolving their descent into a series of moments, and determining its rate of velocity at successive intervals; and curvilinear motions were similarly resolved into the combination of an impulsive with an accelerating force, a method diametrically opposed to that of Bacon, who would not even accept the rough analysis of the apparent celestial motions proposed by Greek astronomers.

It seems strange that Galileo, having gone so far, did not go a step further, and perceive that the planetary orbits, being curvilinear, must result from the combination of a centripetal with a tangential force. But the truth is that he never seems to have grasped his own law of inertia in its full generality. He understood that the planets could not have been set in motion without a rectilinear impulse; but his idea was that this impulse continued only so long as was necessary in order to give them their present velocity, instead of acting on them for ever as a tangential force. The explanation of this strange inconsequence must be sought in a survival of Aristotelian conceptions, in the persistent belief that rectilinear motion was necessarily limited and temporary, while circular motion was natural, perfect, and eternal.[548] Now such conceptions as Nature, perfection, and eternity always rebel against an analysis of the phenomena wherein they are supposed to reside. The same prejudice will explain why Galileo should have so persistently ignored Kepler's Laws, for we can hardly imagine that they were not brought under his notice.

The philosophical affinities of the new science were not exhausted by the atomistic analysis of Democritus and the regulative method of Aristotle. Platonism could hardly fail to benefit by the great impulse given to mathematical studies in the latter half of the sixteenth century. The passionate love of its founder for geometry must have recommended him as much to the most advanced minds of the period as his religious mysticism had recommended him to the theologians of the earlier Renaissance. And the increasing ascendency of the heliocentric astronomy, with its splendid defiance of sense and opinion, was indirectly a triumph for the philosophy which, more than any other, had asserted the claims of pure reason against both. We see this distinctly in Galileo. In express adhesion to Platonism, he throws his teaching into a conversational form, endeavouring to extract the truth from his opponents rather than convey it into their minds from without; and the theory of reminiscence as the source of demonstrative knowledge seems to meet with his approval.[549] He is always ready with proofs drawn from observation and experiment; but nothing can be more in Plato's spirit, nothing more unlike Aristotle and Bacon, than his encomium on the sublime genius of Aristarchus and Copernicus for having maintained a rational hypothesis against what seemed to be the evidence of their senses.[550] And he elsewhere observes how much less would have been the glory of Copernicus had he known the experimental verification of his theory.[551]

The Platonic influence told even more efficaciously on Galileo's still greater contemporary, Kepler. With him as with the author of the Republic, mysticism took the direction of seeking everywhere for evidence of mathematical proportions. With what brilliant success the search was attended, it is needless to relate. What interests us here is the fact, vouched for by Arago, that the German astronomer was guided by an idea of Plato's, that the world must have been created on geometrical principles.[552] Had Bacon known anything about the work on which his adventurous contemporary was engaged, we may be sure that it would have afforded him another illustration for his Idôla, the only difficulty being whether it should be referred to the illusions of the Tribe, the Den, or the Theatre.

Meanwhile Atomism continued to exercise a powerful influence on the method even more than on the doctrines of science. The analytical mode of treatment, applied by Galileo to dynamics, was applied, with equal success, by other mathematicians, to the study of discrete and continuous quantity. It is to the division of numbers and figures into infinitesimal parts—a direct contravention of Aristotle's teaching—that we owe logarithms, algebraic geometry, and the differential calculus. Thus was established a connexion between spiritualism and materialism, the philosophy of Plato and the philosophy of Democritus. Out of these elements, together with what still survived of Aristotelianism, was constructed the system of Descartes.

IV.

To understand Descartes aright, we must provisionally disregard the account given in his work on Method of the process by which he arrived at a new theory of the world; for, in truth, there was nothing new about it except the proportion in which fragments taken from older systems were selected and recombined.

Descartes

As we have already noticed, there is no such thing as spinning philosophies out of one's own head; and, in the case of Descartes, even the belief that he was so doing came to him from Plato; for, along with Aristotle's dogmatic errors, his sound teaching with regard to the derivation of knowledge had fallen into oblivion. The initial doubt of the *Discourse on Method* and the *Meditations* is also Platonic; only it is manifested under an individual and subjective, instead of a universal and objective form. But to find the real starting-point of Descartes' enquiries we must look for it in his mathematical studies. A geometrician naturally conceives the visible world under the aspect of figured extension; and if he thinks the figures away, nothing will remain but extension as the ultimate material out of which all determinate bodies are shaped. Such was the result reached by Plato in his *Timaeus*. He identified matter with space, viewing this as the receptacle for his eternal and self-existent Ideas, or rather the plastic medium on which their images are impressed. The simplest spatial elements are triangles; accordingly it is with these that he constructs his solid bodies. The theory of triangular elements was probably suggested by Atomism; it is, in fact, a compromise between the purely mathematical and the materialistic methods. Like all Plato's fancies, this theory of matter was attacked with such convincing arguments by Aristotle that, so long as his physics remained in the ascendent, it did not find a single supporter; although, as we saw in the last chapter, Plotinus very nearly worked his way back to it from the Peripatetic definition. Even now, at the moment of Aristotle's fall, it might have failed to attract attention, had not the conditions under which it first arose been almost exactly repeated. Geometrical demonstration had again become the type of all reasoning; there was again a sceptical spirit abroad, forcing men to fall back on the most elementary and universal conceptions; an atomistic materialism again threatened to claim at least the whole field of physical enquiry for its own. That Descartes followed the *Timaeus* in identifying matter with extension cannot be doubted; especially when we see that he adopts Plato's analysis of body into elementary triangles; but the theory agreed so well with his intellectual predispositions that he may easily have imagined it to be a necessary deduction from his own *à priori* ideas. Moreover, after the first two steps, he parts company with Plato, and gives himself up, so far as his rejection of a vacuum will permit, to the mechanical physics of Democritus. Much praise has recently been bestowed on his attempt to interpret all physical phenomena in terms of matter and motion, and to deduce them from the unaided operation of natural causes; but this is no more than had been done by the early Greek thinkers, from whom, we may observe, his hypothesis of an initial vortex was also derived. His cosmogony is better than theirs, only in so far as it is adapted to scientific discoveries in astronomy and physiology not made by Descartes himself; for where his conjectures go beyond these they are entirely at fault.

Descartes' theory of the universe included, however, something more than extension (or matter) and motion. This was Thought. If we ask whence came the notion of Thought, our philosopher will answer that it was obtained by looking into himself. It was, in reality, obtained by looking into Aristotle, or into some text-book reproducing his metaphysics. But the Platonic element in his system enabled Descartes to isolate Thought much more completely than it had been isolated by Aristotle. To understand this, we must turn once more to the *Timaeus*. Plato made up his universe from space and Ideas. But the Ideas were too vague or too unintelligible for scientific purposes. Even mediaeval Realists were content to replace them by Aristotle's much clearer doctrine of Forms. On the other hand, Aristotle's First Matter was anything but a satisfactory conception. It was a mere abstraction; the unknowable residuum left behind when bodies were stripped, in imagination, of all their sensible and cogitable qualities. In other words, there was no Matter actually existing without Form; whereas Form was never so truly itself, never so absolutely existent, as when completely separated from Matter: it then became simple self-consciousness, as in God, or in the reasonable part of the human soul. The revolution wrought by substituting space for Aristotle's First Matter will now become apparent. Corporeal substance could at once be conceived as existing without the co-operation of Form; and at the same stroke, Form, liberated from its material bonds, sprang back into the subjective sphere, to live henceforward only as pure self-conscious thought.

This absolute separation of Form and Matter, under their new names of Thought and Extension, once grasped, various principles of Cartesianism will follow from it by logical necessity. First comes the exclusion of final causes from philosophy, or rather from Nature. There was not, as with Epicurus, any anti-theological feeling concerned in their rejection. With Aristotle, against whom Descartes is always protesting, the final cause was not a mark of designing intelligence imposed on Matter from without; it was only a particular aspect of Form, the realisation of what Matter was always striving after by virtue of its inherent potentiality. When Form was conceived only as pure thought, there could be no question of such a process; the most highly organised bodies being only modes of figured extension. The revival of Atomism had, no doubt, a great deal to do with the preference for a mechanical interpretation of life. Aristotle had himself shown with masterly clearness the difference between his view of Nature and that taken by Democritus; thus indicating beforehand the direction in which an alternative to his own teaching might be sought; and Bacon had, in fact, already referred with approval to the example set by Democritus in dealing with teleological enquiries.

Nevertheless Bacon's own attitude towards final causes differs essentially from Descartes'. The French mathematician, had he spoken his whole mind, would probably have denied their existence altogether. The English reformer fully admits their reality, as, with his Aristotelian theory of Forms, he could hardly avoid doing; and we find that he actually associates the study of final with that of formal causes, assigning both to metaphysics as its peculiar province. This being so, his comparative neglect of the former is most easily explained by the famous comparison of teleological enquiries to vestal virgins, dedicated to the service of God and bearing no offspring; for Mr. Ellis has made it perfectly clear that the barrenness alluded to is not scientific but industrial. Our knowledge is extended when we trace the workings of a divine purpose in Nature; but this is not a kind of knowledge which bears fruit in useful mechanical inventions.[553] Bacon probably felt that men would not be very forward to improve on Nature if they believed in the perfection of her works and in their beneficent adaptation to our wants. The teleological spirit was as strong with him as with Aristotle, but it took a different direction. Instead of studying the adaptation of means to ends where it already existed, he wished men to create it for themselves. But the utilitarian tendency, which predominated with Bacon, was quite exceptional with Descartes. Speaking generally, he desired knowledge for its own sake, not as an instrument for the gratification of other wants; and this intellectual disinterestedness was, perhaps, another aspect of the severance effected between thought and matter.

The celebrated Cartesian paradox, that animals are unconscious automata, is another consequence of the same principle. In Aristotle's philosophy, the doctrine of potentiality developing itself into act through a series of ascending manifestations, supplied a link connecting the highest rational with the lowest vegetal life. The identification of Form with pure thought put an end to the conception of any such intermediate gradations.

Brutes must either have a mind like ours or none at all. The former alternative was not even taken into consideration; probably, among other reasons, because it was not easily reconcilable with Christianity; so that nothing remained but to deny sensibility where thought was believed not to exist.

Finally, in man himself, thought is not distinguished from feeling; it is, in fact, the essence of mind, just as extension is the essence of body; and all spiritual phenomena are modes of thought in the same sense that all physical phenomena are modes of space. It was, then, rather a happy chance than genuine physiological insight which led Descartes to make brain the organ of feeling no less than of intellection; a view, as Prof. Huxley has observed, much in advance of that held by Bichat a hundred and fifty years later. For whoever deduced all the mental manifestations from a common essence was bound in consistency to locate them in the same bodily organ; what the metaphysician had joined the physiologist could not possibly put asunder.

We are now in a position to understand the full force of Descartes' Cogito ergo sum. It expresses the substantiality of self-conscious Form, the equal claim of thought with extension to be recognised as an element of the universe. This recognition of self-consciousness as the surest reality was, indeed, far from being new. The Greek Sceptics had never gone to the length of doubting their own personal existence. On the contrary, they professed a sort of subjective idealism. Refusing to go beyond their own consciousness, they found in its undisturbed self-possession the only absolute satisfaction that life could afford. But knowledge and reality had become so intimately associated with something independent of mind, and mind itself with a mere reflection of reality, that the denial of an external world seemed to the vulgar a denial of existence itself. And although Aristotle had found the highest, if not the sole absolute actuality in self-thinking thought, he projected it to such a distance from human personality that its bearing on the sceptical controversy had passed unperceived. Descartes began his demonstration at the point where all the ancient systems had converged, but failed to discover in what direction the conditions of the problem required that they should be prolonged. No mistake can be greater than to regard him as the precursor of German philosophy. The latter originated quite independently of his teaching, though not perhaps of his example, in the combination of a much profounder scepticism with a much wider knowledge of dogmatic metaphysics. His method is the very reverse of true idealism. The Cogito ergo sum is not a taking up of existence into thought, but rather a conversion of thought into one particular type of existence. Now, as we have seen, all other existence was conceived as extension, and however carefully thought might be distinguished from this as absolutely indivisible, it was speedily reduced to the same general pattern of inclusion, limitation, and expansion. Whereas Kant, Fichte, and Hegel afterwards dwelt on the form of thought, Descartes attended only to its content, or to that in which it was contained. In other words, he began by considering not how he thought but what he thought and whence it came—his ideas and their supposed derivation from a higher sphere. Take, for example, his two great methods for proving the existence of God. We have in our minds the idea of a perfect being—at least Descartes professed to have such an idea in his mind,—and we, as imperfect beings, could not have originated it for ourselves. It must, therefore, have been placed there by a perfect being acting on us from without. It is here taken for granted that the mechanical equivalence between material effects and their causes must obtain in a world where spatial relations, and therefore measurement, are presumably unknown. And, secondly, existence, as a perfection, is involved in the idea of a perfect being; therefore such a being can only be conceived as existing.

Here there seems to be a confused notion that because the properties of a geometrical figure can be deduced from its definition, therefore the existence of something more than a simple idea can be deduced from the definition of that idea itself. But besides the mathematical influence, there was evidently a Platonic influence at work; and one is reminded of Plato's argument that the soul cannot die because it participates in the idea of life. Such fallacies were impossible so long as Aristotle's logic continued to be carefully studied, and they gradually disappeared with its revival. Meanwhile the cat was away, and the mice used their opportunity.

That the absolute disjunction of thought from matter involved the impossibility of their interaction, was a consequence not drawn by Descartes himself, but by his immediate followers. Here also, Greek philosophy played its part in hastening the development of modern ideas. The fall of Aristotle had incidentally the effect of reviving not only the systems which preceded, but also those which followed his. Chief among these were Stoicism and Epicureanism. Differing widely in most other respects, they agreed in teaching that body is acted on by body alone. The Cartesians accepted this principle to the fullest extent so far as human perceptions and volitions were concerned; and to a great extent in dealing with the problems of physical science. But instead of arguing from the laws of mechanical causation to the materiality of mind, they argued from its immateriality to the total absence of communication between consciousness and motion. There was, however, one thinker of that age who went all lengths with the later Greek materialists. This was Thomas Hobbes, the founder of modern ethics, the first Englishman to grasp and develope still further Galileo's method of mathematical deduction and mechanical analysis.

V.

The author of the Leviathan has sometimes been represented as one who carried the Baconian method into politics, and prepared the way for its more thorough application to psychology by Locke.

Locke

But this view, which regards the three great leaders of English philosophy in the seventeenth century as successive links in a connected series, is a misapprehension of history, which could only have arisen through leaving out of account the contemporary development of Continental speculation, and through the inveterate habit of looking on the modern distinction between empiricism and transcendentalism as a fundamental antithesis dividing the philosophers of every epoch into two opposing schools. The truth is that, if the three writers just mentioned agree in deriving knowledge solely from experience, they agree in nothing else; and that their unanimity on this one point does not amount to much, will be evident if we consider what each understood by the notion in question.

With Bacon, experience was the negation of mere authority, whether taking the form of natural prejudice, of individual prepossession, of hollow phrases, or of established systems. The question how we come by that knowledge which all agree to be the most certain, is left untouched in his logic; either of the current answers would have suited his system equally well; nor is there any reason for believing that he would have sided with Mill rather than with Kant respecting the origin of mathematical axioms. With Locke, experience meant the analysis of notions and judgments into the simple data of sense and self-consciousness; and the experientialists of the present day are beyond all doubt his disciples; but the parentage of his philosophy, so far as it is simply a denial of innate ideas, must be sought, not in the Novum Organum, nor in any other modern work, but in the old Organon of Aristotle, or in the comments of the Schoolmen who followed Aristotle in protesting against the Platonism of their time, just as Locke protested against the Platonism of Descartes and Malebranche.

The experience of Hobbes differs both in origin and application from either of these. With him, sensible impressions are not a court of appeal against traditional judgments, nor yet are they the ultimate elements into which all ideas may be analysed; they are the channels through which pulsating movements are conveyed into the mind; and these movements, again, represent the action of mechanical forces or the will of a paramount authority. And he holds this doctrine, partly as a logical consequence of his materialism, partly as a safeguard against the theological pretensions which, in his opinion, are a constant threat to social order. The authority of the political sovereign is menaced on the one hand by Papal infallibility, and on the other by rebellious subjects putting forward a claim to supernatural inspiration. To the Pope, Hobbes says: 'You are violating the law of Nature by professing to derive from God what is really given only by the consent of men, and can only be given by them to their temporal head,—the right to impose a particular religion.' To the Puritan, he says: 'Your inward illumination is a superstitious dream, and you have no right to use it as a pretext for breaking the king's peace. Religion has really nothing to do with the supernatural; it is only a particular way of inculcating obedience to the natural conditions of social union.'

Again, Hobbes differs wholly from Bacon in the deductive character of his method. His logic is the old syllogistic system reorganised on the model of mathematical analysis. Like all the great thinkers of his time, he was a geometrician and a mechanical physicist, reasoning from general to particular propositions and descending from causes to effects.[554] His famous theory of a social contract is a rational construction, not a historical narrative. But though a mathematician, he shows no traces of Platonic influence. He is, therefore, all the more governed by Atomist and Stoic modes of thought. He treats human nature, single and associated, as Galileo and Descartes had treated motion and space. Like them, too, he finds himself in constant antagonism to Aristotle. The description of man as a social animal is disdainfully rejected, and the political union resolved into an equilibrium of many opposing wills maintained by violent pressure from without. In ethics, no less than in physics, we find attractive forces replaced by mechanical impacts.

While the analysis of Hobbes goes much deeper than Aristotle's, the grasp of his reconstructive synthesis is wider and stronger in at least an equal proportion. Recognising the good of the whole as the supreme rule of conduct,[555] he gives a new interpretation to the particular virtues, and disposes of the theory which made them a mean between two extremes no less effectually than his contemporaries had disposed of the same theory in its application to the elementary constitution of matter. And just as they were aided in their revolt against Aristotle by the revival of other Greek systems, so also was he. The identification of justice with public interest, though commonly attributed to Epicurus alone, was, like materialism, an idea shared by him with Stoicism, and was probably impressed on modern thought by the weight of their united authority. And when we find the philosopher of Malmesbury making public happiness consist in order and tranquillity, we cannot but think that this was a generalisation from the Stoic and Epicurean conceptions of individual happiness; for it reproduces, under a social form, the same ideal of passionless repose.

On the other hand, this substitution of the social for the personal integer involves a corresponding change in the valuation of individual happiness. What the passions had been to later Greek philosophy, that the individual soul became to Hobbes, something essentially infinite and insatiable, whose desires grow as they are gratified, whose happiness, if such it can be called, is not a condition of stable repose but of perpetual movement and unrest.[556] Here, again, the analogy between physics and ethics obtains. In both, there was an original opposition between the idea of a limit and the idea of infinite expansion. Just as, among the earlier Greek thinkers, there was a physical philosophy of the infinite or, as its impugners called it, the indefinite, so also there was, corresponding to it, a philosophy of the infinite or indefinite in ethics, represented, not indeed by professional moralists, but by rhetoricians and men of the world. Their ideal was not the contented man, but the popular orator or the despot who revels in the consciousness of power—the ability to satisfy his desires, whatever they may be. And the extreme consequence of this principle is drawn by Plato's Callicles when he declares that true happiness consists in nursing one's desires up to the highest point at which they can be freely indulged; while his ideal of character is the superior individual who sets at naught whatever restraints have been devised by a weak and timid majority to protect themselves against him.

The Greek love of balanced antithesis and circumscribing form triumphed over the infinite in both fields. While the two great masters of idealism imprisoned the formless and turbulent terrestrial elements within a uniform and eternal sphere of crystal, they imposed a similar restraint on the desires and emotions, confining them within a barrier of reason which, when once erected, could never be broken through. And although the ground won in physics was lost again for a time through a revival of old theories, this was because true Hellenism found its only congenial sphere in ethics, and there the philosophy of the finite continued to reign supreme. If the successors of Aristotle fell back on cosmologies of ampler scope than his, they retained his limiting method in their speculations on man.

With Christianity, there came a certain inversion of parts. The external universe again became subjected to narrow limitations, and the flammantia moenia mundi beyond which Epicurus had dared to penetrate, were raised up once more and guarded by new terrors as an impassable barrier to thought. But infinity took refuge within the soul; and, while in this life a sterner self-control than even that of Stoicism was enjoined, perspectives of illimitable delight in another life were disclosed. Finally, at the Renaissance, every barrier was simultaneously overthrown, and the accumulated energies of western civilisation expatiated over a field which, if it was vast in reality, was absolutely unbounded in imagination. Great as were the achievements of that age, its dreams were greater still; and what most excites our wonder in the works of its heroes is but the fragment of an unfinished whole. The ideal of life set up by Aristotle was, like his conception of the world, contradicted in every particular; and the relative positions assigned by him to act and power were precisely reversed. It has been shown how Shakespeare reflected the Platonism of his contemporaries: he reflected also the fierce outburst of their ambition; and in describing what they would dare, to possess solely sovereign sway and masterdom, or wear without corrival all the dignities of honour, he borrowed almost the very words used by Euripides to express the feelings encouraged by some teachers of his time. The same spirit is exhibited a generation later in the dramas of Calderon and Corneille, before their thoughts were forced into a different channel by the stress of the Catholic reaction; while its last and highest manifestation is the sentiment of Milton's ruined archangel, that to reign in hell is better than to serve in heaven. Thus, when Hobbes reduces all the passions to modes of the fundamental desire for power,[557] he does but give the scientific theory of that which stands proclaimed in more thrilling accents by the noblest poetry of his age.

Where no danger could deter from the pursuit of power, no balancing of pain with pleasure availed to quench the ardour of desire. With full knowledge that violent delights have violent ends and in their triumph die, the fateful condition was accepted. Not only did Giordano Bruno, in conscious parallelism with his theory of matter, declare that without mutation, variety, and vicissitude nothing would be agreeable, nothing good, nothing delightful, that enjoyment consists solely in transition and movement, and that all pleasure lies midway between the painful longing of fresh appetite and the sadness of its satiation and extinction;[558] but the sedater wisdom of Bacon, in touching on the controversy between Callicles and Socrates, seems to incline towards the side of the former; and, in all cases, warns men not to make too much of the inconveniences attendent on pleasure, but 'so to procure serenity as they destroy not magnanimity.'[559]

These, then, were the principal elements of the philosophical Renaissance. First, there was a certain survival of Aristotelianism as a method of comprehensive and logical arrangement. Then there was the new Platonism, bringing along with it a revival of either Alexandrian or mediaeval pantheism, and closely associated with geometrical studies. Thirdly, there was the old Greek Atomism, as originally set forth by Democritus or as re-edited by Epicurus, traditionally unfavourable to theology, potent alike for decomposition and reconstruction, confirmed by the new astronomy, and lending its method to the reformation of mathematics; next the later Greek ethical systems; and finally the formless idea of infinite power which all Greek systems had, as such, conspired to suppress, but which, nevertheless, had played a great part in the earlier stages of Greek speculation both physical and moral.

On these foundations the lofty edifice of Spinozism was reared; out of these materials its composite structure was built; and without a previous study of them it cannot be understood.

VI.

Whether Spinoza ever read Plato is doubtful. One hardly sees why he should have neglected a writer whose works were easily accessible, and at that time very popular with thinking minds. But whether he was acquainted with the Dialogues at first hand or not, Plato will help us to understand Spinoza, for it was through the door of geometry that he entered philosophy, and under the guidance of one who was saturated with the Platonic spirit; so far as Christianity influenced him, it was through elements derived from Plato; and his metaphysical method was one which, more than any other, would have been welcomed with delight by the author of the Meno and the Republic, as an attempt to realise his own dialectical ideal. For Spinozism is, on the face of it, an application of geometrical reasoning to philosophy, and especially to ethics. It is also an attempt to prove transcendentally what geometricians only assume—the necessity of space.

Spinoza

Now, Plato looked on geometrical demonstration as the great type of certainty, the scientific completion of what Socrates had begun by his interrogative method, the one means of carrying irrefragable conviction into every department of knowledge, and more particularly into the study of our highest good. On the other hand, he saw that geometricians assume what itself requires to be demonstrated; and he confidently expected that the deficiency would be supplied by his own projected method of transcendent dialectics. Such at least seems to be the drift of the following passage:

When I speak of the division of the intellectual, you will also understand me to speak of that knowledge which reason herself attains by the power of dialectic, using the hypotheses not as first principles, but only as hypotheses—that is to say as steps and points of departure into a region which is above hypotheses, in order that she may soar beyond them to the first principle of the whole; and clinging to this and then to that which depends on this, by successive steps she descends again without the aid of any sensible object, beginning and ending in ideas.[560]

The problem, then, which Spinoza set himself was, first, to account for the fundamental assumptions of all science, and more particularly of geometry, by deducing them from a single self-evident principle; and then to use that principle for the solution of whatever problems seemed to stand most in need of its application. And, as usually happens in such adventurous enterprises, the supposed answer of pure reason was obtained by combining or expanding conceptions borrowed without criticism from pre-existing systems of philosophy.

Descartes had already accomplished a great simplification of the speculative problem by summing up all existence under the two heads of extension and thought. It remained to account for these, and to reduce them to a single idea. As we have seen, they were derived from Greek philosophy, and the bond which was to unite them must be sought for in the same direction. It will be remembered that the systems of Plato and Aristotle were bounded at either extremity by a determinate and by an indeterminate principle. With the one, existence ranged between the Idea of Good at the upper end of the scale and empty space at the lower; with the other, between absolute Thought and First Matter. It was by combining the two definite terms, space and thought, that Descartes had constructed his system; and after subtracting these the two indefinite terms remained. In one respect they were even more opposed to each other than were the terms with which they had been respectively associated. The Idea of Good represented unity, identity, and constancy, as against plurality, difference, and change; while Aristotle's Matter was, by its very definition, multiform, fluctuating, and indeterminate. Nevertheless, there were equally important analogies traceable between them. No very clear account could be given of either, and both were customarily described by negatives. If Matter fell short of complete existence, the Good transcended all existence. If the one was a universal capacity for assuming Forms, the other was the source whence all Forms proceeded. When the distinctive characteristics of an individual were thought away, the question might well be mooted into which principle it would return. The ambiguous use of the word Power contributed still further to their identification, for it was not less applicable to the receptive than to the productive faculty. Now we have just seen into what importance the idea of Power suddenly sprang at the Renaissance: with Bruno it was the only abiding reality of Nature; with Hobbes it was the only object of human desire.

Another term occupying a very large place in Aristotle's philosophy was well adapted to mediate between and eventually to unite the two speculative extremes. This was Substance; in logic the subject of predication, in metaphysics the substratum of qualities, the οὐσία or Being of the Ten Categories. Now First Matter might fairly claim the position of a universal subject or substance, since it was invested with every sensible quality in turn, and even, as the common element of all Forms, with every thinkable quality as well. Aristotle himself had finally pronounced for the individual compound of Form and Matter as the true substance. Yet he also speaks as if the essential definition of a thing constituted the thing itself; in which case Form alone could be the true subject; and a similar claim might be put forward on behalf of the Plotinian One.[561]

Such were the à priori elements which a historical synthesis had prepared to satisfy the want of a metaphysical Absolute. Let us now see what result would follow when the newly-recovered idea of space was subjected to a metaphysical analysis. Extension is both one and infinite. No particular area can be conceived apart from the whole which both contains and explains it. Again, extension is absolutely homogeneous; to whatever distance we may travel in imagination there will still be the same repetition of similar parts. But space, with the Cartesians, meant more than a simple juxtaposition of parts; having been made the essence of matter, it was invested with mechanical as well as with geometrical properties. The bodies into which it resolved itself were conceived as moving, and as communicating their movement to one another through an unbroken chain of causation in which each constituted a single link, determining and determined by the rest; so that, here also, each part was explained by reference to an infinite whole, reproducing its essence, while exempt from the condition of circumscribed existence. We can understand, then, that when the necessity of accounting for extension itself once became felt, the natural solution would be to conceive it as holding the same relation to some greater whole which its own subdivisions held to their sum total; in other words it should be at once a part, an emanation, and an image of the ultimate reality. This is, in fact, very nearly the relation which Matter holds to the One in the Neo-Platonic system. And we know that with Plotinus Matter is almost the same as infinite Extension.

Corresponding to the universal space which contains all particular spaces, there was, in the Neo-Platonic system, a universal Thought which contained all particular thoughts,—the Nous about which we heard so much in studying Plotinus. Such a conception is utterly strange to the modern mind, but it was familiar enough to Spinoza; and we can see how it would be suggested by the common forms of reasoning. The tendency of syllogism is either to subsume lower under higher notions until a summum genus is reached, or to resolve all subjects into a single predicate, or to connect all predicates with a single subject. The analogies of space, too, would tell in the same direction, bringing nearer the idea of a vast thought-sea in which all particular thoughts, or what to a Cartesian meant the same thing, all particular minds, were contained. And Neo-Platonism showed how this universal Mind or Thought could, like the space which it so much resembled, be interpreted as the product of a still higher principle. To complete the parallelism, it remained to show that Thought, which before had seemed essentially finite, is, on the contrary, co-infinite with Extension. How this was done will appear a little further on.

Spinoza gathered up all the threads of speculation thus made ready for his grasp, when he defined God as a substance consisting of infinite attributes, each of which expresses his infinite and eternal essence; subsequently adding that the essence here spoken of is Power, and that two of the infinite attributes are Extension and Thought, whereof the particular things known to us are modes. Platonism had decomposed the world into two ideal principles, and had re-created it by combining them over again in various proportions, but they were not entirely reabsorbed and worked up into the concrete reality which resulted from their union; they were, so to speak, knotted together, but the ends continued to hang loose. Above and below the finite sphere of existence there remained as an unemployed surplus the infinite causal energy of the One and the infinite passive potentiality of Matter. Spinoza combined and identified the two opposing elements in the notion of a single substance as infinite in actuality as they had been in power. He thus gave its highest metaphysical expression to that common tendency which we traced through the prospects opened out by the Copernican astronomy, the revival of Atomism, the dynamical psychology of Hobbes, and the illimitable passion of the Renaissance, while, at the same time, preserving the unity of Plato's idealism, and even making it more concentrated than before.

It has been shown how universal space and universal thought at once contain and explain each particular space and each particular concept. In like manner, the infinite substance contains and explains space and thought themselves. Contains them, yes, as attributes; but explains them, how? As two among an infinity of attributes. In other words, if we ask why there should be such an existence as space, the answer is because existence, being infinite, must necessarily include every conceivable thing. The argument is strikingly like a principle of the Epicurean philosophy, and may well have been suggested by it. According to Lucretius, the appearance of design in our world need not be attributed to creative intelligence, because infinite atoms moving in infinite manners through infinite time, must at length arrive, after a comprehensive series of experiments, at the present frame of things;[562] and the same principle is invoked on a smaller scale to account for the origin of organised beings, of memory, and of civil society.[563] In both systems, infinite space is the root-conception; but what Lucretius had legitimately used to explain becoming, Spinoza illegitimately applies to the elucidation of being. At one stroke all empirical knowledge is placed on an à priori foundation. By assuming unlimited credit at the bank of the universe we entitle ourselves to draw a cheque for any particular amount. Thus the idea of infinite attributes is no mere collateral speculation, but forms an essential element of Spinozism. The known varieties of existence are, so to speak, surrounded, supported, and fixed in their places by the endless multitude of the unknown. And this conception of being as absolutely infinite, is another proof of Spinoza's Platonic tendencies, for it involves the realisation of an abstract idea, that is to say, of Being, which the philosopher treats as something more comprehensive than the facts of consciousness whence it is derived.

Or, again, we may say that two principles,—the Nominalistic as well as the Realistic,—are here at work. By virtue of the one, Spinoza makes Being something beyond and above the facts of experience. By virtue of the other he reinvests it with concrete reality, but a reality altogether transcending our powers of imagination. Very much, also, that Plotinus says about his One might be applied to Spinoza's Substance, but with a new and positive meaning. The First Cause is above existence, but only existence as restricted within the very narrow limits of our experience, and only as infinite reality transcends the parts which it includes.

It is well known that Spinoza draws a sharp line of demarcation between the two attributes of Extension and Thought, which, with him, correspond to what are usually called body and mind. Neither attribute can act on the other. Mind receives no impressions from body, nor does body receive any impulses from mind. This proposition follows by rigorous logical necessity from the Platonic principle that mind is independent of body, combined with the Stoic principle that nothing but body can act on body, generalised into the wider principle that interaction implies homogeneity of nature. According to some critics, Spinoza's teaching on this point constitutes a fatal flaw in his philosophy. How, it is asked, can we know that there is any such thing as body (or extension) if body cannot be perceived,—for perceived it certainly cannot be without acting on our minds? The idea of infinite substance suggests a way out of the difficulty. 'I find in myself,' Spinoza might say, 'the idea of extension. In fact, my mind is nothing but the idea of extension, or the idea of that idea, and so on through as many self-reflections as you please. At the same time, mind, or thought, is not itself extended. Descartes and the Platonists before him have proved thus much. Consequently I can conceive extension as existing independently of myself, and, more generally, of all thought. But how can I be sure that it actually does so exist? In this wise. An examination of thought leads me to the notion of something in which it resides—a substance whose attribute it is. But having once conceived such a substance, I cannot limit it to a single attribute, nor to two, nor to any finite number. Limitation implies a boundary, and there can be no boundary assigned to existence, for existence by its very definition includes everything that is. Accordingly, whatever can be conceived, in other words whatever can be thought without involving a contradiction,—an important reservation which I beg you to observe,—must necessarily exist. Now extension involves no contradiction, therefore it exists,—exists, that is to say, as an attribute of the infinite substance. And, by parity of reasoning, there must be an idea of extension; for this also can exist without involving a contradiction, as the simplest introspection suffices to show. You ask me why then I do not believe in gorgons and chimaeras. I answer that since, in point of fact, they do not exist, I presume that their notion involves a contradiction, although my knowledge of natural law is not sufficiently extended to show me where the contradiction lies. But perhaps science will some day be able to point out in every instance of a non-existing thing, where the contradiction lies, no less surely than it can now be pointed out in the case of impossible geometrical figures.' In short, while other people travel straight from their sensations to an external world, Spinoza travels round to it by the idea of an infinite substance.[564]

The relation of Spinoza's Substance to its attributes is ambiguous. It is at once their cause, their totality, and their unity. The highly elastic and indefinite term Power helped these various aspects to play into and replace one another according to the requirements of the system. It is associated with the subjective possibility of multiplying imaginary existences to any amount; with the causal energy in which existence originates; and with the expansiveness characteristic alike of Extension and of Thought. For the two known attributes of the universal substance are not simply related to it as co-predicates of a common subject; they severally express its essential Power, and are, to that extent, identical with one another. But when we ask, How do they express Power? the same ambiguity recurs. Substance is revealed through its attributes, as a cause through its effects; as an aggregate through its constituents; and as an abstract notion through its concrete embodiments. Thus Extension and Thought are identical through their very differences, since these illustrate the versatility of their common source, and at the same time jointly contribute to the realisation of its perfection. But, for all practical purposes, Spinoza deals only with the parallelism and resemblance of the attributes. We have to see how he establishes it, and how far he was helped in so doing by the traditions of Greek philosophy.

VII.

It has been already shown how Extension, having become identified with matter, took on its mechanical qualities, and was conceived as a connected series of causes or modes of motion. The parallel found by Spinoza for this series in Thought is the chain of reasons and consequents forming a demonstrative argument; and here he is obviously following Aristotle, who although ostensibly distinguishing between formal and efficient causes, hopelessly confounds them in the second book of his Posterior Analytics.[565] We are said to understand a thing when we bring it under a general rule, and also when we discover the mechanical agency which produces it. For instance, we may know that a particular man will die, either from the fact that all men are mortal, or from the fact that he has received a fatal wound. The general rule, however, is not the cause of what will happen, but only the cause of our knowing that it will happen; and knowledge of the rule by no means carries with it a knowledge of the efficient cause; as we see in the case of gravitation and other natural forces whose modus operandi is still a complete mystery. What deceived Aristotle was partly his false analysis of the syllogism, which he interpreted as the connexion of two terms by the interposition of a middle answering to the causal nexus of two phenomena; and partly his conception of the universe as a series of concentric spheres, through which movement is transmitted from without, thus combining the two ideas of notional comprehension and mechanical causation.

Be this as it may, Spinoza takes up the Aristotelian identification of logical with dynamical connexion, and gives it the widest possible development. For the Stagirite would not, at any rate, have dreamed of attributing any but a subjective existence to the demonstrative series, nor of extending it beyond the limits of our actual knowledge. Spinoza, on the other hand, assumes that the whole infinite chain of material causes is represented by a corresponding chain of eternal ideas; and this chain he calls the infinite intellect of God.[566] Here, besides the necessities of systematisation, the influence of mediaeval realism is plainly evident. For, when the absolute self-existence of Plato's Ideas had been surrendered in deference to Aristotle's criticism, a home was still found for them by Plotinus in the eternal Nous, and by the Christian Schoolmen in the mind of God; nor did such a belief present any difficulties so long as the divine personality was respected. The pantheism of Spinoza, however, was absolute, and excluded the notion of any but a finite subjectivity. Thus the infinite intellect of God is an unsupported chain of ideas recalling the theory at one time imagined by Plato.[567] Or its existence may be merely what Aristotle would have called potential; in other words, Spinoza may mean that reasons will go on evolving themselves so long as we choose to study the dialectic of existence, always in strict parallelism with the natural series of material movements constituting the external universe; and just as this is determined through all its parts by the totality of extension, or of all matter (whether moving or motionless) taken together, so also at the summit of the logical series stands the idea of God, from whose definition the demonstration of every lesser idea necessarily follows. It is true that in a chain of connected energies the antecedent, as such, must be always precisely equal to the consequent; but, apparently, this difficulty did not present itself to Spinoza, nor need we be surprised at this; for Kant, coming a century later, was still so imbued with Aristotelian traditions as, similarly, to derive the category of Cause and Effect from the relation between Reason and Consequent in hypothetical propositions.[568]

Meanwhile the parallelism between Thought and Extension was not exhausted by the identification just analysed. Extension was not only a series of movements; it still remained an expression for co-existence and adjacency. Spinoza, therefore, felt himself obliged to supply Thought with a correspondingly continuous quality. It is here that his chief originality lies, here that he has been most closely followed by the philosophy of our own time. Mind, he declares, is an attribute everywhere accompanying matter, co-extensive and co-infinite with space. Our own animation is the sum or the resultant of an animation clinging to every particle that enters into the composition of our bodies. When our thoughts are affected by an external impulse, to suppose that this impulse proceeds from anything material is a delusion; it is produced by the mind belonging to the body which acts on our body; although in what sense this process is to be understood remains a mystery. Spinoza has clearly explained the doctrine of animal automatism, and shown it to be perfectly conceivable;[569] but he has entirely omitted to explain how the parallel influence of one thought (or feeling) on another is to be understood; for although this too is spoken of as a causal relation, it seems to be quite different from the logical concatenation described as the infinite intellect of God; and to suppose that idea follows from idea like movement from movement would amount to a complete materialisation of mind; while our philosopher would certainly have repudiated Mr. Shadworth

Hodgson's theory, that states of consciousness are only connected through their extended substratum, as the segments of a mosaic picture are held together by the underlying surface of masonry. Nor can we admit that Spinoza entertained the theory, now so popular, according to which extension and consciousness are merely different aspects of a single reality. For this would imply that the substance which they manifest had an existence of its own apart from its attributes; whereas Spinoza makes it consist of the attributes, that is to say, identifies it with their totality. We are forced, then, to conclude that the proposition declaring thought and extension to be the same thing[570] has no other meaning than that they are connected by the double analogy which we have endeavoured to explain.

The analogy between Thought and Extension under the two aspects of necessary connexion and mere contingent relation in co-existence or succession, was, in truth, more interesting to its author as a basis for his ethical than as a development of his metaphysical speculations. The two orders of relations represent, in their distinction, the opposition of science to opinion or imagination, the opposition of dutiful conviction to blind or selfish impulse. Spinoza borrows from the Stoics their identification of volition with belief; but in working out the consequences of this principle it is of Plato rather than of the Stoics that he reminds us. The passions are in his system what sense, imagination, and opinion were in that of the Athenian idealist; and his ethics may almost be called the metaphysics of the Republic turned outside in. Joy, grief and desire are more or less imperfect perceptions of reality—a reality not belonging to the external world but to the conscious subject itself.[571] When Spinoza traces them to a consciousness or expectation of raised or lowered power, we recognise the influence of Hobbes; but when, here as elsewhere, he identifies power with existence, we detect a return to Greek forms of thought. The great conflict between illusion and reality is fought out once more; only, this time, it is about our own essence that we are first deceived and then enlightened. If the nature and origin of outward things are half revealed, half concealed by sense and imagination, our emotions are in like manner the obscuring and distorting medium through which we apprehend our inmost selves, and whatever adds to or takes away from the plenitude of our existence; and what science is to the one, morality and religion are to the other.

It is remarkable that while Spinoza was giving a new application to the Platonic method, another Cartesian, Malebranche, was working it out more strictly on the old lines of speculative research. The Recherche de la Vérité of this unjustly neglected thinker is a methodical account of the various subjective obstacles which impede our apprehension of things as they really exist, and of the means by which it may be facilitated. Here also, attention is concentrated on the subjective side of philosophy; and if the mental processes selected for study are of theoretical rather than practical interest, we may probably attribute this to the circumstance that every ethical question was already decided for Malebranche by the Church whose orders he had assumed.

But it was not merely in the writings of professed philosophers that the new aspect of Platonism found expression. All great art embodies in one form or another the leading conceptions of its age; and the latter half of the seventeenth century found such a manifestation in the comedies of Molière. If these works stand at the head of French literature, they owe their position not more to their author's brilliant wit than to his profound philosophy of life; or rather, we should say that with him wit and philosophy are one. The comic power of Shakespeare was shown by resolving the outward appearances of this world into a series of dissolving illusions. Like Spinoza and Malebranche, Molière turns the illusion in, showing what perverted opinions men form of themselves and others, through misconceptions and passions either of spontaneous growth or sedulously fostered by designing hands. Society, with him, seems almost entirely made up of pretenders and their dupes, both characters being not unfrequently combined in the same person, who is made a victim through his desire to pass for what he is not and cannot be. And this is what essentially distinguishes the art of Molière from the New Comedy of Athens, which he, like other moderns, had at first felt inclined to imitate until the success of the Précieuses Ridicules showed him where his true opportunities lay. For the New Comedy was Aristotelian where it was not simply humanist; that is to say, it was an exhibition of types like those sketched by Aristotle's disciple, Theophrastus, and already prefigured in the master's own Ethics. These were the perennial forms in a world of infinite and perishing individual existences, not concealed behind phenomena, but incorporated in them and constituting their essential truth. The Old Comedy is something different again; it is pre-philosophic, and may be characterised as an attempt to describe great political interests and tendencies through the medium of myths and fables and familiar domesticities, just as the old theories of Nature, the old lessons of practical wisdom, and the first great national chronicles had been thrown into the same homely form.[572]

The purely intellectual view of human nature, the definition of mind in terms of cognition, is one more fallacy from which Aristotle's teaching, had it not fallen into neglect or contempt, might have guarded Spinoza. Nevertheless, his parallelism between passion and sensuous perception saves him from the worst extravagances of his Greek predecessors. For the senses, however much they might be maligned, never were nor could be altogether rejected; while the passions met with little mercy from Plato and with none from the Stoics, who considered them not only unnecessary but even unnatural. Spinoza more wisely sees in them assertions, however obscure and confused, of the will to be and grow which constitutes individual existence. And he sees that they can no more be removed by pointing out their evil consequences than sense-impressions can be abolished by proving their fallaciousness. On the other hand, when Spinoza speaks as if one emotion could only be conquered or expelled by another emotion, we must not allow his peculiar phraseology to conceal from us the purely intellectual character of his whole ethical system. What he really holds is that emotion can be overcome by reason or better knowledge, because it is itself an imperfect cognition. Point by point, an analogy—or something more than an analogy—is made out between the errors of sensuous perception joined to imagination, and the errors of our spontaneous efforts after happiness or self-realisation. Both are imposed on us from without, and neither can be got rid of by a simple act of volition. Both are affected by illusions of perspective: the nearer object of desire, like the nearer object of perception, assuming a disproportionate place in the field of view. In both, accidental contiguity is habitually confounded with causation; while in both the assignment of causes to effects, instead of being traced back through an infinite series of antecedents, stops short with the antecedent nearest to ourselves. If objects are classified according to their superficial resemblances or the usages of common language, so also are the desires sustained and intensified by imitation and rivalry. By parity of reasoning, moral education must be conducted on the same lines as intellectual education. First, it is shown how our individual existence, depending as it does on forces infinitely exceeding our own, is to be maintained. This is chiefly done by cultivating friendly relations with other men; probably, although Spinoza does not himself make the comparison, on the same principle as that observed in the mutual assistance and rectification of the senses, together with their preservation by means of verbal signs. The misleading passions are to be overcome by discovering their origin; by referring the pleasures and pains which produce them to the right causes; by calling in thought to redress the balance of imagination; by dividing the attention among an infinite number of causes; finally, by demonstrating the absolute necessity of whatever actions excite them, and classifying them according to their relations, in the same way that the phenomena of the material world are dealt with when subjected to scientific analysis.

So far Spinoza, following the example of Stoicism, has only studied the means by which reason conquers passion. He now proceeds to show, in the spirit of Plato or of Platonic Christianity, how immensely superior to the pleasures of sense and opinion are those afforded by true religion—by the love of God and the possession of eternal life. But, here also, as in the Greek system, logic does duty for emotion. The love of God means no more than viewing ourselves as filling a place in the infinite framework of existence, and as determined to be what we are by the totality of forces composing it. And eternal life is merely the adjustment of our thoughts to the logical order by which all modes of existence are deducible from the idea of infinite power.

Thus, while Spinoza draws to a head all the tendencies inherited from Greek philosophy, borrowing from the early physicists their necessarianism; from the Atomists, their exclusion of final causes, their denial of the supernatural, and their infinite worlds; from the Athenian school, their distinction between mind and body and between reason and sense; from Aristotle, his parallelism between causation and syllogism; from the Epicureans, their vindication of pleasure; and from the Stoics, their identification of belief with action, their conquest of passion and their devotion to humanity;—it is to the dominant Platonism of the seventeenth century that his system owes its foundation, its development, and its crown; for he begins by realising the abstract conception of being, and infers its absolute infinity from the misleading analogy of space, which is not an abstraction at all; deduces his conclusions according to the geometrical method recommended by Plato; and ends, like Plato, by translating dialectic formulas into the emotional language of religious faith.[573]

VIII.

From this grand synthesis, however, a single element was omitted; and, like the uninvited guest of fairy tradition, it proved strong enough singly to destroy what had been constructed by the united efforts of all the rest. This was the sceptical principle, the critical analysis of ideas, first exercised by Protagoras, made a new starting-point by Socrates, carried to perfection by Plato, supplementing experience with Aristotle, and finally proclaimed in its purity as the sole function of philosophy by an entire school of Greek thought.

Notwithstanding the sterility commonly associated with mere negation, it was this which, of all the later Greek schools, possessed the greatest powers of growth. Besides passing through more than one stage of development on its own account, Scepticism imposed serious modifications on Stoicism, gave birth to Eclecticism, and contributed to the establishment of Neo-Platonism. The explanation is not far to seek. The more highly organised a system is, the more resistance does it offer to change, the more does its transmission tend to assume a rigidly scholastic form. To such dogmatism the Sceptics were, on principle, opposed; and by keeping the problems of philosophy open, they facilitated the task of all who had a new solution to offer; while mind and its activities being, to some extent, safe from the universal doubt, the sceptical principle spontaneously threw back thought on a subjective instead of an objective synthesis of knowledge—in other words, on that psychological idealism the pregnancy and comprehensiveness of which are every day becoming more clearly recognised. And we shall now see how the same fertilising power of criticism has been manifested in modern times as well.

The sceptical philosophy, already advocated in the Middle Ages by John of Salisbury, was, like every other form of ancient thought, revived at the Renaissance, but only under the very superficial form which infers from the co-existence of many divergent opinions that none of them can be true. Even so, however, It led Montaigne to sounder notions of toleration and humanity than were entertained by any of his contemporaries. With Bacon, and still more with Descartes, it also appears as the necessary preparation for a remodelling of all belief; but the great dogmatic systems still exercised such a potent influence on both those thinkers that their professed demand for a new method merely leads up to an altered statement of the old unproved assumptions.

Meanwhile the old principle of universal doubt could no longer be maintained in presence of the certainties already won by modern science. Man, in the time of Newton, had, as Pope tersely puts it, 'too much knowledge for the sceptic side.' The problem was not how to establish the reality, but how to ascertain the origin and possible extent of that knowledge. The first to perceive this, the first to evolve criticism out of scepticism, and therefore the real founder of modern philosophy, was Locke. Nevertheless, even with him, the advantage of studying the more recent in close connexion with the earlier developments of thought does not cease; it only enters on a new phase. If he cannot, like his predecessors, be directly affiliated to one or more of the Greek schools, his position can be illustrated by a parallel derived from the history of those schools. What Arcesilaus and

Carneades had been to Socrates and his successors, that Locke was, in a large measure, to Bacon and the Cartesians. He went back to the initial doubt which with them had been overborne by the dogmatic reaction, and insisted on making it a reality. The spirit of the Apologia is absent from Plato's later dialogues, only to reappear with even more than its original power in the teaching of the New Academy. And, in like manner, Descartes' introspective method, with its demand for clear ideas, becomes, in the Essay concerning Human Understanding, an irresistible solvent for the psychologyy and physics of its first propounder. The doctrine of innate ideas, the doctrine that extension is the essence of matter, the doctrine that thought is the essence of mind, the more general doctrine, held also by Bacon, that things have a discoverable essence whence all their properties may be deduced by a process analogous to mathematical reasoning,—all collapsed when brought to the test of definite and concrete experience.

We have here, indeed, something comparable not only to the scepticism of the New Academy, but also to the Aristotelian criticism of Plato's metaphysics; and, at first sight, it might seem as if the Peripatetic philosophy was destined once more to regain the position taken from it by the resuscitation of its ancient foe. But Locke was not inclined to substitute one form of scholasticism for another. By applying the analytical method of Atomism to knowledge itself, he created a weapon equally fatal to the two competing systems. Under his dissection, the concrete individual substance of the one vanished no less completely than the universal ideas of the other. Nothing remained but a bundle of qualities held together by a subjective bond.

Similarly, in political science, the analytical method of assuming civil government to result from a concurrence of individual wills, which with Hobbes had served only to destroy ecclesiastical authority, while leaving intact and even strengthening the authority of secular rulers, was reinterpreted by Locke as a negation of all absolutism whatever.

It is interesting to observe how, here also, the positive science of the age had a large share in determining its philosophic character. Founded on the discovery of the earth's true shape, Aristotle's metaphysics had been overthrown by the discovery of the earth's motion. And now the claims of Cartesianism to have furnished an exact knowledge of matter and a definition of it whence all the facts of observation could be deduced à priori, were summarily refuted by the discovery of universal gravitation. The Cartesians complained that Newton was bringing back the occult qualities of the Schoolmen; but the tendency of bodies to move towards one another proved as certain as it was inexplicably mysterious. For a time, the study of causes was superseded by the study of laws; and the new method of physical science moved in perfect harmony with the phenomenism of Locke. One most important consequence of this revolution was to place the new Critical philosophy on a footing quite different from that occupied by the ancient sceptics. Both restricted certain knowledge to our own states of consciousness; but it now appeared that this might be done without impeaching the value of accepted scientific conclusions, which was more than the Academic philosophy would have admitted. In other words, granting that we were limited to phenomena, it was shown that science consisted in ascertaining the relations of these phenomena to one another, instead of to a problematic reality lying behind them; while, that such relations existed and were, in fact, part of the phenomena themselves, was what no sceptic could easily deny.

Nevertheless, in each case, subjective idealism had the effect of concentrating speculation, properly so called, on ethical and practical interests. Locke struck the keynote of eighteenth century philosophy when he pronounced morality to be 'the proper science and business of mankind in general.'[574] And no sooner had morality come to the front than the significance of ancient thought again made itself apparent. Whether through conscious imitation, or because the same causes brought about the same effects, ethical enquiries moved along the lines originally laid down in the schools of Athens. When rules of conduct were not directly referred to a divine revelation, they were based either on a supposed law of Nature, or on the necessities of human happiness, or on some combination of the two. Nothing is more characteristic of the eighteenth century than its worship of Nature. Even the theology of the age is deeply coloured by it; and with the majority of those who rejected theology it became a new religion. But this sentiment is demonstrably of Greek origin, and found its most elaborate, though not its most absolute, expression in Stoicism. The Stoics had inherited it from the Cynics, who held the faith in greater purity; and these, again, so far as we can judge, from a certain Sophistic school, some fragments of whose teaching have been preserved by Xenophon and Plato; while the first who gave wide currency to this famous abstraction was, in all probability, Heracleitus. To the Stoics, however, is due that intimate association of naturalism with teleology which meets us again in the philosophy of the last century, and even now wherever the doctrine of evolution has not been thoroughly accepted. It was assumed, in the teeth of all evidence, that Nature bears the marks of a uniformly beneficent design, that evil is exclusively of human origin, and that even human nature is essentially good when unspoiled by artificial restrictions.

Yet if teleology was, in some respects, a falling-off from the rigid mechanicism first taught by the pre-Socratic schools and then again by the Cartesian school, in at least one respect it marked a comparative progress. For the first attempts made both by ancient and modern philosophy to explain vital phenomena on purely mechanical principles were altogether premature; and the immense extension of biological knowledge which took place subsequently to both, could not but bring about an irresistible movement in the opposite direction. The first to revive teleology was Leibniz, who furnished a transition from the seventeenth to the eighteenth century by his monadology. In this, Atomism is combined with Aristotelian ideas, just as it had previously been combined with Platonic ideas by Descartes. The movement of the atoms is explained by their aspiration after a more perfect state instead of by mechanical pressure. But while Leibniz still relies on the ontological argument of Descartes to prove the existence of God, this was soon abandoned, along with the cosmological argument, for the argument from design, which was also that used by the Stoics; while in ethics the fitness of things was substituted for the more mechanical law of self-preservation, as the rule of conduct; and the subjection of all impulse to reason was replaced by the milder principle of a control exercised by the benevolent over the malevolent instincts. This was a very distinct departure from the Stoic method, yet those who made it were more faithful to teleology than Stoicism had been; for to condemn human feeling altogether was implicitly to condemn the work of Nature or of God.

The other great ethical method of the eighteenth century, its hedonism, was closely connected with the sceptical movement in speculative philosophy, and, like that, received an entirely new significance by becoming associated with the idea of law. Those who isolate man from the universe are necessarily led to seek in his interests as such the sole regulator of his actions, and their sole sanction in the opinion of his fellows. Protagoras went already so far, notwithstanding his unwillingness to recognise pleasure as the supreme end; and in the system of his true successor, Aristippus, the most extreme hedonism goes hand in hand with the most extreme idealism; while with Epicurus, again, both are tempered by the influence of naturalism, imposing on him its conceptions of objective law alike in science and in practice. Still his system leaned heavily to the side of self-gratification pure and simple; and it was reserved for modern thought to establish a complete equilibrium between the two competing tendencies of Greek ethics. This has been effected in Utilitarianism; and those critics are entirely mistaken who, like M. Guyau, regard that system as a mere reproduction of Epicureanism. It might with full as much reason be called a modern version of Stoicism. The idea of humanity is essentially Stoic; to work for the good of humanity was a Stoic precept; and to sacrifice one's own pleasure for that higher good is a virtue which would have satisfied the most rigorous demands of a Cleanthes, an Epictêtus, or an Aurelius.

Utilitarianism agrees with the ancient hedonism in holding pleasure to be the sole good and pain the sole evil. Its adherents also, for the most part, admit that the desire of the one and the dread of the other are the sole motives to action; but, while making the end absolutely universal and impersonal, they make the motive into a momentary impulse, without any necessary relation to the future happiness of the agent himself. The good man does his duty because doing it gives him pleasure, or because the failure to do it would give him pain, at the moment; although he knows that a contrary course would save him from greater pain or win him greater pleasure hereafter. No accurate thinker would call this acting from a selfish or interested motive; nor does it agree with the teaching of Epicurus. Were all sensitive beings to be united in a single organism, then, on utilitarian principles, self-interest, interpreted in the sense of seeking its own preservation and pleasure, would be the only law that the individualised aggregate could rationally obey. But the good of each part would be rigorously subordinated to the good of the whole; and utilitarian morality desires that we should act as if this hypothesis were realised, at least in reference to our own particular interests. Now, the idea of humanity as forming such a consolidated whole is not Epicurean. It belongs to the philosophy which always reprobated pleasure, precisely because its pursuit is associated with the dereliction of public duty and with bitter rivalry for the possession of what, by its very nature, exists only in limited quantities, while the demand for it is unlimited or, at any rate, far exceeds the supply. According to the Stoics, there was only one way in which the individual could study his private interest without abandoning his position as a social being, and this was to find it exclusively in the practice of virtue.[575] But virtue and public interest remained mere forms scantily supplemented by appeals to the traditional morality, until the idea of generalised happiness, of pleasure diffused through the whole community, came to fill them with substance and life.

It has also to be observed that the idea of utility as a test of moral goodness is quite distinct from hedonism. Plato proclaims, in the most unequivocal terms, that actions must be estimated by their consequences instead of by the feelings of sympathy or antipathy which they excite; yet no one could object more strongly to making pleasure the end of action. Thus, three distinct doctrines seem to converge in modern English ethics, of which all are traceable to Greek philosophy, but only one to Epicureanism in particular, and not ultimately to that but to the older systems whence it sprang.

And here we unexpectedly find ourselves confronted by a new relation between ancient and modern thought. Each acts as a powerful precipitant on the other, dissolving what might otherwise have passed for inseparable associations, and combining elements which a less complete experience might have led us to regard as necessarily incompatible with one another. The instance just analysed is highly significant; nor does it stand alone. Modern spiritualists often talk as if morality was impossible apart from their peculiar metaphysics. But the Stoics, confessedly the purest moralists of antiquity, were uncompromising materialists; while the spiritualist Aristotle taught what is not easily distinguishable from a very refined sort of egoism. Again, the doctrine of free-will is now commonly connected with a belief in the separability of consciousness from matter, and, like that, is declared to be an indispensable condition of morality. Among the Greeks, however, it was held by the materialist Epicureans more distinctly than by any other school; while the Stoics did not find necessarianism inconsistent with self-sacrificing virtue. The partial derivation of knowledge from an activity in our own minds is another supposed concomitant of spiritualism; although Aristotle traces every idea to an external source, while at the same time holding some cognitions to be necessarily true—a theory repudiated by modern experientialists. To Plato, the spirituality of the soul seemed to involve its pre-existence no less than its immortality, a consequence not accepted by his modern imitators. Teleology is now commonly opposed to pantheism; the two were closely combined in Stoicism; while Aristotle, although he believed in a personal God, attributed the marks of design in Nature to purely unconscious agencies.

IX.

The naturalism and utilitarianism of the eighteenth century are the last conceptions directly inherited from ancient philosophy by modern thought. Henceforward, whatever light the study of the former can throw on the vicissitudes of the latter is due either to their partial parallelism, or to an influence becoming every day fainter and more difficult to trace amid the multitude of factors involved. The progress of analytical criticism was continually deflected or arrested by the still powerful resistance of scholasticism, just as the sceptical tendencies of the New Academy had been before, though happily with less permanent success; and as, in antiquity, this had happened within no less than without the critical school, so also do we find Locke clinging to the theology of Descartes; Berkeley lapsing into Platonism; Hume playing fast and loose with his own principles; and Kant leaving it doubtful to which side he belongs, so evenly are the two opposing tendencies balanced in his mind, so dexterously does he adapt the new criticism to the framework of scholastic logic and metaphysics.

Meanwhile the strength of the analytical method was doubled by its extension to the phenomena of growth and change; for, as applied to these, it became the famous theory of Development or Evolution. No idea belongs so completely to modern philosophy; for even the ancient thinkers who threw their cosmology into a historical form had never attempted to explain the present by the past. If anything, they explained the past by the present, assuming a rough analogy to exist between the formation of the universe as a whole and the genesis of those natural or artificial bodies which were continually growing or being built up before their eyes. Their cosmology was, in fact, nothing but the old mythology stripped of its personal or conscious element; and, like it, was a hypothesis unsupported by any external evidence;—a criticism not inconsistent with the admission that to eliminate the supernatural element from speculation was, even in the absence of any solid addition to human knowledge, an achievement of inestimable value. The evolutionary method is also an elimination of the supernatural, but it is a great deal more. By tracing the history of compound structures to their first origin, and noting the successive increments to which their gradual growth is due, it reveals, as no statical analysis ever could, the actual order of synthesis, and the meaning of the separate constituents by whose joint action their movements are determined; while, conversely, their dissolution supplies us with a number of ready-made experiments in which the influence of each particular factor in the sum total may be detected by watching the changes that ensue on its removal. In a word, the method of evolution is the atomistic method, extended from matter to motion, and viewed under the form of succession instead of under the form of co-existence.

As a universal philosophy, the theory of Development, like every other modern idea, has only been permitted to manifest itself in combination with different forms of the old scholasticism. The whole speculative movement of our century is made up of such hybrid systems; and three, in particular, still divide the suffrages of many thinking men who have not been able entirely to shake off the influence of reactionary ideas. These are the systems of Hegel, of Comte, and of Mr. Herbert Spencer. In each, the logic and metaphysics inherited from Greek thought are variously compounded with the new science. And each, for that very reason, serves to facilitate the transition from one to the other; a part analogous to that played among the Greeks themselves by the vast constructions of Plato and Aristotle, or, in an age of less productivity, by the Stoic and Alexandrian philosophies.

The influence of Aristotle has, indeed, continued to make itself felt not only through the teaching of his modern imitators, but more directly as a living tradition in literature, or through the renewed study of his writings at first hand. Even in the pure sciences, it survived until a comparatively recent period, and, so far as the French intellect goes, it is not yet entirely extinct. From Abélard on, Paris was the headquarters of that soberer scholasticism which took its cue from the Peripatetic logic; and the resulting direction of thought, deeply impressed as it became on the French character and the French language, was interrupted rather than permanently altered by the Cartesian revolution, and, with the fall of Cartesianism, gradually recovered its old predominance. The Aristotelian philosophy is remarkable above all others for clear definitions, full descriptions, comprehensive classifications, lucid reasoning, encyclopaedic science, and disinterested love of knowledge; along with a certain incapacity for ethical speculation,[576] strong conservative leanings, and a general tendency towards the rigid demarcation rather than the fruitful commingling of ideas. And it will probably be admitted that these are also traits characteristic of French thinking as opposed to English or German thinking. For instance, widely different as is the Mécanique Céleste from the astronomy of Aristotle's treatise On the Heavens, both agree in being attempts to prove the eternal stability of the celestial system.[577] The destructive deluges by which Aristotle supposes civilisation to be periodically interrupted, reappear on a larger scale in the theory of catastrophes still held by French geologists. Another Aristotelian dogma, the fixity of organic species, though vigorously assailed by eminent French naturalists, has, on the whole, triumphed over the opposite doctrine of transformism in France, and now impedes the acceptance of Darwin's teaching even in circles where theological prepossessions are extinct. The accepted classifications in botany and zoology are the work of Frenchmen following in the footsteps of Aristotle, whose genius for methodical arrangement was signally exemplified in at least one of these departments; the division of animals into vertebrate and invertebrate being originally due to him. Bichat's distinction between the animal and the vegetable functions recalls Aristotle's distinction between the sensitive and nutritive souls; while his method of studying the tissues before the organs is prefigured in the treatise on the Parts of Animals. For a long time, the ruling of Aristotle's Poetics was undisputed in French criticism; and if anything could disentitle Montesquieu's Esprit des Lois to the proud motto, Prolem sine matre creatam, it would be its close relationship to the Politics of the same universal master. Finally, if it be granted that the enthusiasm for knowledge, irrespective of its utilitarian applications, exists to a greater degree among the educated classes of France than in any other modern society, we may plausibly attribute this honourable characteristic to the fostering influence of one who has proclaimed more eloquently than any other philosopher that theoretical activity is the highest good of human life, the ideal of all Nature, and the sole beatitude of God.

It remains to add a few words on the position which ancient and modern philosophy respectively occupy towards theology. Here their relation is one of contrast rather than of resemblance. The Greek thinkers start at an immense distance from religious belief, and their first allusions to it are marked by a scornful denial of its validity. Gradually, with the transition from physical to ethical enquiries, an approximation between the two is brought about, though not without occasional returns to their former attitude of hostility. Finally, in presence of a common danger they become interwoven and almost identified with one another; while the new religion against which they make common cause, itself presents the same spectacle of metaphysical and moral ideas entering into combination with the spontaneous products of popular mythology. And be it observed that throughout the whole of this process action and reaction were equal and contrary. The decline and corruption of philosophy was the price paid for the elevation and purification of religion. While the one was constantly sinking, the other was constantly rising, until they converged on the plane of dogmatic theology. By the very circumstances of the case, an opposite course has been imposed on the development of modern philosophy. Starting from an intimate union with religion, it slowly disengages itself from the compromising alliance; and, although, here also, the normal course of ideas has been interrupted by frequent reactions, the general movement of European thought has been no less decidedly towards a complete emancipation from the popular beliefs than the movement of Greek thought had been towards their conciliation and support.

FOOTNOTES:

1 See Vol. I., pp. 78-83.

2 Aristotle, Metaph., VIII., iii., 1043, b, 25.

3 Zeller, Phil. d. Gr., II., a, 277.

4 Diog. L., VI., 3.

5 According to the very probable conjecture of Zeller, l. c.

6 Zeller, l. c.; Diog. L., VI., 12.

7 Diog., VI., 3.

8 For the authorities, see Zeller, op. cit., p. 263.

9 Diog., IX., 62.

10 Metaph., IV., iv., 1008, b, 12 ff.

11 Diss., III., xxii.

12 Diog., VIII., i. ff.

13 Diog., VI., 96.

14 Zeller, Ph. d. Gr., III., a, 29.

15 Diog., VII., 5.

16 Diog., VII., 183.

17 Ibid., 179.

18 Ibid., 25.

19 Ibid., 180 L.

20 Plutarch, De Stoic. Repug., iii., 2.

21 It is significant that the only Stoic who fell back on pure Cynicism should have been Aristo of Chios, a genuine Greek, while the only one who, like Aristotle, identified good with knowledge was Herillus, a Carthaginian.

22 Op. cit., p. 18, cf. p. 362.

23 Diog., VII., 144 ff.

24 Posidonius estimated the sun's distance from the earth at 500,000,000 stades, and the moon's distance at 2,000,000 stades, which, counting the stade at 200 yards, gives about 57,000,000 and 227,000 miles respectively. The sun's diameter he reckoned, according to one account, at 440,000 miles, about half the real amount; according to another account at a quarter less. Zeller, op. cit., p. 190, Note 2.

25 For the authorities, see Zeller, op. cit., p. 139, Note 1.

26 Zeller, p. 155.

27 The Stoic necessarianism gave occasion to a repartee which has remained classical ever since, although its original authorship is known to few. A slave of Zeno's, on receiving chastisement for a theft, tried to excuse himself by quoting his master's principle that he was fated to steal. 'And to be flogged for it,' replied the philosopher, calmly continuing his predestined task. (Diog., VII., 23.)

28 Soph., 247, D.

29 Plutarch, De Comm. Notit., xxx., 2; Cicero, Acad., I., xi., 39; Diog., VII., 150; Zeller, p. 117.

30 Plutarch, De Stoic. Repug., xliii., 4.

31 Zeller, p. 201, ff.

32 Cicero, De Nat. Deor., II., xv., 39.

33 Sextus Empiricus, Adv. Math., IX., 18.

34 Cicero, De Nat. Deor., I., xiii., 32.

35 Zeller, p. 309 ff.

36 See Cicero, De Divinatione, I., passim.

37 Plutarch, De Placit. Phil., IV., xi.

38 This seems the best explanation of the various statements on the subject made by our authorities, for which see Zeller, pp. 71-86.

39 Sextus Emp., Adv. Math., VIII., 375.

40 Zeller, p. 109.

41 Zeller, p. 93.

42 Stobaeus, Eclog., II., p. 132, quoted by Ritter and Preller, p. 394; Diog., VII., 89.

43 'Quid est sapientia? Semper idem velle atque idem nolle. Licet illam exceptiunculam non adicias ut rectum sit quod velis. Non potest cuiquam semper idem placere nisi rectum.' Seneca, Epist., xx., 4.

44 Cicero, De Fin., I., ix., 30. In this he followed the Cyrenaics; see Diog., II., 87.

45 Sextus Emp., Adv. Math., XI., 73.

46 'Das platonische Gedicht vom himmlischen Gottesstaat hatte durch diestoische Auffassung der Welt als eines vom Göttlichen durchdrungenen und beseelten Körpers einen Leib bekommen, in dessen zwingenden Organismus der Einzelne als Glied beschlossen ist und sich fügen muss.' Bruno Bauer, Christus u. d. Cäsaren, p. 328.

47 Zeller, p. 168, Note 2.

48 Diog., VII., vii., 85.

49 Gellius, Noct. Att., XII., v., 7, quoted by Ritter and Preller, p. 395.

50 Dissert., I., xix., II.

51 Ibid., xxii., 9, ff.

52 Cicero, Tusc. Disput., IV., xix. ff.

53 Cic., Tusc. Disput., IV., vi.

54 Zeller, p. 229.

55 See the Dissertations of Epictêtus throughout.

56 Plutarch, De Communibus Notitiis, cap. xxxiii., p. 1076 B.

57 Cf. Zeller, p. 583.

58 Zeller, pp. 260-1.

59 Ibid., pp. 267-8.

60 Ibid., p. 270.

61 Cicero, De Fin., III., xvii., 58; Acad., I., x., 37; De Off., I., iii., 8.

62 De Off., I., vi.

63 I., viii.

64 I., xviii-xxiii.

65 Pyrrh. Hyp., III., 201.

66 Cic., De Off., III., xxiii., 91.

67 Cic., De Off., III., xii., 51.

68 Ibid., xxiii., 89.

69 Plutarch, De Comm. Notit., xi., 8.

70 Cf. Zeller, pp. 263-4, 278-84.

71 Diog., VII., 130; Cic., De Fin., III., xviii., 60; Zeller, pp. 305-9.

72 Diog., VII., 31, 176.

73 Plutarch, De Stoic. Repug., xviii., 5.

74 'Omnia scelera, etiam ante effectum operis, quantum culpae satis est, perfecta sunt.'—Seneca, De Const. Sap., vii., 4. Cf. Zeno apud Sext. Emp., Adv. Math., XI., 190.

75 'Prope est a te Deus, tecum est, intus est ... sacer intra nos spiritus sedet bonorum malorumque nostrorum observator et custos.'—Seneca, Epp., xli., 1. Cf. Horace, Epp., I., i., 61; Lucan, IX., 573; Persius, III., 43; Juvenal, XIII., 192-235.

76 It may be desirable to give some reasons in support of this opinion, as the contrary has been stated by scholars writing within a comparatively recent period. Thus Welcker says: 'Das Gewissen ward bei den Griechen als ein göttliches Wesen, Erinys, gescheut und wie wir es sonst nicht finden, zur Gottheit erhoben' (Griechische Götterlehre, I., 233); and again (p. 699) 'Ερινύς ... ist das Gewissen.' Similarly, M. Alfred Maury observes that, 'les remords se personnifiaient sous la forme de déesses Erinnyies, chargées de punir tous les forfaits' (Histoire des Religions de la Grèce Antique, I., 342). And Preller, while entertaining sounder views respecting their origin, contents himself with the caution that, 'Man sich hüten muss die Furien blos fur die subjectiven Mächte des menschlichen Gewissen zu halten' (Griechische Mythologie, I., 686, 3rd ed.). Now, in the first place, the Erinyes did not punish all crime, as they ought to have done had they represented conscience. According to Aeschylus (Eumen., 604-5), they considered that the murder of her husband by Clytaemnestra was no affair of theirs, there being no blood relationship between the parties concerned.

They did not persecute Electra, who, short of striking the fatal blow, had as much hand in her mother's death as Orestes. And even when a father was killed by his son, they do not always seem to have taken up the matter; for in the Odyssey it is not by the Erinyes of Laius, but by those of Epicastê that Oedipus is pursued—a conception very unlike that of Sophocles, who makes him feel as much remorse for the parricide as for the incest and its consequences. In the next place, the Erinyes are let loose not by the action itself but by the curses of the injured or offended blood-relation, as we see by Homer, Il., IX., 454 and 566; which seems to show that if they personified anything human it was the imprecations of the victim, not the self-reproach of the aggressor. Thirdly, the Orestes of Aeschylus, so far from feeling conscience-smitten, disclaims all responsibility for his mother's death, inflicted as it was in consequence of a direct command from the higher gods, accompanied by threats of heavy punishment in case of disobedience. (Eumen., 443 ff.). And, finally, the office assigned to the Erinyes of seeing that the laws of nature are not broken (vol. I., 67) shows that the Greeks conceived their existence as something altogether objective and physical. [There is a short but very sensible account of the Erinyes in Keightley's Mythology, p. 175, 4th ed.]

77 Cicero, De Off., I., xxxi.; Epictêtus, Man., 17, b., 30; Diss., I., ii., 33; xvi., 20; xxix., 39; II., v., 10; ib., 21; x., 4, xiv., 8; xxiii., 38; xxv., 22; Antoninus, Comm., VI., 39, 43; IX., 29; cf. Seneca, Epp., lxxxv., 34, and the saying of Marcus Aurelius quoted by Dion Cassius (Epit., LXXI., xxxiv., 4), that we cannot make men what we wish them to be; we can only turn what faculties they have to the best account in working for the public good.

78 For the references to these and other similar passages, see the last note.

79 Plutarch, De Alex. Virt., I., vi.; Diog., VII., 33.

80 It need hardly be observed that here also the morality of natural law has attained its highest artistic development under the hand of George Eliot—sometimes even to the neglect of purely artistic effect, as in Daniel Deronda and the Spanish Gypsy.

81 Zeller, p. 297, followed by Mr. Capes, in his excellent little work on Stoicism (p. 51).

82 Seneca, De Irâ, I., v., 2 ff.; II., xxxi., 7; De Clem., I., iii., 2; De Benef., IV., xxvi., l, Epp., xcv., 51 ff.; Epictêtus, Diss., IV., v., 10; Antoninus, VII., 13; together with the additional references given by Zeller, p. 286 ff. It is to be observed that the mutual love attributed to human beings by the Stoic philosophers stands, not for an empirical characteristic, but for an unrealised idea of human nature. The actual feelings of men towards one another are described by Seneca in language recalling that of Schopenhauer and Leopardi. 'Erras,' he exclaims, 'si istorum tibi qui occurrunt vultibus credis: hominum effigies habent, animos ferarum: nisi quod illarum perniciosior est primus incursus. Nunquam enim illas ad nocendum nisi necessitas inicit: aut fame aut timore coguntur ad pugnam: homini perdere hominem libet.'—Epp., ciii., 2.

83 Plato, Protagoras, 337, D.

84 'He [Charles Austin] presented the Benthamic doctrines in the most startling form of which they were susceptible, exaggerating everything in them which tended to consequences offensive to any one's preconceived feelings.'—Mill's Autobiography, p. 78.

85 Zeller, p. 281.

86 'Homo sacra res homini jam per lusum et jocum occiditur ... satisque spectaculi ex homine mors est.'—Seneca, Epp., xcv., 33. 'Servi sunt? Immo homines. Servi sunt? Immo contubernales. Servi sunt? Immo humiles amici. Servi sunt? Immo conservi.'—Ibid., xlvii., 1. Compare the treatise De Irâ, passim.

87 Seneca once lets falls the words, 'fortuna aequo jure genitos alium alii donavit.'—Consol. ad Marciam, xx, 2; but this is the only expression of the kind that we have been able to discover in a Stoic writer of the empire.

88 Seneca, Epp., lxxx.

89 'L'empereur avait pour principe de maintenir les anciennes maximes romaines dans leur intégrité.' (Renan's Marc-Aurèle, p. 54.) The authority given by M. Renan is Dion Cass., LXXI., xxxiv.; where, however, there is nothing of the kind stated. Capitolinus says (Anton. Phil., cap. xi.): 'Jus autem magis vetus restituit quam novum fecit.'

90 Renan, p. 30; Capitolinus, Anton. Phil., xii.; Dion Cass., Epit., LXXI., xxix., 3.

91 Antoninus, Comm., VI., 46; X., 8.

92 The expressions used by M. Ernest Renan when treating of this subject are somewhat conflicting. In reference to the penal enactments against Christianity under Marcus Aurelius, he first states that, however objectionable they may have been, 'en tout cas dans l'application la mansuétude du bon empereur fut à l'abri de tout reproche' (Marc-Aurèle, p. 58.) Further on, however we are told that when the martyrs of Lyons appealed to Rome, 'la réponse impériale arriva en fin. Elle était dure et cruelle.' (p. 329.) And subsequently M. Renan makes the Emperor personally responsible for the atrocities practised on that occasion by observing, 'Si Marc-Aurèle, au lieu d'employer les lions et la chaise rougie,' &c. (p. 345.) But perhaps such inconsistencies are to be expected in a writer who has elevated the necessity of perpetual self-contradiction into a principle.

93 Epictêtus, Diss., III., xxiv.

94 Seneca, De Irâ, I., xiv., 2; De Clement., I., vi., 2.

95 Diog., VII., 91. Ziegler (Gesch. d. Ethik, Bonn, 1882, I., 174) holds, in opposition to Zeller, that originally every Stoic, as such, was assumed to be a perfect sage, and that the question was only whether the ideal had ever been realised outside the school. This, however, goes against the evidence of Plutarch, who tells as (De Stoic. Repug., xxxi., 5) that Chrysippus neither professed to be good himself nor supposed that any of his friends or teachers or disciples was good.

96 Seneca, Epp., cxvi., 4. It must be borne in mind that Panaetius was speaking at a time when the object of passion would at best be either another man's wife or a member of the demi-monde.

97 Comm., VII., 26; XII., 16.

98 See especially Antoninus, Comm., IX., 1.

99 Friedländer, Römische Sittengeschichte, I., 463; Duruy, Histoire des Romains, V., 349 ff., 370; cf. Gaston Boissier, La Religion Romaine, II., 152 ff., 212 ff.

100 This idea is most distinctly expressed by Marcus Aurelius, II., 1, and VII., 13.

101 For the authorities, see Zeller, p. 176.

102 See especially Seneca, Epp., lxiv., and the whole treatise De Providentiâ.

103 See, inter alia, Comm., IV., 3; VI., 15, 37; VII., 21, 49; XI., 1; XII., 7, 21, 23, 24, 26, 31, 32.

104 Comm., XI., 28, xii. 14. A modern disciple of Aurelius has expressed himself to the same purpose in slightly different language:—

'Long fed on boundless hopes, O race of man,

How angrily thou spurn'st all simpler fare!

"Christ," some one says, "was human as we are.

No judge eyes us from heaven our sin to scan;

We live no more, when we have done our span."

"Well, then, for Christ," thou answerest, "who can care?

From sin, which Heaven records not, why forbear?

Live we, like brutes, our life without a plan!"

So answerest thou; but why not rather say:

"Hath man no second life?—Pitch this one high!

Sits there no judge in Heaven, our sin to see?

More strictly, then, the inward judge obey!

Was Christ a man like us?—Ah! let us try

If we then, too, can be such men as he!"'

—The Better Part, by Mr. Matthew Arnold. The italics are in the original.

105 *First Principles, § 177.*

106 See an article entitled 'Pantheism and Cosmic Emotion,' by Frederic Harrison, in the Nineteenth Century for August, 1881.

107 From the Hymn of Cleanthes, translated by Mr. Francis Newman in The Soul, p. 73, fifth edition.

108 *Epicureanism, p. 1.*

109 Ph. d. Gr., III., a, p. 380.

110 Op. cit., p. 72.

111 Short Studies, III., p. 246.

112 *Gesch. des Mater., I., p. 92.*

113 Pollock's Spinoza, p. 64.

114 Epicuro e l'Epicurismo, Florence, 1877, p. 29.

115 *Lucretii Philosophia cum fontibus comparata, Groningen, 1877, p. 137.*

116 *Dialogues Philosophiques, p. 54, quoted by Woltjer, loc. cit.*

117 Diog. L., X., 142.

118 Ibid., 113.

119 Diog. L., X., 134.

120 Cicero, Acad., II., xxxiii., 106.

121 Cicero, De Fin., II., xxx., 96; Diog., X., 22. Cicero translates the words διαλογισμῶν μνήμη, 'memoria rationum inventorumque nostrorum.' They may refer merely to the pleasure derived from intellectual conversation.

122 The authorities for the life of Epicurus are given by Zeller, op. cit., p. 363 ff.

123 Diog., II., 92.

124 Zeller, Ph. d. Gr., II., a, 294.

125 Cf. Plato, Protag., 353, C, ff., with Epicurus in the letter to Menoeceus, quoted by Diog., X., 129.

126 *Morale d'Épicure, p. 20.*

127 Wallace's Épicureanism, p. 154; Guyau, Morale d'Épicure, p. 34.

128 Cicero, Tusc. Disput., III., xviii., 41; Zeller, III., a, p. 444.

129 Zeller, p. 460.

130 Ibid., p. 581.

131 Diog., II., 72.

132 Diog., X., 131.

133 Guyau, Morale d'Épicure, p. 55.

134 Diog., X., 118.

135 Lucret., IV., 1057-66.

136 Diog., X., 117, 118.

137 Cicero, De Fin., V., xxvii., 80; Diog., X., 118.

138 That is, if we assume what Aristotle says on the subject to be derived from common usage (Eth. Nic., III., ix., p. 1115, a, 33).

139 Cicero, Tusc. Disp., II., xii., 28.

140 Cicero, De Fin., I., xv.; Tusc., V., xxviii.

141 Diog., X., 150 ff.

142 Wallace, p. 162; Diog., X., 150.

143 Epicureanism, pp. 162-3.

144 Cicero, De Fin., II., vii., 20; De Nat. Deor., I., xvii., 45, xxx., 85.

145 Diog., X., 150-1.

146 V., 1145-59.

147 Cicero, De Fin., II., xvii., 57.

148 Op. cit., p. 163.

149 The lamented Prof. T. H. Green may be mentioned as another example of a high-minded thinker who was also an ardent and active politician. With regard to antiquity, see the splendid roll of public-spirited philosophers enumerated by Plutarch, Adv. Col., xxxii.

150 Op. cit., p. 164.

151 J. S. Mill observed, in a conversation with Mr. John Morley, reported by the latter, that 'in his youth mere negation of religion was a firm bond of union, social and otherwise, between men who agreed in nothing else.'—Fortnightly Review, vol. XIII., p. 675.

152 Cicero, De Nat. Deor., L., 18-24.

153 Woltjer, Lucret. Ph., p. 74.

154 'Das Staatsgesetz oder das dem Gesetz gleichkommende väterliche Herkommen bildet einen Gegensatz gegen ein abgeschlossenes Priesterthum und dessen natürlichen Einfluss.' Welcker, Gr. Götterlehre, II., p. 45. 'La religion romaine, comme toutes celles où domine l'esprit laïque, diminue le rôle du prêtre.' Gaston Boissier, La Religion Romaine, I., p. 16.

155 This reminds one of the 'pèlerinages,' which figure along with 'pigeon-shooting' among the attractions offered by French country hotels to idle visitors.

156 Republic, II., 364, C, ff; Jowett's transl., III., 234-5. Elsewhere Plato proposes that these 'bestial persons' who persuade others that the gods can be induced by magical incantations to pardon crime, should be punished by imprisonment for life (Legg, X., 909, A, f.).

157 Villemain, Life of Gregory VII., Engl, transl., I., p. 305. As a further illustration of the same subject, it may be mentioned that there is a cemetery near Innsbruck (and probably many more like it throughout the Tyrol) freely adorned with rude representations of souls in purgatory, stretching out their hands for help from amid the flames. The help is of course to be obtained by purchase from the priesthood.

158 Lucret., I., 108-12.

159 Agamemnon, 369 (Dindorf).

160 Zeller, pp. 428-9.

161 Prof. Sellar observes, as we think, with perfect truth, that 'there is no necessary connexion between the atomic theory of philosophy and that view of the ends and objects of life which Lucretius derived from Epicurus.'—Roman Poets of the Republic, p. 348, 2nd ed.

162 Lucret., I., 1020 ff.; V., 835 ff; IV., 780 ff.; V., 1023; V., 1307 ff.

163 That Democritus attributed weight to his atoms has been proved, in opposition to Lewes and others, by Zeller, Ph. d. Gr., I., p. 713 (3rd ed.)

164 Woltjer, Lucr. Phil., p. 38.

165 Arist., Phys., IV., viii., 216, a, 20.

166 II., 257 ff.

167 Lucret., IV., 875 ff.

168 Lucret., V., 437 ff.

169 Zeller, Ph. d. Gr., III., a, pp. 397-8. Reichel's transl., pp. 412-3 (1st ed.)

170 Woltjer (Lucret. Ph., p. 126) charges Lucretius with having misunderstood his master on this point. As the sun and moon appear larger when near the horizon than at other times, Epicurus thought that we then see them either as they really are or a little larger. This, Lucretius, according to Woltjer, took to mean that their general apparent size may be a little over or under their real size.

171 Zeller, p. 413.

172 See, for instance, Woltjer, op. cit., p. 88.

173 Zeller, p. 443, note 3.

174 Zeller, pp. 417-8.

175 Diog., X., 125.

176 III., 922.

177 Cicero, De Fin., I., ix., 30.

178 'Aeque enim timent ne apud inferos sint, quam ne nusquam.'—Seneca, Epp., lxxxii., 16.

179 Cf. Plutarch, Non posse suaviter vivi, cap. xxvii.

180 Among other feelings consequent on the first experience of death among the posterity of Cain, the following are specified:—

'It seemed the light was never loved before,

Now each man said, "'Twill go and come no more."

No budding branch, no pebble from the brook,

No form, no shadow but new dearness took

From the one thought that life must have an end;

And the last parting now began to send

Diffusive dread through love and wedded bliss,

Thrilling them into finer tenderness.'

181 III., 59 ff.

182 Ethic., Pars. IV., Prop. vii.

183 Ethic. Nic., III., xii., 1117, b, 10 ff. Sir Alexander Grant, in his note on the passage, appositely compares the character of Wordsworth's Happy Warrior, who is 'More brave for this that he has much to love.'

184 For the authorities, see Zeller, p. 388.

185 Lucret., IV., 354, 728, 761.

186 Such at least seems to be the theory rather obscurely set forth in Diog., X., 32.

187 Diog., X., 33, Sextus Emp., Adv. Math., VII., 211-16; Zeller, p. 391.

188 For additional authorities see Zeller, pp. 385-95, and Wallace's Epicureanism, chap. x.

189 See Woltjer, Lucr. Ph., p. 141 ff.

190 *Morale d'Épicure, p. 157.*

191 In a fragment quoted by Sextus Empiricus, Adv. Math., IX., 54.

192 *Fragmenta Tragicorum, Didot, p. 140.*

193 Zeller, p. 416, note 1.

194 See the whole concluding portion of Lucr., bk. V.

195 Chiefly by Ritter, Gesch. d. Phil., IV., p. 94, on which see the clear and convincing reply of Zeller, op. cit., p. 47.

196 For details we must refer to the masterly treatise of Dr. Woltjer, already cited more than once in the course of this chapter.

197 Cf. II., 18, with II., 172.

198 The single exception to this rule that can be quoted is, we believe, the argument against impassioned love derived from its enslaving influence (quod alterius sub nutu degitur aetas, V., 1116). But to live under another's nod is a condition eminently unfavourable to the mental tranquillity which an Epicurean prized before all things; nor, in any case, does it seem to have counted for so much with Lucretius as the 'damnation of expenses' which was no less formidable a deterrent to him than to the 'unco guid' of Burns's satire.

199 V., 1153-4.

200 V., 1125.

201 Ziegler (Gesch. a. Ethik, I., p. 203) quotes Lucret., III., 136, to prove that the poet recognised the existence of mental pleasures as such. But Lucretius only says that the mind has pleasures not derived from an immediate external stimulus. This would apply perfectly to the imagination of sensual pleasure.

202 Woltjer, op. cit., p. 5.

203 IV., 966.

204 Woltjer, op. cit., pp. 178 ff.

205 There is an unquestionable coincidence between Lucretius, II., 69 ff. and Plato, Legg., 776 B, pointed out by Teichmüller, Geschichte der Begriffe, p. 177. Both may have drawn from some older source.

206 We think, however, that Prof. Sellar attributes more importance to this element in the Lucretian philosophy than it will bear. His words are: 'The doctrine proclaimed by Lucretius was, that creation was no result of a capricious or benevolent exercise of power, but of certain processes extending through infinite time, by means of which the atoms have at length been able to combine and work together in accordance with their ultimate conditions. The conception of these ultimate conditions and of their relations to one another involves some more vital agency than that of blind chance or an iron fatalism. The foedera Naturai are opposed to the foedera fati. The idea of law in Nature as understood by Lucretius is not merely that of invariable sequence or concomitance of phenomena. It implies at least the further idea of a "secreta facultas" in the original elements.' (Roman Poets of the Republic, p. 335, 2nd ed.) The expression secreta facultas occurs, we believe, only once in the whole poem (I., 174), and is used on that single occasion without any reference to the atoms, which do not appear until a later stage of the exposition. Lucretius is proving that whatever begins to exist must have a cause, and in support of this principle he appeals to the fixed laws which govern the growth of plants. Each plant springs from a particular kind of seed, and so, he argues, each seed must have a distinct or specific virtue of its own, which virtue he expresses by the words secreta facultas. But, according to his subsequent teaching, this specific virtue depends on a particular combination of the atoms, not on any spontaneous power which they possess of grouping themselves together so as to form organic compounds. With regard to the properties of the atoms themselves, Lucretius enumerates them clearly enough. They are extension, figure, resistance, and motion; the last mentioned being divided into downward gravitation, lateral deflection, and the momenta produced by mutual impact. Here we have nothing more than the two elements of 'iron fatalism' and 'blind chance' which Prof. Sellar regards as insufficient to account for the Lucretian scheme of creation; gravitation and mutual impact give the one, lateral deflection gives the other. Any faculty over and above these could only be conceived under the form of conscious impulse, or of mutual attractions and repulsions exercised by the atoms on one another. The first hypothesis is expressly rejected by the poet, who tells us (I., 1020) that the primordial elements are destitute of consciousness, and have fallen into their present places through the agency of purely mechanical causes. The second hypothesis is nowhere alluded to in the most distant manner, it is contrary to the whole spirit of Epicurean physics, it never occurred to a single thinker of antiquity, and to have conceived it at that time would have needed more than the genius of a Newton. As a last escape it may be urged that Lucretius believed in 'a sort of a something' which, like the fourth element in the soul, he was not prepared to define. But besides the utter want of evidence for such a supposition, what necessity would there have been for the infinite chances which he postulates in order to explain how the actual system of things came to be evolved, had the elements been originally endowed with the disposition to fall into such a system rather than into any other? For Prof. Sellar's vital agency must mean this disposition if it means anything at all.

While on this subject we must also express our surprise to find Prof. Sellar saying of Lucretius that 'in no ancient writer' is 'the certainty and universality of law more emphatically and unmistakably expressed' (p. 334). This would, we think, be much truer of the Stoics, who recognised in its absolute universality that law of causation on which all other laws depend, but which Lucretius expressly tells us (II., 255) is broken through by the clinamen. A more accurate statement of the case, we think, would be to say that the Epicurean poet believed unreservedly in uniformities of co-existence, but not, to the same extent, in uniformities of sequence; while apart from these two classes neither he nor modern science knows of any laws at all.

207 V., 695-73, 730-49.

208 Cicero, De Nat. Deor., I., xxiv., 66.

209 Comm., IX., 28.

210 Coleridge's Friend, Section II., Essay II., sub in.

211 'In the higher ranks of French society there are men who merit to be called professors of the art of happiness; who have analysed its ingredients with careful fingers and scrutinising eyes; who have consummated their experience of means and ends; who, like able doctors, can apply an immediate remedy to the daily difficulties of home-life; whose practice is worthy of their theory, and who prove it by maintaining in their wives' hearts and in their own a perennial never-weakening sentiment of gratitude and love.' (French Home Life, p. 324.) Although Mr. Marshall's observations are directly applicable to the happiness of married life only, they tend to prove that all happiness may be reduced to an art.

212 Wallace's Epicureanism, p. 37.

213 Cicero, De Rep., III., vi.-xx.

214 Plutarch, Cato Major, xxii. ff.

215 Pindar, Pyth., III., 96.

216 Vol. I., p. 46.

217 It is said that the same ironical attitude continues to characterise the Greeks of our time. Col. Leake (quoted by Welcker, Gr. Götterl., II., p. 127) informs us that travellers in Greece are continually entertained with local fables which are everywhere repeated, but believed by nobody, least of all by the inhabitants of the district where they first originated. And Welcker adds, from his own experience, that the young Greeks who act as guides in the religious houses related the miraculous legends of the place with an enthusiasm and an eloquence which left him in doubt whether or not they themselves believed what they expected him to believe.

218 Il., II., 80; XII., 238; XVI., 859; Od., I., 215; XI., 363; XXIII., 166; Agamem., 477 ff.

219 Sextus Empiricus, Adv. Math., VII., 89 ff; Zeller, Ph. d. Gr., I., pp. 464, 652, 743, 828. (3rd ed.)

220 For the theses of Gorgias see Sextus Empiricus, Adv. Math., VII., 65 ff.

221 Sext. Emp., Adv. Math., VII., 170 ff.

222 Xen., Mem., IV., iii., 14.

223 Timaeus, 37, B, 43, D ff.

224 Examples of these questions are: 'Have you lost your horns?' and, 'Did Electra know that Orestes was her brother?' Stated in words, she knew that he was; but she did not recognise him as her brother when he came to her in disguise.

225 Plutarch, Adv. Col., xxii.-xxiii.; Seneca, Epp., ix.

226 Zeller, Ph. d. Gr., III., a, 481; Diog. L., IX., xi.

227 Zeller, op. cit., p. 484; Ritter and Preller, Hist. Ph., p. 336.

228 ὡς χαλεπὸν εἴη ὁλοσχερῶς ἐκδῦναι ἄνθρωπον. For this and the other stories, see Diog. L., IX., 66-8.

229 Pyrrh. Hyp., I., 28 ff.

230 Diog. L., VII., 171.

231 Cicero, Acad., II., xxiv., 77; Sext. Emp., Adv. Math., VII., 150-7; Zeller, Ph. d. Gr., III., a, pp. 492 ff.

232 Plutarch, De Comm. Notit., i., 4; Zeller, op. cit., p. 81 (where, however, the reference to Plutarch is wrongly given).

233 Εἰ μὴ γὰρ ἦν Χρύσιππος οὐκ ἂν ἦν ἐγώ. (Diog. L., IV., 62.) The original line ran, εἰ μὴ γὰρ ἦν Χρύσιππος οὐκ ἂν ἦν στοά.

234 Sext. Emp., Adv. Math., VII., 159-65.

235 That Carneades was the first to start this difficulty cannot be directly proved, but is conjectured with great probability by Zeller (op. cit., p. 504).

236 Sext. Pyrrh. Hyp., II., 186. Adv. Math., VIII., 463.

237 Pyrrh. Hyp., II., 195, 204.

238 Cicero, De Nat. Deor., I., xxiii., 62; III., iv., 11; xvi., 42; xxi., 53.

239 Sext., Adv. Math., IX., 182-3.

240 Cic., De Nat. Deor., III., xviii., 47.

241 Cic., Acad., II., xxxviii., 120; Zeller, op. cit., p. 506.

242 Cic., Acad., ibid., 121; Zeller, op. cit., p. 507.

243 Cic., De Nat. Deor., III., x., 24.

244 ibid., III., xi., 27.

245 ibid., ix., 21.

246 ibid., III., xii., 29; I., xxxix., 109.

247 Sext. Adv. Math., IX., 139-47.

248 ibid., 152-77.

249 Cic., De Nat. Deor., III., vi.; De Divin., II., passim; De Nat. Deor., III., xxvi. ff.

250 *Le Christianisme et ses Origines, II., p. 3.*

251 Sext., Pyrrh. Hyp., III., 2.

252 Sext., Adv. Math., VII., 166-89.

253 Cic., De Fin., III., xii., 41; Zeller, op. cit., p. 519.

254 According to Zeller's interpretation of Cicero, Acad., II., xi., 34.

255 Zeller, op. cit., p. 602.

256 ibid., p. 603.

257 For the authorities see Zeller, op. cit., pp. 599-601.

258 Zeller, op. cit., pp. 603-8.

259 Zeller, op. cit., pp. 554, 561 ff.

260 Zeller, op. cit., p. 575.

261 Zeller, op. cit., p. 621.

262 Cic., Acad., II., xlv.

263 *The treatises entitled De Stoicorum Repugnantiâ and De Communibus Notiliis.*

264 Lucret., IV., 1154-64; Juven., VI., 186-95.

265 Varro observes that for 170 years the ancient Romans worshipped their gods without images; 'quod si adhuc,' inquit, 'mansisset castius Dii observarentur.' And in the same passage, speaking of mythology, he says, 'hoc omnia Diis attribuuntur quae non modo in hominem, sed etiam in contemtissimum hominem cadere possunt.' Augustin., De Civit. Dei, IV., iii., and xxxi., quoted by Zeller, op. cit., p. 674.

266 Ritter and Preller, Hist. Phil., p. 426; Woltjer, Lucretii Philosophia, p. 5.

267 The services of Posidonius seem to have been overlooked by M. Gaston Boissier when he implies in his work on Roman Religion (vol. ii., p. 13) that Fabianus, a Roman declaimer under Augustus, was the first to give an eloquent expression to Stoicism.

268 Zeller, op. cit., pp. 597-8.

269 Acad., II., xxii., 69.

270 ibid., xxxi., 99.

271 De Fin., V., xxi., 59.

272 Acad., II., xxxix.

273 For the literary studies of Socrates, see Xenoph., Mem., I., vi., 14; those of Cicero are too manifest to need any special reference.

274 See the passages quoted by Zeller, op. cit., pp. 659-60.

275 Acad., I., x.

276 De Fin., IV., viii.

277 De Off., III., iii., 11.

278 The passage occurs near the beginning of his Essay on Bacon.

279 *See the Somnium Scipionis, De Repub., VI., xvii.*

280 ibid., xxvi.

281 De Divin., II., lxxii., 148; Zeller, op. cit., p. 667.

282 I. 724 ff.

283 I. 5-7, and 34-36.

284 I., 231-51.

285 The very passage (Georg., II., 475-92) which is supposed to refer to Lucretius contains a line (frigidus obstiterit circum praecordia sanguis) embodying the Stoic theory that the soul has its seat in the heart, and is nourished by a warm exhalation from the blood. See Zeller, Ph. d. Gr., III., a, p. 197.

286 Zeller does indeed call Seneca and Marcus Aurelius 'Platonising Stoics' (Ph. d. Gr., III., b, p. 236, 3rd. ed.); but the evidence adduced hardly seems to justify the epithet.

287 Metamorph., XV., 60.

288 Zeller, Ph. d. Gr., III., a, p. 681.

289 Epp., I., i., 18.

290 M. Gaston Boissier (Religion Romaine, I., p. 206), on the strength of a passage in one of Horace's Satires (II., iii., 11), where the poet speaks of carrying Plato about with him on his travels, infers that the study of the Dialogues had a good deal to do with his conversion. It is, however, more than probable that the Plato mentioned is not the philosopher, but the comic poet, for we find that his companions in Horace's trunk were Menander, Eupolis, and Archilochus.

291 Zeller is inclined to place Aenesidêmus a hundred years earlier than the date here assigned to him (Ph. d. Gr., III., b, p. 9); but two pieces of evidence which he himself quotes seem to militate strongly against this view. One is a statement of Aristocles the Peripatetic, who flourished 160-190 A.D., that Scepticism had been revived not long before his time (ἐχθὲς καὶ πρώην; apud Euseb., Pr. Ev., XIV., xviii., 22; Zeller, op. cit., p. 9); the other is Seneca's question, Quis est qui tradat praecepta Pyrrhonis? (Nat. Quaest., VII., xxxii. 2; Zeller, p. 11). On the other hand, Epictêtus, lecturing towards the end of the first century, alludes to Scepticism as something then living and active. The natural inference is that Aenesidêmus flourished before his time and after Seneca, that is about the period mentioned in the text; and we cannot make out that there are any satisfactory data pointing to a different conclusion.

292 Zeller, III., b, p. 18.

293 Zeller, III., a, pp. 495 and 514; Cic., Acad., I., xii., 45; ibid., II., ix., 28.

294 With all deference to so great a scholar as Zeller, it seems to us that he has misinterpreted a passage in which Sextus Empiricus observes that a particular argument of his own against the possibility of reaching truth either by sense or by reason, is virtually (δυνάμει) contained in the difficulties raised by Aenesidêmus (Adv. Math., VIII., 40). Zeller (op. cit., III., b, p. 20, note 5) translates δυνάμει, 'dem Sinne nach,' 'in substance,' a meaning which it will hardly bear. What Sextus says is that the untrustworthiness of reason follows on the untrustworthiness of sense, for the notions supplied by the latter must either be common to all the senses—which is impossible, owing to their specialised character—or limited to some, and therefore equally liable with them to dispute and contradiction. Moreover, he argues, rational notions (τά νοητά) cannot all be true, as they conflict both with each other and with sensation. And the reference to Aenesidêmus means simply that this kind of argument amounts to a further extension of his attack on the credibility of the senses; it does not imply that Aenesidêmus had ever attacked reason himself. The whole passage is quite in the usual style of exhaustive alternation followed by Sextus, and its extreme awkwardness seems to show that he is forcing his arguments into parallelism with those of his predecessor. It is possible also that the different members of the argument have been transposed; for the part connecting reason with sense (44) ought logically to stand last, and that relating to the discrepancy of different notions with one another (45-7), second. Cf. Adv. Math., VII., 350, where Aenesidêmus is said to have identified the understanding with the senses, quite in the style of Protagoras and quite unlike the New Academy.

295 Sext. Emp., Pyrrh. Hyp., I., 180 ff.

296 Adv. Math., IX., 228.

297 The ten Tropes were evidently suggested by the ten Categories of Aristotle. The five grounded on differences of disposition, place, quantity, relation, and habits, show at once by their names that they are derived from κεῖσθαι, ποῦ, ποσόν, πρός τι, and ἔχειν. The Trope of comparative frequency would be suggested by πότε; the disturbing influence of bodies on one another combines ποιεῖν and πάσχειν; the conflict of the special senses belongs, although somewhat more remotely, to ποιόν; and, in order to make up the number ten, οὐσία, which answers to the percipient in general, had to be divided into the two Tropes taken respectively from the differences among animals and among men,—an arrangement that would occur all the more readily as οὐσία included the two notions of Genus and Species, of which the one answers, in this instance, to animals, and the other to men.

298 Zeller, III., b, p. 23.

299 Zeller, op. cit. pp. 29-37.

300 Sext. Emp., Pyrrh. Hyp., I., 164 and 178; Zeller, op. cit., pp. 37 and 38.

301 *Adv. Math., V., 1.*

302 ibid., IX., 208.

303 These are the four principles enumerated by Sextus, Pyrrh. Hyp., I., 24.

304 Diog. L., X., 9.

305 The materials and, to a certain extent, the ideas of this chapter are chiefly derived from Zeller's Philosophie der Griechen, Vol. III., Duruy's Histoire des Romains, Vol. V., Gaston Boissier's Religion Romaine, and above all from Friedländer's Darstellungen aus der Sittengeschichte Rom's, Part III., chapters iv. and vi.

306 Friedländer, Römische Sittengeschichte, III., pp, 483, 681.

307 As a striking instance of the solidarity which now connects all forms of irrationalism, it may be mentioned that Livy's fables are accepted, in avowed defiance of modern criticism, by the clericalising English students of archaeology in Rome.

308 Using the word In Its modern rather than in its ancient sense, so as to include the whole empire outside the city of Rome.

309 Epp., II., i., 20 ff.

310 Carm., I., xi., and III., xxiii.

311 Carm., III., vi., and the Carmen Seculare.

312 Boissier, Religion Romaine, I., p. 336.

313 Friedländer, III., p. 510.

314 See the note on Honestiores and Humiliores appended to the fifth volume of Duruy's Histoire des Romains.

315 *Lucian, Adversus Indoctum.*

316 Juvenal, Satt., XVI., 14.

317 Persius, Satt., III., 77.; cf. V., 189.

318 Matth., viii., 9; Luke, vii., 8.

319 Thucydides, II., iv. The other women alluded to are, the wife of Admêtus, who tells Themistocles how he is to proceed in order to conciliate her husband (I., cxxxvi.); Stratonice, the sister whom Perdiccas gives in marriage to Seuthes (II., ci.); and Brauro, the Edonian queen who murders her husband Pittacus (IV., cvii.). The wife and daughter of Hippias the Peisistratid and the sister of Harmodius are mentioned in bk. VI., lv. ff, but they take us back to an earlier period of Greek history than that of which Thucydides treats consecutively; while the names of Helen and Procne, which also occur, belong, of course, to a much remoter past (I., ix., and II., xxix.)

320 It has even been maintained that the condition of the Roman matron was superior to that of the modern Frenchwoman. (Duruy, Histoire des Romains, V., p. 41.)

321 Boissier, Religion Romaine, II. p. 200.

322 Boissier, op. cit., II., pp. 214 ff.

323 Friedländer, Romische Sittengeschichte, I., pp. 441 ff.

324 Lucian, De Mercede Conductis, xxvi.; Friedländer, I., p. 447.

325 Epict., Fragm., 53 Dübner.

326 Juvenal, V., and Lucian, De Mercede Conductis.

327 Friedländer, III., p. 502.

328 Friedländer, ibid.

329 Boissier, op. cit., I., p. 362.

330 *Havet, Le Christianisme et ses Origines, II., p. 150.*

331 Hor., Satt., I., ix., 67-72.

332 Ibid., I., iv., 142.

333 Opera, ed. Tauchnitz, V., p. 209.

334 Philo, Vita Mos. p. 136, M.; Joseph., Contr. Ap., II., xxxix.; Friedländer, III., p. 583.

335 Ovid., Ars Am., I., 415; Rem. Am., 219; Pers., V., 179; Juv., XIV., 97; Friedländer, loc. cit.

336 Havet, II., p. 328.

337 Friedländer, I., p. 451.

338 Ars Am., I., 76.

339 Friedländer, III., pp. 518, 539 ff, 553 ff.

340 Xenophon, Mem., I., i., 9.

341 Friedländer, III., p. 523.

342 ibid., pp. 524 ff.

343 Friedländer, III., pp. 527 ff.

344 Plutarch, De Defect. Oracul., cap. xlv., p. 434.

345 Lucian, Alexander, 25, 47.

346 According to Friedländer (III., p. 531), this happened between 167 and 169.

347 Friedländer, p. 532.

348 Friedländer, III., p. 533.

349 Ibid., p. 534.

350 For details see Friedländer, loc. cit.

351 Friedländer, pp. 535 ff. This form of superstition still flourishes in great force among at least the lower class of Italians at the present day; and the continual stimulation afforded to it by the public lottery is not the least mischievous consequence of that infamous institution.

352 Aelian, Fragm., 98; Friedländer, p. 494.

353 Friedländer, loc. cit.

354 Friedländer, p. 549.

355 For the whole subject of Aristeides see Friedländer, pp. 496 ff.

356 'Et parum sane fuit quod illi honores divinos, omnis aetas, omnis sexus, omnis condicio ac dignitas dedit, nisi quod etiam sacrilegus judicatus est qui ejus imaginem in suo domo non habuit qui per fortunam vel potuit habere vel debuit. Denique hodieque in multis domibus M. Aurelii statuae consistunt inter deos penates. Nec defuerunt homines qui somniis eum multa praedixisse augurantes futura et vera concinnerunt.'—Vita M. Antonini Phil., cap. xviii.

357 Friedländer, p. 513.

358 Friedländer, III., p. 683. Cp. Clifford's epitaph: 'I was nothing and was conceived; I loved and did a little work; I am nothing and grieve not.'

359 Comm., IV., 21; XII., 5, 26.

360 Zeller, Ph. d. Gr., III., a, p. 798.

361 Quoted by Friedländer, pp. 681 f.

362 Ibid., p. 688.

363 *Ibid.*

364 Zeller, op. cit., p. 828.

365 See in particular, Satt., II, 149.

366 Friedländer, I., p. 465 f.

367 Duruy, Hist. d. Rom., V., p. 463.

368 III., p. 692.

369 Friedländer, III., p. 701.

370 A mesure que le temps s'avance les traits par lesquels se produit la croyance à une autre vie, d'abord vagues et confus, loin de s'effacer, se prononcent et se précisent. On se fait de la destinée des âmes des idées de plus en plus hautes; on rend aux morts des honneurs de plus en plus grands. En outre, ces idées, ces pratiques s'étendent de plus en plus au grand nombre. Au commencement il semble qu'on ne s'inquiète que du sort des rois et des héros, enfants ou descendants directs des dieux; avec le temps beaucoup d'autres ont part aux mêmes préoccupations, puis tous ou presque tous. La félicité est réservée a qui ressemble aux dieux; c'est une maxime antique qui subsiste immuable. Avec le temps on se fait de la ressemblance avec les dieux ou, ce qui revient au même, de la perfection, des idées qui permettent à tous d'y prétendre.' Ravaisson, Le Monument de Myrrhine et les bas-reliefs funéraires, 1876, quoted by Duruy, op. cit., p. 463.

371 See Vol. I., p. 68.

372 For references see Friedländer, III., pp. 706 ff.

373 Epod., xvii., 79.

374 Friedländer, pp. 710 f.

375 Sen., Epp., xvi., 5; xcv., 52; xli., 1 and 2.

376 Perhaps, however, Zeller's contention amounts to no more than that Seneca follows Posidonius in his adoption of the Platonic distinction between reason and passion, which were identified by the older Stoics. But the object of the latter was apparently to save the personality of man, which seemed to be threatened by Plato's tripartite division of mind; and as Seneca achieves the same result by including the passions in the ἡγεμονικὸν[377] the difference between them and him is after all little more than verbal. For the general attitude of Seneca towards religion see Gaston Boissier, Religion Romaine, II., pp. 63-92.

377 Epp., xcii., 1., (Zeller, by mistake refers to Epp., xciv., in Ph. d. Gr., III., a, p. 711.)

378 As ψυχάριον, σωμάτιον, σαρκίδιον.

379 Epict., Fragm., 175, Diss., I., xvi., 1-8; II., xvi., 42; III., xxii., 2; xxiv., 91-94. Zeller, III., a, p. 742.

380 Zeller, p. 745.

381 Friedländer, III., p. 493.

382 Comm., VI., 30.

383 Oratt., VI., p. 203.

384 Diss., II., xxxvi.

385 Ph. d. Gr., III., b, pp. 88 ff.

386 Seneca, Epp., lxiv., 2; cviii., 17.

387 Seneca, De Irâ, III., xxxvi., 1.

388 Seneca, Epp., cviii., 22.

389 For a detailed account of the Neo-Pythagorean school, see Zeller, op. cit., III., b, pp. 79-158, from which the above summary is entirely derived.

390 De Defect. Orac., xvii., p. 419.

391 Diss., I., xv., 2.

392 *Plutarch, De Is. et Osir., xxv. and xxvi; De Fac. in Orbe Lun., xxx.*

393 *Op. et D., 120.*

394 Diss., I., xv., 7.

395 Zeller, III., b, pp. 189 ff.

396 De Superstit., viii., p. 169.

397 Metamorph., XI., xxv.

398 Zeller, III., b, pp. 257 ff.

399 For references, see Ritter and Preller, Hist. Phil., pp. 467-73.

400 For references, see Zeller, III., b, pp. 148 f.

401 Suidas, quoted by Ritter and Preller, p. 485.

402 Vacherot, Histoire de l'Ecole d'Alexandrie, pp. 214-17; Zeller, III., b, pp. 387 ff. The original authority is Irenaeus.

403 Politicus, p. 270 ff.

404 Legg., X., pp. 896, D ff, 898, C, 904, A.

405 De Isid. et Osir., xlv. f.; De Vir. Moral., iii.; De Anim. Procr., v., 5. Plutarch supposes that the irrational soul in man is derived from the evil world-soul which he regards rather as senseless than as Satanic. It would thus very closely resemble the delirious Demiurgus of Valentinus and the 'absolut Dumme' of Eduard v. Hartmann.

406 Diss., III., xxiii.

407 Zeller, Ph. d. Gr., III., a, pp. 807 ff.

408 Porph., Vita Plot., cap. iii.

409 Ibid., cap. vii.

410 Ibid., cap. xiii.

411 Not, as is commonly stated, on the model of Plato's Republic, which would have been a far more difficult enterprise, and one little in accordance with the practical good sense shown on other occasions by Plotinus.

412 Porph., Vita, cap. xii.; Hegel, Gesch. d. Ph., III., p. 34.

413 Porph., Vita, cap. ix.

414 Ibid., xi. Leopardi has taken the incident referred to as the subject of one of his dialogues; Plotinus, the great champion of optimism, being chosen, with bitter irony, to represent the Italian poet's own pessimistic views of life. The difficulty was to show how the Neo-Platonist philosopher could, consistently with the principles thus fathered on him, still continue to dissuade his pupil from committing suicide. Leopardi voluntarily faces the argumentum ad hominem by which common sense has in all ages summarily disposed of pessimism: 'Then why don't you kill yourself?' ('Your philosophy or your life,' so to speak.) The answer is singularly lame.

Porphyry is to think of the distress which his death would cause to his friends. He might have replied that if the general misery were so great as Plotinus had maintained, a little more or less affliction would not make any appreciable difference; that, considering the profound selfishness of mankind, an accepted article of faith with pessimism, his friends would in all probability easily resign themselves to his loss; that, at any rate, the suffering inflicted on them would be a mere trifle compared to what he would himself be getting rid of; and that, if the worst came to the worst, they had but to follow his example and ease themselves of all their troubles at a single stroke. A sincere pessimist would probably say: 'I do not kill myself because I am afraid: and my very fear of death is a conclusive argument in favour of my creed. Nothing proves the deep-rooted necessity of pain more strongly than that we should refuse to profit by so obvious a means of escaping from it as that offered by suicide.' Of course where pessimism is associated with a belief in metempsychosis, as among the Buddhists, there is the best of reasons for not seeking a violent death, namely, that it would in all probability transfer the suicide to another and inferior grade of existence; whereas, by using the opportunities of self-mortification which this world offers, he might succeed in extinguishing the vital principle for good and all. And Schopenhauer does, in fact, adopt the belief in metempsychosis just so far as is necessary to exclude the desirability of suicide from his philosophy. But the truth is, that while Asiatic pessimism is the logical consequence of a false metaphysical system, the analogous systems of European pessimists are simply an excuse for not pushing their disgust with life to its only rational issue.

415 Porph., Vita, cap. xviii.

416 Porphyry says six, but there must be a mistake somewhere, as Plotinus was fifty-nine when their friendship began, and died in his sixty-sixth year; while Porphyry's departure for Sicily took place two years before that event, leaving, at most, five years during which their personal intercourse can have lasted, if the other dates are to be trusted.

417 Enn., III., ii. and iii.

418 Plotini Opera recognovit Adolphus Kirchhoff, Lipsiae, 1856, in Teubner's series of Greek and Latin authors. H. F. Müller, the latest editor of Plotinus, has returned to the original arrangement by Enneads. His edition is accompanied by a very useful German translation, only half of which, however, has as yet appeared. (Berlin, 1878.)

419 Zeller, Ph. d. Gr., III., b, p. 472. (Third edition.)

420 Porph., Vita, iv. ff., xxiv. ff.

421 Ibid., cap. x.

422 *Ibid.*

423 Ibid., cap. xxii.

424 Ibid., capp. i. and ii.

425 Zeller, op. cit., pp. 451 ff.

426 Porph., Vita, cap. xx.

427 A single example will make our meaning clear. Plotinus is trying to prove that there can be no Form without Matter. He first argues that if the notes of a concept can be separated from one another, this proves the presence of Matter, since divisibility is an affection belonging only to it. He then goes on to say, εἱ δὲ πολλὰ ὂν ἀμέριστόν ἐστι, τὰ πολλὰ ἐν ἑνὶ ὄντα ἐν ὕλῃ ἐστὶ τῷ ἑνὶ αὐτὰ μορφαὶ αὗτου ὄντα. (Enn., II., iv., 4; Kirchhoff, I., p. 113, l. 7.) The meaning is, that if the notes are inseparable, the unity in which they inhere is related to them as Matter to Form.

428 See the index to Kirchhoff's edition.

429 For references see Kirchner, Die Philosophie des Plotin, p. 185; Steinhart, Meletemata Plotiniana, pp. 9-23; Zeller, Ph. d. Gr., III., b, pp. 430 f.

430 Steinhart, op. cit., pp. 30 ff.; Kirchner, op. cit., pp. 186 ff.

431 Porph., Vita, cap. xv.

432 Enn., I., vi.

433 Meno, 86, A. Compare Vol. I., p. 212.

434 Theaetêtus, 176, A. Phaedo, 67, B ff.

435 Op. cit., p. 427.

436 Enn., IV., vii.

437 Enn., III., i., 3.

438 Enn., III., i.

439 Ἀλλὰ γὰρ δεῖ καὶ ἕκαστον εἶναι καὶ πράξεις ἡμετέρας καὶ διανοίας ὑπάρχειν. III., i., 4, Kirchh., I., p. 38, l. 22. So utterly incapable is M. Vacherot of placing himself at this point of view, that he actually reads into the words quoted an argument in favour of free-will based on the testimony of consciousness. His version runs as follows:—'Nous savons et nous croyons fermement par le sentiment de ce qui se passe en nous que les individus (les âmes) vivent, agissent, pensent, d'une vie, d'une action, d'une pensée qui leur est propre.'—Histoire Critique de l'École d'Alexandrie, I., p. 514. So far as our knowledge goes, such an appeal to consciousness is not to be found in any ancient writer.

440 See Legg., 861, A ff. for an attempt to prove that men may properly be punished for actions committed through ignorance of their real good. This passage is one of the grounds used by Teichmüller, in his Literarische Fehden, to establish the rather paradoxical thesis that Aristotle published his Ethics before Plato's death.

441 III., i., 10.

442 Cap. 4, sub fin.

443 Capp. 6 and 7. Cp. Enn., II., iii.; Zeller, op. cit., pp. 567 ff; Kirchner, Ph. d. Plot., p. 195.

444 Plato, Phaedo, 79, A ff.; Aristot., De An., III., iv., sub fin.

445 Phaedr., 245, C; Legg., 892, A.

446 Adv. Col., ix., 3.

447 Enn., IV., ii., i.

448 Enn., IV., ii., sub fin.; Tim., 35, A.

449 Enn., V., ix.

450 Enn., IV., viii.

451 Enn., V., ix., 2.

452 Readers of Pope's Essay on Man will recognise this argument. It was, in fact, borrowed from Plotinus by Leibnitz, and handed on through

Bolingbroke to Pope. There is no better introduction to Neo-Platonism than this beautiful poem.

453 Kirchner, Ph. d. Plot., p. 35. The triad of body, soul, and spirit is still to be met with in modern popular philosophy; but, contrary to the Greek order of priority, there is a noticeable tendency to rank soul, as the seat of emotion, higher than spirit or pure reason, particularly among persons whose opinions receive little countenance from the last-mentioned faculty.

454 Rep., VI., 508, C ff.; VII., 517, C.

455 Vol. I., p. 229.

456 Ibid., p. 235.

457 Aristot., Metaph., I., vi.

458 Enn., V., iv., 2; Kirchh., I., p. 72, l. 8.

459 This is the method of Fichte's Wissenschaftslehre, which seems to show that Fichte was acquainted with Neo-Platonism, probably at second-hand.

460 Enn., IV., ix.

461 Ibid., 3; Kirchh., I., p, 75, l. 24.

462 Enn., VI., ix., 1.

463 Enn., VI., ix., 3; Kirchh., I., pp. 81 ff.

464 In the introductory essay prefixed to his work De l'École d'Alexandrie.

465 οὕτω δὲ καλῶν ἀμφοτέρων ὄντων, γνώσεώς τε καὶ ἀληθείας, ἄλλο καὶ κάλλιον ἔτι τούτων.—Rep., 508, E. οὐκ οὐσίας ὄντος τοῦ ἀγαθοῦ, ἀλλ' ἔτι ἐπέκεινα τῆς οὐσίας πρεσβείᾳ καὶ δυνάμει ὑπερέχοντος.—Ibid., 509, B. The first of these passages is bracketed by Stallbaum, but not the second.

466 Symp., 211, E f.

467 Enn., V., i.

468 Enn., VI., ix., 3, sub fin.; ibid., 6, p. 764, E. (Kirchh., I., p. 87, l. 16); Enn., V., v., 6, p. 525, D. (Kirchh., II., p. 24, l. 24).

469 Enn., VI., ix., 9, sub fin.

470 Ibid., V., ii., I, p. 494, A. (Kirchh., I., p. 109, l. 7).

471 Ibid., V., i., 5, p. 487, C. (Kirchh., I., p. 101, l. 32).

472 Enn., V., i., 6, p. 487, B. (Kirchh., I., p. 101, l. 21).

473 Enn., V., i., 4, p. 485, E (Kirchh., I., pp. 99 f.).

474 Enn., V., ii., 1, p. 494, A; VI., ix., 2, p. 759, A; II., iv., 5, p. 162, A.

475 Enn., IV., iv., 16, p. 409, C (Kirchh., I., p. 283, l. 31).

476 Enn., V., ii., 2.

477 Enn., II., iv.

478 Aristot., Metaph., VII., x., sub fin.

479 Tim., 48, E, ff.

480 Ibid., 47, E.

481 Enn., II., iv., 5, p. 161, E (Kirchh., I., p. 114, l. 1).

482 Enn., II., iv., 11, sub fin.

483 Enn., III., vi., 14 f.

484 Enn., II., iv., 15, p. 169, A (Kirchh., I., p. 124, l. 17).

485 Ibid., 5, p. 162, A (Kirchh., I., p. 114, l. 12).

486 Ibid., III., ix., 3, p. 358, A (Kirchh., I., p. 128, l. 22).

487 Enn., III., iv., i.

488 Enn., II., iv., 15, p. 169, B (Kirchh., I., p. 124, l. 22).

489 Enn., IV., iii,, 9, p. 379, A (Kirchh., I., p. 244, l. 17). In one of his latest essays (Enn., I., viii., 7) Plotinus for a moment accepts the Platonic theory that evil must necessarily coexist with good as its correlative opposite, but quickly returns to the alternative theory that evil results from the gradual diminution and extinction of good (cp. Zeller, Ph. d. Gr., III., b, p. 549).

490 Enn., III., viii., 4 and 8.

491 Our own word 'paragon' is a curious record of the theory in question. It is derived from the Greek participial substantive ὁ παράγων, the producer. Now, according to Neo-Platonism, in the hierarchic series of existences, the product always strives, or should strive, to model itself on the producer, hence παράγων came to be used in the double sense of a cause and an exemplar. As such, it is one of the technical terms employed throughout the Institutiones Theologicae of Proclus. But, in time, the second or derivative meaning became so much the more important as to gain exclusive possession of the word on its adoption into modern languages.

492 Enn., III., iv., 2.

493 Enn., I., ii., 1.

494 Ibid., 3.

495 Enn., I., ii., 6, sub fin.

496 Ibid., 5.

497 Ibid., ix.

498 Enn., I., iii.

499 Rep., VI., 511.

500 See the conclusion of the Posterior Analytics.

501 Enn., III., vii., 1, p. 325, C (Kirchh., II., p. 282, l. 13).

502 Zeller's last volume, giving a full account of the Neo-Platonic school, has recently reached a third edition, but it belongs to a connected work, and contains, in addition, a mass of information possessing special interest for theologians. It has not, however, been translated into English, nor apparently is there any intention of translating it. Our own literature on the subject is represented by a worthless book of Kingsley's, entitled Alexandria and her Schools, and a novel by a lady, called the Wards of Plotinus.

503 Enn., VI., ix., sub fin.

504 Enn., III., ii., 15, p. 266, E (Kirchh., II., p. 336, l. 31). M. Renan talks of the period from 235 to 284 as 'cet enfer d'un demi-siècle où sombre toute philosophie, toute civilité, toute délicatesse' (Marc-Aurèle, p. 498). As, however, this epoch produced Neo-Platonism, the expression 'toute philosophie' is rather misplaced.

505 Enn., IV., iv., 17, p. 410, B. (Kirchh., I., p. 285, l. 1).

506 Ph. d. Gr., III., b, pp. 69 ff, 419 ff.

507 Op. cit., pp. 419 ff.

508 Zeller, p. 447.

509 Enn., V., v., p. 520, A. (Kirchh., II., p. 18, l. 3). This is the only passage in the Enneads where the Sceptics seem to be alluded to.

510 *Loc. cit.*

511 *Vita, x., sub fin.*

512 For specimens of his treatment, see Zeller, pp. 622 ff.

513 For the theology of Plotinus see Zeller, pp. 619 ff, and for the daemons, p. 570. In our opinion, Zeller attributes a much stronger religious faith to Plotinus than can be proved from the passages to which he refers.

514 Enn., V., vii.

515 Enn., V., vii., I, p. 539, B. (Kirchh., I., p. 145, l. 23).

516 For references, see Zeller, pp. 588 ff.

517 Enn., VI., ii., 3, p. 598, A. (Kirchh., II., p. 227).

518 Enn., II., ix.

519 Ibid., cap. 6.

520 Ibid., 14.

521 Enn., II., ix., 15.

522 Kirchner, Die Ph. d. Plot., pp. 1-24, 175-208. Cp. Steinhart, Meletemata Plotiniana, p. 4.

523 Two other popular misconceptions may be traced back, in part at least, to the exclusively transcendental interpretation of Plato's philosophy. By drawing away attention from the Socratic dialogues, it broke the connexion between Socrates and his chief disciple, thus leaving the former to be estimated exclusively from Xenophon's view of his character as a moral and religious teacher. True, Xenophon himself supplies us with the data which prove that Socrates was, above all things, a dialectician, but only in the reflex light of Plato's subsequent developments can their real significance be perceived. On the other hand, the attempt to combine

Aristotle with Plato led to a serious misunderstanding of the actual relation between the two. When the whole ideal element of his philosophy had been drawn off and employed to heighten still further the transcendentalism of his master's teaching, the Stagirite came to be judged entirely by the residual elements, by the logical, physical, and critical portions of his system. On the strength of these, he was represented as the type of whatever is most opposed to Plato, and, in particular, of a practical, prosaic turn of mind, which was quite alien from his true character.

524 Χαλεπὸν μὲν γνωσθῆναι ... γιγνωσκόμενον δὲ μᾶλλον τῷ ἀπ' αὐτοῦ γεννήματι τῇ οὐσίᾳ. (Enn., VI., ix., 5, p. 763, B.) Πᾶν τὸ θεῖον αὐτὸ μὲν διὰ τὴν ὑπερούσιον ἕνωσιν ἄρρητόν ἐστι καὶ ἄγνωστον πᾶσι τοῖς δευτέροις· ἀπὸ δὲ τῶν μετεχόντων ληπτόν ἐστι καὶ γνωστόν. (Proclus, Institutiones Theologicae, cxxiii.), cp. Proclus, ibid., clxii.

525 De Princip., ii., quoted by Ritter and Preller, p. 536 f.

526 Inst. Theol., lxxii., cp. Zeller, p. 808, where it is denied, wrongly, as we think, that Plotinus held the same view.

527 The following sketch is based on the accounts given of the period to which it relates in the works of Zeller and Vacherot.

528 De Civit. Dei, VIII., v., quoted by Kirchner, p. 208.

529 Enn., II., ix., 18, p. 217, C; for Syrianus and Proclus, see Zeller, p. 738. The Emperor Constantine is said to have remained a sun-worshipper all his life (Vacherot, II., p. 153); and even Philo Judaeus speaks of the stars as visible gods (Zeller, p. 393).

530 Quoted by Ritter and Preller, p. 539.

531 Compare the report of Agathias with the series of questions put to Priscian, quoted in the Dissertation by M. Quicherat, prefixed to Dübner's edition of Priscian's Solutiones (printed after Plotinus in Didot's edition, pp. 549 ff).

532 M. Vacherot says (II., p. 400), without giving any authority for his statement, that the Neo-Platonists were driven from Persia by the persecution of the Magi; and that they returned home 'furtivement,' which is certainly incorrect. They returned openly, under the protection of a treaty between Persia and Rome.

533 *Repub., IX., sub fin.*

534 *Hauréau, Histoire de la Philosophie Scolastique, I., p. 372.*

535 For Gilbert de la Porrée see Hauréau, I., chap. xviii.

536 *Jourdain, Recherches critiques sur les Traductions latines d'Aristote.*

537 The term Nominalist is here used in the wide sense given to it by Hauréau. See the last chapter of his work on the Scholastic Philosophy.

538 Works I., p. 405 in Ellis and Spedding's edition.

539 'Historia naturalis ... materia prima philosophiae.' De Aug., II., iii.

540 The 'notions and conceptions' of the Advancement of Learning (Works, III., p. 356) is rendered by 'axiomata' in the De Augmentis (I., p. 567), where in both instances the question is entirely about Forms. Cp. § 8 of Prof. Fowler's Introduction to the Novum Organum.

541 *Analyt. Prior., II., xxx.*

542 Prof. Bain, after mentioning that the second book of the Topics 'sets forth in a crude condition the principal canons of inductive logic,' goes on to say that 'these statements cannot be called germs for they never germinated' (Grote's Minor Works, p. 14). May they not have germinated in the Novum Organum?

543 Descartes showed a much deeper insight into the scientific conditions of industrial progress than Bacon. His words are, 'On peut trouver une philosophie pratique par laquelle connoissant la force et les actions du feu, de l'eau, de l'air, des astres, des cieux, et de tous les autres corps qui nous environnent, aussi distinctement que nous connoissons les divers mestiers de nos artisans, nous les pourrions employer en même façon à tous les usages auxquels ils sont propres, et ainsi nous rendre comme maistres et possesseurs de la Nature.' Discours de la Méthode, Sixième Partie. This passage has been recently quoted by Dr. Bridges ('Comte's Definition of Life,' Fortnightly Review for June 1881, p. 684) to illustrate what seems a very questionable position. He says that the Copernican astronomy, by revealing the infinitude of the universe, made men despair of comprehending nature in her totality, and thus threw them back on enquiries of more directly human interest and practical applicability; particularly specifying 'the lofty utilitarianism of the Novum Organum and of the Discours de la Méthode,' as 'one of the first concomitants' 'of this intellectual revolution.' There seems to be a double misconception here: for, in the first place, Bacon could hardly have been influenced by a theory which he persistently rejected; and, in the next place, neither Bacon nor Descartes showed a trace of the positivist tendency to despair of attaining absolute and universal knowledge. Both of them expected to discover the inmost essences of things; and neither of them imagined that a different set of conditions might come into play outside the boundaries of the visible universe. In fact they believed themselves to be enlarging instead of restricting the field of mental vision; and it was from this very enlargement that they anticipated the most momentous practical results. It was with Locke, as we shall see hereafter, that the sceptical or agnostic movement began. In this same article, Dr. Bridges repeats, probably on Comte's authority, the incredible statement that 'Thales taught the Egyptian priests those two or three elementary truths as to the laws of triangles, which enabled them to tell the height of the pyramid by measuring its shadow.' Comte's ignorance or carelessness in relating this story as a well-attested fact was long ago noticed with astonishment by Grote. (Life of George Grote, p. 204.)

544 Whewell notices this 'Stationary Interval' (History of the Inductive Sciences, Bk. XVI., chapter iii., sect. 3), but without determining either its just limits or its real cause.

545 Compreso che sarà il moto di quest' astro mondano in cui siamo ... s'aprirà la porta de l'intelligenza de li principi veri di cose naturali. De l'Infinito Universo e Mondi, p. 51, Wagner's Ed.

546 'Sono amputate radici che germogliano, son cose antiche che rivegnono. Ibid., p. 82.

547 Principio Causa et Uno, p. 225. For David of Dinan, whose opinions are known only through the reports of Albertus and Aquinas, see Hauréau, II., iv.

548 Galileo's words are:—'Il moto circulare è naturale del tutto e delle parti mentre sono in ottima disposizione.' Dialoghi sui Massimi Sistemi. Opere, Vol. I., p. 265; see also p. 38.

549 Dialoghi, p. 211.

550 'Non posso trovar termine all'ammirazione mia come abbia possuto in Aristarco e nel Copernico far la ragione tanta violenza al senso che contro a questo ella si sia fatta padrona della loro credulità.' Dialoghi, p. 358.

551 Ibid., p. 370.

552 'Kepler était persuadé de l'existence de ces lois en suivant cette pensée de Platon: que Dieu, en créant le monde, avait dû faire de la géometrie.' Arago, Œuvres III., p. 212.

553 De Aug., III., v. Works, I., p. 571.

554 This is well brought out in a remarkable series of articles on the Philosophy of Hobbes recently published by Tönnies in the Vierteljahrsschrift fur wissenschaftliche Philosophie.

555 *Leviathan, chap. xv., sub fin.*

556 *Leviathan, chap. xi., sub fin.*

557 Leviathan, chap. vi.

558 *Spaccio della Bestia Trionfante, sub in.*

559 Advancement of Learning, Ellis and Spedding, III., p. 428.

560 Republic, VI., 511, Jowett's Trans. III., p. 398.

561 Plotinus himself expresses a doubt as to whether the One is, properly speaking, all things or not (Enn., V., ii., sub in.); but in his essay on Substance and Quality, he defines qualities as energies of the substance to which they belong (Enn., II., vi. 3). Now all things are, according to his philosophy, energies of the One. There would, therefore, be no difficulty in considering it as their substance.

[562]

—— Quia multimodis, multis, mutata, per omne

Ex infinito vexantur percita plagis,

Omne genus motus, et coetus experiundo,

Tandem deveniunt in taleis dispositturas,

Qualibus haec rebus consistit summa creata. (I., 1023-7.)

563 V., 853; IV., 780-800; V., 1025.

564 Just the same remark applies to the monads of Leibnitz. Each monad reflects all the others, and infers that its reflections represent a reality from the infinite creative power of God. Descartes' appeal to the divine veracity represents the same method in a less developed stage. The root-idea here is to be sought for, not in Greek thought but in the Christian doctrine of a supernatural revelation.

565 The formal cause of a thing is its species, the concept under which it is immediately subsumed; the efficient cause is what brings it into existence. Thus the formal cause of a man is humanity, the efficient cause, his father.

566 Eth., I., prop. xvi.; II., prop. iii.; prop. v.; prop. xviii., schol.; prop. xxviii.; prop. xl., schol. ii.; V., prop. xxix., schol.; prop. xl., schol. (The passage last referred to is the clearest and most decisive.)

567 See the passage from the Republic quoted above.

568 The tendency of logicians is now, contrariwise, to force reasoning into parallelism with mathematical physics by interpreting the proposition as an equation between subject and predicate.

569 III., prop. ii., schol.

570 II., vii., schol.

571 III., ix. and xi.

572 Greek tragedy is just the reverse—an expansion of the old patriarchal relations into a mould fitted to receive the highest thought and feeling of a civilised age.

573 For the whole subject of Spinoza's mathematical method, see Windelband's paper on Spinoza in the Vierteljahrsschrift für wissenschaftliche Philosophie, 1877. Some points in the last paragraph were suggested by Mr. Pollock's Spinoza (pp. 255, 264).

574 Essay, Bk. iv., ch. 12.

575 See the references to Epictêtus, supra, p. 21.

576 What Aristotle has written on the subject is not ethics but natural history.

577 'Ne remarque-t-on comment chaque recherche analytique de Laplace a fait ressortir dans notre globe et dans l'univers des conditions d'ordre et de durée?'—Arago, Œuvres, III., p. 496.

Printed in Great Britain
by Amazon

65461202R00280